MISREADING
ANITA BROOKNER

LIVERPOOL ENGLISH TEXTS AND STUDIES 80

MISREADING ANITA BROOKNER

Aestheticism, Intertextuality, and the Queer Nineteenth Century

PETA MAYER

LIVERPOOL UNIVERSITY PRESS

First published 2020 by
Liverpool University Press
4 Cambridge Street
Liverpool
L69 7ZU

Copyright © 2020 Peta Mayer

The right of Peta Mayer to be identified as the author of this work has been asserted by her in accordance with the Copyright, Designs and Patents Act 1988.

All rights reserved. No part of this book may be reproduced, stored in a retrieval system, or transmitted, in any form or by any means, electronic, mechanical, photocopying, recording, or otherwise, without the prior written permission of the publisher.

British Library Cataloguing-in-Publication data
A British Library CIP record is available

ISBN 978-1-78962-059-7 cased

Typeset by Carnegie Book Production, Lancaster
Printed and bound by CPI Group (UK) Ltd, Croydon CR0 4YY

To Sasha and Linus

Contents

List of Illustrations   ix

Acknowledgements   x

List of Abbreviations   xii

Glossary of Rhetorical Terms   xiii

Introduction   1

1   The Military Man, the Analysand, and the Queer in *A Friend from England* (1987)   33

2   The Aesthete in *A Misalliance* (1986)   74

3   The Dandy in *Brief Lives* (1990)   117

4   The *Flâneur* in *Undue Influence* (1999)   160

5   The Degenerate in *Falling Slowly* (1998)   192

Epilogue: The Storyteller Returns: *Hotel du Lac* (1984)   224

Bibliography   247

Index   261

Illustrations

1 Giorgione, *The Tempest*, 1506–08. Oil on canvas, 83 cm × 73 cm. Gallerie dell'Accademia, Venice — 35

2 X-ray of Giorgione, *The Tempest*, 1506–08. Gallerie dell'Accademia, Venice — 36

3 1934 Lucien Lelong silk velvet evening gown. Illustration by Tom Tierney. Reproduced by kind permission of Dover Books — 119

4 1936 Madame Grès draped silk jersey gown. Illustration by Tom Tierney. Reproduced by kind permission of Dover Books — 120

5 1929 Patou evening ensemble. Illustration by Tom Tierney. Reproduced by kind permission of Dover Books — 121

6 Map of *Undue Influence* — 162

Acknowledgements

Misreading Anita Brookner was made possible due to the tireless support of Clara Tuite at the University of Melbourne. Clara's enthusiasm for the project, and the insights and opportunities she provided along the way were invaluable to its evolution. Clara's knowledge is boundless, yet her understanding of Brookner is both so intimate and expansive; more than once did I have cause to appreciate Clara proffering a timely Brookner quote that I myself had forgotten or overlooked. And more than once did we find ourselves laughing in accord over the exact same Brookner phrasing. Clara was a fabulous PhD supervisor, but she has also been a significant mentor.

Our mutual excitement at the possibilities of Brookner's oeuvre culminated in 'Latecomers: Anita Brookner Then and Now', the first international symposium on Anita Brookner, held in March 2017 at the University of Melbourne. I am most grateful to Clara for initiating the symposium, for the assistance of the University of Melbourne, and for the lifelong connections it enabled.

I am thankful to Grace Moore, University of Melbourne, for bringing fresh energy, enthusiasm, and expertise to the project in its later stages. Patricia Juliana Smith at Hofstra University added a new breadth of knowledge and charm, as well as personal support. It was fabulous to have Laurence Petit spend an extended amount of time in Melbourne, and delightful to have another Brooknerphile in the neighbourhood with her own limitless perspectives of Brookner's work.

I thank my friends and family, Kez Hughes, Troy Colvin, Alice and Eli Grant, Nicola Dracoulis, Jennie Lang, Anna Jackson, Lynette Frey, Melita Granger, Caroline Johnston, Norma Babo, Gai Palmer, Nicholas Hansen, Helen Day, Greg Wadley, Lauren Markwell, Margaret Wright,

ACKNOWLEDGEMENTS

Nicholas Wright, Michael Wright, and Veronica Clarke. Their willingness to listen, distract, act sane, and embrace Brookner makes me love them all the more. I have been so lucky to work with an incredible team at Liverpool University Press, who made this journey smooth and even enjoyable.

My sister, Olivia Mayer, is a brilliant reader and editor. I have especially appreciated her unwavering support, charisma, and perseverance.

I could not have completed this book without the love and support of my parents: Wendy Mayer, who first introduced me to Brookner, and the unceasing kindness, generosity, and good humour of my father, Erich Mayer.

Abbreviations

Full citations appear in the footnotes when each of these sources is first mentioned. Thereafter, these works are cited in the text in parentheses, using the following abbreviations.

AI	*The Anxiety of Influence*, by Harold Bloom
AN	*Against Nature*, by Joris-Karl Huysmans
BJ	*The Beast in the Jungle*, by Henry James
BL	*Brief Lives*, by Anita Brookner
D	'Fragment of an Analysis of a Case of Hysteria ("Dora") (1905 [1901])', by Sigmund Freud
DGN	*Degeneration*, by Max Nordau
FE	*A Friend from England*, by Anita Brookner
FS	*Falling Slowly*, by Anita Brookner
GF	*The Genius of the Future*, by Anita Brookner
HB	*The Life of Henri Brulard*, by Stendhal
HL	*Hotel du Lac*, by Anita Brookner
L	*On Love*, by Stendhal
M	*A Misalliance*, by Anita Brookner
MV	*The Muse of the Violets*, by Renée Vivien
PML	*The Painter of Modern Life and Other Essays*, by Charles Baudelaire
RD	*Romanticism and Its Discontents*, by Anita Brookner
SB	*Scarlet and Black: A Chronicle of the Nineteenth Century*, by Stendhal
UI	*Undue Influence*, by Anita Brookner
WA	*A Woman Appeared to Me*, by Renée Vivien

Glossary of Rhetorical Terms

A Friend from England
'Hendiadys': the expression of an idea by linking two words or ideas, e.g., 'sound and fury' rather than 'furious sound'. In *Misreading Anita Brookner*, Georges Kliebenstein's more expansive adaptation of hendiadys is used. Kliebenstein uses the notation 'a + A', where 'A' represents a repeat event that clarifies the significance of 'a' across the given narrative.

'Homiologia': tedious and inane repetition.

'Preterition': the act of mentioning something through omission, inference, or circumlocution.

A Misalliance
'Metaleptic prolepsis': a backwards–forwards movement in narrative in which the story flashes backwards in time to retrieve information and then once again moves forwards. We understand metalepsis as the retrospective assignation of a relationship between past and present and prolepsis as the anticipation of a future event or fulfilment in and from the point of the present.

Brief Lives
'Detail': the proliferation or refinement of information across a narrative.

Undue Influence
'Peripeteia': reversal or sudden change within the narrative.

Falling Slowly
'Syllepsis': the figure for understanding the same word or concept in two different ways at the same time, one meaning being literal and the other being figurative; the shift between or deconstruction of the literal and the figurative.

Hotel du Lac
'Anagnorisis': the making of a critical discovery.

'Paraprosdokian': when a surprise discovery or unexpected event causes the reader to reinterpret an earlier part of the narrative.

Introduction

> [I]t was not always clear what Blanche meant. If you had not read the same books you did not always make sense of her allusions.
>
> Anita Brookner, *A Misalliance*

In Anita Brookner's only television interview, broadcast in September 1985, Hermione Lee asks the novelist to define the differences between her male and female readers.[1] 'Let me think', she pauses, before reflecting that 'the most pertinent criticism I've had from a male reader is "you write French books, don't you?" which I loved'.[2]

But what is the 'French book'? Brookner's casual realignment of her novels with the French canon of literature sends, at the very least, a covert glance to the writers and artists who constitute the subject matter of her first career as a historian of French Romantic art: Stendhal, Charles Baudelaire, Karl-Joris Huysmans, and their cohorts. Born in London to Jewish parents in 1928, Brookner had already received international recognition as an art historian before the 1981 publication of her first novel, *A Start in Life*.[3] And, contrary to her reputation as a middlebrow women's novelist, it is, on the other hand, the subversive behaviour of the male Romantics that Brookner emphasises throughout her criticism: 'Romanticism is essentially about dissidence, about rejection, about protest, about breaking the old rules', she writes in *Romanticism and Its*

---

1 Anita Brookner, interview by Hermione Lee, *Book Four*, Channel 4 (8 September 1985). VHS cassette accessed at British Film Institute National Archive (9 May 2006). No. 131309.
2 Anita Brookner, interview by Hermione Lee, *Book Four*, Channel 4.
3 Anita Brookner, *A Start in Life* (London: Jonathan Cape, 1981).

Discontents.⁴ In this way, Brookner's summonsing of the French book also calls to mind 'the poisonous book' invoked by Dorian Gray in Oscar Wilde's *The Picture of Dorian Gray*, and revealed at Wilde's 1895 trial for gross indecency to characterise those intellectual and moral experiments undertaken by fellow nineteenth-century aesthete Duc des Esseintes in Huysmans's *Against Nature*.⁵

In *The History of Sexuality*, Michel Foucault famously draws a network of associations between the historical period of the nineteenth century during which Romanticism unfolded and an emergent cultural apparatus for producing sexuality.⁶ In the context of the new nineteenth-century capitalist politics of gender and sexuality, which aligned bourgeois masculinity with production, utilitarianism, rationality, logic, and public-sphere working life, and femininity with consumption, decoration, display, and domesticity, the aesthetes and Romantics at the centre of Brookner's art-history oeuvre experimented with modes of self-conscious artifice that dramatically complicated emerging categories of gender and sexual identity.

The historical pressures on and opportunities for nineteenth-century subjects became expressed in a range of different textual devices, discourses, and narratives of the (generally male) aesthetes and Romantics. Many of these devices also become familiar in the discursive formation of homosexuality.⁷ Several of Brookner's predecessors—Diderot, Balzac, Baudelaire, Theophile Gautier, Émile Zola, and Henry James—are enlisted by Elizabeth Ladenson as the nineteenth-century aesthetes and Romantics who mobilised the figure of the lesbian as a posterchild of the 'art for art sake's' movement, based on the figure's ability to represent pleasure and subversion outside a use-value economy.⁸ Monique Wittig crowned Baudelaire as 'the lesbian poet'; the fact that his sapphic poems

---

4 Anita Brookner, *Romanticism and Its Discontents* (London: Viking, 2000), 21. Hereafter cited in text as *RD*.
5 Oscar Wilde, *The Picture of Dorian Gray* (Ware: Wordsworth Classics, 1992), 101. Hereafter cited in text as *DG*.
6 Michel Foucault, *The History of Sexuality*, vol. 1, *An Introduction*, trans. Robert Hurley (Harmondsworth: Penguin, 1981).
7 'The French possess a strong tradition of writing on homosexuality which since the late eighteenth century has nurtured its own growth'. George Stambolian and Elaine Marks, Introduction to *Homosexualities and French Literature: Cultural Contexts/Critical Texts*, ed. George Stambolian and Elaine Marks (Ithaca, NY: Cornell University Press, 1979), 25.
8 Elisabeth Ladenson, *Dirt for Art's Sake: Books on Trial from 'Madame Bovary' to 'Lolita'* (Ithaca, NY: Cornell University Press, 2007), 75.

in *The Flowers of Evil* (initially entitled 'The Lesbians') were banned are indicative of the perceived transgressive value of female same-sex desire at the time.[9] In his book on Baudelaire, Walter Benjamin characterised the lesbian as 'the heroine of modernity', marking the way the aesthetes and Romantics valorised the figure of the lesbian in their efforts to scandalise and also to make sense of contemporary experience.[10] Other critics have rightfully complicated the notion that the male Romantics were indeed so subversive. For Rita Felski, aestheticism's shifts between traditional male and female spheres were nothing more than 'an imaginary identification with the feminine'.[11] And Thaïs E. Morgan sees the aspirational transgressive discourse of Baudelaire, Manet, and Swinburne as encoded with 'a fundamentally conservative sexual politics'.[12] Furthermore, some Romantics and aesthetes were in fact women, and in *Misreading Anita Brookner* the work of Renée Vivien and Germaine de Staël will also become important in helping to decode the signs and symbols of Brookner's work.

In the 1990s, the advent of queer theory brought about the phenomenon known as 'the queering of the nineteenth century', in which the nineteenth-century discursive formulation of homosexuality became invested with new meaning. In *Epistemology of the Closet*, for instance, Eve Kosofsky Sedgwick examines how the trope of preterition and the narrative of the secret in Henry James's 1903 novella, *The Beast in the Jungle*, can be read (in conjunction with James's biography) to suggest homoerotic desire in a story that had previously been read straight.[13] These contemporary queer interventions have been enormously influential in my reading of how nineteenth-century motifs live and breathe in Brookner's twentieth-century novels. Widely recognised as one of Brookner's significant precursors, James is central to both Romantic aestheticism and queer theory, and his

---

9 Monique Wittig, 'Paradigm', in Stambolian and Marks, *Homosexualities and French Literature*, 117.
10 Walter Benjamin, *Charles Baudelaire: A Lyric Poet in the Era of High Capitalism*, trans. Harry Zohn (London: Verso, 1997), 90.
11 Rita Felski, 'The Counterdiscourse of the Feminine in Three Texts by Wilde, Huysmans, and Sacher-Masoch', *PMLA* 106.5 (1991): 1094.
12 Thaïs E. Morgan, 'Male Lesbian Bodies: The Construction of Alternative Masculinities in Courbet, Baudelaire, and Swinburne', *Genders* 15 (1992): 53.
13 Henry James, *The Beast in the Jungle*, in *Complete Stories, 1898–1910* (New York: Library of America, 1966), 496–541. Hereafter cited in text as *BJ*; Eve Kosofsky Sedgwick, *Epistemology of the Closet* (Berkeley: University of California Press, 1990), 202, 204.

work can be said to invest Brookner's novels with queer literary potential through the intertextual network.[14] More specifically, then, the 'French book' can be thought of as signalling a range of contestatory or queer behaviours that are synonymous with social and political upheaval in the nineteenth century. These tropes and behaviours offer ways to rethink the boundaries around gender identity, sexuality, family life, and representation, both then and now. As a canonical springboard across multiple contexts, the French book as invoked by Brookner therefore opens up a vast repertory of queer hermeneutic possibilities that will be explored in *Misreading Anita Brookner*.

Strange Brooknerines

In her review of Brookner's 2000 novel, *The Bay of Angels*, Miranda Seymour coined the term 'Brooknerine' in what constitutes a blurring of Brookner's individual characters into one archetype. In Seymour's mind, the heroine of the story was yet another member of a 'sad group of Brooknerines who must walk through a long, dark valley of clouded understanding'.[15] While pending judgement on the efficacy of the queer arguments presented in *Misreading Anita Brookner*, it is worth noting an early tendency in Brookner's reception for critics to remark that the novels were 'strange' (*FS*, 187).[16] Well, we live in hope.

14 While Smith is the only critic directly to connect *The Beast in the Jungle* to Brookner in a queer context, both Sadler and Adeline R. Tinter draw direct links between Brookner's fiction and James's seminal story. Patricia Juliana Smith, *Lesbian Panic: Homoeroticism in Modern British Women's Fiction* (New York: Columbia University Press, 1997), 5; Lynn Veach Sadler, *Anita Brookner*, Twayne's English Author Series, 473 (Boston: Twayne, 1990), 135; Adeline R. Tintner, 'Henry James's Fiction "Swallowed, Digested and Assimilated": A Strong "Whiff" of Henry James in 1997's Overflow', *Henry James Review* 19.3 (1998): 257.
15 Miranda Seymour, 'The Mistress of Gloom', *Atlantic Monthly* (June 2001): 108.
16 'A strange and disturbing book'. Sally Emerson, 'Recent Fiction', *Illustrated London News* (August 1981): 76; 'Strangely static'. Brenda Niall, 'Alone Again, Naturally', *Weekend Australian* (7–8 April 2001): R15; 'Accept them on their own strange terms'. Elizabeth Judd, 'Plotless Wonder', *Atlantic Monthly* (April 2003): 109; 'Strangely devoid of friends'. Brian McFarlane, 'A Small, Tenacious Addiction to Life', *Saturday Age* (7 April 2001): E11; 'Truly strange … a strange, interesting novel'. Caroline Moore, 'Baby, It's Cold Outside', *Spectator* (19 February 2005): 38. Brookner's 24th novel is entitled *Strangers* (London: Fig Tree, 2009); while Romantic biographer Graham Robb's *Strangers: Homosexual Love in the Nineteenth Century* (London: Picador, 2003) discusses nineteenth-century homosexual culture under the designation 'strangers'.

INTRODUCTION

A Misalliance, published in 1986, is Brookner's sixth novel of a total of twenty-four novels and one novella, and one of the six novels under consideration in *Misreading Anita Brookner*. In it, protagonist Blanche Vernon rejects a dinner invitation by claiming a subversive connection to one of the previous century's pre-eminent writers: 'I might make an injudicious remark or start raving on about Henry James', she warns her ex-husband, Bertie.[17] The heroine's intertextual practices do not, however, stabilise meaning; rather, they underscore the contingent nature of meaning-making. To Blanche, 'it seemed that she constantly misread the situation', a practice we hope to embrace in this analysis of Brookner in order to stretch out the possible options for interpretation (*M*, 101). An inveterate patron of the National Gallery of London and the Wallace Collection—where her 'obsession' with the nymphs of Italian Renaissance painting spawns a real-life fascination with the nymph-like Sally Beamish—Blanche's '*insupportably* eccentric' behaviour is shared in different ways by all the heroines of the five other Brookner novels that are under scrutiny in this book (*M*, 54, 30).

So, while narrator Rachel Kennedy of *A Friend from England*, a novel set in 1980s London, is identified by others as a 'feminist', Rachel herself professes a preference for innocent women.[18] 'It pleases me, in some obscure way, to conceive of women as timorous, delicate, in need of special treatment, of deference', she says (*FE*, 171). But despite her interest in Heather Livingstone Rachel's opinion of her friend is not always flattering. 'When I first met her', Rachel says of Heather, 'I thought she must be deaf. When I got to know her better I revised my opinion slightly: I thought she was retarded' (*FE*, 91). The problematic relationship between the women forces Rachel to confront some uncomfortable facts throughout the novel about herself and Heather, remarking of Heather that her 'particular form of nurturing made someone like me sound unrealistic as if my entire formation were out of order' (*FE*, 159). Thus, Rachel vaguely apprehends her own eccentricities in *A Friend from England*.

Brookner once described female friendship as 'an undervalued and underfictionalised topic', implicitly illuminating the homosocial dimension of her contribution to the literary canon in the genre of

---

17 Anita Brookner, *A Misalliance* (London: Grafton Books, 1987), 73. First published 1986. Hereafter cited in text as *M*.
18 Anita Brookner, *A Friend from England* (London: Grafton Books, 1988), 67. First published 1987. Hereafter cited in text as *FE*.

women's writing.[19] As its title suggests, *A Friend from England* chronicles the relationship between two female acquaintances, as do *A Misalliance* and Brookner's ninth novel—*Brief Lives*, published in 1990.[20]

The narrator of *Brief Lives*, Fay Dodworth, is burdened with that chronically taboo contemporary inconvenience: self-doubt. Fay represents herself as 'marginal', 'inconsequential', and 'weak and incapable' (*BL*, 86, 80, 122). Fay's tendency to see herself as flawed is exacerbated by her relationship with the brilliant and scandalous Julia Morton, a former '*diseuse*' (*BL*, 2). In the novel, Fay describes her 'thraldom' to 'cult object' Julia—'a woman who at her best was bored by one and at worst seemed antagonistic' (*BL*, 207, 136, 160). Over the course of her adult life, Fay charts her subjection to and rebellion against Julia, confessing that, 'Although I did not like her any more than she liked me, she was always in my thoughts' (*BL*, 198). Like many of Brookner's protagonists, Fay and Julia are childless. In interview with Hermione Lee, Brookner emphasised her solitary heroines' capacity to disrupt the domestic fiction when she commented that '[t]he solitary woman has a much longer life simply because she outlives the family'.[21] In *Misreading Anita Brookner*, Brookner's solitary heroines, their female friendships, and their creative subjectivities enable alternative narratives to the heterosexual romance of domestic fiction, which is found in varying degrees to be aesthetically repellent, inauthentic, comedic, unsatisfactory, and unappealing.

In *Undue Influence*, published in 1999, and also set in the late twentieth century, narrator Claire Pitt categorises herself as someone who cannot be categorised.[22] Such 'unclassifiability' is partly owing to her 'aberrant imagination' (*UI*, 165, 91). This narrator cultivates a 'dangerously unhealthy attitude' that manifests as an 'odd habit of making up people's lives for them' (*UI*, 24, 176). Claire's hobby becomes contentious when she mistakes imagination for reality; towards the end of the novel, she reports: 'I am left with the feeling that I have comprehensively failed' (*UI*, 187). In a 1985 interview, Brookner stated that she was 'interested in the reasons for failure' and in 2001 she described failure as '[m]uch more

---

19 Anita Brookner, interview by Olga Kenyon, in Olga Kenyon, *Women Writers Talk: Interviews with 10 Women Writers* (Oxford: Lennard Publishing, 1989), 23.
20 Anita Brookner, *Brief Lives* (Harmondsworth: Penguin, 1991). First published 1990. Hereafter cited in text as *BL*.
21 Anita Brookner, interview by Hermione Lee, *Book Four*, Channel 4.
22 Anita Brookner, *Undue Influence* (London: Viking, 1999), 165. Hereafter cited in text as *UI*.

interesting than success'.²³ In privileging failure over success (like many artists), Brookner disavows happy endings and signals a willingness to explore conflicting motivations and complex outcomes.

In *Falling Slowly*, published in 1998, Miriam Sharpe acknowledges that she and her sister Beatrice are 'outside the norm'.²⁴ Younger sister Miriam is 'a connoisseur of various forms of dullness' and suffers from 'a delirium of ennui', while older sister Beatrice's 'ruinous inability to understand what was being enacted' results in a form of social isolation that precedes her premature death (*FS*, 7, 8, 58). With a mother who had 'schooled both girls in the arts of discouragement', Beatrice and Miriam's difficult adulthoods have their roots in rumpled starts (*FS*, 126). While detailing themes of female friendship and the solitary woman, Brookner's novels are all deeply invested in the genre of domestic fiction. In *The History of Sexuality*, Foucault branded the family as 'the most active site of sexuality'.²⁵ This is a reminder that when the conventions of the domestic fiction are under duress, there is a chance to probe a range of ways in which the family enables queer connections and desires. Therefore, in *Misreading Anita Brookner*, the domestic fiction becomes the stage from which to view the queer renegotiation of a range of familial roles and relations.²⁶

Finally, in Brookner's Booker-winning novel, *Hotel du Lac*, published in 1984, and which predicts many of the themes that unfold in her oeuvre, the writer–protagonist, Edith Hope, is a self-described 'unnatural daughter' (*HL*, 145).²⁷ Sent into exile for scandalous behaviour, Edith finds

---

23 Anita Brookner, interview by Amanda Smith, 'Anita Brookner', *Publishers Weekly* (6 September 1985): 67; Anita Brookner, interview by Robert McCrum, 'Just Don't Mention Jane Austen', *Observer* (28 January 2001): www.theguardian.com/books/2001/jan/28/fiction.janeausten.
24 Anita Brookner, *Falling Slowly* (London: Viking, 1998), 187. Hereafter cited in text as *FS*.
25 Foucault, *History of Sexuality*, 1: 109.
26 Laurence Petit's work offers a dynamic exposé of how Brookner disrupts the conventions of the domestic fiction. Petit contextualises Brookner's *Family and Friends* (1995) as a 'meta-photographic text' to analyse the way in which the novelist is able 'to rewrite and subvert the established genre of the family chronicle' by combining familial self-representation with a narrative that questions the family cohesion presented. Laurence Petit, 'Romance of a Family or Inverted "Family Romance": Familial Gaze and Narratorial Look in Anita Brookner's *Family and Friends*', *Literature Interpretation Theory* 17 (2006): 379.
27 Anita Brookner, *Hotel du Lac* (Harmondsworth: Penguin, 1993). First published 1984. Hereafter cited in text as *HL*.

herself 'out of place', and serves out her 'probation' at the eponymous hotel 'out of season' (*HL*, 10, 61, 32). While Edith is cast by others into the role of the 'old maid, or at least a maiden lady', her private behaviour suggests otherwise (*HL*, 85). Over the course of the novel Edith rejects two proposals of marriage (once leaving the groom at the altar) while simultaneously involved in a long-term relationship with a married man. Readers expressed surprise that, as a writer of romance fiction, Edith Hope would rebuff suitors. However, in Brookner's novels the marriage plot frequently fails to constitute a desirable option for the heroines. For Edith Hope, the identity of writer is far more preferable to the fiction of romance.

But, though Brookner's heroines are outsiders, they are also conformists. Brookner's novels predominantly depict women whose impeccable grooming, knowledge of the arts, and financial and social independence also reflect the acts, practices, and discourses of late twentieth-century, bourgeois femininity. In *A Misalliance*, for example, Blanche 'calculated that she could spend up to an unwanted hour every morning by simply putting herself to rights, and producing a pleasing effect to lavish on the empty day' (*M*, 7). In *Brief Lives*, Fay Dodworth perfects the art of making carrot mousse, performs volunteer work at the Women's League, and affects a cultivated modesty about her past singing career. 'I was always theoretically preparing for a dinner party', Fay confides (*BL*, 36). In *Falling Slowly*, both Miriam and Beatrice claim to be 'in search of the ideal family' (*FS*, 57). And in *Hotel du Lac*, Edith Hope confesses of her romance novels that 'I believed every word I wrote' (*HL*, 181). This conjunction of the subversive and the normative partly explains the 'strangeness', or perhaps queerness, of Brookner's fiction.

Brookner's literary expertise, her prolific publishing career (spanning over sixty years), and her international success might have all combined to underscore her credentials as a leader within the contemporary canon, a feminist icon and intellectual. In 1967, Brookner was appointed the first-ever female Slade Professor of Art at Cambridge. Her monograph on Jacques-Louis David was renowned as 'a model of the genre'; she was widely celebrated as an inspiring teacher; and she had been credited as a 'major exponent of the so-called New Art History'; indeed, a leader of the paradigm shift from Formalism to the New Art History.[28] After Brookner's parents refused to support her financially when she won a

---

28 Shusha Guppy, 'The Art of Fiction XCVIII: Anita Brookner', *Paris Review* 104 (Fall 1987): 163; Shusha Guppy, 'The Secret Sharer: An Interview and Profile of

scholarship in the 1950s to study at the École du Louvre in Paris, she supplemented her income by writing reviews for the *Burlington Magazine* and went on to write hundreds of reviews for publications including the *Times Literary Supplement* and the *Spectator*.[29] She recalled that during these three years of writing her thesis, she had 'never been so happy' and claimed that she was 'liberated by poverty before [she] knew what the women's movement was all about'.[30] In 1984, *Hotel du Lac* was the 'surprise' winner of the Booker Prize.[31] Two years later the novel was adapted by Christopher Hampton into a BAFTA Award-winning BBC drama starring Anna Massey and Denholm Elliot. Brookner was awarded a CBE (Commander of the Order of the British Empire) in 1990. As a novelist, Brookner commanded 'a cult following', with many book bloggers participating in online celebrations to mark 'International Anita Brookner Day' on her eightieth birthday in 2008.[32]

Early Reception

Richard Mayne's interview with Brookner immediately following the announcement of her Booker Prize win bursts with sexist assumptions that are symptomatic of the mainstream view of women writers in the 1980s. 'This is a rather personal question', Mayne warns Brookner: 'but the heroine of the book, Edith, is a writer, a novelist; she looks a little like Virginia Woolf; she's obviously beautiful. These are characteristics which you share with her. Do you share others?'[33] As indicated by Mayne's almost sleazy approach, Brookner's early reception (roughly dating from 1980 to 2010) was a fraught and controversial space, particularly regarding

---

Anita Brookner', *World and I* 13.7 (1998): 285; *Dictionary of Art Historians*, s.v. 'Brookner, Anita': http://arthistorians.info/brooknera (accessed 15 January 2010).
29 Guppy, 'Secret Sharer', 285.
30 Anita Brookner, interview by Mick Brown, 'A Singular Woman', *Telegraph* online (19 February 2009): www.telegraph.co.uk/culture/books/authorinterviews/4639980/A-singular-woman.html (subscription required); Anita Brookner, interview by Sheila Hale, 'Self Reflecting', *Saturday Review* 11.3 (1985): 37.
31 Richard Mayne, 'Kaleidoscope', BBC Radio 4 (18 October 1984), transcript, 3–4. In 1985, Brookner commented that 'Many people thought Ballard's *Empire of the Sun* should have won. And, being British, went on saying this 'til about last week. It's a very good book'. Brookner, in *Publishers Weekly*, 68.
32 Guppy, 'Secret Sharer', 282; See *International Anita Brookner Day* (blog): brooknerday.blogspot.com.au/ (last modified 18 May 2019).
33 Mayne, 'Kaleidoscope', 4. Brookner's response is genius and entirely characteristic: 'Practically all of them, I should think. But I'm not going to go into detail'.

the status of her female characters. In Britain from 1979 to 1990, Margaret Thatcher's Conservative prime ministership championed traditional patriarchal values such as motherhood and domesticity, actively opposed women's education issues, disrespected equal pay legislation and cut back welfare payments which forced women back into the home.[34] At the time of Brookner's dual career success, there was still huge pressure on women to conform to old-fashioned female domestic and sexual stereotypes. The international second-wave feminist movement evolved against this hostile political context, fashioning its own particular version of the subject of woman, while internal divisions erupted into different yet interlacing streams including radical, lesbian, and black feminisms. The feminist movement exerted a different kind of pressure on women, with its encouragement and insistence that women break out of conservative roles and seize control of their own lives. Globalisation, the technological revolution, the growth of new media economies, the rise of the celebrity author and the continued systemic dominance of the white, male writer also impacted on reading cultures at the time, shaping how, what, and why things were broadcast about gender and sexuality in mainstream presses.[35]

Yet Brookner's women were neither home-makers nor go-getters, although they often stayed at home and were frequently in the professional classes. It was in this problematic context that reviewers regularly condemned Brookner's female protagonists as 'losers', 'failures', and 'fools', while deeming the novels to be 'plotless', 'repetitive', 'boring', and 'depressing'.[36] Clashing with the assertive image of the contemporary liberal feminist heroine, the passive femininity of Brookner's heroines was

---

34 Ann K. McClellan, *How British Women Writers Transformed the Campus Novel: Virginia Woolf, Dorothy L. Sayers, Margaret Drabble, Anita Brookner, Jeanette Winterson* (Lewiston, NY: Edwin Mellon Press, 2012), 198–99.

35 In 'The Paratextual Construction of Anita Brookner: Chronotopic Conflict in the Book Review and Author Interview', *Women: A Cultural Review* 19.1 (2008): 49–68, I discuss the ways in which the paratextual genres of the book review and author interview are in temporal conflict with the intertextual Brookner narrative. I emphasise the importance of genre analyses when discussing the interpretation of Brookner's novels in book reviews and academic criticism as well as considering the gendered construction of the woman writer in the author interview.

36 Alison Light, 'A Family Romance', *New Statesman and Society* 6.260 (9 July 1993): 33; Sally Blakeney, 'Failing Females', *Australian* (26 September 1998); Barbara Hardy, 'A Cinderella's Loneliness', *Times Literary Supplement* (14 September 1984): 1019; Lindsay Duguid, 'The Downward Drag and the Loss of Allure', *Times Literary Supplement* (24 August 1990): 889; Jacqueline Seewald, 'Private View', *Library Journal* 122.6 (April 1997): 145; Rochelle Ratner, 'The Next Big Thing',

a dominant focus of critics. In the *Times Literary Supplement*, Candice Rodd deduced that Brookner's heroines were even '[t]oo well-behaved for a full-blown nervous breakdown'.³⁷ In *Hotel du Lac*, Edith Hope's publisher Harold encouraged his protégé to make her novels more sexy. 'It's sex for the young woman executive now', he instructed: 'she wants something to reassure her that being liberated is fun' (*HL*, 26). Harold's recommendation reflects the expectations around women writers in the 1980s, which both Edith and Brookner seemingly failed to live up to. Thus, sexuality 'remains largely unexplored in Brookner's texts', surmised Daphne Watson.³⁸ Matt Schudel's obituary of Brookner in the *Washington Post* reconfirmed this stereotype at the time of the author's death: 'For books so intensely mature and private, they contained little overt passion or sex', he wrote.³⁹ In general, commentators followed the logic that Brookner's novels were organised by lack.⁴⁰ The belief was that the 'lack of a man' in Brookner's fiction, combined with the absence of (hetero)sexuality, equated to the absence of happiness. And this made critics angry.⁴¹ Consequently, 'the desire to kick Anita Brookner's heroines is always strong' was not a lone sentiment during the era of the novelist's original reception.⁴²

Library Journal 128.12 (July 2003): 145; Hermione Lee, 'Melancholia in Maida Vale', *Observer* (27 March 1983): 32.

37 Candice Rodd, 'Drawing-Room Despair', *Times Literary Supplement* (21 August 1992): 17.
38 Daphne Watson, *Their Own Worst Enemies: Women's Writers of Women's Fiction* (London: Pluto Press, 1995), 54; Aranzuzu Usandizaga, 'The Female *Bildungsroman* at the Fin de Siècle: The "Utopian Imperative" in Anita Brookner's *A Closed Eye* and *Fraud*', *Critique: Studies in Contemporary Fiction* 39.4 (1998): 333.
39 Matt Schudel, 'Anita Brookner, Booker Prize-Winning Author of Ruminative Novels, Dies at 87': www.washingtonpost.com/entertainment/books/anita-brookner-booker-prize-winning-author-of-ruminative-novels-dies-at-87/2016/03/15/c6601012-eac6-11e5-a6f3-21ccdbc5f74e_story.html.
40 Ann Fisher-Wirth states, 'All of Brookner's heroines are defined by lack. They exist, by their own choice, almost entirely within the patriarchal structures—particularly the conventional heterosexual rituals of courtship and marriage—that offer them only meagre satisfaction'. Ann Fisher-Wirth, 'Hunger Art: The Novels of Anita Brookner', *Twentieth-Century Literature* 41.1 (1995): 1.
41 Daphne Watson maintains that Brookner's heroines are 'limited and indeed diminished by a sense of hollowness—a hollowness which marks the lack of a man'. Watson, *Their Own Worst Enemies*, 54.
42 Jan Dalley, 'Sympathy for the Bedevilled: Fraud', *Independent on Sunday* online (23 August 1992): www.independent.co.uk/arts-entertainment/book-reivew--sympathy-for-the-bedevilled-fraud--anita-brookner-cape-1499-1542086.html.

Across a variety of critical media, commentators also reported an absence of historical context in Brookner's novels. 'Brookner's characters occupy only the vaguest of times and places', wrote Jan Zita Grover.[43] 'It is almost a novel written out of time', remarked Barbara Hardy of *Hotel du Lac*.[44] Frederic Jameson's 1981 exhortation to 'always historicise!' seemed to be lost on Brookner, with the added irony that the novelist was herself a historian. Indeed, one unusual criticism of Brookner's *Romanticism and Its Discontents* came from Patrice Higonnet, in the *Times Literary Supplement*, who declared that what was 'striking about this text is its context, or wilful lack of it'.[45] However, when discussing her fiction in a 2009 interview, Brookner flagged an interest in experimenting with context as a core philosophy of her literary practice. 'Life without a context, which is a writer's life, is very unpleasant. I wanted to explore what you do not with a blank page, but with a blank day'.[46] Brookner's ownership of the writer's life as the inspiration to dissect issues of context is also interesting in light of her labelling as an autobiographical writer. In much autobiographical criticism, the focus is on questions of gender and heterocentric developmental milestones which have tended to obfuscate Brookner's identifications as Romanticist, writer, and critic.

In Brookner's early reception, in fact, her expertise in eighteenth- and nineteenth-century art history sometimes resulted in critics levelling charges of mimicry and lack of imagination against her. Brookner herself was openly 'content to claim' both Henry James and Charles Dickens as her mentors, and, over the years, her novels drew frequent comparisons to the works of the former.[47] However, the impact of James on Brookner was sometimes restaged as a stereotypical opposition between the original male master and the derivative female apprentice:

'We ... perhaps begin to long ... for someone to give her characters a good shaking and a sensible talking to'. David Allen, 'Lovers and Other Dangers', *Australian* (19 October 1996); 'I used to think Brookner was a genius, but now I just want to kick her in the shins'. Heather Mallick, 'Depressive Tale Lacks Substance', *Toronto Sun* (6 September 1998).

43 Jan Zita Grover, 'Small Expectations: Anita Brookner's Novels', *Women's Review of Books* 11.10–11 (July 1994): 39.
44 Hardy, 'A Cinderella's Loneliness', 1019.
45 Patrice Higonnet, 'Artists of Indefinite Longing', *Times Literary Supplement* (3 November 2000): 16.
46 Brookner, in Brown, 'A Singular Woman'.
47 Brookner, in Smith, 'Anita Brookner', 67.

'Brookner has devoured James, and she drops what she has learned from him wholesale into her books. She is overly fond of mimicking his qualifying phrases'.[48] Or, as a different reviewer put it, 'Anita Brookner's novels are expert copies of nineteenth-century novels'.[49] For Lynn Veach Sadler, Brookner's trailblazing first career as an academic set her at a disadvantage in other ways. In her 1990 book, *Anita Brookner*, Sadler claimed that 'Brookner is a very attractive woman and the devotion of such hours to research may account for her remaining unmarried'.[50] By contrast, feminist critics battling for change in antagonistic institutions expressed anger at Brookner's apparent anachronisms. 'How can she offer that, I ask myself again and again, as an image of life, of womanhood?' Wendy Steiner demanded to know. 'How can this still be the way of the world at the end of the twentieth century?' asked Ann Fisher-Wirth.[51] 'Reading Brookner one might think the whole Feminist movement had never occurred', declared Watson.[52] Brookner's failure either to bedeck her heroines in the armour of contemporaneity, or to sign her allegiance with updated representational strategies, antagonised multiple audiences.

The problem was aggravated by Brookner's explicit resistance to feminism, which coexisted with more ambiguous indicators in her life and work. 'You'd have to be crouching in your burrow to see my novels in a feminist way', Brookner told John Haffenden in 1984.[53] With Brookner's Anglo-Jewish nationality and its pressure to assimilate at the forefront of her developing sense of self, combined with her intellectual commitment to Romanticism (and Darwinism), she evinced suspicion of the concept of female solidarity. 'What women want is the clean part of the programme; how they get it is the dirty part', she also remarked to Haffenden.[54] Likewise, it was Brookner-the-Romanticist speaking when she told Gail Caldwell that men 'have the same emotions [as women]. Bedrock emotions: hope, fear, loneliness'.[55] Throughout Brookner's interviews, there is a sense that the regulatory aspects of gender, with

---

48 Deborah Friedell, 'Disengagement', *New Republic* (9 February 2004): 32.
49 Sven Birkerts, 'Private View', *New Republic* (24 April 1995): 41.
50 Sadler, *Anita Brookner*, 4.
51 Wendy Steiner, 'She Who Won't Be Obeyed', *New York Times Book Review* (23 January 2000): 34; Fisher-Wirth, 'Hunger Art', 1.
52 Watson, *Their Own Worst Enemies*, 42.
53 Anita Brookner, interview by John Haffenden, in John Haffenden, *Novelists in Interview* (London: Methuen, 1985), 70.
54 Brookner, in Haffenden, *Novelists in Interview*, 7.
55 Anita Brookner, interview by Gail Caldwell, *Boston Globe* (5 June 1985), 31.

its naive dichotomous identifications, was something that Brookner was unwilling to parse emotionally, intellectually, and experientially. When asked about her time at male-dominated Cambridge in the 1960s, she commented that 'Nobody looked all that male and I didn't look all that female'.[56] In Brookner's spoken commentary there exists a tendency for the intellectual novelist to resist any type of simplistic or reductive world view, moral high ground, or commercial pose.[57] And, despite her belated dismissal of the interview genre, Brookner's interviews are nevertheless attractive for the degree to which she provides beautiful answers to unclean questions.

There have been other women writers who resist allying with the feminist movement. Kate Fullbrook aligned Brookner with Katherine Mansfield, Gertrude Stein, and Margaret Atwood, stating 'This tendency … is both understandable in terms of the need for women writers of fiction to secure their independence *as* writers, and deserves much more attention by feminist critics as we, equally legitimately, analyse their work'.[58] Albeit from the perspective of my own feminist 'burrow', there are countless vignettes in Brookner's novels supporting the intelligence, independence, and idiosyncratic behaviour of the Brooknerine that seem to qualify as feminist behaviour. For instance, the runaway bride motif of *Hotel du Lac* rejects the conventional female domains of commitment, security, and obedience. Rather, Edith Hope chooses her path as a women's writer with her own sexual independence, and humorously dismisses the less attractive options where women are defined by marriage through their relationships to men. Similarly, Blanche Vernon's study of nymphs in *A Misalliance* can be seen to constitute a self-motivated and unconventional private study about female sexuality which seeks knowledge about woman and selfhood outside patriarchal norms. In this way, Brookner's impetus to write complex outsider female characters leaves the door wide open to a queer feminist analysis of her novels.

Fullbrook, along with other critics, also emphasised a strong, positive connection between Brookner's work as a Romantic art historian and

---

56 Guppy, 'Secret Sharer', 285.
57 In 'The Paratextual Construction of Anita Brookner', I try and follow Brookner's distaste for the interview genre by examining how Brookner's comments have been circulated out of context to construct an unreal persona for the author. Mayer, 'The Paratextual Construction of Anita Brookner', 49–68.
58 Kate Fullbrook, 'Anita Brookner: On Reaching for the Sun', in *British Women Writing Fiction*, ed. Abby H.P. Werlock (Tuscaloosa and London: University of Alabama Press, 2000), 103–04n4.

her novels. 'All her writing is notably shaped by her work as a historian of ideas ... For Brookner, romanticism is not an exhausted movement of the past, but the framework on which the contemporary world is pinioned', she states.[59] John Skinner, Richard Vidaud, Eileen Williams-Wanquet, Ann V. Norton, and Margaret D. Stetz are among those who tirelessly documented Brookner's nineteenth-century (and contemporary) intertextual practice, with Vidaud stating in 2000 that 'each of the eighteen novels published so far gather together multiple previous texts: texts of all genres with no immediately obvious relationship to each other'.[60] The intertextual dimension of Brookner's novels, and the stunning way it works across her fiction, history, and criticism, as well as across historical context, is a particular passion of *Misreading Anita Brookner*. For some critics it also accounts for Brookner's membership within the contemporary canon of postmodernity.[61]

In 2002, *The Independent*'s Boyd Tonkin publicly recognised that a skewered view of Brookner's novels had been presented through the powerful yet seemingly benign book review. 'There was always something facile, even hysterical, about these reviews (I should know; I wrote one). The annual Brookner offered a cheap shot to young critics, eager to savage a scandalous bearer of bad tidings about ageing and loneliness', Tonkin confessed.[62] While Tonkin's disclaimer reflected a particular stream of Brookner criticism, it also bore witness to the changing tide of

---

59 Fullbrook, 'Anita Brookner', 92.
60 John Skinner, *The Fictions of Anita Brookner: Illusions of Romance* (Basingstoke: Macmillan, 1992); Eileen Williams-Wanquet, *Art and Life in the Novels of Anita Brookner: Reading for Life, Subversive Re-writing to Live* (Berne: Peter Lang, 2004); Richard Vidaud, 'L'écriture palimpsestueuese d'Anita Brookner: de la transtextualité à l'autotextualité', *Études britanniques contemporaines* 19 (2000): 81 (translation privately commissioned by author); Ann V. Norton, 'Anita Brookner Reads Edith Wharton and Henry James: The Problem of Moral Imagination', *Tulsa Studies in Women's Literature* 29.1 (2010): 19–33; Margaret D. Stetz, 'Anita Brookner's Visual World', *Tulsa Studies in Women's Literature* 29.1 (2010): 35–46.
61 See Deborah Bowen, 'Preserving Appearances: Photography and the Postmodern Realism of Anita Brookner', *Mosaic* 28.2 (June 1995): 123; Norton, 'Anita Brookner Reads Edith Wharton and Henry James, 19–33; Laurence Petit, 'Romance of a Family or Inverted "Family Romance"', 379–97; and Laurence Petit, 'Between Iconophilia and Iconophobia: Anita Brookner's Museum of Words', *Word & Image* 30.1 (2014): 7–12: doi.org/10.1080/02666286.2013.771924.
62 Boyd Tonkin, 'Anita Brookner: "You Should Play Russian Roulette with Your Life"', *Independent Magazine* (29 June 2002): www.independent.co.uk/arts-entertainment/books/features/anita-brookner-you-should-play-russian-roulette-with-your-life-182287.html.

critical contexts, including the deconstruction of gender categories that accompanied the publication of Judith Butler's *Gender Trouble: Feminism and the Subversion of Identity* in 1990, and the rise of queer theory.[63] In 1997, Patricia Juliana Smith was the first to contextualise Brookner in the canon of queer criticism when Smith included *A Friend from England* in her book, *Lesbian Panic: Homoeroticism in Modern British Women's Fiction*, propelling a momentum which this book hopes to build on.[64] Louise Sylvester was among just a handful of critics who brilliantly illuminated the significance of Brookner's Jewishness in her writing, through the trope of foreignness.[65] By defining the trope of foreignness as something 'which is amenable to being hidden, but which is feared may reveal itself'; by remarking that the novels generally contain 'no overt references' to Jewish identity; and by commenting that Brookner 'refuses to name' the Holocaust, Sylvester's formulation of Brookner's Jewish troping indeed bears strong resemblance to some of the historical tropes for queerness which are explored in *Misreading Anita Brookner*.[66] Sylvester's inquiry into how Brookner's novels reference Jewish contexts is also significant for underscoring that Brookner has a representational strategy that is largely *representational*; that is, she is among thousands of authors who name through inference, metaphor, symbol, trope, motif, figure, etc., and whose writing freights importance on how the work is read. A further high point in Brookner's reception came in 2008 when Lassner, Norton, and Stetz convened a panel on Brookner at the Modern Language Association conference that called for a 'new appraisal of [Brookner's] achievements' and 'a new framework in which to evaluate them in order to bring attention to the unacknowledged breadth and ambition of her fiction'.[67] Examining Brookner's European Jewish subjects, Lassner praised the novelist for creating 'a collective memory and memorial to the lost as well as a narrative that expands and complicates contemporary British culture'.[68] Norton spearheaded further intertextual research by delving

---

63 Judith Butler, *Gender Trouble: Feminism and the Subversion of Identity* (New York: Routledge, 1990).
64 Smith, *Lesbian Panic*.
65 Louise Sylvester, 'Troping the Other: Anita Brookner's Jews', *English: The Journal of the English Association* 50.196 (2001): 47–58.
66 Sylvester, 'Troping the Other', 49, 51, 53.
67 Phyllis Lassner, Ann V. Norton, and Margaret D. Stetz, 'Introduction: Anita Brookner in the World', *Tulsa Studies in Women's Literature* 29.1 (2010): 15.
68 Phyllis Lassner, 'Exiles from Jewish Memory: Anita Brookner's Anglo-Jewish Aesthetic', *Tulsa Studies in Women's Literature* 29.1 (2010): 60.

into Brookner's influence by Edith Wharton and Henry James.[69] And Stetz expanded Brookner's investment in visual and intertextual spaces, arguing that storytelling in the novels is accomplished through visual means and open 'limitlessly' into the world of European art.[70] So, despite the contentious mainstream encoding of Brookner as the boring novelist of repetitive tales about lonely, single women, there has always been a groundswell behind a more nuanced interpretation of her work.

Performative Romanticism

The momentum around investigating Brookner's Romantic, intertextual, and queer dimensions directly informs the work of *Misreading Anita Brookner*. This book argues that Brookner's novels exhibit a form of 'performative Romanticism', which emerges across intertextual, historical, and temporal literary practices. First, the novels host an array of both nineteenth-century and contemporary tropes, motifs, narratives, and discourses. Laurent Jenny usefully distinguishes between explicit and implicit intertextuality to discriminate between overt references to literary or visual texts and subjects, such as when Miriam Sharpe 'marvelled that Henry James knew so much about women and children' in *Falling Slowly*, and the covert or implicit forms of intertextuality manifested by references to various narrative tropes and motifs (*FS*, 189).[71]

In particular, it can be seen that Brookner's implicit intertextual references are generally references to the literary tropes and narrative devices of Romantic aestheticism. Romantic aestheticism is defined broadly to include Romanticism, symbolism, and decadence, French and English aestheticism, and Henry James, whose work engages with a variety of European aestheticist themes despite his American nationality. In *Romanticism and Its Discontents*, Brookner specifies that Romanticism emerges at different times in French, British, and German forms, and with different emphases depending on context: 'although Romanticism does not erupt into painting until the very end of the eighteenth century it is comparatively untrammelled in literature long before this date' (*RD*, 7–8). As such, the broad rubric of 'Romantic aestheticism'

---

69 Norton, 'Anita Brookner Reads Edith Wharton and Henry James', 19–33.
70 Stetz, 'Anita Brookner's Visual World', 36–40.
71 Laurent Jenny, 'The Strategy of Form', in *French Literary Theory Today*, ed. Tzvetan Todorov, trans. R. Carter (Cambridge: Cambridge University Press, 1982), 34.

used herein supports a more fluid movement across genres and national interests as they emerge in Brookner's contemporary fiction.

Brookner's earliest novels more overtly embrace an explicit intertextual practice; in the later novels, the practice becomes more implicit. In Brookner's first novel, *A Start in Life*, the protagonist, Ruth Weiss, is publishing a three-volume series entitled *Women in Balzac's Novels* and teaches a course on *Eugénie Grandet*.[72] The novel's title—*A Start in Life*—makes an intertextual reference to the 1844 novelette by Balzac entitled *Un debut dans la vie* (*A Start in Life*). As a woman whose 'appearance and character were exactly half-way between the nineteenth and twentieth centuries', Ruth Weiss embodies the historical conundrum posed by Brookner's fiction.[73] In Brookner's second novel, *Providence*, the protagonist, Kitty Maule, is a Benjamin Constant specialist whose students are studying *Adolphe*.[74] Brookner states that 'Kitty Maule was difficult to place', ostensibly because of her French–English background.[75] Haffenden draws attention to Brookner's nineteenth-century intertextual writing strategy, remarking: 'Two of your novels are critiques of other fictions, *A Start in Life* utilizes *Eugénie Grandet*, and *Providence* a novel by Constant … I think the analogies and correspondences you draw between *Adolphe* and *Providence* are particularly striking and illuminating'.[76] 'It's a little bit mechanical, I think, or forced: I wouldn't do that again', Brookner replies, in what constitutes an acknowledgement of a developing intertextual practice.[77]

In the six Brookner novels that feature in this present study—generally through gestures to the literary and artistic tastes of her protagonists—Brookner explicitly references works by Stendhal, Ivan Goncharov, Charles Dickens, Giorgione, Henry James, J.M.W. Turner, Honoré de Balzac, Staël, Plato, Alfred Tennyson, Arthur Rimbaud, Theodor Fontane, the Dutch masters, Eugène Galien-Laloue, Sigmund Freud, Colette, and Marcel Proust. By invoking these artists and their works, Brookner draws a variety of tropes, discourses, and narratives into her own fictional worlds. Intertextuality becomes a freeway of meaning, enabling the reader to travel into different histories and stories

---

72 Brookner, *A Start in Life*, 7.
73 Brookner, *A Start in Life*, 8.
74 Anita Brookner, *Providence* (Harmondsworth: Penguin, 1991). First published 1982.
75 Brookner, *Providence*, 5.
76 Brookner, in Haffenden, *Novelists in Interview*, 66.
77 Brookner, in Haffenden, *Novelists in Interview*, 66.

INTRODUCTION

and return with a new bag of interpretative tricks. Brookner's intertextuality encompasses the canon of Western art and literature, creating a situation where contemporary meaning is always under pressure from the past. This juxtaposition of multiple meanings can effectively be used to highlight how certain meanings become privileged in a historical context. For example, the 'strange' Brooknerine, who is an anomaly in her contemporary world, conversely brings to light the preferred behaviours of contemporary femininity.

Secondly, in addition to the intertextual strategies of the novels, Brookner's texts and subjects can be said to perform a variety of nineteenth- and twentieth-century acts that span multiple historical contexts. In *Gender Trouble*, Butler frames gender as 'a stylised repetition of acts through time', drawing attention to how gender is historically constituted through behaviour.[78] For Butler, performative acts are types of behaviours, gestures, desires, or enactments that create the gendered subject and are played out in temporal ways. In *Romanticism and Its Discontents*, Brookner states that 'Romanticism is about behaviour, it is therefore recognisable', suggesting that Romantic acts are also quantifiable as behaviour that is performed in time (*RD*, 1). She hints at the possibility that Romantic behaviour can be discernible within a contemporary context when she maintains that the 'traces are perceptible today, even though the context has been lost' (*RD*, 20).[79] In interviews in the

---

78 Judith Butler, *Gender Trouble*, 140. Butler's contention that 'we regularly punish those who fail to do their gender right' sheds light on the personal type of criticism levelled at the strange Brooknerine. Butler, *Gender Trouble*, 139.

79 Brookner's interest in contextual disjunction, and the ongoing relevance of Romantic contexts, resonates with other critics. In *The Romanticism of Contemporary Theory: Institution, Aesthetics, Nihilism*, Justin Clemens outlines a historical tradition that maintains that Romanticism continues to organise perceptions of self and other in contemporary thought. He notes that 'Romanticism—if not precisely a *historical* formation—still has an uncircumventable historical *force* ... those who believe themselves still Romantic are essentially correct, but in ways that they are not necessarily aware of; on the other hand, those who believe themselves anti-Romantic fall back into Romanticism by way of the very gestures by which they believe that they escape it'. Justin Clemens, *The Romanticism of Contemporary Theory: Institution, Aesthetics, Nihilism* (Aldershot: Ashgate, 2003), 38. Similarly, when Brookner was asked to respond to Isaiah Berlin's contention that 'all the problems of our age can be traced back to Romanticism', she agreed that he was 'absolutely right. It was hearing him lecture on the subject that impressed me so much as made me decide to take it up and teach it myself'. Guppy, 'The Art of Fiction', 156, 156.

mid-80s, Brookner occasionally described certain types of contemporary behaviour as Romantic or nineteenth-century. Referring to the capital R Romanticism of the heroine of *Hotel du Lac*, Brookner claimed that 'Edith Hope is not a twentieth-century heroine, she belongs to the nineteenth century'.[80] Likewise, Brookner described the Dorn family of her fifth novel, *Family and Friends*, published in 1985, as 'a nineteenth-century family without a nineteenth century to support it'.[81]

The argument presented in *Misreading Anita Brookner* is that the cross-historical nature of Brookner's work confounds attempts to read her novels through any one particular historical context.[82] Historical context is traditionally confined to one historical period; Brookner's work, however, expands context to cover multiple historical periods. Subsequently, the notion that subjectivity can be a performance assembled from cross-historical discourses has an interesting effect on how contemporary gender and sexuality can be considered.[83] In Brookner's novels, female characters execute a cross-historical performance that draws predominantly on nineteenth-century male codes of behaviour. The performative

80 Brookner, in Guppy, 'The Art of Fiction', 161.
81 Brookner, interview Hermione Lee, *Book Four*, Channel 4.
82 In 'Forms of Time and of the Chronotope in the Novel', Mikhail Bakhtin coined the term 'chronotope' (literally, 'time space') to express 'the intrinsic connectedness of temporal and spatial relationships that are artistically expressed in literature'. Bakhtin's chronotope can be thought of as the literary term for historical context. However, it is interesting to note that an overly literal interpretation of the 'connectedness' of time and space can inhibit readers from thinking of behaviour as informed by multiple historical contexts or chronotopes. Mikhail Bakhtin, 'Forms of Time and of the Chronotope in the Novel', in *The Dialogic Imagination: Four Essays*, trans. Caryl Emerson and Michael Holquist (Austin: University of Texas Press, 1981), 84.
83 When Judith Butler discusses gender as temporal performance, she links gender to historical context, thereby illuminating how normative gender can be regulated through the production of historical context. The effect is that the framing of historical context becomes one way in which gender can be policed, as witnessed by Claire Pitt's admission in *Undue Influence* that she 'failed to conform to what a woman should do and be, even in this unregulated age' (*UI*, 130). Following Butler, it can also be seen how the interdependence of normative gender and historical context yokes, by extension, the production of historical context to the regulation of sexual identity. In *Misreading Anita Brookner*, I use the term 'hetero-chronic' to reference how the production of historical context as an exclusive period of time can be used to privilege heterosexual identity. Hetero-chronic refers to the privileging of heterosexuality grounded in a singular, unitary historical context or period as the natural developmental model for subjectivity.

Romanticism of Brookner's texts and subjects can therefore be said to defy the periodising regulation of gender and sexuality.

Thirdly, the intertextual, cross-historical Brookner novel is also a temporal text. I distinguish between the historical and the temporal by identifying 'the historical' as referring to behaviours or events that emerge as effects of a particular time and 'the temporal' as referring to tropological or narrative forms that mobilise concepts of time to convey information. In her novels, Brookner employs different temporal tropes to represent her contemporary characters as anachronistic, outdated, and old-fashioned, and these tropes (along with those of absence and invisibility) are historically associated with the figure of the lesbian. In *Brief Lives*, the 'strikingly old-fashioned' Julia Morton incarnates the anachronistic to the extent of being associated with the figure of a broken clock: 'if ever Julia went to a shop, which was rarely, it was to produce a hopelessly shattered clock to be mended', Fay reports (*BL*, 4, 6). Rachel Kennedy of *A Friend from England* attributes to the 'docile' Heather Livingstone 'a temperament as undemanding as that of a Victorian matron' (*FE*, 15, 15). While in *A Misalliance* Blanche condemns herself for having 'so many inaccurate or outdated thoughts' (*M*, 83). In *The Apparitional Lesbian*, Terry Castle contends that 'women who desire other women repeatedly find themselves vaporised by metaphor and translated into (empty) fictional space', calling to mind the way in which Brookner's temporal tropes effect an evacuation from the privileged historical context.[84] Castle's reading of the 'derealisation' of the lesbian complements Annamarie Jagose's interrogation of the narrative mechanisms that produce the lesbian as 'the figure most comprehensively worked over by sequence, secondary and inconsequential in all senses'.[85] And, in *Feeling Backward*, Heather Love contextualises 'figures of backwardness as allegories of queer historical experience'.[86] Love's explicit parsing of the backward turn through queer discourses further illuminates links between Brookner's themes of the outdated, the unfashionable, and the anachronistic and their queer temporal contexts.

84 Terry Castle, *The Apparitional Lesbian: Female Homosexuality and Modern Culture* (New York: Columbia University Press, 1993), 45.
85 Castle, *The Apparitional Lesbian*, 6; Annamarie Jagose, Introduction to *Inconsequence: Lesbian Representation and the Logic of Sexual Sequence* (Ithaca, NY: Cornell University Press, 2002), x.
86 Heather Love, *Feeling Backward: Loss and the Politics of Queer History* (Cambridge, Mass.: Harvard University Press, 2007), 5.

Temporal tropes also operate as dualities: the anachronistic presupposes an idea of the contemporary, for instance. And, with dualities come hierarchies: in a linear narrative, the contemporary is privileged over the historical or anachronistic; a backward turn to historical forms may be seen as derivative and secondary to original forms. By contrast, Brookner's novels juxtapose temporal tropes and historical periods, enabling readers to test concepts of progress, generation, and reproduction. Therefore, while many critics originally dismissed the novelist herself as anachronistic, Brookner's own mobilisation of anachronism within a literary and historical vernacular reflects a more strategic approach than is widely recognised. Crossing intertexts, historical periods, and temporalities, Brookner's texts, subjects, and contexts complicate representations of gender, sexuality, historical context, family, and intersubjectivity.[87] The intertextual, cross-historical, and temporal investigations of *Misreading Anita Brookner* will additionally attempt to illuminate vulnerabilities around Brookner's representation as a women's writer and her status in the literary field, as well as highlighting the difference between literal and figurative readings of the novels.

In *Misreading Anita Brookner*, a queer methodology is employed which operates across historical, temporal, gendered, erotic, semiotic, and generic modes. This study features a cast of intertextual Romantic personae—comprised of the military man, the analysand, the queer, the aesthete, the

---

87 The notion of 'crossing' has significant application in queer theory. In early queer contexts, 'gender crossing' referred to a subject's potential to mix different gender signifiers, thereby 'crossing' between male and female categories. Crossing became a way to recombine signifiers from supposedly known categories in order to complicate and challenge meaning, intervene in or suspend predetermined forms of knowledge and presuppositions, and signify the fluidity that was thought more fully to represent the subject's experience. In 'Packing History, Count(er)ing Generations', Elizabeth Freeman discusses 'temporal drag' and temporal crossing, formulating ways to acknowledge 'the interesting threat that the genuine *past*-ness of the past sometimes makes to the political present'. Elizabeth Freeman, 'Packing History, Count(er)ing Generations'. *New Literary History* 31 (2000): 728–29. She also notes how temporal crossings can be executed in generational and familial models, mapping out a way 'to complicate the idea of horizontal political generations succeeding one another, with a notion of "temporal drag"'. Freeman, 'Packing History', 730. In *Misreading Anita Brookner*, I draw on concepts of gender, historical, and generational crossings to describe the way in which Brookner's subjects perform cross-gendered, cross-historical, and cross-generational behaviours. These crossings form part of the Brooknerine's ability to disturb conventional readings and disrupt normative expectations of the historical subject's sexuality and behaviour.

out to other periods of time to reinvest itself with a plethora of possible meanings and as self-consciously aware of the meaning that is produced through textual interpretation. Dealing as it does in tropes, motifs, textual devices, intertextuality, and signifying matrices, *Misreading Anita Brookner* is not a purveyor of literal interpretation. I follow Julia Kristeva's belief that everything is intertextual, and Lee Edelman's understanding that literal signification is itself a figurative form that follows its own logic of construction.[89] All forms of interpretation which seem natural have been learned.

What you will find in *Misreading Anita Brookner* is an attempt to do something different with Brookner's novels. For me, Brookner writes about alternative ways of being and living which have not always been parsed by conventional filters for reading subjectivity. Her novels provide a different model for life, where women (and men) think, feel, laugh, and desire independently of mainstream patriarchal regulation. You will find me dipping into the Brookner intertextual archive to try to find different ways to narrate the patterns in her novels. My reliance on the intertextual network for epistemological help is an attempt to escape from the stranglehold of presupposition around meaning. We all get meaning from somewhere, so transparency is important. In a literary context, it seems especially relevant to use the canon as context, rather than prevailing mainstream discourses. I call on the hermeneutic assistance of a cast of Romantic figures in the hope that their behaviours help liberate our knowledge of how it is possible to be and act in our time. And I engage a collection of rhetorical devices, not because they have complex names, but because they have historical and literary resonance within the canon with which Brookner works, and because they help unlock the myriad of narrative puzzles she leaves in the text. Finally, I hope you will find unceasing respect for and recognition of one the greatest writers of our time.

The Chapters

The military man, the analysand, the queer, the aesthete, the dandy, the *flâneur*, the degenerate, and the storyteller are all figures of the nineteenth-century literary landscape. While differing in style and

---

89 Julia Kristeva, 'Word, Dialogue and Novel', in *The Kristeva Reader*, ed. Toril Moi (Oxford: Basil Blackwood, 1986), 37. Lee Edelman, *No Future: Queer Theory and the Death Drive* (Durham, NC: Duke University Press, 2004), 15.

INTRODUCTION

form, their idiosyncratic behaviours each exhibit responses that can be called queer, and which contest the homosexual/heterosexual opposition that emerged in the nineteenth century. Through recombinant modes of social and literary behaviours, these queer figures all appear in the Brookner novels that are explored in the following chapters.

Each chapter (with the exception of the Epilogue) follows a similar four-part structure. First is the introduction, where the novel's key themes are foregrounded. Secondly, there is a plot summary and a review of the novel's original reception. Third, comes a section in which the selected intertexts are engaged, in conjunction with themes and motifs from Brookner's novel, to produce the chapter's key Romantic persona. Finally, I use the organising narrative forms to stage the performance of the intertextual figure back through Brookner's novel to generate a new reading of the text.

A further exception to this structure is Chapter 1, where, in addition to the figure of the military man, two further minor figures are delineated in the text: the analysand and the queer. However, the military man is the major figure whose performance will unlock the main interpretation of the text, due primarily to the dominance of themes relating to adventure and failure in both Rachel's personality and the narrative structure itself.

In Chapter 1, Brookner's seventh novel, *A Friend from England*, takes centre stage. The text narrates the problematic relationship between the 'orphan' narrator, Rachel Kennedy, a bookseller, and twenty-nine-year-old 'bovine' beauty Heather Livingstone, a boutique owner (*FE*, 178, 65). In the novel's early reception, critics decried Rachel as 'monstrous and pathological', structural problems were detected in Brookner's writing style, and she was found to lack knowledge of contemporary female friendships.[90] An alternative way to read Rachel's personality and relationships, and Brookner's literary strategies, is to accept an array of identifications, desires, and expressions that are not limited to normative ways of relating in a given historical context.

In *Lesbian Panic*, Smith describes Rachel as striking 'a theatrically "butch" pose'.[91] But Rachel's 'butch' behaviour might also be thought to echo the militant psyche of nineteenth-century France, bedevilled

---

90 Fisher-Wirth, 'Hunger Art', 1; Skinner, *The Fictions of Anita Brookner*, 119; David Plante, 'They Won Their Life on the Football Pools', *New York Times Book Review* (20 March 1988), sect. 7.
91 Smith, *Lesbian Panic*, 128.

dandy, the *flâneur*, the degenerate, and the storyteller—whom I construct as hermeneutic devices for reading Brookner's novels. Each Romantic persona is constituted from a set of behaviours, an organising rhetorical device, and a narrative form, to reflect the performative, historical, and literary nature of Brookner's oeuvre.[88] Each figure becomes representative of a set of behaviours that emerge from a particular Brookner novel, and the various intertexts referenced therein, which are matched with texts by authors who all have strong ties to the 'French book': Stendhal, Henry James, Oscar Wilde, Freud, Charles Baudelaire, Renée Vivien, Balzac, Walter Pater, Harold Bloom, Joris-Karl Huysmans, Max Nordau, Colette, and Proust. These behaviours are combined with a complementary rhetorical device that demonstrates a particular pattern of representation in the text (in the glossary that precedes this introduction, you will find a list of the rhetorical terms and their definitions). Finally, an organising narrative form is mapped out for the individual persona that imparts information about the structure of the text. The narrative forms that are designated for each persona are encoded with their own sequence of events or plot points. Based on the structure and design of the rhetorical device and narrative form, the performance of the persona is staged across this new set of plot points to produce a fresh reading of the text. In each chapter, the combination of nineteenth- and twentieth-century epistemologies, and their illumination across a new sequence of markers in the text, brings new meaning to the novel and to the relationships between Brookner's female protagonists in the domestic fiction.

What you will not find in *Misreading Anita Brookner* is an overly conventional analysis which privileges normative ways of doing, being, or thinking. You will not find anything that explains the author through the novels, or the novels through the author, unless you take into account the author's superlative intellect and legacy as a Romanticist. This book is not an attempt to say that Brookner was a queer feminist, although we probably all have the capacity to be stronger and richer in what we do and who we are. Nor will you encounter an interpretation that pins the novels solely to their time of publication, unless you see our particular 'postmodern' historical context as constantly reaching

---

88 In the following chapters, I use Roland Barthes's term 'signifying matrix' to refer to the specialised field of signifiers that I designate around the texts and behaviours that combine to form each Romantic persona. Roland Barthes, *The Fashion System*, trans. Matthew Ward and Richard Howard (New York: Hill & Wang, 1983), 59.

through the 1800s by war and revolution. By 1863, the military man is such an established feature of the boulevards of nineteenth-century Paris that Charles Baudelaire consecrates a section to this figure in *The Painter of Modern Life*: 'Taken as a class, the military man has his beauty, just as the dandy and courtesan have theirs', he enthuses.[92]

Yet the true 'soldier–philosopher' of the nineteenth century was Stendhal (*GF*, 43). In *The Genius of the Future*, Brookner emphasises that Stendhal's military experience as a solider in Napoleon's army impacted on his personal and literary philosophies (*GF*, 36). In a moment of explicit intertextual referencing in *A Friend from England*, Rachel exits her austere flat for an implied sexual adventure, leaving behind a half-read copy of Stendhal's memoir *The Life of Henri Brulard*.[93] It follows that the three intertexts deployed to produce the military man are all by Stendhal: *Scarlet and Black: A Chronicle of the Nineteenth Century*, which Brookner reads as characterised chiefly by energy, passion, and adventure; *On Love*, Stendhal's pamphlet on romantic love in which he compares the amorous chase to military strategy; and *The Life of Henri Brulard* (*GF*, 43).[94] From across the intertextual matrix, the set of behaviours that can be said to constitute the military man are energy, passion, risk, duty, strategy, romantic love, obstacles, failure, and curiosity about experience and innocence. Like Brookner, Georges Kliebenstein identifies adventure as a key theme of the Stendhalian narrative.[95] He supplies the rhetorical figure of hendiadys as a way to interpret the Stendhalian narrative. In addition, the adventure narrative, as analysed by Margaret Bruzelius in *Romancing the Novel*, is also deployed to stage the performance of the military man across the plot points designated by the Stendhalian hendiadys.[96]

The second persona to be identified in *A Friend from England* is the figure of the analysand. In *Freud's Women*, Lisa Appignanesi and John

---

92 Charles Baudelaire, *The Painter of Modern Life and Other Essays*, ed. and trans. Jonathan Mayne (London: Phaidon Press, 1964), 25. First published 1863. Hereafter cited in text as *PML*.

93 Stendhal, *The Life of Henri Brulard*, trans. Catherine Alison Phillips (New York: Vintage Books, 1955). First published 1890. Hereafter cited in text as *HB*.

94 Stendhal, *Scarlet and Black: A Chronicle of the Nineteenth Century*, trans. Margaret R.B. Shaw (Harmondsworth: Penguin, 1953). First published 1830. Hereafter cited in text as *SB*; Stendhal, *On Love*, trans. Sophie Lewis (London: Hesperus Press, 2009). Hereafter cited in text as *L*.

95 *Figures du destin stendhalien* (Nancy: Presses Sorbonne Nouvelle, 2004) (translation privately commissioned by author).

96 Margaret Bruzelius, *Romancing the Novel: Adventure from Scott to Sebald* (Lewisburg, Pa.: Bucknell University Press, 2007).

Forrester write that 'psychoanalysis, like feminism, emerges as a response to the "hysterical" woman whose condition was emblematic of a collective malaise, and in turn a response to the untenable place of women in the late nineteenth century'.[97] Thus, Appignanesi and Forrester recognise how psychoanalysis combines a number of disparate signifying effects or symptoms around a particular type of nineteenth-century female subjectivity. This subject can be located within a network of psychoanalytic narrative associations in *A Friend from England* to produce the figure of the analysand. In the novel, Rachel's behaviour is shaped by her chronic hydrophobia. As she puts it, 'I cannot look at weeping skies or raindrops pattering on windows, or, least of all, at the falling rain itself without getting up to wander nervously from room to room, wringing my hands, and wondering if I can last out until it stops' (*FE*, 177). 'Fragment of an Analysis of a Case of Hysteria' ("Dora") (1905 [1901]) sees Freud make a number of claims around psychic symptoms and lesbian desire that can be matched to Rachel's representation of hydrophobia and her homologia (inane repetition) to characterise the analysand.[98] This figure is sketched in *A Friend from England* to emphasise a second historical formation of lesbian desire in the novel.

The final persona to map out in *A Friend from England* is the queer. To describe Heather's first husband, Michael Sandberg, Rachel combines narrative strategies from James's *A Beast in the Jungle* and Wilde's *The Picture of Dorian Gray*; it is a portrayal best decoded through the representational matrix that establishes the nineteenth-century figure of the queer. Therefore the texts of James and Wilde help produce the figure of the queer from a set of characteristics that signify youth, beauty, and monstrosity, in conjunction with the narrative of the secret and the rhetorical device of preterition.

In Chapter 2, Brookner's sixth novel, *A Misalliance*, is under consideration. A 'peculiar mixture of raciness and delicacy', Blanche Vernon, the novel's heroine, is fascinated by the nymphs of Renaissance painting (*M*, 92). When she meets the nymph-like Sally Beamish, Blanche's fascination shifts from art to life. The narrative of *A Misalliance* is dappled with evocations of visual, oral, olfactory, and sensual pleasures

---

97 Lisa Appignanesi and John Forrester, *Freud's Women* (London: Virago, 1993), 5.
98 Sigmund Freud, 'Fragment of an Analysis of a Case of Hysteria ("Dora") (1905 [1901])', in *Case Histories, 1, 'Dora' and 'Little Hans'*, Penguin Freud Library, 8, ed. Angela Richards trans. Alix Strachey and James Strachey (Harmondsworth: Penguin, 1990), 31–164. Hereafter cited in text as *D*.

that implicitly invoke Sapphic and Hellenic imagery. In nineteenth-century Romantic aestheticism, Sapphic motifs in the work of two of Brookner's precursors, Baudelaire and Vivien, converged around the transgressive figure of the lesbian. In this chapter, Baudelaire's Sapphism is supplemented with Vivien's proto-feminist appropriation of Sappho's works to emphasise the women's writer, female experience, and challenges to hetero-patriarchal institutions. Subsequently, the figure of the aesthete is produced through a combination of the idolatry of the senses, the nineteenth-century exhortation to live life as art, the 'backward turn', the heightened significance of the gaze, and filtered through the subversive power of nineteenth-century aestheticism.

Walter Benjamin's figure of history as an image, and Timothy Bahti's reading of Benjamin's 'angel of history', are marshalled to inform how the rhetorical figure of metaleptic prolepsis becomes the organising rhetorical device of the aesthete.[99] Mikhail Bakhtin's narrative of metamorphosis completes the figure of the aesthete.[100] The performance of the aesthete is thereby staged over the contours of metamorphosis: guilt, punishment, redemption, purification, and blessedness.[101]

In Chapter 3, Brookner's tenth novel, *Brief Lives*, is brought into focus. In this story, the self-described 'dull' and 'boring' narrator, Fay Dodworth, tells of her awe of and subjection to Julia Morton, a celebrated former performer (*BL*, 93, 52). Critics objected to the text's proliferation of 'inconsequential' detail, which led to accusations of inappropriate titling. 'The lives portrayed in this novel … are hardly brief', wrote one critic.[102] But such critiques overlooked the implications of Fay's depiction of Julia— her outstanding appearance, her scandalous discourse, her ability to command a range of services from others, her capacity to protest at the boredom caused by mere mortals, and her transgressive nature— which all bear resemblance to the narrative constitution of the nineteenth-century figure of the dandy.

---

99 Walter Benjamin, 'Theses on the Philosophy of History', in *Illuminations: Essays and Reflections*, ed. Hannah Arendt, trans. Harry Zohn (New York: Schocken Books, 1968), 253–65; Timothy Bahti, 'History as Rhetorical Enactment: Walter Benjamin's Theses "On the Concept of History"', in *Allegories of History: Literary Historiography after Hegel* (Baltimore, Md.: Johns Hopkins University Press, 1992), 183–204.
100 Bakhtin, 'Forms of Time', 113.
101 Bakhtin, 'Forms of Time', 113.
102 Cheryl Alexander Malcolm, *Understanding Anita Brookner* (Columbia: University of South Carolina Press, 2002), 118; 'Brief Lives', *Time* (5 August 1991): 14.

INTRODUCTION

Recent interpretations of the *Brief Lives* compiled by seventeenth-century antiquarian John Aubrey also afford a different perspective from the dominant readings of Brookner's novel upon its release.[103] The significance of detail is examined in Aubrey's biographical compendium that bears the same title as Brookner's book, and further connected to the *Imaginary Lives* penned by nineteenth-century symbolist poet, Marcel Schwob.[104] Throughout the nineteenth century, exclusivity of detail became associated with the figure of the dandy. Barthes explains the value ascribed to the detail as symptomatic of the emergence of an aesthetic category whose purpose was to circulate 'a new value: *taste*, or better still, as the word is appropriately ambiguous, *distinction*'.[105] The importance attributed to the detail in nineteenth-century dandy narratives informs the decision herein to nominate the detail as the organising rhetorical figure of the dandy.

In his 1830 manifesto of dandyism, *Treatise on Elegant Living*, Balzac outlines the categories central to refined modern living: 'Speak, walk, eat or dress yourself, and I will tell you what you are ', he undertakes.[106] In conjunction with the concerns about boredom and transgression delineated by Barbey in *On Dandyism and George Brummell* and Baudelaire's *The Painter of Modern Life*, then, acts of talking, dressing, eating, and walking emerge as key behaviours of the dandy.[107] The nineteenth-century dandy's appropriation of feminine characteristics are brought to light to illuminate the figure's historical brand of gendered and sexual transgression. These are subsequently linked to Julia's masculinity in *Brief Lives*, the asexual sexuality evinced across the centuries, and the forms of 'recessed homosexuality' that Clara Tuite flags as more typical of British dandy texts.[108]

---

103 Kate Bennett, 'John Aubrey's Collections and the Early Modern Museum', *Bodleian Library Record* 17.3–4 (2001): 213–45; John James Purdon, 'John Aubrey's "Discourse in Paper"', *Essays in Criticism* 55.3 (2005): 226–47.
104 Marcel Schwob, *Imaginary Lives*, trans. Lorimer Hammond (New York: Avon Book Division, 1952).
105 Roland Barthes, 'Dandyism and Fashion', in *The Language of Fashion*, trans. Andy Stafford, ed. Andy Stafford and Michael Carter (Oxford: Berg, 2006), 66.
106 Honoré de Balzac, *Treatise on Elegant Living*, trans. Napoleon Jeffries (Cambridge, Mass.: Wakefield Press, 2010), 23.
107 Jules Barbey d'Aurevilly, 'On Dandyism and George Brummell', trans. George Walden, in George Walden, *Who's a Dandy?* (London: Gibson Square Books, 2002).
108 Clara Tuite, 'Trials of the Dandy: George Brummell's Scandalous Celebrity', in *Romanticism and Celebrity Culture, 1750–1850*, ed. Tom Mole (Cambridge: Cambridge University Press, 2009), 161.

Tuite also construes the rise-and-fall narrative as the organising narrative of the dandy.¹⁰⁹ It follows that the performance of the dandy is staged across the categories of talking, dressing, walking, and eating, and along the generic contours of glamour, ruination, and ephemeral endurance that Tuite depicts as the markers of the rise-and-fall narrative.¹¹⁰

In Chapter 4, Brookner's nineteenth novel, *Undue Influence*, is under scrutiny. The narrative focuses on Claire Pitt, a thirty-two-year-old bookseller who invents stories about the strangers and acquaintances she passes on her way to work at a Gower Street bookshop. Claire meets Martin Gibson, a former London University academic and fellow walker, when he becomes a customer of the bookshop, and subsequently the focus of her miscalculating imagination. At work, Claire is also responsible for editing a manuscript of 'Walks with Myself', compiled by the late father of her employers and designed 'to be a companion for the solitary walker' (*UI*, 61).

Another figure famously associated with walking and imagination, albeit a male figure, is the nineteenth-century *flâneur*. The *flâneur's* material and immaterial freedoms signal the figure's distance from the reproductive unit of the heterosexual family. The *flâneur's* queerness, then, stems from a rejection of the heterosexual romance and his simultaneous adoption of the intertextual relationship as his narrative of origin.

This chapter's analysis opens with a literal map outlining the routes of two different walks around central London—one for Claire and one for Martin. As walks that predominately reflect the female narrator's transgressive appropriation of creative and public space, they challenge Michel de Certeau's contention in 'Walking in the City' that maps of walking routes 'constitute procedures for forgetting' the anarchical proclivities of walking subjects.¹¹¹ Assembling narratives of creative masculine imagination and walking from Baudelaire's *The Painter of Modern Life* and Bloom's *The Anxiety of Influence*, while combining them with Claire Pitt's contemporary female imagination, the figure of the *flâneur* is activated across behaviours of imagination, walking, misreading, and queer reversals. Matching the peripatetic with the

---

109 Tuite, 'Trials of the Dandy', 146.
110 Tuite, 'Trials of the Dandy', 146.
111 Michel de Certeau, 'Walking in the City', in *The Practice of Everyday Life*, trans. Steven Rendall (Berkeley: University of California Press, 1984), 97.

INTRODUCTION

peripeteiac, the rhetorical figure of peripeteia (reversal) seems like the obvious choice as the primary rhetorical device of the *flâneur*. As the organising narrative form of the *flâneur*, Bloom's narrative of influence rounds out the constitution of the figure. The performance of the *flâneur* is thereby staged across the six 'revisionary ratios' that Bloom delineates as the contours of the narrative of influence (*AI*, 10). Based around key themes of this study—misreading, and the status of contemporary female creativity in relation to nineteenth-century Romantic aestheticism—the performance of the *flâneur* also acts as a metatextual figure for the broad methodological work of *Misreading Anita Brookner*.

In Chapter 5, Brookner's eighteenth novel, *Falling Slowly*, is called to reckoning. The novel tells the story of Beatrice and Miriam Sharpe, two sisters with a 'terminal closeness' to each other who are identified by a spectrum of behaviours broadly premised around figures of absence and invisibility (*FS*, 7). The qualities associated with the Sharpe sisters, which tend to represent a deviation from the most commonly accepted definitions of desirability, include 'dullness', 'decline', 'invisibility', and 'vacancy' (*FS*, 7, 8, 171, 61).

The publication of *Falling Slowly* became the occasion for critics to declare that Brookner's writing style had degenerated.[112] But across the intertextual matrix of *Falling Slowly*, Huysmans's *Against Nature*, and Max Nordau's *Degeneration*, the figure of the degenerate itself emerges through a selection of behavioural signifiers grafted onto an opposition between the literal and the figurative, as well as a 'no future' narrative, and the rhetorical figure of syllepsis.[113] Based around signifiers of absence, invisibility, and backwardness, and staged in the familial symbolic, the figure of the degenerate manifests as lesbian sisters in the queer family matrix. The performance of the degenerate is staged along three palimpsestic tableaux in *Falling Slowly*. In these three different scenes, I shift between literal and figurative readings to demonstrate the mutable nature of so-called rigid designators and to illuminate the life-affirming properties of degenerate signs. Mobilising themes of rereading, the deconstruction of the literal/figurative opposition, and the figure of the lesbian in the domestic fiction, the performance of the

---

112 Gillian Tindall, 'Safe Sorrow', *Times Literary Supplement* (10 July 1998): 23.
113 Joris-Karl Huysmans, *Against Nature*, trans. Margaret Mauldon (Oxford: Oxford University Press, 1998). Hereafter cited in text as *AN*; Max Nordau, *Degeneration*, 4th edn, translated from the 2nd German edn (New York: D. Appleton, 1895). First published in English 1892. Hereafter cited in *DGN*.

degenerate is a metatextual figure for the broad epistemological work of this book.

In the Epilogue, this study draws to a close by returning to Brookner's early period. The spotlight falls on how *Hotel du Lac* is animated by a narrative of return that conjures the figure of the storyteller. Drawing on intertextual indications with Colette, as well as multiple literary techniques including a narrative orality, I finally locate Brookner as the consummate storyteller and women's writer.

CHAPTER ONE

The Military Man, the Analysand, and the Queer in *A Friend from England* (1987)

> Looking back much later I came to see it as something from the pages of a nineteenth-century novel.
>
> Anita Brookner, *A Friend from England*

Introduction

In the final chapter of *A Friend from England*, Rachel Kennedy, the 'spirited and relentless' thirty-two-year-old eponymous friend and narrator of Brookner's seventh novel, pursues the 'outlandishly chic' twenty-eight-year-old boutique owner, Heather Livingstone, from London to Venice (*FE*, 190, 56). Rachel represents her journey as an 'adventure', a 'quest', and a 'mission', the aim of which is 'to retrieve Heather from her hiding place and bring her safely home again' (*FE*, 192, 194, 185, 185). This adventure, however, is fuelled by 'fury', 'violence', 'panic', and 'monumental anger'—emotions that incite her to 'a pitch of opposition which had something murderous about it' (*FE*, 106, 172, 187, 185, 181). To complete her mission, Rachel thinks 'in terms of victory and defeat' and of 'handcuffing [Heather] and removing her by force', before she imagines corralling Heather back to London: 'I would take her by the arm and lead her back in triumph to the Pensione Wildner, where I would sit her on the bed and invite her to a final accounting' (*FE*, 192, 193, 190).

But before her final assignation with Heather takes place, Rachel visits the Gallerie dell'Accademia to see a canonical Renaissance painting: Giorgione's *Tempest* (Figure 1).

In a deserted room I found the only picture I wanted to see. The woman suckling her child had a heavy face, immanent with meaning, but from which all explanation had been withdrawn. To her right, on the edge of the picture, stood the mysterious and elegant knight, intense and remote, his face in shadow. The storm that broke on the scene bound the two together in puzzling complicity. In the background, a banal hill village. In the middle distance, two broken columns. (*FE*, 191)

Rachel's pilgrimage is lent significance when she later compares Heather to the mother in Giorgione's painting: Heather's 'face seemed to have the same moody distant expression as the woman suckling her baby in the picture' (*FE*, 201). Throughout the novel, Rachel emphasises Heather's feminine 'innocence', noting that 'Heather would always need to be accompanied in order that no one should take advantage of her', and contrasting such observations with those about her 'matronly calm … her Giaconda-like smile' and the way 'she looked like the bride in a Brueghel painting' (*FE*, 21, 21, 51, 47). In comparison, the militancy that characterises Rachel's own performance throughout the text suggests that she herself identifies with the intense and elegant knight or military man.

At the start of her academic career, Brookner studied history at the University of London, but switched disciplines after discovering the special potential of the visual medium. 'I hated history without the images', she said: 'And I find that pictures gave me a great deal imaginatively, emotionally and intellectually'.[1] In art-historical critical discussions, Giorgione's *Tempest* is notorious for inspiring conflicting readings.[2] No authoritative interpretation exists: biblical, iconographical, mythological, biographical, and historical analyses have alternatively read the male figure as a shepherd, a poet, a soldier, and an artist.[3] In 1939, speculation about the meaning of *The Tempest* intensified when X-ray technology exposed a pentimento which revealed that a figure of a nude female bather had preceded that of the male knight (Figure 2).[4]

---

1 Anita Brookner, interview by Sue MacGregor, 'Woman's Hour', BBC Radio 4 (13 January 1982).
2 'More has probably been written about the subject matter of this small but exquisite painting than about any other'. Deborah Howard, 'Giorgione's *Tempesta* and Titian's *Assunta* in the Context of the Combrai Wars', *Art History* 8.3 (1985): 272.
3 Rudolf Schier, 'Giorgione's *Tempest*: A Virgilian Pastoral', *Renaissance Studies* 22.4 (2008): 482.
4 Schier, 'Giorgione's *Tempest*', 497.

Giorgione, *The Tempest*, 1506–08. Oil on canvas, 83 cm × 73 cm.
Gallerie dell'Accademia, Venice

The palimpsest of an intimate scene between two naked women, laid bare by X-rays of *The Tempest*, suggests the female homoerotic scene that Patricia Simons reads as characteristic of Renaissance images of *donna con donna*.[5] Rachel's designation of the standing figure as a 'knight'

---

5 Patricia Simons, 'Lesbian (In)Visibility in Italian Renaissance Culture: Diana and Other Cases of *donna con donna*', in *Gay and Lesbian Studies in Art History*, ed. Whitney Davis (New York: Harrington Park Press, 1994), 85.

X-ray of Giorgione, *The Tempest*, 1506–08. Gallerie dell'Accademia, Venice

recalls the controversial issues of interpretation that *The Tempest* has historically inspired. Rachel's identification with the figure of the knight transports her, as a contemporary female subject, into the persona of the military man and next to Heather, whom Rachel understands as occupying the figure of the nude female bather in the painting's *mise en scène*. Analogously, as per the X-ray's findings, shifts between the figure of the military man and the earlier, perching nude female bather place Rachel and Heather together in a Sapphic homoerotic frame.

These shifts across character, gender, and context are demonstrative of the queer possibilities that emerge in Brookner's fiction when reading through a cross-historical lens. Therefore, Rachel's knightly quest, culminating in her identification with Giorgione's soldier, provides a conceptual framework for a queering of nineteenth-century tropes and narratives in *A Friend from England*. In this chapter, intertextual readings of Stendhal, Sigmund Freud, Henry James, and Oscar Wilde are presented in order to cast the personae of the military man, analysand, and queer as historical narrative formations that emblematise (sets of) queer nineteenth-century behaviours which are reconstituted and performed in Brookner's contemporary text. By bringing to life the figures of the military man, analysand, and queer it is possible to narrate multiple discourses of homoerotic desire in *A Friend from England*.

In part 2 of the chapter, Rachel's key modes of nineteenth-century behaviour are revealed to inform her fascination with the Livingstone family and Heather's two engagements. In the early reception of *A Friend from England*, reviewers largely perceived the novel to have failed; they thread the proairetic code of the novel to a contemporary context and a hetero-centric narrative. In this early mode of reading/ reception, Rachel's 'cold, hard … brute' instincts are perceived to be incongruous with contemporary gender, while charges of hyperbole are levelled against Brookner's writing style (*FE*, 186). This mode of analysis conflates Rachel's behaviour with heterosexual failure and narrative failure. In finding Rachel's behaviour unacceptable because she does not conform to contemporary gender and sexuality codes, and Brookner unacceptable for not conforming to contemporary women's representational strategies, reviewers participate in regulating gender and sexuality through normative expectations around literary representation and historical context.

This chapter attempts to do something different with *A Friend from England*—with Rachel's contentious persona and discourse, her romanticisation of the Livingstone family, and her eroticisation of Heather as alternately virgin and mother—by deploying the figure of the military man as an alternative epistemological formation through which to decode key narratives in the text. In 1863, in *The Painter of Modern Life*, Charles Baudelaire introduces the military man as one of the iconic personae of the boulevards of nineteenth-century Paris (*PML*, 24). For Baudelaire, the military man has 'a beauty characterised by energy', reveals an 'exceptional quality of independence and bravado', possesses 'a deep impetuous desire of war, love and gaming', and is 'ready to face death at any moment' (*PML*, 25). Baudelaire's military man displays an 'outward splendour' that matches Rachel's: 'I armed myself with courage, sought out my finest clothes, smoothed the leather of my conqueror's boots', she recalls of her preparations for Venice (*PML, 24*; *FE*, 186). And, just as Baudelaire's soldier's 'military coquetry' attracts admirers (*PML*, 24), the performance of the military man in *A Friend from England* propels Rachel's desire for Heather through the text (*PML*, 24).

A generation before Baudelaire, Stendhal had a definitive personal experience of war as a soldier in Napoleon's army. Brookner's *A Friend from England* and Stendhal's *Scarlet and Black* share a number of common themes and motifs concerning the energy of the outsider hero protagonist, their confrontational natures and aspirational values, and their curiosity about experience, innocence, romantic love, obstacles, failure, duty, and strategy. Drawing on Stendhal's memoir, *The Life of Henri Brulard*, in which the author reveals his great passion for his mother who died when he was seven, Rachel's attraction to the figure of the mother in *A Friend from England* can be newly elucidated. In addition, Stendhal's treatise on Romantic love and masculinity, *On Love*, illuminates how ambition and energy intersect with military discourses and narratives of Romantic love in Stendhal's oeuvre.

Along with the military man, two further queer personae can be excavated from *A Friend from England*: the analysand and the queer. Sigmund Freud's 'Dora' becomes useful for reading Rachel's hydrophobia, as well as the text's water/fire metaphors, its word associations and its homiologia (inane repetition) (*D*, 31–155). In 'Dora', Freud belatedly concluded that his patient's symptoms stemmed from her unresolved desire for a family friend, Frau K. In staging the performance of the analysand in *A Friend from England*, then, another historical trope of female same-sex desire is unveiled. This reading is distinct from a medical and pathologising rendering of lesbian desire; rather, the aim is to explore the historical construction and reconstitution of discursive formations of sexuality.

For the performance of the queer, Henry James's *The Beast in the Jungle* and Oscar Wilde's *The Picture of Dorian Gray* are recruited to read Rachel's characterisation of Michael Sandberg, Heather's first husband, through the rhetorical device of preterition and the narrative of the secret. Rachel's representation of Michael is full of smoke and mirrors, leaving a number of question marks around his masculinity, authenticity, maturity, and honesty.

Her strategy for characterising Michael is given homosexual meaning when she 'unmasks' Michael wearing make-up at a 'peculiar' wine bar and discovers his 'terrible' 'secret' (*FE*, 116, 116, 120, 115). Patricia Juliana Smith accused Brookner of 'willful and highly sophisticated suppressions of the knowledge of sexuality' in *A Friend from England*.[6] Against Smith, the defence presented here suggests that Brookner's multiple narratives of desire, drawing on historical, temporal, and familial forms of queer discursivity, reflect a deep and nuanced understanding of the history of sexuality.

Plot Summary and Original Reception

In *A Friend from England*, Rachel Kennedy recalls a period during which she acts on her fascination with the social and sexual decisions of Heather Livingstone, the daughter of her accountant, Oscar Livingstone. A self-described 'orphan' and 'liberated woman' of the twentieth century, with 'extensive' sexual experience, Rachel is the part-owner of a Notting Hill bookstore (*FE*, 178, 81, 52). A friend of Rachel's late father Oscar— along with his wife Dorrie—befriend Rachel and begin to include her in their family social events. Rachel is attracted to the parvenu Livingstones, whom she sees as providing some stability in her otherwise untenanted life. 'My odd relationship with the Livingstones was of great value to me; they were fixed points of reference in a slipping universe, abiding by rules which everybody else had broken' (*FE*, 31). Rachel believes the Livingstones perceive her as a type of 'Bohemian' and 'feminist', in contrast to the 'innocence' of Heather (*FE*, 31, 67, 51). Thus, Rachel understands that the Livingstones require her help with their daughter: 'that I would somehow look after Heather, guide her towards a radiant future, that I might in fact inherit Heather from her parents'—and she unofficially appoints herself Heather's 'protector' and 'chaperone' (*FE*, 33, 19, 31). While Rachel admires Heather's 'scornful and up-to-date appearance' and observes that Heather 'was capable of a kind of outlandish chic', she nevertheless claims that she feels 'rather little' for her (*FE*, 15, 56, 34). She recalls, 'When I first met her I thought she must be deaf. When I got to know her better I revised my opinion slightly: I thought she was retarded' (*FE*, 91) This ambivalence seems to be reflected back from Heather. 'I was not sure that Heather had ever really accepted me as a friend', Rachel says. 'In some ways I was almost sure that she disliked me' (*FE*, 121).

Rachel's reactions to Heather's announcements about her changing marital status fuel the action throughout the novel. After an expedited courtship, Heather marries Michael Sandberg, a man who 'had the air

---

6 Smith, *Lesbian Panic*, 124.

of dreading the spotlight but playing up to it' (*FE*, 43). When Heather and Michael return from their honeymoon, Rachel initiates a series of confrontations with Heather, raising objections to the younger woman's handling of her first marriage, her divorce, her second courtship with an Italian named Marco, and, finally, her decision to move to Venice to live with Marco. Ostensibly on Dorrie's wishes, Rachel pursues Heather to Venice to bring her back to London. After one of the 'worst' afternoons of her life, Rachel returns to London and has little future contact with the Livingstones (*FE*, 201).

Despite Rachel's own concession that her 'murderous' responses to the unremarkable behaviour of Heather were 'disproportionate', early critics of the novel were unconvinced and unforgiving (*FE*, 181, 181). 'Rachel seems monstrous, pathological', declared Ann Fisher-Wirth.[7] In the *Times Literary Supplement*, Deborah Singmaster found Rachel 'repellently cold and cerebral'.[8] John Skinner described her as 'obsessive' and 'psychotic', going so far as to suggest that there might even be a 'structural fault in the novel'.[9] Indeed, widespread doubts were voiced about Brookner's technical competency. In the *New York Times Book Review*, David Plante remarked on the novel's 'unreality' and claimed that 'complexity and drama is forced on material that is not very complex or dramatic'.[10] Critics warned that readers might be left irritated, confused, angry, or unmoved by Brookner's representations of character and events.[11] The novel was the catalyst for declaring that Brookner's fiction had degenerated, a practice which then became commonplace in her critical reception.[12]

---

7 'Fisher-Wirth, 'Hunger Art', 1.
8 Deborah Singmaster, 'Sorting Out the Arrangements', *Times Literary Supplement* (21 August 1989): 899.
9 Skinner, *The Fictions of Anita Brookner*, 120, 120, 119.
10 Plante, 'They Won Their Life', sect. 7.
11 Alice Bloom describes *A Friend from England* as a 'slight, sad novel'. 'A Friend from England', *Hudson Review* 41 (1988–89): 544; Skinner warns that the 'reader's irritation may be reinforced by a kind of world-weary superiority in Rachel's references to "paying one's dues" or the tedious *rite de passage* of Heather's fiancé being introduced to the family'. *The Fictions of Anita Brookner*, 119; and R.Z. Sheppard reports that the 'reader is left to wonder how bovine the bride must be to have been led into this situation'. Sheppard, 'A Friend from England', *Time* (21 March 1988): 76.
12 'The writing in *A Friend from England* is not as alert as it is in her previous novels'. Plante, 'They Won Their Life', sect. 7; 'I wish now that Brookner would try again the larger canvas of *Family and Friends*'. Bloom, 'A Friend from England', 545.

In the novel, a range of references situate narrative time in the 1980s, consistent with the date of the novel's publication: references to the Livingstones' win on the football pools; to Heather's avant-garde garments and women wearing casual shoes to work; to acupuncturists, feminism, Harrods, Japanese tourists, fitness habits, nightlife, aeroplanes, obscene telephone calls, and waiters battling with dry-cleaning bags. Yet critics were left with more questions than answers. In the *New York Times Book Review*, David Plante was unable to parse the historical context inhabited by the two main female protagonists. 'When one reads of Heather tucking a rug around Rachel's legs in the car, one wonders if a young woman of twenty-seven would do that for another young woman, hardly older, even in England', he mused.[13] In an essay that includes an analysis of *A Friend from England*, academic critic Ann Fisher-Wirth begins: 'I read Anita Brookner with chagrin and fascination. I have never before been addicted to a writer with whose values and vision I so consciously disagree. Every time a new Brookner novel is published, I buy it the day it arrives—in hard cover, no less. My life remains on hold until the new novel is finished. Yet when I close the book, more often than not, I am angry. How can she offer that, I ask myself again and again, as an image of life, of womanhood?' For Fisher-Wirth, then, passion for Brookner's fiction could not assuage her anxiety over the novelist's representations of contemporary women.

Despite Rachel's critique of marriage throughout the novel, Lynn Veach Sadler diagnoses the narrator with 'a severe case of sour grapes' on account of Rachel's dramatic responses to Heather's engagements.[14] The heterosexual normativity organising Sadler's reading of the text is further evidenced by her desire to solve the narrator's problems by matchmaking Rachel with Robin, her business partner. 'What we cannot understand is why Robin and Rachel do not make a couple', Sadler laments, despite the fact that, as Smith points out, Robin's manicured appearance and gym-and-nightclub lifestyle more snugly fit the portrait of a gay man.[15] In *Understanding Anita Brookner*, Cheryl Alexander Malcolm's reading of *A Friend from England* divines 'the absence of any romantic interest in the narrative'.[16] Locating the historical context of the text squarely in the twentieth century, Malcolm portrays Rachel as 'a comfortably

---

13 Plante, 'They Won Their Life', sect. 7.
14 Sadler, *Anita Brookner*, 129.
15 Sadler, *Anita Brookner*, 135; Smith, *Lesbian Panic*, 125.
16 Malcolm, *Understanding Anita Brookner*, 84.

well-off middle class Londoner'.[17] Malcolm maintains that 'the focus is on the relationship between daughters and parents as opposed to women and men' and that Rachel is 'perfectly content with her single status'.[18] Malcolm's reading of the text reinforces the notion that the heterosexual family romance is the transcendent authority in the genre of domestic fiction. Marooned on the text's contemporary time/space chronotope, critics' overly literal interpretations were unable to escape retelling a narrative about normative gender and sexuality. Alternatively, in the following three sections, historical and tropological readings are mobilised to investigate the way multiple forms of homoerotic desire circulate in *A Friend from England*.

Producing the Figure of the Military Man

In *A Friend from England*, Rachel Kennedy describes a restless evening at home reading Stendhal's reflections on post-Napoleonic life:

> I picked up a book from the pile on the table at my elbow, and read, 'Lacking more serious occupation since 1814, I write, as one might smoke a cigar after dinner, in order to pass the time.' I put down the book again, disheartened by this dandyish attitude, so impossibly urbane as to be permanently beyond my reach. (*FE*, 129)

Rachel's reading matter resembles a passage from Catherine Alison Phillips's translation of Stendhal's *Life of Henri Brulard* in which he writes, 'In the evening, on returning rather bored from the ambassador's reception, I said to myself: I ought to write my life; then perhaps, at last, when it's finished, I should know what I have been, whether gay or sad, a clever man or a fool, brave or timid' (*HB*, 6). In *The Genius of the Future*, Brookner emphasises the degree to which Stendhal's experience as a soldier in Napoleon's army impacted on his life. 'Of great importance for an understanding of Stendhal's attitude to his age is his actual military career, and this is considerable' (*GF*, 36). Brookner describes Stendhal's persona as 'unique, highly personal, very idiosyncratic, and stamped with a virile, almost military character', and she represents his study of Italian art history, *The History of Painting in Italy*, as written by 'a soldier–philosopher' (*GF*, 33, 43). In 1830, Stendhal published *Scarlet and Black*, a novel which narrates the plight of a young male protagonist who tries to

---

17 Malcolm, *Understanding Anita Brookner*, 79.
18 Malcolm, *Understanding Anita Brookner*, 79.

improve his social, romantic, and professional status in post-Napoleonic France but is ultimately defeated by circumstances of birth, class, and historical context. Brookner distinguishes energy and adventure as key traits of the Stendhalian narrative when she states:

> For Stendhal, the principal element of passion is energy, a truth to be held to be self-evident in the eighteenth century, but already faded from the mind's eye by 1839, and by the end of the [*Scarlet and Black*], when this passion and its energy have taken him through more fatiguing adventures and ended in tragedy, Stendhal is nevertheless able to finish the novel with the dedication TO THE HAPPY FEW, which in this connection means those who use themselves to the very limit of their capacities and ideals. (*GF*, 43)

Therefore, we come to see that a military effect is not only integral to understanding Stendhal, in whose work it manifests over a number of different character and narrative behaviours, it is also a critical component in the Stendhal–Brookner intertextual relationship.

Georges Kliebenstein confirms Brookner's contention that the adventure narrative is a key discursive feature of Stendhal's writing.[19] Kliebenstein further suggests that the Stendhalian narrative is organised by the rhetorical figure of hendiadys.[20] Richard Lanham defines hendiadys as the 'expression of an idea by two nouns connected by "and" instead of by a noun and its qualifier: "by length of time and siege" for "by a long siege"'.[21] Kliebenstein expands the definition of hendiadys to encompass its broad occupation of the narrative; to explain how hendiadys works as a narrative sequence, he uses the notation of 'a+A', where 'A' represents a repeat event that clarifies the significance of 'a'.[22] Kliebenstein offers a number of examples of his thesis, including the one from *Scarlet and Black* when Julien shoots Madame de Rênal once and misses ('a'), and when he shoots her a second time and hits her ('A').[23] Kliebenstein's recalibration of the Stendhalian hendiadys is useful for providing a more complex, non-literal reading of repetition in a text. Insofar as the figure of hendiadys projects knowledge backwards, it is valuable for the

---

19 Kliebenstein, *Figures du destin stendhalien*.
20 Francesco Manzini, 'Figures du destin stendhalien', *French Studies: A Quarterly Review* 60.1 (January 2006): 128.
21 Richard Lanham, *A Handlist of Rhetorical Terms*, 2nd edn (Berkeley: University of California Press, 1991), 82.
22 Benjamin McRae Amoss, 'Figures du destin stendhalien', *Nineteenth-Century French Studies* 35.2 (2007): 498.
23 Amoss, 'Figures du destin stendhalien', 498.

strategies of rereading and close reading that can be applied to Brookner's notoriously repetitive novels. The rhetorical device of hendiadys becomes significant here, primarily to consider events in the text, but also to shed light on the repetition of certain words.

In *Scarlet and Black*, the protagonist, Julien Sorel, is a young man of 'boundless ambition' from a peasant family (*SB*, 364). Set in the aftermath of Napoleon's downfall, at a time when it was still legal for men to kill their wives, the novel explores the limited options for a young man without financial or social status, such as 'a soldier or a priest, according to the profession that's fashionable in France' (*SB*, 91). In the golden age of Napoleon, the military had enabled new forms of social mobility for men, and Julien harboured 'dreams of military glory' (*SB*, 124). In Julien's town of Verrières, the rising spectre of capitalist industrialisation assumes prominence after Napoleon's demise.

Julien's character also impacts on his fate. Like Rachel Kennedy in *A Friend from England*, Julien is 'bold and enterprising', a 'man of spirit', 'courageous', but also an outsider: 'he could please nobody—he was too different' (*SB*, 118, 156, 220, 364). Others find Julien 'sly' and 'offensive' (*SB*, 98, 211). He is also 'suspicious', commands a 'stiff self-consciousness', is a 'failure' in the art of hypocrisy, and naive in love (*SB*, 156, 107, 200). Julien's sense of duty and his thirst for risk-taking and adventure underscore aspects of his Romantic masculinity. At the same time, Julien has a noticeably feminine disposition: 'This young peasant had such a fair complexion and his eyes were so gentle that Madame de Rênal's somewhat romantic nature made her at first imagine it might be some young woman in disguise who had come to ask a favour of the Mayor' (*SB*, 46). Julien's femininity is mirrored by that of Stendhal-as-narrator in *The Life of Henri Brulard* when he says, 'I have too fine a skin, a woman's skin … in a word, the surface of my body is feminine' (*HB*, 135). While Naomi Schor labels Stendhal's identification 'strictly epidermal', it prompts Julia Kristeva's contention that 'the Stendhalian lover is secretly a lesbian'.[24]

Indeed, in *The Life of Henri Brulard*, Stendhal pre-empts Freud's discovery of the centrality of the mother as love object, advancing the possibility of a feminine-identified subject desiring a feminine object. 'In loving her at the age of perhaps six (1789)', Stendhal writes, 'I had exactly

---

24 Naomi Schor, *Reading in Detail: Aesthetics and the Feminine* (New York: Methuen, 1987), 392; Julia Kristeva, *Tales of Love*, trans. Leon S. Roudiez (New York: Columbia University Press, 1987), 361.

the same character as when, in 1828, I loved Alberthe de Rubempré with a mad passion. I wanted to cover my mother with kisses and for her to have no clothes on. She loved me passionately and often kissed me; I returned her kisses with such ardour that she was often obliged to go away' (*HB*, 29). When his mother died when he was seven, Stendhal's life changed irreparably. It ushered in 'a time of profound suffering and moral vexation', which was formative and enduring (*HB*, 57). As he reveals in comparing his passionate love for his mother with that of prospective girlfriend Alberthe de Rubempré, Stendhal's eroticisation of the mother figure is transported across his subsequent (always failed) relationships.

Like Stendhal, Julien Sorel in *Scarlet and Black* and Rachel Kennedy in *A Friend from England* both suffer from the premature deaths of their mothers. In *The Life of Henri Brulard*, the death of the eroticised mother is accompanied by a passionate induction into literary cultures. 'From the age of seven I had resolved to write comedies like Molière', Stendhal recalls (*HB*, 80). Underscoring the way in which the eroticised mother figure is interlaced with romantic love and literary production in his oeuvre, Stendhal states that 'my compositions have always filled me with the same modesty as my loves' (*HB*, 99). He weights love and literature with the same value: he claims that 'love has always been to me the greatest of all affairs, or, rather, the only one' but also states that 'literature ... is the sole labour of my whole life' (*HB*, 198, 244).

In *Scarlet and Black*, Julien's literacy marks his outsider status in his family and yet seemingly assists his professional and romantic life. Considered potentially corrupting and dangerous, Julien's class-defying ability to read propels his hazardous social ascent and decline in the novel, first as tutor to the mayor's children during which time he embarks on an illicit affair with the innocent Madame de Rênal, secondly as Besançon seminarist, third as aspiring Parisian dandy and the lover of Mathilde de la Mole, and finally as fugitive and criminal. In *A Friend from England*, bookseller Rachel Kennedy's investment in reading cultures triggers the explicit Stendhalian intertextuality in the novel. The bookshop necessitates Rachel's relationship with the Livingstones through her business with Oscar, the accountant she inherits from her father. While spending time with the Livingstones, Rachel documents a repeated refrain in which Oscar Livingstone asks Heather, 'seen your mother?' (*FE*, 25, 57, 79, 112). However, for Rachel the refrain becomes something else: 'much later, when these things had come to mind rather forcefully, I seemed to hear him saying something else. "Where's your mother?" And ... he would, in my mind at least, repeat this. "Where's your mother?" I would hear. And again, "Where's your mother?"' (*FE*, 25). Lacking her own mother, and adopting the Livingstones as family-substitute, Rachel's misreading of the refrain, and her association of it with Heather, the object of her desire, constitutes the erotic triumvirate of mother, romantic love, and literary culture—a key component of the Stendhal–Brookner intertextual matrix.

Throughout *Scarlet and Black*, multiple historical, social, and personal influences conspire to cause problems for Julien. 'We fear we may weary the reader with the recital of our hero's countless misfortunes', warns the narrator (*SB*, 203). As a feature of the Stendhalian narrative, obstacles create movement within the text, and in *Scarlet and Black* obstacles are frequently impediments to love. Julien's attraction to Madame de Rênal is 'the first reef on which his career foundered' (*SB*, 54). Yet, with her, his 'love was still another name for ambition' (*SB*, 107). Mathilde de la Mole reinforces the connection between obstacles and romantic love when she reflects on her attraction to Julien:

> If, while still poor, Julien had been noble, my loving him would be nothing more than a vulgar act of folly, a commonplace misalliance; I wouldn't want such a thing; it would have nothing of what characterises a grand passion—the enormous obstacles to override, the dark uncertainty of the outcome. (*SB*, 324)

The novel's interweaving of love and difficulty inform the way in which courtship is formulated as a military strategy in a post-Napoleonic context. Julien, who sleeps with a photo of Napoleon under his bed, represents sexual acts as acts of 'heroic duty' (*SB*, 73). Like Rachel Kennedy, he thinks in terms of being 'defeated' in love, of drawing up 'a detailed plan of campaign' of 'the battle about to take place', the 'siege' he undertakes to win love, and his states of self-examination: 'Like a soldier returning from parade Julien was busily absorbed in reviewing every detail of his conduct' (*SB*, 73, 98, 341, 410, 103). However, Julien's compulsive attention to detail does not translate into romantic success. Romantic obstacles enhance the energy and passion of the man of spirit, but love is not resolved favourably for Julien Sorel in *Scarlet and Black*.

In *Romancing the Novel*, Margaret Bruzelius explains that the generic world of adventure is defined by a recognisable plot, setting, and cast of characters. She argues that the hero of the adventure narrative is always a 'profoundly literary' young man with an absent father, whose organising mission is based around the inheritance of a social role.[25] Also described as the 'adventure romance' or the 'masculine romance', the adventure narrative 'contains obvious elements of extremely conservative fantasy, all of which are put in the service of the discovery of the hero's adult masculinity'.[26] In the adventure narrative, the hero meets unexpected obstacles and challenges which he frequently fails to surmount, fantasises the ideal of female docility in his desire for a 'marriageable maiden', and journeys to an exotic landscape.[27] The exotic landscape envelopes a 'generative space, an enclosed area nearly always containing water, in which he finds some essential piece of information he needs to know to bring his plot to a conclusion'.[28] With its emphasis on stereotypical male and female gender roles and exotic and normal spaces, the adventure romance is, Bruzelius states, 'a deeply conservative genre'.[29] Like the traditional domestic fiction, the adventure romance relies on normative gender narratives to help tell its story. In the domestic fiction, the heroine's femininity unfolds as she surmounts the trials of the private realm while navigating the heterosexual romance to secure an appropriate marriage. In the adventure narrative, the hero's masculinity develops in tandem with his exploration of the public world and alongside his courtship of a marriageable maiden. Therefore, both domestic and adventure narratives are organised around the developmental movement of the heterosexual romance which naturalises masculine and feminine difference by sponsoring separate plot lines for the main characters who eventually converge or diverge for the purpose of the story.

My reading of *A Friend from England* repurposes the adventure narrative as a queer misadventure. In *Scarlet and Black*, Julien's 'adventure' and 'misadventures' relate to his sexual conquests and failures. In *A Friend from England*, Rachel's desire is framed through an adventure narrative. She speaks of 'my adventurous single state', refers to herself as 'a true adventuress' with 'extensive' sexual experience, and dubs Heather's affair with Marco 'a foreign adventure of the most banal kind' (*FE*, 113, 149 52, 152). Therefore, the adventure narrative in *A Friend from England* operates as a narrative of sexual misadventure. Calibrated through the performance of the military man, the queer misadventure

---

25 Bruzelius, *Romancing the Novel*, 78, 23.
26 Bruzelius, *Romancing the Novel*, 23.
27 Bruzelius, *Romancing the Novel*, 25.
28 Bruzelius, *Romancing the Novel*, 1–24.
29 Bruzelius, *Romancing the Novel*, 26.

narrative moves Rachel's desire through the text via a discourse of Romantic militant masculinity. This interpretation engages subversive resignifications of gender, highlighting Julien's merging of feminine and masculine characteristics and Rachel Kennedy's 'brave' feminism; her ambivalence towards normative gender roles: 'I had always thought [Heather] a dull person, hardly a woman at all, and she had apparently thought of me in the same way'; and her assumption of a Romantic masculine militancy (*FE*, 67, 199). It supports fluid genre boundaries by remixing the domestic fiction with the adventure romance. It champions a form of temporal 'crossing' by bringing historical meaning into the present. And it reinforces how romance narratives can go in multiple directions. In this reading, the narrative of sexual misadventure does not idealise happy endings. 'In passionate love', Stendhal writes, 'intimacy is not perfect happiness in itself but the last step on our way to perfection' (*L*, 78). This position is reinforced by D.A. Miller when he argues that, in Stendhalian terms, 'love fully realised is a love that loses its value'.[30] In *Misreading Anita Brookner*, therefore, the queer narrative of sexual misadventure does not idealise romantic coupling but experiments with energy, passion, and failure in the moment.

Staging the Performance of the Military Man

To stage the performance of the military man in *A Friend from England*, Rachel is cast as the orphan adventurer anti-hero, the 'intense and elegant' soldier with whom she identifies from Giorgione's *Tempest* (*FE*, 191). Rachel states that her goal with the Livingstones is 'to preserve that little family in all its pristine innocence'. She thinks, 'I might in fact inherit Heather from her parents' and believes that 'Heather was simply required not to change' (*FE*, 158, 33, 176). In this way, Rachel's fantasy of her deployment with the Livingstone family is consistent with the adventure narrative's fantasy of social continuity.[31] Drawing its strength from the public–private dichotomy, Rachel's relationship with the Livingstones allows her to assert her own public viability and, in so doing, her sexual authority: 'their rootedness gave me the security to be rootless, to test my

---

30 D.A. Miller, *Narrative and its Discontents: Problems of Closure in the Traditional Novel* (Princeton, NJ: Princeton University Press, 1981), 226.
31 Bruzelius states that 'the most important element of the adventure form is the fantasy of a genetic identity, an inheritance either of value or of social role, that remains constant'. Bruzelius, *Romancing the Novel*, 23.

vagrancy against their stability, my preparedness for adventure against their bourgeois world' (*FE*, 67). Purporting to act as Heather's 'passport to the world' and 'the agent of Heather's advancement', Rachel's social function rationalises her 'mission' (*FE*, 21, 49, 184). 'Men deal with things rationally', comments Stendhal's narrator in *On Love* (*L*, 16). Rachel's sense of duty can therefore be seen as a signifier of Romantic masculinity that propels her actions through the novel.

In restaging a queer narrative of misadventure in *A Friend from England*, Heather becomes the 'marriageable maiden' and the object of Rachel's desire. Rachel's attraction to Heather's 'pale milk-fed appearance, effortlessly triumphing over her modish black garments' can be seen as an instance of the Stendhalian lover's obsession (*FE*, 16). As Stendhal writes in *On Love*, 'these misguided souls smother the true person in an imaginary charm drawn from their own inexhaustible source ... they see their darling not as they are but as they have made them and, while believing they take great delight in their loved one, they are simply delighting in their own conceptions' (*L*, 40). Just as Bruzelius maintains that the 'marriageable maiden' of the adventure represents 'a masculine fantasy of female submission and availability', Rachel fantasises Heather's innocence and vulnerability: 'I would bear some vague responsibility for Heather, always to my mind the least capable of looking after herself in this cruel world, always absent, always in need of care' (*FE*, 64).[32]

However, as Kristeva observes, the Stendhalian lover thinks in terms of 'feminine duets' and 'adores a virgin, forbidden mother'.[33] Combining two points along a trajectory of desire that fantasises Heather as both an innocent and as the suckling mother in Giorgione's *Tempest*, the marriageable maiden is an iconic Stendhal–Brookner love object. At twenty-seven years old, Heather is one year off the age Stendhal nominates as the ideal age for 'crystallisation' to occur—Stendhal's term for how the mind invents and processes romantic love (*L*, 6). Rachel's fantasy of Heather's innocence complements Stendhal's analysis of how lovers fantasise the sublime aspects of the object of their desire: 'For romantic hearts, the more sublime the soul of your beloved, the more celestial and the further removed from the mire of all vulgar concerns will be the pleasures you find in her arms' (*L*, 24). For Stendhal, the projected innocence of the desired object intensifies the pleasure of the lover. In *A Friend from England*, the convergence of Rachel's sense

---

32 Bruzelius, *Romancing the Novel*, 28.
33 Kristeva, *Tales of Love*, 359, 354.

of masculine duty and Heather's feminine innocence brought to light through the performance of the military man—are integral to the text's queer historical narrative and assist the configuration of Rachel's desire for Heather.

Venice features as the exotic landscape and 'wet, private, generative space' in which the denouement of the adventure takes place in Bruzelius's treatment.[34] Situating the hermeneutical key of the narrative with the 'generative space' of the exotic landscape, Bruzelius's analysis of plotting complements Kliebenstein's emphasis on belated explanations encoded in the 'a+A' sequence of Stendhalian hendiadys. Following the narrative sequence plotted in the Stendhalian hendiadys, point 'a' correlates to the events surrounding Heather's first engagement to Michael and point 'A' corresponds with the Venetian revelations surrounding Heather's engagement to Marco.

Setting Venice as the exotic space that hosts the cataclysmic scenes around Giorgione's *Tempest* brings together multiple layers of intertextual meaning. Italy was a focal point in Stendhal's personal and professional life. His published works on Italy include *A History of Painting in Italy* (1817), *The Italian Chronicles* (1837–39), and a number of Italian travel narratives, and he served as a French consul in Trieste and Civitavecchia. Shakespeare was a great influence on Stendhal, and in Shakespeare's *Tempest*, Prospero's summoning of the tempest is the event which brings relationships to a head on the island of the duke's exile.[35] In Latin, 'tempus' literally means 'time'; in analysing Stendhal's 'amatory genius', Kristeva claims that the novelist, in his own words, 'wanted to "get out" of his century in order to extol a love that "lives in storms", "convulsive" love that might relate him to Shakespeare, Corneille, Mozart, and Madame Roland'.[36] In *Scarlet and Black*, motifs of storms and tempests are adumbrated by representations of the Italian passions. The narrator uses the metaphor of the storm to describe both Julien's character—'with a being so extraordinary almost every day was stormy weather'—and the state of love—'a man in love, like a traveller in a storm, can do no more than cling to his resolution never to alter the truth and always to listen to his heart' (*SB*, 82, 81).[37] In *A Friend from England*, Rachel's passions

---

34 Bruzelius, *Romancing the Novel*, 26
35 Like Julien and Rachel, *The Tempest*'s Miranda is also motherless.
36 Kristeva, *Tales of Love*, 347.
37 The epigraph for Chapter 10, part 1 of *Scarlet and Black* comes from Byron's *Don Juan*: But passion most dissembles, yet betrays / Even by its darkness; as the

climax in Venice during her pilgrimage to Giorgione's *Tempest*. In an otherwise heterocentric reading of *A Friend from England*, Malcolm underscores the queer signification of Venice when she notes that:

> few cities are also as intertextually packed as this one. With allusions to works ranging from Henry James's *The Aspern Papers* (1888) and Thomas Mann's *Der Tod in Venedig* (*Death in Venice*, 1912) to Ian McEwan's *The Comfort of Strangers* (1981), *A Friend from England*, which begins in 'humdrum circumstances' is thus transformed by its Venetian setting into something altogether more dramatic and complex than would at first appear to be the case ... In common with Thomas Mann's and McEwan's 'Venice texts', death and homoerotic elements combine to build dramatic tension in *A Friend from England*.[38]

As Malcolm documents, Brookner's intertextual references to Venice not only draw on the dramatic passions but are steeped in references to the queer canon. As such, Venice surfaces as the ideal location for the erotic denouement of the queer misadventure.

A series of confrontations between Rachel and Heather, in which Rachel's passion and energy manifest as effects of an excessive and confronting romantic love, are embedded between the narrative points 'a' and 'A' of the Stendhalian hendiadys: 'One should dare everything when it comes to women', states Stendhal (*L*, 51). These confrontations occur at Heather's flat when she returns from her honeymoon (*FE*, 106), at the hospital when Heather announces the end of her marriage to Michael (*FE*, 147), back at Heather's flat when Rachel attempts to convince Heather not to remarry (*FE*, 153), and once again at the hospital (*FE*, 174). The four-part confrontation sequence functions as necessary obstacles to the satisfaction of Rachel's desire; as such, it conforms to the 'structure of frustration' that Miller regards as central to Stendhalian narrative.[39] The confrontations are organised by the same circular narrative structure of the sexual adventure narrative, and their failure functions as a stimulation which propels the narrative of

---

blackest sky / Foretells the heaviest tempest (*SB*, 79). Byron also refers to Venice as 'Sea-Sodom'. George Gordon Byron et al., *The Life, Letters and Journals of Lord Byron*, rev. edn (1830; repr., London: J. Murray, 1932), 4: 271. *Scarlet and Black*, Chapter 20, part 1 draws its epigraph from Shakespeare's *The Tempest*: Do not give dalliance / Too much the rein; the strongest oaths are straw / To the fire i' the blood (*SB*, 136).

38 Malcolm, *Understanding Anita Brookner*, 85.
39 Miller, *Narrative and its Discontents*, 208.

sexual misadventure forward: an act of Heather's (of libidinal content) causes Rachel to react in a particular way; Rachel voices an objection to Heather's act; Heather fails to respond in the way Rachel desires; Rachel suffers extreme discomfort and vows to try again. The circular nature of these confrontations is brought to conclusion at narrative point 'A', which in itself complies with a broader circular narrative that returns Rachel to everyday life in London.

Initially, Heather and Michael's engagement leaves Rachel feeling 'superfluous'; it threatens the social role which enables Rachel's desire for Heather and Heather's sexual accessibility to Rachel (*FE*, 32). This threat is restaged when Heather and Michael marry: 'it seemed as if Heather had been gathered in, and I began to wonder, rather sadly, if I should be needed any more' (*FE*, 64). Nevertheless, as the engagement collapses into marriage, Rachel musters a number of strategies for interpreting the 'sexless arrangement' between Heather and Michael (*FE*, 47). First intuited as a threat to her desire for Heather, Rachel shifts the social capital connoted by Heather's engagement and marriage to signify instead something 'unrealistic and insignificant' and 'pompous and futile' (*FE*, 79, 134). Rachel's analysis of the marriage has the effect of intensifying her eroticisation of Heather and executes a reversal of status in which the heterosexual union at its heart is rendered fraudulent. By repudiating as an 'impossibility' the likelihood that Heather 'had been subjected to repeated assaults from her husband', Rachel replays Heather's sexual submission, simultaneously undermining Michael as the agent of its effect (*FE*, 64). Concluding that, in relation to Heather, Michael is 'a partner who would certainly not remove her to an alien world of brutal depths and unwanted rancours' (*FE*, 52), Rachel, on the other hand, represents herself as someone who 'takes some pleasure speaking to her brutally' (*FE*, 174). Taking a cue from the figure of hendiadys, this form of repetition can be read backwards to suggest that Rachel's brutal pleasure in Heather accrues the sexual content that is expunged from the Heather/Michael relationship. In Rachel's narrative, both marriage and the domestic fiction are transformed into queer sites which enable her desire. Heather and Michael's marriage becomes the occasion for Rachel to advertise her own potential to fulfil a set of erotic criteria and through which she is able metonymically to place herself in the role reserved for Heather's sexual partner.

Rachel's confrontations with Heather ignite after Rachel senses Heather's inability to conform to the rules of her sexless marriage. Following Heather and Michael's honeymoon, Rachel's first confrontation with

Heather is motivated by the desire to conduct 'the conversation we always avoided' (*FE*, 105). In *Epistemology of the Closet*, Sedgwick describes two nineteenth-century narrative strategies for the representation of desire. First, she invokes 'the erotic negative' to describe the ways in which desire is made discursive through its negation, a formulation which suggests the subject of Rachel and Heather's deferred conversation is sexual.[40] Secondly, Sedgwick outlines a narrative in which 'knowledge' and 'sex' are conflated, 'so that knowledge in the first place means sexual knowledge; ignorance, sexual ignorance'.[41] This sex–knowledge equation complements the indications that Rachel seeks, in the exchange of sexual information: confirmation that marriage is for Heather a 'continuation of her virgin life' (*FE*, 105). Rachel's need to construct a dialogue with Heather through the rhetorical strategies of negation and instruction demonstrate how the confrontations between the women constitute an exchange of knowledge which is eroticised. 'I knew what mattered and she did not', Rachel declares (*FE*, 52). 'I knew more about the ways of the world than Heather ... I certainly did not intend to be on hand to guide her', and: 'I did not relish the task of lining up my experience with Heather's and taking on the burden of inducting Heather into a fully adult life' (*FE*, 78, 66). In the first confrontation, Rachel advises Heather that 'the getting of wisdom should be her first priority' (*FE*, 112). This is consistent with the narrator's self-representation as an experienced figure of wisdom, reinforcing the erotic nature of their exchange. However, acknowledging that 'there might be something obscene about this goading of Heather', Rachel fails in her application to win Heather over. In accordance with the programming of the military man, this failure enhances the intensity of the sexual misadventure. As Stendhal observes: 'Always some small doubt to soothe—this is what gives energy to each moment; what shapes the trajectory of happy love. Since fear will never completely disappear, its pleasures will never fade' (*L*, 81). Therefore, in spite of being unable to extract the information that her interrogative seeks to elicit, and in spite of the illness that sees her arrive at Heather's 'on slightly uncertain legs', Rachel reports that she found herself 'striding home, fuelled more by indignation than by returning strength, but recovering a little strength from the indignation itself' (*FE*, 107, 102, 112).

The second major obstacle in Rachel's adventure manifests as Heather's decision to leave Michael, a fact which emerges when Heather attends

---

40 Sedgwick, *Epistemology of the Closet*, 202.
41 Sedgwick, *Epistemology of the Closet*, 73.

her mother's hospital bedside after a trip to Venice. Having determined that Michael enables rather than threatens her eroticisation of Heather, Rachel's attitude towards him changes from critical to supportive. Variously denounced as a 'liar', a 'child', a 'clown', and a 'criminal' (*FE*, 42), he eventually becomes 'poor Michael', just as Rachel, in keeping with the textual logic of metonymical substitution, becomes 'poor Rachel' (*FE*, 111, 201). Heather's absence in Venice has left Rachel 'longing for her return' (*FE*, 142). But when Heather reappears with the news of her marriage break-up and her imminent return to Venice, Rachel responds with 'stupefaction' and 'indignation' (*FE*, 146):

> I must confess to feeling furious with her ... using my time and energy to enjoy the equivalent of my habitual adventures. And ... once she realized that such adventures were preferable to more complex and burdensome attachments, who knew what path she might not follow? ... She did not have ... the taste for danger. (*FE*, 148)

Read through the performance of the military man, Rachel's extreme response reflects her desire for Heather. 'The sensitive soul goes mad with the excess of feeling', Stendhal explains in *On Love*, adding that 'the sensitive lover has none of the coolness required to make the most of his situation' (*L*, 45). Thus, the new obstacles have the effect of encouraging Rachel to reformulate and reinforce her mission: 'my supreme, my ultimate task would be to talk sense to Heather, to persuade her, in my own inimitable way, that what awaited her in Venice could be postponed *sine die* ... and that it would be more seemly on her part to inaugurate a period of official spinsterhood' (*FE*, 152). In *On Love*, Stendhal sympathises that: 'Willpower's lack of influence over love is clear to see ... exasperated by your mistress and yourself, with what enthusiasm would you embrace indifference, if you could!' (*L*, 49). In the face of love, however, willpower crumbles. 'Love is the strongest of the passions', Stendhal claims. 'In others, desires have to adapt to cold reality; with love, reality is eagerly reshaped according to your desires' (*L*, 23, 23). Ceding to the inevitable demise of Heather's first marriage, Rachel is newly invigorated by the fantasy of Heather's spinsterhood. And, just as Heather's status as a Victorian daughter existed—a status Rachel formerly idealised—spinsterhood similarly exists outside heterosexual enforcement.

Heather's decision to move to Venice is the subject of Rachel's next major objection. Rachel negotiates a meeting with Heather that elicits the 'nervous receptivity' she always experiences in Heather's company

(*FE*, 153). 'The thought of the visit's end hangs over us right from the start, so we cannot enjoy any of it', Stendhal surmises of the lover's anxiety in *On Love* (*L*, 47). In this confrontation, Rachel continues to contest the value of marriage: 'you set too much store by marriage ... The whole idea is preposterous', she says, upbraiding Heather with 'alarm', 'passion', and 'despair' (*FE*, 155, 155, 157, 157). Stendhal warns his troops to 'accept no slights from other men' and Rachel attempts to shatter any romantic feeling attached to Marco. Yet Heather is nonplussed, and the confrontation leaves Rachel 'feeling bulky and superfluous ... breathing irregularly ... exhausted and ashamed ... disconsolate and downgraded' (*L*, 64; *FE*, 158–59). 'Only its embarrassing consequences are true proof of a grand passion', Stendhal states in *On Love*. 'You feel yourself compelled like a lunatic to execute strange actions, you feel as if you had two selves: one that acts, and another that condemns your actions' (*L*, 48). Thus, Rachel recognises that 'it was clear that [she] could not attempt to come to terms with Heather again, nor could [she] even face her' (*FE*, 159). As Rachel puts it: 'I felt that I had lost her, and that the loss was entirely my fault' (*FE*, 159). However, eight pages later, Rachel meets Heather at the hospital where Rachel acknowledges that she is 'prepared to go all through it again' (*FE*, 167). In a now familiar pattern, Rachel fails, and the failure spurs her onwards. 'I would have time to try again', she says. (*FE*, 168). Subsequently, after meeting with Heather's parents, Rachel undertakes to go to Venice and return to England with Heather in tow.

Rachel's militant performance intensifies around her departure for Venice as momentum builds towards point 'A' of the Stendhalian hendiadys, yet her mood is subject to various changes throughout her trip. 'I vowed silently that if Heather were to make me suffer one moment longer than was necessary I would have a reckoning with her that she would never forget', she snarls at the outset of her trip (*FE*, 187). As Bruzelius records, 'In adventure, the exotic world does not give the hero a chance to display his acumen or industry, but is rather a place in which he demonstrates his ignorance and inexperience at the risk of his life'.[42] Therefore, in Venice, Rachel recalls, 'I found myself at a loss' (*FE*, 191). Waiting to meet Heather, Rachel visits the Gallerie dell'Accademia, where her identification with the queer palimpsests of *The Tempest* ignited this book's parallel interpretation of *A Friend from England* which layers contemporary female subjectivity with nineteenth-century narratives of Romantic masculinity. But where love is a siege for the military man,

---

42 Bruzelius, *Romancing the Novel*, 41.

energy lies in pursuit not capture. With her anger diminished, Rachel is without power. 'Suddenly I felt genial, good-natured … I no longer felt strongly about the outcome. I relinquished the idea of handcuffing her and removing her by force' (*FE*, 193). In this new mood, the final confrontation between the two women is diluted, directed for once by Heather and wrought with uncharacteristic meekness by Rachel. Finally, the 'mulish' Heather remakes Rachel as her mule, charging her with the task of delivering packages to Heather's parents in London (*FE*, 91, 199). Rachel recalls: 'I was almost bereft of words by this time and looked to Heather for my cue' (*FE*, 201). In contrast to Heather's first engagement at point 'a', in which Rachel's epistemological authority is unchallenged, Heather's second engagement at point 'A' culminates in a renegotiation of (sexual) knowledge and power between the women.

Once Heather retreats, however, Rachel recovers, pursuing her in an Aschenbach-like chase along the canals of Venice:

> 'Heather,' I shouted. 'Come back!'
> I got clumsily to my feet, impeded by what seemed to me to be increasing bulk or weight. I tried to follow her, but I had only vaguely noted the direction in which she had disappeared. I ran blindly down a side street. It was intensely quiet and very dark. I stumbled against bags of rubbish stacked against walls. Then I was blocked by water. Panicking, I retraced my steps. I was in the centre of Venice, somewhere behind the Fenice, but there was no one about. I crossed a little bridge, and then another. Everything was silent. I retraced my steps once again and passed fearfully through the dusky alleys like an unquiet spirit, careful to make no sound. … As I looked back I saw a black form disappearing into a doorway.
> … I felt as if I had traversed miles of hostile territory, and I noticed in myself that peculiar deadness that comes with a recognition of defeat. I had failed, but that was not what counted. What counted was that I was guilty of an error. It was not Heather who was endangered, but myself. I felt shame, penury, and the shock of truth. Something terrible had happened. I did not see how I could ever face those who knew me. … The fact of the matter was that the wonders of this earth suddenly meant nothing to me. Without a face opposite mine the world was empty; without another voice it was silent. (*FE*, 203–04)

Overwhelmed by losing Heather, Rachel encounters 'the shock of truth', made discursive as the absence of the romantic other. 'In love, men run the risk of secret torment of the soul', Stendhal muses (*L*, 19). Bruzelius maintains that information processed in the exotic space of the conventional adventure narrative ends up reinforcing the political and moral authority of the normative, public world to which the hero inevitably returns.[43] Indeed, when Rachel returns home alone, she sinks back into her own life. Further connection with the Livingstone family occurs only by chance when Rachel encounters Oscar Livingstone in the street.

Read through a narrative of sexual misadventure, however, the performance of the military man imbues *A Friend from England* with historical and erotic significance, even as Rachel assimilates back into her bookstore days. Through this interpretation, Rachel can be seen as a sensitive Stendhalian lover whose actions are not regulated by the correct and appropriate codes of gender, sexual, and historical behaviour in either nineteenth- or twentieth-century contexts. Instead, the figuration of the military man reassembles cross-historical codes to produce a passionate and fleeting narrative of love and desire which effects a queering of the adventure narrative and the domestic fiction. In the following sections, two further nineteenth-century homoerotic tropes are brought to light in *A Friend from England*. From the intertextual indications between Freud's case study 'Dora' and the narrative matrix surrounding Rachel's hydrophobia, the figure of the analysand is summoned from the text. Subsequently, the figure of the queer emerges from the intertextual correspondence between *A Friend from England*, Henry James's *The Beast in the Jungle*, and Oscar Wilde's *The Picture of Dorian Gray*.

Staging the Figure of the Analysand

In *A Friend from England*, Rachel's debilitating hydrophobia manifests itself alongside a series of water allusions and throughout her confrontations with Heather (*FE*, 34, 62). In the following passage, Rachel describes a hydrophobic incident prior to her trip to Venice, 'the ultimate nightmare: a city filled with water' (*FE*, 186):

> [A]bout that time it rained heavily for a part of every day, usually in the morning, so that I awoke to streaming windows and that sense of oppression that always accompanies wet weather. This is not mere antipathy (nobody likes rain, after all) but a terrible nervousness that connects with my other fears. I cannot look at weeping skies or raindrops pattering on windows, or, least of all, at the falling rain itself without getting up to wander nervously from room to room, wringing my hands, and wondering if I can last out until it stops. And if I am out, of course, it is a hundred times worse. With every splash of water on my face or my leg I have to suppress an

---

43 Bruzelius, *Romancing the Novel*, 41.

involuntary cry. In the end I have to run for cover ... If I am home, I try not to look at the windows, but I find I am drawn to them, as if made to watch, repelled yet fascinated by the falling sheet of water, wondering what it would be like to stand in and let my head fall back and my mouth and eyes fill. But this, of course, is to be resisted, as is any kind of relaxation of my vigilance. The temptation is both horrifying and enduring, and can never be resolved. (*FE*, 177)

In this section, the figure of the analysand is used to read Rachel's hydrophobia as a trope of female same-sex desire. In the nineteenth century, the rise of Freudian psychoanalysis brought with it a new narrative patterning for the construction of sexual identity. In 'Dora', Freud contends that 'a symptom signifies a sexual situation' (*D*, 80). Freud also links symptoms to homoerotic figuration when he maintains that 'all psychoneurotics are persons with strongly marked perverse tendencies' (*D*, 84). Toril Moi emphasises that 'Dora' is entirely an act of narrative construction on the part of Freud when she states that 'it is Freud himself who has imposed a fictional coherence on Dora's story ... Dora's story *is* largely Freud's story'.[44] Therefore, in seeking to illuminate the narrative strategies and rhetorical devices which produce intertextual personae, the figure of the analysand can be read as the effects of a narrative model based around medical and psychological approaches to representing, interpreting, eroticising, and pathologising an array of disparate symptoms, word associations, and homosexual desires. Establishing pathways along the intertextual matrix between 'Dora' and *A Friend from England*, the figure of the analysand is produced across the signification of Rachel's hydrophobia, her unconscious motivations for illness, the text's word play, its water/fire motifs, and repetition. In 'Dora', Freud represents an 'incessant repetition of the same thought' as an essential component of his analysand's narrative (*D*, 88). In narratology, 'inane repetition' is represented by the device of homiologia; therefore, this device is nominated as the organising rhetorical figure of the analysand. Freud also claims that the narratives of psychoneurotics are characterised by 'altering the chronological order of events' (*D*, 47). In this way, it becomes possible to read the repetitive refrains in the text as devices that effectively disrupt the hetero-chronic sequence of the text. The reconstituted figure of the analysand in *A Friend from*

---

44 Toril Moi, 'Representation of Patriarchy: Sexuality and Epistemology in Freud's "Dora"', in *In Dora's Case: Freud—Hysteria—Feminism*, ed. Charles Bernheimer and Claire Kahane (New York: Columbia University Press, 1985), 187.

England can be read against the pathologising psychoanalytic model of same-sex desire, and offers an additional queer trope through which to read Rachel's desire for Heather. The redistribution of Freud's epistemological threads into the intertextual figure of the analysand weakens the pathways that naturalise ideological formations and suggests new ways of thinking about the relationship between desire and narrative that draw on historical and rhetorical forms and patterns. Like the military man, the analysand results from a recombination of historical discourses that enact a queer resistance to the way in which the production of historical context privileges the heterosexual subject.

In 'Dora', Freud's narrative centres around his analysis with Ida Bauer, a patient who initially presented with aphonia (loss of voice), whom he nicknamed 'Dora'. Over the course of the analysis, Bauer asserted that her father had had an affair with a family friend, Frau K, and that her father tried to legitimate the affair in part by offering Bauer to Frau K's husband, Herr K, a man who had repeatedly made sexual advances towards her. Initially, Freud attempted to persuade Bauer of her desire for both her father and Herr K, but the analysis failed when Bauer ended it after eleven weeks. In a later footnote to his essay, Freud appended his first, hetero-centric response with the following statement: 'Behind the almost limitless series of displacements which were thus brought to light, it was possible to divine the operation of a single simple factor—Dora's deep-rooted homosexual love for Frau K' (*D*, 146 n. 1). In what Mandy Merck describes as a difficult and belated move for Freud, 'Dora' became an important study for the narrative construction of female same-sex desire.[45]

In the original reception of *A Friend from England*, the erotic connotations of Rachel's hydrophobia are effaced despite the historical sexual connotations of water. Sadler states, 'Brookner, always rather eccentric in conception and perception, seems increasingly to combine the sardonic and the whimsical. The use of water in *A Friend from England* is a case in point'.[46] Skinner at least wonders whether 'the whole complex of hydrophobia in *A Friend from England* may even represent the imaginative transference of some unspecified personal fear', but immediately undercuts the erotic possibilities of Brookner's novel by

---

45 Mandy Merck, 'The Train of Thought in Freud's "Case of Homosexuality in a Woman"', in *Perversions: Deviant Readings by Mandy Merck* (London: Virago, 1993), 13–32.
46 Sadler, *Anita Brookner*, 138.

suggesting that 'the persistent water motif may be read in terms of some of its commonest associations within our culture: *currents* of feeling, *streams* of consciousness, *depth* of emotion, fertility, birth and even life itself'.[47] Exemplifying the denial of any form of erotic investment between Rachel and Heather in the first reception of *A Friend from England*, a handful of Brookner critics consistently read the wetness in the text as an overbearing poetic device.

Alternatively, Freud's methodology in 'Dora', and its narrative reconstitution in *A Friend from England*, can be mobilised to read the water motifs as a poetics of lesbian desire. In addition to hydrophobia's erotic status when read through the performance of the analysand, water itself has sexual valence in 'Dora'. Freud states that '"wet" was connected with … the group of ideas relating to sexual temptation … [and to] a kind of getting wet involved in sexual intercourse' (*D*, 128). In *A Friend from England*, the significance of Rachel's hydrophobic response to water is intensified by an array of water motifs in the text. Rain dampens Heather and Michael's wedding, saturates Rachel's discovery of Michael's 'secret' at a bar named 'The Titanic', and invades Heather's mother's hospital debacle, where Rachel concludes that Dorrie 'looked as if she were drowning' (*FE*, 59, 113, 115 162). Rachel's raincoat constitutes an integral part of her armature in her confrontations with Heather, whom she characterises as a 'swimmer in calm and protected waters' (*FE*, 158, 28). In Freudian narratives, symptoms are traced to childhood experiences and Rachel relates a memory of swimming to her father. However, the pleasant associations that Rachel makes between water and men are abrogated later in her life through a sexual imaginary that rejects the figure of male ejaculation. An attempted swimming excursion with Robin leaves Rachel 'fearful … of the mess and foam' created in the pool (*FE*, 61). After 'coughing in a hysteria of fear', Rachel vows to 'avoid all expanses of water'—a promise that proves impossible to maintain in Venice (*FE*, 61, 62). By contrast, Rachel refers to 'the safe anchorage of Heather's flat' (*FE*, 153). Rachel's hydrophobia makes her trip to Venice more hazardous (and therefore more pleasurable according to the figure of the military man) and her erotic identifications take place around the storms of *The Tempest*. In this sense, the significance of the water motif in *A Friend from England* finds erotic complement in both the figure of the military man and the analysand.

47 Skinner, *The Fictions of Anita Brookner*, 127, 128.

In 'Dora', Freud interprets allusions to fire in Dora's dreams as 'to the contrary, [about] water' (*D*, 108). In *A Friend from England*, Brookner charges fire/water motifs with symbolic power to describe bedroom activities, the site traditionally associated with sexual intercourse. Rachel displays an ongoing interest in Heather's marital bedroom: 'I seemed to see her marooned in that cruel blue bedroom', she states (*FE*, 99). 'She should have lived out her life in that bedroom I had once seen', she remarks of Heather's childhood bedroom (*FE*, 100). Through the reverse logic of hendiadys, Rachel situates herself in the bedroom with Heather: 'for a moment or two I identified so completely with Heather and her gentle upbringing that it was I who had issued from that suburban villa, from that virginal bedroom', she states after discovering Michael's secret, which, as the following section reveals, will also unveil itself through icy blue hues (*FE*, 118, 114). For Rachel, Heather and Michael's bedroom is notable for the absence of sexual activity, which she renders through the Freudian fire/water prism:

> I remember noting the bedroom as a cold blue room with one wall taken up by a range of white fitted wardrobes, and an immense bed covered by a pale blue satin counterpane. It looked icy and unused, and I wondered how she could bear it. There were none of Michael's things scattered around, and by now his absence was rather noticeable. ...
>
> I reminded myself that there was nothing necessarily unusual about this, although the image of that icy bedroom followed me back into the drawing-room, and I went to the fire to warm my hands. (*FE*, 72)

Later, when Rachel returns to inspect the bedroom again, she is motivated to increase Heather's pleasure. 'Mentally I changed the furnishings in that terrible bedroom—I could quite see that she would have no desire to languish there' (*FE*, 107). In combining fire/water motifs alongside a story about unused masculine sexual absence and feminine sexual healing, the figuration of the analysand is given heightened erotic significance in *A Friend from England*.

Indeed, the voluminous water references in *A Friend from England* might be read as re-enacting the analysand's proclivity for repetition, and as a strategic component in the trope of female same-sex desire. Ironically, Brookner is no stranger to the accusation of repetition, and Rachel Kennedy is an exemplary repetitive subject.[48] However, far from

---

48 'Obsessional themes need not result in repetitive fictions, if the writer can invent reasonably new characters, situations and plots to express them; unfortunately there is little that is new or original in *Undue Influence*'. Joyce Carol Oates,

underlining Brookner's lack of imagination, the analysand persona illuminates repetition as a strategy for narrating particular types of erotic dispositions. As previously suggested, Rachel's incantation of the refrain 'where's your mother?' participates in a Stendhalian eroticisation of the mother which is reinforced as a prototypical Freudian sentiment through the figure of the analysand (*FE*, 25, 57, 79, 112). Furthermore, Rachel describes Heather as 'shrewd' on eleven separate occasions, only to finally reveal that 'I persisted in thinking this, although, when I turned it over in my mind, I could not remember a single circumstance in which Heather had ever demonstrated her legendary shrewdness' (*FE*, 14, 15, 30, 40, 53, 65, 79, 91, 104, 150, 176). In 'Dora', Freud suggests that 'a string of reproaches against other people leads one to suspect the existence of a string of self-reproaches with the same content' (*D*, 67). With the hermeneutic assistance of the figure of the analysand, therefore, Rachel presents as a 'shrewd' character. The existence of a shrewd narrator constitutes a warning against an overly literal interpretation of the text, and suggests a more self-conscious and transparent interpretation is warranted.

In 'Dora', Freud generates an epistemology around the analysand's 'motives for illness' to produce a narrative of cause and effect (*D*, 75). Throughout his analysis, Freud draws definitive associations between representations that recur in a patient's narrative. Through the figure of the analysand, it follows that associations can be drawn between recurring phrases in Rachel's narrative, and her common responses to Heather, water, and their intersecting erotic connotations. In *A Friend from England*, the 'nervous receptivity' brought on by Rachel's hydrophobia resembles 'the nervous exasperation that the thought of Heather's company always induced' (*FE*, 153, 102). As such, because water evokes the same feelings as does Heather's proximity to Rachel, illness for Rachel reinvents a sense of Heather's presence. When Oscar Livingstone urges Rachel to 'keep an eye on Heather', Rachel subsequently falls ill (*FE*, 94). Rachel's spectral consumption of Heather has the same immobilising effect on her as her hydrophobia does, which 'put a stop to all social movements' (*FE*, 120). Illness reminds Rachel of Heather,

---

'Writing for the Tortoise Market', *Times Literary Supplement* (30 July 1999): 19; 'Last June, when the British edition of this book was published, the *London Review of Books*' assessment began as follows: "Anita Brookner's first novel appeared in 1981. Since then she has published it again, slightly altered, almost every year"'. Paul Gray, 'Understated Outrage at Growing Old', *New Leader* 85.6 (2002): 44.

and, in Keatsian fashion, Rachel is 'more than half in love with easeful death' (*FE*, 96). By associating Heather with illness and death, Rachel transfers her symptoms to Heather in order to effect Heather's eroticised subordination. Thus does Rachel imagine Heather prepared for the guillotine—'a potential victim ... her rather long pale neck would emerge from her black sweater as if she had been prepared for execution'—while later Rachel assumes the complementary position in the relationship: 'I felt like a murderer' (*FE*, 29, 165).

Freud recounts that 'When Dora talked about Frau K, she used to praise her "adorable white body" in accents more appropriate to a lover than a defeated rival' (*D*, 96). Similarly, Rachel admires Heather's 'marvellously white skin' (*FE*, 99). In 'Dora', Ida Bauer journeys to a Dresden gallery where she 'remained *two hours* in front of the *Sistine Madonna*, rapt in silent admiration' (*D*, 137). Freud states that Dora identifies with the Madonna, in a kind of counter-transference of her own sexuality (*D*, 145 n. 1). In *A Friend from England*, Rachel's pilgrimage to the Gallerie dell'Accademia results in her identification with the figure of the military man, which also licenses a counter-transference of her sexuality. In 'Dora', Freud reads communication between Dora and Frau K as the subject of an erotic exchange: they had 'read and discussed forbidden topics' (*D*, 97). Similarly, in *A Friend from England*, Rachel and Heather's confrontations—based around jousting for positions of experience and innocence—can be read as circulating a mode of sexual knowledge. In 'Dora', Freud suggests that Ida Bauer's surname denotes an object which indicates something 'ambiguous' and 'improper' (*D*, 145 n. 1). In Brookner's novel, Rachel asserts that she 'slept like a stone', thereby discursively constituting her desire to sleep with Heather Livingstone (*FE*, 133). Alternatively, the surname of Heather's husband, Michael Sandberg, is emblematic of a shore-based resistance to Rachel's tempestuous desires. In rendering the figure of the analysand in *A Friend from England*, it becomes possible to harmonise the detail of Freud with Brookner's text in order to create a coherent epistemology of female same-sex desire in *A Friend from England*.

In *Desire and Domestic Fiction*, Nancy Armstrong frames 'Dora' as a 'rewriting of domestic fiction'.[49] According to Armstrong, 'Dora' was historically significant for the changing way kinship was represented.[50]

---

49 Nancy Armstrong, *Desire and Domestic Fiction: A Political History of the Novel* (New York: Oxford University Press, 1987), 253.
50 Armstrong, *Desire and Domestic Fiction*, 253.

Armstrong states that, before 'Dora', the language of family relationships was enmeshed in 'the women's domain', while after 'Dora', kinship moved to become the discursive domain of the counsellor and therapist.[51] She argues that by turning rhetorical strategies into psychological symptoms, this shift separated 'the authority of a professional (male) institution' from its productive effects in language and thereby compounded the depoliticisation of female subjectivity.[52] Brookner reverses this process. By rendering the tropes of Freudian kinship in her domestic fiction, Brookner highlights their narrative origins to depathologise the female psychological subject and regains authority of kinship narratives from patriarchal institutions. In addition, her juxtaposition of the historical and contemporary enacts the analysand's repetitive perversion of chronology to reinvigorate tropes of female same-sex desire in the novel. In this way, the intertextual figure of the analysand is also invested in the queering of kinship narratives.

Staging the Figure of the Queer

Concurrent with the naming of homosexuality in 1869 and heterosexuality in 1870, nineteenth-century literature witnessed the emergence of a generally unmarried and childless persona who was characterised by seemingly eccentric behaviour be it through gender performance, sexuality, in the family domain, or according to temporal or representational codes.[53] The spinsters and bachelors of Brookner's precursors, Henry James, Honoré de Balzac, and Charles Dickens, all introduce character types who are distanced from the dominant chords of heterosexual culture. Queer theorists have illuminated some of the rhetorical devices and strategies through which these personae were discursively constituted. In *The Apparitional Lesbian*, Terry Castle argues that the figure of the lesbian was historically subject to a process of narrative derealisation, a process assisted in the nineteenth century by the French aesthetes' use of spectral metaphors.[54] She states that 'at least until around 1900 lesbianism manifests itself in the Western literary imagination

---

[51] Armstrong, *Desire and Domestic Fiction*, 253.
[52] Armstrong, *Desire and Domestic Fiction*, 259.
[53] Chris White states that the term 'homosexuality' was coined by Karl-Maria Benkert in 1869 who added 'heterosexuality' to the language in 1870. Introduction to *Nineteenth-Century Writings on Homosexuality: A Sourcebook*, ed. Chris White (London: Routledge, 1999), 4.
[54] Castle, *The Apparitional Lesbian*, 6.

primarily as an absence, as chimera or *amor impossibilia*—a kind of love that, by definition, cannot exist'.[55] Annamarie Jagose asserts that the narrative mechanisms of chronology and retrospection produce the lesbian as a figure of invisibility, belatedness, and secondariness.[56] Sedgwick ties the narrative of the unspeakable to 'the centuries-long historical chain of substantive uses of space-clearing negatives to void and at the same time to underline the possibility of male same-sex genitality'.[57]

Sedgwick nominates the narrative of the secret and the rhetorical device of preterition as implicit pointers to homosexual meaning in nineteenth-century narratives. The *New Shorter Oxford English Dictionary* defines preterition as 'summary mention made of a thing by professing to omit it ... the action of passing over a matter; the fact of being passed over without notice; omission, disregard'.[58] Preterition therefore refers to all types of circumlocution, inference, and non-literal forms of signification. In the nineteenth century, the changing legal and medical status of homosexual acts, criminality, and perversion impacted on both the way in which homosexuality emerged in discourse and the naturalisation and institution of normative heterosexuality through literal discourse. Queer theorists such as Sedgwick and Alan Sinfield frame the Wilde trials as a key influence on how the tropes and discourses associated with the Jamesian bachelor and the Wildean dandy were retrospectively homoeroticised and homosexualised.[59]

How do we get to the figure of the queer? In this section, a host of eccentric character indictors are brought together with the narrative of the secret and the rhetorical device of preterition to produce the figure of the queer. Drawing on the narrative matrix that Henry James establishes in *The Beast in the Jungle*, as well as Oscar Wilde's narrative of the secret, and of youth, beauty, and monstrosity, in *The Picture of Dorian Gray*, the figure of the queer is staged through Rachel's representation of Heather's first husband, Michael Sandberg, in *A Friend from England*. Sedgwick's seminal analysis in *The Beast in the Closet*, Jagose's interpretation of narrative sequencing, and Sinfield's historical analysis in *The Wilde Century* assist in demonstrating that the performance of

---

55 Castle, *The Apparitional Lesbian*, 30.
56 Jagose, *Inconsequence*, xi.
57 Sedgwick, *Epistemology of the Closet*, 204.
58 *New Shorter Oxford English Dictionary*, 4th edn, s.v. 'preterition'.
59 Sedgwick, *Epistemology of the Closet*, 203; *Wilde Century*, 3.

the queer in *A Friend from England* constitutes a third historical trope of homosexuality in the text after the figures of the military man and the analysand.

The Beast in the Jungle tells the story of a man, John Marcher, who spends his life anxiously waiting for something to happen to him, though what that could be is unknown. As Sedgwick illuminates, there are actually two forms of secrets in *The Beast in the Jungle*: Marcher has a secret, the content of which itself is secret, both to himself and the world.[60] Marcher shares the fact of having an unknown 'secret' with a friend, May Bartram, who, after many years, suggests to Marcher that the thing he was waiting for has already happened (*BJ*, 502). Some time after Bartram's death, Marcher comes to his own form of realisation about his secret.

In the story, James identifies Marcher through a series of character indicators which emphasise his discomfort and 'singularity' (*BJ*, 509). 'The rest of the world of course thought him queer', the narrator informs us (*BJ*, 510). His secret marks Marcher as having a problematic relationship to discursivity and temporality; because Marcher cannot 'name' it, he is sentenced to a world of figuration—what Sedgwick calls 'the reifying grammar of periphrasis and preterition' (*BJ*, 515).[61] According to Sedgwick's logic, a logic reinforced by the work of Sinfield, the nineteenth-century language that produces the figure of the queer connotes homosexual meaning without yet connoting a twentieth-century homosexual identity.[62]

In *The Beast in the Jungle*, Marcher's contested relationship to literal symbolisation affects the way he is located in time and space. The very title of James's text figuratively points to Marcher's predicament as a temporal conundrum, a factor that holds him in a state of suspense. However, Bartram's belated insistence that Marcher has already suffered his fate turns his horrified anticipation around, directing it to a past event (*BJ*, 531). Unaware of both what was to have happened and what did happen, Marcher's absence of knowledge is also an absence of the present. His inability to name his condition means his character is never commensurate with the historical time connoted as reality. In

---

60 Sedgwick, *Epistemology of the Closet*, 204.
61 Sedgwick, *Epistemology of the Closet*, 203.
62 Sedgwick, *Epistemology of the Closet*, 203; Alan Sinfield, *The Wilde Century: Effeminacy, Oscar Wilde and the Queer Moment* (New York: Columbia University Press, 1994), 3.

Inconsequence, Jagose implicates both chronological narrative sequencing and the retrospective narrating of relations between present and past as temporal devices that stage the figure of the lesbian.⁶³ Either suspended in chronological time or projected into the past, Marcher's double-edged temporal conundrum mirrors the figuration of lesbianism as delineated by Jagose. As Castle indicates in *The Apparitional Lesbian*, the trope of preterition has been a foundational historical trope in the representation of lesbianism.⁶⁴ In the present analysis, therefore, the figure of the queer crosses both male and female historical same-sex imaginaries.

Pre-dating *The Beast in the Jungle* by 13 years, Oscar Wilde's *The Picture of Dorian Gray* also tells the story of a man with a secret. At the start of the novel, Dorian Gray is a young lad with 'extraordinary good looks', 'wonderfully handsome, with his finely curved scarlet lips, his frank blue eyes and his crisp gold hair' (*DG*, 84, 16). Gray wishes for 'eternal youth' when he catches sight of his image in a portrait painted by artist Basil Hallward, and when Gray's wish comes true, he embodies the act of chronological suspension and a resistance to those narratives of chronological and generational progress that Jagose indicts as an organising mechanism of lesbian figuration (*DG*, 171, 174).⁶⁵ Gray is able to preserve his persona of youth and beauty and indulge in a 'new Hedonism' while his ageing process and the consequences of his actions are realised by his image in the canvas, an image that degenerates into a 'monstrous' and 'shameful' picture of 'ugliness' (*DG*, 21, 102, 122, 112). A prototypical aestheticist consumer, Gray is influenced by Lord Henry to read certain material. Gray thus becomes intrigued by Gautier's 'Venice poems' and absorbed in a novel that will be identified at Wilde's trial as Huysmans's *Against Nature*: texts which have significance in Brookner's oeuvre and in the 'exotic' space of Venice in *A Friend from England*.

Wilde's 1895 conviction for gross indecency had the further effect of retrospectively imbuing key discourses of Wilde's text, and Romantic aestheticism, with homosexual meaning. 'The trials helped to produce a major shift in perceptions of the scope of same-sex passion', claims Sinfield. 'The principal twentieth-century stereotype entered our cultures: not just the homosexual ... but the queer'.⁶⁶ Accordingly, Wilde's trials,

---

63 Jagose, *Inconsequence*, xi.
64 Castle, *The Apparitional Lesbian*, 30.
65 Jagose, *Inconsequence*, x.
66 Sinfield, *The Wilde Century*, 3.

along with the discourses of the secret, of terrible monstrosities, of male youth and beauty, of transgression, preterition, and chronological perversion—all of which could be read and recombined through any number of narrative paradigms—served to firmly conflate the figure of the queer with homosexual meaning.

Of course, the term 'homosexual' is never used in *The Beast in the Jungle*, *The Picture of Dorian Gray*, or *A Friend from England*, although the historical context of Brookner's text is quite different from that of the former two works. In *A Friend from England*, however, Rachel's representation of Michael Sandberg reconstitutes key discourses from the nineteenth-century archives of James and Wilde. In the first-person voice, Rachel stages the figure of the queer across character signifiers which connote Michael's beauty, youth, and preteritive resistance to discursive, temporal, and heterosexual normativity (most dramatically in the family matrix), in conjunction with the narrative of his 'terrible' secret. In generating a signifying schematic around Michael Sandberg, Rachel represents him as a young man with 'Victorian overtones' whose physical appearance recalls the Greek beauty and youth of Dorian Gray (*FE*, 45). Michael's hair, Rachel notes, was 'conspicuously golden, thick and wavy, hair that is rarely seen on a man once he has passed adolescence' (*FE*, 43). Lord Henry's characterisation of Gray as a 'wilful sunbeam' is revisited in Rachel's observation that 'Michael had a sort of sunniness about him which seemed to preclude any baffling depths of character' (*DG*, 43; *FE*, 46). And Gray's 'appearance of aristocracy' is recalled in Michael's presentation as 'the loafer of the family, rich, infantile, well-heeled, not to be taken entirely seriously, happiest and most himself in places of light entertainment' (*DG*, 53; FE, 104). With his 'habitual wink', too, Michael has the mannerisms of a man with a secret (*FE*, 114). Despite his youth, beauty, and charm, Michael is burdened by the type of nervous anxiety which also afflicts both John Marcher and Dorian Gray. 'His very movements were exaggerated: his clothes seemed agitated, as if hard put to contain him. There was a fearful restlessness about him, something florid and opaque', Rachel notes (*FE*, 43). In *The Beast in the Jungle* and *The Picture of Dorian Gray*, the nervous restlessness of the protagonists is a physical manifestation of the secret each man harbours. Similarly, Michael's affect in *A Friend from England* causes Rachel to sense in him 'the hidden imprint of secret, private, unhappiness', an apprehension which seems to bear truth when she has later 'unmasked' Michael's 'secret' and his 'terrible life' (*FE*, 108, 116, 115, 119).

Rachel first introduces Michael to readers by conjoining representations of his physical beauty and physical unease with the figure of the liar:

> My first impression of Michael Sandberg was that he was blessed with, or consumed by, radiant high spirits. My second impression was that a man of such obvious and exemplary charm must be a liar. He broadcast a sort of hilarity which went well with his fair hair ... I judged him to be playing his part well but with slight exaggerations. ... too much charm was being displayed, and ... the expressions of rapture that played across his extremely mobile features were perhaps a little premature, a little out of place and a little excessive. (*FE*, 42)

According to Rachel, Michael's personal discourse exhibits a false relationship to knowledge and truth. 'He spoke in clichés, and no doubt some psychic trick had taught him to think in clichés' (*FE*, 119). Michael's social persona is unclear: 'His tie seemed to signify some association or other which I could not hope to understand' (*FE*, 43). He evinces an 'unfocussed radiance' and can 'look as if he had just arrived from out of town', bearing the affect of 'a foreigner' (*FE*, 53, 104). Michael's marriage and engagement to Heather deliver to Rachel neither a satisfying performance of heterosexual masculinity nor a convincing image of heterosexual coupling. 'As far as I could judge, they were not wildly attracted to each other', remarks Rachel of Heather and Michael 'for the frequent claspings of the hand that went on were between Michael and his father rather than between Michael and Heather' (*FE*, 46). Michael, concludes Rachel, 'was not the sort of man to rouse a woman from the slumbers of virginity' (*FE*, 51). In Rachel's speculative narrative, Michael's personal failings are directly connected to his failure to perform heterosexual masculinity.

For Rachel, Michael's multiple absences are begot in collusion with his father, Teddy Sandberg, whom she deems 'equally unreliable' (*FE*, 44). Therefore, preterition is part of the family domain. While Michael and Heather's questionable courtship unfolds, Sandberg senior approaches Rachel with an 'unpleasant' sexual invitation. 'You look like a girl who could be a very good friend', he leers in an unwanted phone call which leaves her feeling 'disgusted' (*FE*, 80). Characterised by Rachel as 'one of those men who think they are good at getting women to change their minds', Sandberg's lack of authenticity, and the absence of reciprocal interest issuing from Rachel, compounds the aura of fabrication around the father–son couple (*FE*, 48). Teddy bears the military-styled nickname of 'the Colonel', even though 'he was not a Colonel, nor had he ever been one' and 'acted rather like his son's manager' (*FE*, 73, 44). Through some anxiety over their proper names, the father and son incarnate a problematic relationship between literal symbolisation, the speakable, and the truth. Rachel remarks that the 'curious name of Sandberg was conferred on them by some slightly complicated ancestry ... but I never got this properly worked out' (*FE*, 49). She does note, however, that there was 'a very slight blurring of the sibilants in their speech ... It was like a little code between them' (*FE*, 49). Similarly, Rachel fathoms the financial status of the Sandbergs through a narrative of dishonesty. The Colonel's money, she notes, 'didn't seem ... to be as straightforward as the Livingstones', and wherever it came from or wherever it went to seemed to be hedged with restrictions' (*FE*, 57). Rachel's inability to penetrate the truth of the Sandbergs' existence results in her suspicions being projected onto the male–male couple in the absence of heterosexual reinforcement. She notes that the Sandberg family unit is distinctive for 'the absence of a woman', while being 'more maternal than paternal' and that the men 'touched each other a great deal' (*FE*, 45, 52, 46). By stressing physicality in the homosocial Sandberg family, Rachel emphasises the pederastic Greek model to evoke a queer eroticism at the heart of the family matrix.

The performance of the queer in *A Friend from England*, enacted through preterition and the narrative of the secret, takes form most dramatically across family axes. In addition to Colonel Sandberg's parodic heterosexual masculinity, Michael's youth, his passionless marriage to Heather, and the figuration of a same-sex erotic between father and son all function to erode heterosexual authority over the domestic fiction. Like Dorian Gray, Michael's golden charm accentuates his youth, but for Rachel it also signifies his childishness. He is 'the child-husband', 'not very grown up', and 'frozen in childhood bewilderment' (*FE*, 42, 43, 65). Rachel's representations of Michael's childishness accentuate the queer possibilities of kinship structures in multiple ways. When she concludes that 'Michael was a son, he would never be a husband', Rachel mobilises familial appellations to represent a resistance to the vertical modes of chronological and generational narratives that underwrite heterosexual privilege (*FE*, 65). Similarly, Rachel denaturalises Michael and Heather's marriage through representations of the couple's childishness. The wedding is like 'a children's party', Heather and Michael look like 'good children from another age', and 'danced like brother and sister' (*FE*, 58, 58, 65). In contrast to the erotic coupling between father and son, Rachel's commentary on the childishness of Michael and Heather operates to undermine the value of heterosexual coupling by conjuring the figures of brother and sister. By illuminating the cultural and social over the natural and romantic, the performance of the queer is invested in contesting heterosexual authority as the foundational origin of family narratives.

Published nearly a century after Wilde's text, Rachel's twentieth-century portrait of Michael invokes his queerness through nineteenth-century strategies of elision and preterition which existed before the more definitive and contemporary discursive actions around homosexual identity. As a retrospective narrator, Rachel is aware of Michael's perceived 'sexual peculiarities and aberrations' throughout her telling of the story (*FE*, 116). Nevertheless, she withholds the imputed homosexual content of Michael's 'secret' until midway through the novel when she discovers Michael wearing make-up at a 'peculiar' wine bar. (*FE*, 115, 112). 'I had never come across this little idiosyncrasy before ... The burden of this secret must be borne by each of us in isolation', Rachel says, denying knowledge of the content of the secret while simultaneously invoking the unspeakable with the monstrous, despite her self-representations as a cosmopolitan, bohemian, sexually experienced feminist in late twentieth-century London (*FE*, 115). In *Lesbian Panic*, Smith indicts Brookner for what she regards as the novelist's practice of reconstituting homophobic nineteenth-century representational strategies.[67] Smith's reading of *A Friend from England* was the first published text to locate Brookner in queer contexts. However, according to Smith:

> willful and highly sophisticated suppressions of the knowledge of sexuality inform the plot of Brookner's suggestively enigmatic reworking of *The Beast in the Jungle* ... Brookner eschews any use of the term denoting homosexuality in her text, thus harking back to the nineteenth-century uses of non-denotation ... the Jamesian elision of self-knowledge that underscores the text serves to illustrate the impossibility of enacting a nineteenth-century plot in a twentieth-century epistemology.[68]

For Smith, the perceived 'impossibility' of recombining historical tropes in a productive capacity implicates Brookner in a regressive campaign to occlude homosexuality. On the contrary, Brookner's strategies can be read queer on the following counts. First, Rachel's summoning of the

---

67 Smith, *Lesbian Panic*, 124.
68 Smith, *Lesbian Panic*, 124.

figure of the queer in Michael Sandberg invokes celebrated discursive, gendered, and temporal modes which are integral to forms of queer historical discursivity. Sedgwick and Sinfield argue that nineteenth-century modes of queer preterition accrue homosexual meaning most definitively in the twentieth century. Therefore, it is precisely Brookner's twentieth-century invocation of the narrative of the secret that imbues it with the power to connote historically non-normative, homosexual meaning. Brookner's appropriation of preteritive modes of expression deployed by the French aesthetes and Romantics is invested in types of 'gender crossing' that is significant to both aestheticist and queer forms of representation. By deploying modes of anticipation and chronological suspension (implied by Michael's youth), and through a retrospective narrative in which homosexuality is never commensurate with present time, Brookner produces the figure of the queer through the temporal mechanisms that Jagose connects to lesbian figuration. On the one hand, Brookner's historicising, tropological form supports Jagose's contention that a superficially remedial narrative that restores visibility to the lesbian merely embraces the same process of literal symbolisation through which sexual hierarchy is enacted. On the other hand, Smith's criticism of Brookner, which conflates Brookner's nineteenth-century representational practice with homophobia, creates an unquestioning relationship between historical time and sexual identity. Negating the degree to which sexual identities are genealogical, historical, and temporal constructs, Smith maps a progressive chronology from the nineteenth century to the present which naturalises and reproduces the temporal narrative mechanisms that produced lesbian invisibility and normalised heterosexual privilege. In framing female homoeroticism through an intelligible and legible category of identification, Smith herself delineates a set of normative historical and temporal conditions which function to regulate the ways in which desire is lived and produced. Effectively, Smith implies that lesbian desire pre-dates its discursive construction and, in so doing, she naturalises literal symbolic practices that construct the self-evidence of the hierarchical heterosexual/homosexual opposition. Against Smith, my contention is that the performance of the queer in *A Friend from England* engages modes of temporal switching integral to queer, anti-homophobic discursivity at the same time as it rejects the normative regulation of sexual identity through historical periodisation.

Secondly, throughout the novel, Rachel emphasises her own 'extensive' sexual experience (*FE*, 52). In the performance of the military man, Rachel's focus on Heather's innocence progresses Rachel's own goal of self-eroticisation. In the performance of the analysand, Rachel's symptoms connote a knowledge of sexual experience which fuels her confrontations with Heather. Now, in the performance of the queer, Rachel's infantilisation of both Michael and Heather enables her to assume an obverse position of authority which simultaneously disables Michael's potential as a suitor while advertising herself as the more desirable companion. In this incarnation, the performance of the queer is supported by the Greek cross-generational model of homosexuality that will be further elucidated in the following chapter on the aesthete. Rachel's critical analysis of marriage and her staging of the queer across the family matrix are constitutive elements in the queering of this domestic fiction.

Finally, the production of the queer, along with the figures of the military man and the analysand, illuminates three historical formations of same-sex desire in *A Friend from England*. In the introduction to this chapter, Rachel's identification with the palimpsests of Giorgione's *Tempest* was framed as a key moment in the staging of homoerotic desire in the novel. In each of the hermeneutic personae subsequently delineated, the historical and intertextual analyses presented have revealed multiple dimensions of homoerotic performance within Brookner's contemporary narrative. In the next chapter, the figure of the aesthete will join the cast of Romantic personae, with the aim of bringing out a select new set of queer nineteenth-century themes and motifs.

CHAPTER TWO

The Aesthete in *A Misalliance* (1986)

> It seemed that she constantly misread the situation.
>
> Anita Brookner, *A Misalliance*

Introduction

In this chapter, Blanche Vernon, the main protagonist of *A Misalliance*, is diagnosed with an advanced case of nympholepsy. 'Nympholepsy' describes a condition whereby a subject has come under the significant influence of nymphs. Initially, Blanche's condition makes her an obsessive spectator of the nymphs of Renaissance painting in the Italian Rooms of London's National Gallery. A 'peculiar mixture of raciness and delicacy', Blanche compulsively returns to the gallery, seeking to obtain knowledge of the nymphs' 'world of love and pleasure' (*M*, 92, 10). For Blanche, the nymphs represent a 'passport to the landscape where the sun shone eternally and where cornucopias of fruit scented the warm air', thereby becoming companions on a particular type of journey (*M*, 20). Following her divorce from Bertie, Blanche is compelled to seek a hot place: 'she was statistically sure that somewhere there was heat, there was sunshine, and radiance, and that this happy climate was reserved for those who had the determination to seek it' (*M*, 31). In tracing Blanche's quest for happiness, *A Misalliance* is decorated with sensual motifs of hot sun, cool groves, moist springs, and the breezy draught of wings—all of which transform the text into an enchanted nymphs' playground.

Blanche Vernon's nympholepsy shifts from art to life when she meets the 'spectacular, vivid, obtrusive' Sally Beamish and her aphasic stepdaughter Elinor at a local hospital (*M*, 39). Blanche is struck by Sally's enigmatic qualities:

> The ichor of extreme and abundant youth and fertility made its pulse felt in the sheen of her skin, the coarseness of the red hair, the limbs swimming in their layered cotton garments, the small feet bare in their black leather sandals. An air of wealth surrounded her and glinted from gold bracelets she wore on either wrist. (*M*, 39)

Blanche's encounter with Sally brings a 'shock of recognition':

> The girl's expression was the same as the expression of those nymphs who seemed to mock her progress through the Italian Rooms of the National Gallery on long slow April afternoons. She had the smile of a true pagan. (*M*, 40)

For Blanche, the sight of Sally brings out a form of 'latent madness' (*M*, 41). It causes Blanche to deduce that 'Elinor's putative mother was in fact a sort of a nymph' (*M*, 59). Thereafter, Blanche conspires to immerse herself in Sally's life in order to study the 'anarchic' style of the younger woman's behaviour (*M*, 65).

Nymphs enjoy a colourful symbolic history that frequently coincides with representations of female sexuality. In *Greek Nymphs: Myth, Cult, Lore*, Jennifer Larson describes nymphs as highly ambiguous figures: sexually desirable and assertive while free of familial restrictions and domestic responsibilities, possessed of healing properties, and found in predominantly female communities.[1] The warning behind Charles Stewart's depiction of nymphs' 'mischievous, dangerous and ambiguous behaviour' and their ability 'to steal the voice or mind of people who chance upon them' is reconstituted in *A Misalliance* in the form of the concern demonstrated for Blanche by her sister-in-law, Barbara.[2] 'Don't go to the National Gallery, Blanche', implores Barbara. 'It is bad for you to wander about on your own like this' (*M*, 55). At other times, the nymphs pervade Blanche's unconscious and 'steal up on her in unguarded moments, even in sleep' (*M*, 48). Once possessed, the nympholept commands a heightened awareness and elevated verbal

---

[1] Jennifer Larson, *Greek Nymphs: Myth, Cult, Lore* (New York: Oxford University Press, 2001).

[2] Charles Stewart, 'Nymphomania: Sexuality, Insanity and Problems in Folklore Analysis', in *The Text and Its Margins: Post-Structuralist Approaches to Twentieth-Century Greek Literature*, ed. Margaret Alexiou and Vassilis Lambropoulos (New York: Pella, 1985), 225.

skills, experiences a state of mental and physical rapture, and may invest substantial resources to nymph-devotion.³ Likewise, in the course of her friendship with Sally Beamish, Blanche confers small cash payments on the 'unscrupulous' beauty, which finance the mixed pleasures of Sally's company (*M*, 124).

In the nineteenth century, when pathologised medical models of sexuality were becoming increasingly predominant, the term 'nymphomania' was coined to refer to an overdeveloped sexual drive in women.⁴ The connection of nymphs to female sexuality and, in particular, to lesbianism is emphasised by Freud. In 'Dora', Freud points out that 'nymphae' is another name for the labia minora (*D*, 139). Freud reads Dora's fascination with the nymphs of Secessionist painting—a fascination mirrored by Blanche's obsession with the nymphs of Renaissance painting—as tantamount to a declaration of lesbian sexuality. 'At this point a certain suspicion of mine became a certainty', he asserts, 'due to the fact that "nymphae" ... is the name given to the labia minora' (*D*, 139). Throughout history, nymphs have represented archetypes of (lawless) female sexuality, female community, and a lesbian erotic.

Blanche's nympholepsy operates within a field of signifiers that emphasise an idolatry of the senses through floral, fruity, and climatic references. Across the intertextual matrix, these motifs can be traced to the ancient Greek poet Sappho (630–570 BC), whose female-centric, synaesthetic fragments of love poetry combine lush, fragrant, sensual, and erotic motifs with themes of female voice, subjectivity, same-sex desire, and memory.

In *Lesbian Peoples: Material for a Dictionary*, Monique Wittig's decision to consecrate a blank page in the entry for Sappho is indicative of the contested nature of Sapphic interpretation.⁵ The highly mediated nature of Sappho's oeuvre, in which surviving fragments of women's poetry have been appropriated and reworked by subsequent artists wielding varying ideologies across the ages, has disarmed the notion that the figure of Sappho possesses any inherent meaning. At the same time, as Nicole Albert points out, the appearance of Sapphic motifs in a text can be 'a

---

3 Larson, *Greek Nymphs*, 13–14.
4 An 1819 definition of nymphomania in the *Dictionnaire des sciences médicales* implicates hot weather in the scourge of nymphomania. See Roddey Reid, *Families in Jeopardy: Regulating the Social Body in France, 1750–1910* (Stanford, Calif.: Stanford University Press, 1993), 92.
5 Monique Wittig and Sande Zeig, *Lesbian Peoples: Material for a Dictionary* (New York: Avon Books, 1979).

means of anticipating the Sapphic plot'.[6] In *Fictions of Sappho, 1546–1937*, Joan DeJean explores the myriad ways Sappho's literary descendants shaped the Sapphic plot in order to portray the poet as lover, fighter, self-harmer, heterosexual victim, political exile, heroine, or lesbian icon.[7] Thaïs E. Morgan argues that, led by Baudelaire, the nineteenth-century French and British aesthetic movements deployed Sappho to express their unconventional personal and erotic styles.[8] Yopie Prins maintains that in the nineteenth century Sappho stood for multiple significations, including 'the construction of Sappho herself as the first woman poet, singing at the origin of the Western lyric tradition'.[9] The location of Sappho the women's writer at the helm of lyric voice is an important one. As the authority on first-person singular, the lyric genre should perhaps establish the strength of the woman writer's voice. However, Sappho's centrality to lyric voice was compromised insofar as the simultaneous construction of the Sapphic myth dispossessed the female subject of the authorial 'I'.[10] This makes an interesting historical allegory for how we might think of the construction of Brookner as an autobiographical women's writer. Despite Brookner's protestations, many commentators have been keen to label her work as autobiographical, at times using material from the novels to fill in a portrait of the author or taking commentary from earlier reviews as fact about Brookner herself.[11] In this

6   Nicole Albert, 'Sappho Mythified, Sappho Mystified or the Metamorphoses of Sappho in Fin-de-Siècle France', *Journal of Homosexuality* 25.1/2 (1993): 87–104.
7   Joan DeJean, *Fictions of Sappho, 1546–1937* (Chicago: University of Chicago Press, 1989), 1–28.
8   Morgan, 'Male Lesbian Bodies', 50.
9   Yopie Prins, *Victorian Sappho* (Princeton, NJ: Princeton University Press, 1999), 3.
10 Prins contends that 'Sappho circulated as proper name for the "Poetess" in Victorian women's verse' and that 'in the course of the nineteenth century, the Poetess and Sappho become increasingly interchangeable names for another generic category, namely "Woman"'. Prins, *Victorian Sappho*, 174, 183.
11 In a 1985 interview with Brookner, Sheila Hale attempts to evoke Brookner's childhood, when she writes: 'An only child, she grew up in the dim, airless, comfortable surroundings that prosperous European immigrants used to re-create for themselves. One imagines the smell of regular, meaty meals emanating from the ponderous dark-wood furniture'. Sheila Hale, 'Self Reflecting', *Saturday Review* 11.3 (1985): 36. However, Hale appears to have drawn this material from Brookner's *Providence* (1982), thereby using Brookner's fiction to create autobiographical content for Brookner's life. In *Providence*, Brookner describes the house of her protagonist, Kitty Maule's, French grandparents: 'once inside the front door, one encountered the smells, the furnishings … An air of dimness, of stuffy comfort, an emanation of ceremonious meals, long past, an airlessness' (P, 6). In

sense, the collective (therefore public and masculinised) construction of the autobiographical women's writer has a history which extends from Sappho to Brookner. Prins maintains that the wealth of reconstructions of Sappho, which make the poet a 'non-originary figure', exemplifies the ways in which interpretation proceeds via a recursive structure, complicating the notion of historical progress and the seemingly fixed station of the reader in the present.[12] Brookner's identifications as a Romanticist, a historian, and a contemporary women's writer always underscore the importance of the backwards turn, historical attribution, and gender indexing. In navigating the Sapphic plot in *A Misalliance*, it therefore becomes necessary to be transparent about which forms of the Sapphic myth are used and why. In this chapter, the nineteenth-century readings of Sappho that are presented expressly combine sensual motifs of lesbian eroticism with strategies of critical and political subversion that were significant to the aesthetic movement.

Despite its themes of love and pleasure, early critics were not enamoured with *A Misalliance*. Highlighting the tendency of commentators to lament the absence of a man for either Blanche or the nymphs, the original reception of *A Misalliance* takes its cues from the contemporary setting, bedevilled as it is with assumptions about its privileged heterosexual subject. Meanwhile, the text's nineteenth-century intertextuality lay neglected. In this stream of Brookner criticism, the original reception implicitly replots the Sapphic blueprint of the voiced and voiceless women's writer. Brookner is positioned as the hapless authoress who struggles along not quite up to speed with her contemporaries, scant attention is paid to the Romantic subtext of her work, and her oeuvre is devalued.

In part 3 of this chapter, an alternative reading of *A Misalliance* is cast through the figure of the aesthete. As with each of the main chapters in *Misreading Anita Brookner*, effort is made to establish the novel's signifying matrix, rhetorical device, and organising narrative form in order to produce its signature emblematic figure and propel the movement of the figure through the text. Through readings of Sappho, Plato, Charles Baudelaire, Renée Vivien, and Walter Pater, the Sapphic intertextuality

---

'The Paratextual Construction of Anita Brookner', I show how Brookner distances herself from the autobiographical at the same time as critics participate in creating Brookner's autobiographical content themselves. Mayer, 'The Paratextual Construction of Anita Brookner', 49–69.

12 Prins, *Victorian Sappho*, 15, 246.

of *A Misalliance* is framed specifically as a form of nineteenth-century sapphism—and related to a mode of Romantic Hellenism—which forms part of the signifying matrix of the aesthete. Prins's deconstruction of Sapphic hierarchies is useful here, enabling me to draw on both Baudelaire's mid-nineteenth-century sapphic poetry as well as Vivien's fin-de-siècle oeuvre. Vivien's indexing as part of the movement known as 'Sapho 1900' by French nationalist André Billy in the mid-twentieth century emphasises a belated and derivative contribution to the aesthetic movement and Sapphic readings.[13] However, in recursively recombining the Sapphic motifs of Baudelaire and Vivien, the production of the aesthete can be used to highlight Vivien's subversive Sapphic narratives of the lesbian, the women's writer, female community, and heterosexual masculinity while also challenging the asymmetrical relationship between high, male Romanticism and the effacing construction of the women's writer. By threading an intertextual genealogy through Sappho, Vivien, and Brookner, it is possible to reassert the status of female creativity in the figure of the aesthete. This backward restoration of women's contribution to Romantic aestheticism becomes the ground upon which Brookner can be read as both women's writer and aesthete.

In his analysis of the 'art for art's sake' movement, Pierre Bourdieu underscores the subversive power of the aesthete, establishing a useful alternative historical context for reading *A Misalliance*. Following Bourdieu, the production of the figure of the aesthete presented herein draws on Sapphic and Hellenic narratives, the 'backward turn', the idolatry of the senses, the exhortation to live life as art, the heightened significance of the gaze—and its configuration in a narrative of subjectification that contests bourgeois, social, and hetero-chronic norms. In specifying the rhetorical figure of metaleptic prolepsis and the narrative of metamorphosis as the organising narrative and rhetorical forms of the figure of the aesthete, the work of Walter Benjamin, Thomas Bahti, and Yopie Prins are all recruited to the cause.[14]

In part 4, the performance of the aesthete in *A Misalliance* is staged across the narrative contours of guilt, punishment, redemption, purification, and blessedness that Mikhail Bakhtin supplies as the problematic knots of the metamorphosis narrative.[15] Based on readings of Jacques

---

13 DeJean, *Fictions of Sappho*, 285.
14 Benjamin, 'Philosophy of History', 253–65; Bahti, 'History as Rhetorical Enactment', 183–204.
15 Bakhtin, 'Forms of Time', 128.

Lacan, Bourdieu, Benjamin, and Plato, the performance of the aesthete in *A Misalliance* travels along Blanche's guilt and punishment in the present, her redemptive flashback in encounters with the nymphs, and the purification and blessedness that follow her relationship with Sally and her final journey to the sun.

Plot Summary and Original Reception

Blanche Vernon, the heroine of *A Misalliance*, is a 'habitually elegant' figure and a talented conversationalist who excels in the culinary arts and is interested in philosophy, painting, and literature (*M*, 12). In *A Woman Appeared to Me*, Vivien's 'Decadent style' lesbian novel about 'a doomed love affair', or misalliance, the narrator contends that 'women's names are strangely suggestive … the souls of Blanches are pure as Easter lilies' (*WA*, 46).[16] In Vivien's poetry, lilies are also 'the eager lilies of your breasts'; the whiteness signified by the name Blanche corresponds to the white light of the moon in Vivien's work, and to virginity, which represents a state of resistance to the patriarchal order.[17] As Arianna Marmo explains, the pseudonymous name of Renée Vivien is also significant. 'The poet wanted to underline her double birth', Marmo states. 'Re-née, in fact, means re-born in French, and the name Vivien also alludes to a new birth.'[18] Like Brookner's French/English identifications and influences, Vivien's 'bilingualism and biculturalism are recurrently present in her work by means of intertextual quotation, translation and re-writing', Marmo maintains.[19] And, as with Brookner's personal and thematic feel for 'exile', the 'geographical displacements' of Vivien also resonate with the Sapphic themes of exile and subversion that are explored in part 4.[20]

16 Martha Vicinus, 'The Adolescent Boy: Fin-de-Siècle Femme Fatale?' in *Victorian Sexual Dissidence*, ed. Richard Dellamora (Chicago: University of Chicago Press, 1999), 93; Gayle Rubin, Introduction to Renée Vivien, *A Woman Appeared to Me*, trans. Jeanette H. Foster (Tallahassee, Fla.: Naiad Press, 1982), iv. Hereafter cited in text as *WA*.

17 See especially the poems 'Sapho' and 'All is White'. Renée Vivien, *The Muse of the Violets*, trans. Margaret Porter and Catherine Kroger (Tallahassee, Fla.: Naiad Press, 1982), 37, 62. Hereafter cited in text as *MV*; Arianna Marmo, 'Purity and Perversion: Renée Vivien's Ophelia Poetry', *New Readings* 12 (2012): 69.

18 Marmo, 'Purity and Perversion', 66.

19 Marmo, 'Purity and Perversion', 66.

20 'I'm a sort of Jewish exile, but I have this straightforward English public school upbringing, and the two sides war with each other for supremacy from time

Like many Brooknerines, Blanche is a committed reader of Henry James, who, as Eric Haralson states, valorised the figure of the aesthete as a way of exploring alternative representations of nineteenth-century masculinity.[21] James, Richard Ellmann also reminds us, mobilises the aesthete as an enabling figure for the portrayal of 'homosexuals', thus marking the figure's lability as a queer signifier.[22] The aesthetes of James's novels widely proclaim the aestheticist injunction to 'live life as art'. To 'make one's life a work of art' is a principal espoused by Gilbert Osmond, the imperious aesthete of Henry James's *The Portrait of a Lady*.[23] In 'The Author of Beltraffio', the son of the eponymous author and aesthete is hailed by James's narrator as 'like some perfect work of art'.[24] Similarly, in *The Tragic Muse*, when asked 'Are you then an aesthete?' Gabriel Nash declares, 'I've no profession ... Merely to be is such a *métier* to live such an art; to feel such a career!'[25] In addition to her reading for pleasure, Blanche harbours an unfinished thesis on Madame de Staël, a literary descendant of Sappho, whose life and work mapped out the figure of the woman genius. Ellen Moers states that in Staël's *Corinne ou l'Italie*, 'Corinne is superspecial: the heroine of genius who writes poetry, improvises, sings, lectures, dances, acts, has a wider range of talents and audience for their display than any woman before or after her'.[26] And yet Corinne's life is undone by romantic failure. In *Soundings*, Brookner's at times unkind portrait of Staël describes her as 'the most famous woman in Europe and the only enemy who Napoleon feared' as well as embodying 'history's most outstanding case

---

to time'. Brookner, in Smith, 'Anita Brookner', 67; Elaine Marks, *Marrano as Metaphor: The Jewish Presence in French Writing* (New York: Columbia University Press, 1996), 43.

21 Eric Haralson, *Henry James and Queer Modernity* (Cambridge: Cambridge University Press, 2003), 3. In *Hotel du Lac*, Edith's involuntary social exile is served out in Switzerland.

22 Richard Ellmann, 'Henry James among the Aesthetes', *Proceedings of the British Academy* 69 (1983): 211.

23 Henry James, *The Novels and Tales of Henry James*, vols. 3–4, *The Portrait of a Lady* (New York: Charles Scribner's Sons, 1907–09), 15.

24 Henry James, *The Novels and Tales of Henry James*, vol. 16, 'The Author of "Beltraffio"' (New York: Charles Scribner's Sons, 1907–09), 21.

25 Henry James, *The Novels and Tales of Henry James*, vols. 7–8, *The Tragic Muse* (New York: Charles Scribner's Sons, 1907–09), 33.

26 Ellen Moers, 'Mme de Staël and the Woman of Genius', *American Scholar* 44.2 (1975), 226. Madame de Staël, *Corinne, or Italy*, trans. Sylvia Raphael (Oxford: Oxford University Press, 2008).

of *Torschlusspanik*: the panic at the shutting of the door'.²⁷ DeJean attests that Staël, predominately in her novels *Delphine* and *Corinne* and in her play *Sapho, drame en cinq actes*, maintains a 'continuously evolving identification with Sappho'.²⁸ Blanche Vernon shares her surname with the character of Madame de Vernon in *Delphine*, in which, DeJean notes, 'Staël creates a heroine who, like Sappho, represents a pure challenge to what she terms the familial "chain of affection", the patriarchal order'.²⁹ However, repeatedly betrayed and abandoned by men, Staël's Sappho is also burdened by the heterosexual romance and 'a piteous creature', according to DeJean.³⁰ Brookner's invocation of Staël adds a further Sapphic dimension to *A Misalliance*, while Blanche's unfinished thesis reflects some difficulty in reconciling the contested Sapphic legacy.

Blanche is also a reader of Plato, from whom she understands that 'all knowledge is recollection', a concept which complements Prins's analysis of the recursive constructions of Sappho (*M*, 31). In the *Phaedrus*, Plato's discussion about whether it is preferable for a pederastic relationship also to be a love relationship invokes the 'beautiful Sappho'; it is also staged in a grove that is 'just right for young girls' and sacred to the nymphs.³¹ Both the explicit and implicit intertextual indicators of *A Misalliance* not only underscore Blanche's 'cultivated tastes' they also signal her association with texts steeped in the Sapphic, Hellenic, and homoerotic codings that circulate around the figure of the aesthete, and with traditions of the women's writer (*M*, 6).

In addition to her cultural inclinations, Blanche's culinary divagations reveal a taste for distinction. Her brother-in-law's illness occasions the brewing of asparagus soup, braised wing of chicken, and a casserole: 'The delicate steam of her soup, scenting the kitchen, made her think of greenhouses, of wet grass, and of the sun breaking through to shine on rain-spotted windows' (*M*, 53). Asparagus also conjures the smell of urine, the vegetable's 'celestial' stems capable of 'transforming my

---

27 Anita Brookner, 'Corinne and Her *Coups de Foudre*', in *Soundings* (London: Harvill Press, 1997), 162, 163. First published in the *Times Literary Supplement* (14 March 1980).
28 DeJean, *Fictions of Sappho*, 161.
29 DeJean, *Fictions of Sappho*, 165; along with Benjamin Constant, de Staël is credited with inventing the catchphrase of the aesthetic movement: *'l'art pour l'art'*. John Wilcox, 'The Beginnings of *L'art pour l'art*', *Journal of Aestheticism and Art Criticism* 11 (1952–53): 363–65.
30 DeJean, *Fictions of Sappho*, 138.
31 Plato, *Phaedrus*, trans. Christopher Rowe (London: Penguin, 2005), 12, 5.

chamber pot into a vase of aromatic perfume', as the narrator in *Swann's Way* recalls.³² Blanche's well-documented fondness for wine—Vouvray (*M*, 15), Sancerre (*M*, 33), Madeira (*M*, 34), Malaga (*M*, 34), Muscadet (*M*, 73), Hock (*M*, 83), Meursault (*M*, 111), Sauternes (*M*, 128), Liebfraumilch (*M*, 165), and Frascati (*M*, 191)—is indicative of a Sapphic love of pleasure and ceremony. 'With the gladness of our festivities and pour the libation', instructs Sappho 2, where libation might also symbolise the female sexual juices.³³ After her divorce from Bertie, Blanche perceives herself as part of the 'fallen creation', experiencing 'an inner desolation that no one must be allowed to suspect' and becoming 'oddly fearful of revealing herself to others' (*M*, 108, 47, 52). In this condition, Blanche turns to the National Gallery, where the nymphs provide a particular form of visual, sensual, and erotic enlightenment.

Once she meets the 'scornful and anarchic' Sally Beamish with her 'delinquent ... weightless ... unscrupulous' personality, Blanche's visits to the gallery are suspended (*M*, 65, 124). Instead, Blanche determines, 'like a spy', to make a study of Sally—to 'befriend her, to contemplate her'—and her stepdaughter, Elinor (*M*, 108, 81). By way of engaging Sally in a relationship, Blanche bestows her with small cash payments 'to tide [her] over' (*M*, 82, 101, 181). As Sally becomes increasingly demanding, Blanche realises their situation is untenable. She makes final arrangements to assist the Beamishes before casting them off and taking a long overdue summer holiday.

Brookner's sixth novel, *A Misalliance*, attracted two prominent critics, both of whom substantially reduced the scope of the text. For Frank Kermode, *A Misalliance* 'is about a woman abandoned by her husband of 20 years'.³⁴ By setting the subject of the novel around heterosexual absence, Kermode diminishes his own power to interpret the text's

---

32 Marcel Proust, *In Search of Lost Time*, vol. 1, *Swann's Way*, trans. C.K. Scott Moncrieff and Terence Kilmartin, rev. edn (New York: Modern Library, 2003), 169. As Brookner tells Shusha Guppy in her *Paris Review* interview, Proust is 'an exceptional case and very precious to me. He kept himself in a state of mind so hypnotic and dangerous that one approaches rereading him almost with fear. He remained always marginal, observing. The cost was too high, when all is said and done. The periods of remaining in that childlike state of receptivity are terrifying. The awful thing is that he got it *right all the time*. It is all true!' Brookner, in Guppy, 'The Art of Fiction', 157–58.
33 Sappho, *The Poetry of Sappho*, trans. Jim Powell (Oxford: Oxford University Press, 2007), 5.
34 Frank Kermode, 'The Obedient and the Free', *Guardian* (29 September 1986): 21.

Sapphic codes, despite stating that 'perhaps some of the motifs and symbols are a bit too heavily marked'.[35] John Bayley also takes a swipe at Brookner's intertexts, though he fails to unpack them further. He states, 'As in all Brookner novels, there is a good deal of emphasis, not really needed, on the metaphysics and the meaning, underpinned by analogies and examples from the world of painting and art'.[36] Subsequently, Bayley proceeds to compare negatively Brookner's motifs with those of Anthony Powell: 'All this art is well enough, though it lacks the generic point and fantasy of Anthony Powell's excursions into the fine arts in *A Dance to the Music of Time*. Far from being pretentious, or a form of showing off, it reveals a touching lack of self-confidence'.[37] Not only is this criticism amplified when considered in the context of Brookner's international reputation as an art historian, but Bayley's use of gender stereotypes, by comparing the male master's genius to Brookner's 'touching lack of self-confidence', is indicative of how the representation of Brookner as a women's writer is concomitant with an emphasis on absence in her oeuvre. 'I was invisible until then; I became briefly visible', Brookner herself observes on her 1984 Booker Prize win.[38] Prins's analysis of the construction of the women's writer seems pertinent once again. 'Sapphic voice is mediated by text and marked feminine precisely because it does not speak', she states, emphasising how women's writing paradoxically becomes known through discourses of invisibility, fragmentation, and lack.[39] DeJean's observation that the 'scholarly tradition ... remains prudently mute on the subject of Vivien' illuminates further connections between Sappho, Vivien, and Brookner as women's writers, based on critical opportunism or neglect.[40]

In Brookner's *Paris Review* interview, the novelist notes the poor reviews of *A Misalliance*, stating that there is 'a personal dislike directed against Blanche Vernon, because you can't blame her for anything, except perhaps for being a prig. Now that is a very minor vice in my book'.[41] In *A Woman Appeared to Me*, Vivien's Sapphic poet character San Giovanni explicitly laments 'the unhappy role of feminine writer' and 'the organised public spying on the private life of the writer'

35 Kermode, 'The Obedient', 21.
36 John Bayley, 'Ladies', *London Review of Books* (4 September 1986): 20.
37 Bayley, 'Ladies', 20.
38 Brookner, in Guppy, 'The Secret Sharer', 283.
39 Prins, *Victorian Sappho*, 16.
40 DeJean, *Fictions of Sappho*, 250.
41 Brookner, in Guppy, 'The Art of Fiction', 166.

(*WA*, 37). Less explicitly, Brookner distinguishes between the type of autobiographical literary criticism to which she is subject as a women's writer and an alternative, intertextual 'Jamesian' reading. She comments that the 'bad reviews were partly a dislike of Blanche, and of me since I'm supposed to be all these women I create. In America they liked it because they thought it was Jamesian, which I would not have dared to presume'.[42] Both Kermode and Bayley are representative of the canonising bent of the literary field, trivialising Brookner's subject matter for its heterosexual femininity, while failing to grapple with the elements of the text that subvert the very subject they denounce. However, the present interpretation of *A Misalliance* alternatively emphasises both the strength of women's writing and avant-garde literary practice.

The theme of failed heterosexuality was the leading obsession of most critics of *A Misalliance*. In her book, *Anita Brookner*, Lynn Veach Sadler declared: 'What is missing from the parade of characters in Blanche's world (and the world of Brookner's novels) is a male who is a match for Sally, Mousie, and the nymphs'.[43] For Sadler, Brookner's innovation manifests itself in her depiction of Blanche's relationship with Sally's stepdaughter Elinor. 'Ironically, given the search for fulfilment through a man that is constant with Brookner's heroines, the title of the sixth novel, *A Misalliance* (1986), refers principally to a relationship that Blanche Vernon has tried to effect with an approximately three-year-old child, Elinor', Sadler states.[44] However, even this relationship gives Sadler pause:

> For a writer who is unmarried and has no children and whose heroines have no children, Anita Brookner pays unusual attention to children beyond the anticipated need of her protagonists to find their identities by breaking away from their parents. *A Misalliance* is especially filled with references to children. All the good women in the novel are childless ... Miss Elphinstone, the old maid, is naturally childless; Blanche and Mrs Duff, unnaturally so.[45]

Here, Sadler's bewilderment at Brookner's interest in children leads her to reinscribe a naturalising narrative of heterosexual reproduction in the novel, despite the text's inherent distance from such a narrative. Finally, Sadler asks whether there are 'women, even a few, much less the majority, really like those in Brookner's novels? ... How could any contemporary

---

42 Brookner, in Guppy, 'The Art of Fiction', 166.
43 Sadler, *Anita Brookner*, 97.
44 Sadler, *Anita Brookner*, 95.
45 Sadler, *Anita Brookner*, 104.

woman, particularly one like Blanche, with individual means, some knowledge of the brighter social world, and a partially written thesis on Mme de Staël started apparently before her marriage, remake herself in the image she thinks her husband demands?'[46] Unfortunately, Sadler's pseudo-feminist posturing ignores both the trajectory of Blanche's development in the novel and the myriad alternative images and intertextual narratives in the text that can be marshalled into the figure of the aesthete.

The unwillingness of some critics to penetrate the domestic plot is a prominent thread in Brookner's early reception. In the *New York Times Book Review*, Fernanda Eberstadt sends a promising nod to the nineteenth-century effect in *A Misalliance* when she describes Blanche as 'a female dandy'. But she later concludes, in an apparent contradiction to her earlier insight, that Brookner's heroines 'simply want husbands to cook for'.[47] When certain critics sense Brookner's deviation from conventional reproductive narratives, the compulsion to restate the primacy of biological stereotypes ensues. For Anne Wyatt-Brown, it is the trope of the biological clock that demands attention:

> Blanche has reached a stage of life when she has begun to accept the fact that her biological time clock is running out … Blanche must find some good method of contributing to the successful evolution of the species. Although she ultimately concludes that her attempt indirectly to adopt an autistic child is fruitless and abandons the attempt, the instinct Brookner celebrates is a deeply felt one.[48]

For John Skinner, Blanche's femininity is both the cause and the effect of her reproductive failure. 'With twenty years of marriage behind her, Blanche therefore represents the furthest along an evolutionary path, although even she is obviously an attractive and well-preserved woman', he notes.[49] In Brookner's original reception, narratives of normative gender, sexuality, and reproduction appear to be so culturally embedded as to make it very difficult for critics to perceive a way of remixing and rereading any other signs and symbols in the text. In the *Times Literary Supplement*, a paper which has published countless reviews written

---

46 Sadler, *Anita Brookner*, 99.
47 Fernanda Eberstadt, 'Good Works and Bad Lovers', *New York Times Book Review* (29 March 1987): 10.
48 Anne M. Wyatt-Brown, 'Creativity in Midlife: The Novels of Anita Brookner', *Journal of Aging Studies* 3.2: 179.
49 Skinner, *The Fictions of Anita Brookner*, 108.

by Brookner, Patricia Craig's response to *A Misalliance* reflects the ideological stranglehold of heterosexual narratives in Brookner criticism. Craig claims that Brooknerines 'are ill-fitted to be the recipients of erotic overtures, unless these come from an unusually discerning man'.[50] Like other Brookner critics, Craig squarely blames the personality of Brookner's heroines for any problems that emerge in the Brookner text. 'Such women can neither experience, nor inspire, the smallest impulse towards anarchic behaviour', Craig contends.[51] On the contrary, by reading the text through the performance of the aesthete, Blanche and *A Misalliance* can be transformed into a locus of literary subversion where pleasures are indulged outside bourgeois values of reproduction and utilitarianism.

In the next section, alternative epistemologies of *A Misalliance* sally forth. Back-crossing the intertextual network between Brookner's novel, Sappho's oeuvre, the nineteenth-century archive of the 'art for art's sake' movement, and Vivien's 'Sapho 1900' texts, the figure of the aesthete emerges across sensual Sapphic motifs of the nymphs' playground, figures of the lesbian, and the women's writer, and of subversion, the backwards turn, the intersection of art and life, and the spectator's response to the object and subject. Staging the performance of the aesthete through the rhetorical device of metaleptic prolepsis and an organising narrative of metamorphosis, Blanche Vernon's true path is revealed including her exile in the present, her Sapphic re-education, and her erotic journey of self-discovery to the sun.

Producing the Figure of the Aesthete

As Blanche Vernon emerges from her divorce, she senses her equilibrium might be restored by a blast of heat, 'as if only in the coming of such sunshine as she could remember or imagine would she relax' (*M*, 7). Blanche's heat-seeking fantasies are intermingled with visual, aural, olfactory, and physical sensual pleasures:

> In the uncertain light of these uncertain days, her thoughts turned to images of an illusory but brilliant heat, the sky turned to whiteness, the air dry and filled with scent, the whine of a passing vehicle receding as the afternoon emptied and discouraged movement. She thought of the evenings of these

---

50 Patricia Craig, 'On Not Being Overwhelmed', *Times Literary Supplement* (29 August 1986): 932.
51 Craig, 'On Not Being Overwhelmed', 932.

imaginary days, the sun intensifying into redness, the sky cooling to a light bright green, and then to a white that seemed laid over indigo. And of the nights, balmy enough to encourage open windows, late music, the drifting smoke of a last cigarette, sheets cool and dry to welcome the still-warm limbs. (*M*, 7)

The appeal to a range of the senses throughout *A Misalliance*, as exemplified by this passage, can be situated as an implicit intertextual pointer to Sappho's poetry as a precursor oeuvre. Sappho 2, for example, imagines apple groves scented with 'frankincense fuming', babbling streams, musk roses, a place where 'breezes blow here honey sweet and softer' and 'flickering leafage settles entrancement', and 'goblets of gold mix nectar' raised in celebration.[52] Nymphs are also a feature of Sappho's poems, both explicitly, as companions to the gods—'Cypris and you Nereids, bring my brother / back to me unharmed'—and implicitly, as constituting the female community of Lesbos where Sappho spent most of her life.[53]

In *Studies of the Greek Poets*, nineteenth-century aesthete John Addington Symonds illuminates the sensual and fertile environment of Sappho's Lesbos: 'Nowhere in any age of Greek history, or in any part of Hellas, did the love of physical beauty, the sensibility to radiant scenes of nature, the consuming fervour of personal feeling, assume such grand proportions and receive so illustrious an expression as they did in Lesbos'.[54] Demetrios explicitly ties Sapphic botany to nymphs and eroticism when he notes that: 'Virtually the whole of Sappho's poetry deals with nymphs' gardens, wedding songs, eroticism'.[55] E.E. Pender includes the winged figure of Eros and the winged figure of the chariot in Sappho as symbols of desire when he comments that 'in Sappho, the fluttering response is caused by the sight of the beloved'.[56] Indeed, the erotic connotations implied by the fluttering of the wings can be a symbol of the wings of the labia, also known as 'nymphae'. Pender argues that the wing motif is one of multiple Sapphic symbols that Plato mobilises in the *Phaedrus*, a text that will become significant in

---

52 Sappho, *Poetry of Sappho*, 4–5.
53 Sappho, *Poetry of Sappho*, 5.
54 John Addington Symonds, *Studies of the Greek Poets*, vol. 1, 3rd edn (London: Adam and Charles Black, 1893), 290. John Addington Symonds was reputedly Henry James's muse for the aesthete in 'The Author of "Beltraffio"' (1884).
55 Demetrios, quoted in Jack Winkler, 'Gardens of Nymphs: Public and Private in Sappho's Lyrics', *Women's Studies* 8 (1981): 78.
56 E.E. Pender, 'Sappho and Anacreon in Plato's *Phaedrus*', *Leeds International Classical Studies* 6.4 (2007): 30.

staging of the performance of the aesthete across Blanche's heat-seeking journey.[57] In *Phaedrus*, Socrates playfully objects to the sunny site of his discussion of cross-generational pederastic relationships by stating, 'Don't you know I'll be patently possessed by the Nymphs, to whom *you* deliberately exposed me?'[58] Pender maintains that the groves and meadows in which nymphs frolic depicted in Sappho's sensual landscapes constitute 'scenes of seduction'.[59] Therefore, Brookner's reconstitution of Sapphic motifs of hot sun, cool groves, breezy wings, and nymph activity can be read as cultivating a sapphic *mise en scène* which informs this queer, lesbian, cross-historical reading of *A Misalliance*.

DeJean asserts that it was Baudelaire who unequivocally constructed a sapphic lesbianism: 'Baudelaire not only gave his readers a homosexual Sappho; he also made Sappho synonymous with the "femmes damnées," redefining thereby the literary lesbian in her antique image'.[60] In *The Flowers of Evil*, Baudelaire hails 'Lesbos!' as an island of 'honey-dew kisses, full of the sun's heat!' and installed himself as protector of 'lusty, young' Sappho's legacy.[61] Sappho 94 depicts a subject anointed with 'flowery perfumes', 'on beds of soft luxury' where 'you would satisfy all your longing / for that tender girl' and constitutes a precursor text to Baudelaire's 'Women Damned: Delphine and Hippolyta'.[62] In this poem, Baudelaire spies his lesbian heroines 'amid deep cushions steeped in musky scents' before the women are plunged into a cavernous Hell 'where the sun has never shone'.[63] In 'Women Damned', the nymphs' playground again becomes the scene of a lesbian frisson:

> Some, half-seduced by confidences shared
> Beside the babbling brook or budding grove,
> Would carve their names on saplings, if they dared—
> An apt confessional for blushing love.[64]

In this imagery, Baudelaire reconstitutes Sapphic motifs that are significant to constructing the figure of the aesthete. It is the connotative

---

57 Pender, 'Sappho and Anacreon', 1–57.
58 Plato, *Phaedrus*, 20.
59 Pender, 'Sappho and Anacreon', 3.
60 DeJean, *Fictions of Sappho*, 273.
61 Charles Baudelaire, *Complete Poems*, trans. Walter Martin (Manchester: Carcenet, 1997), 291, 292.
62 Sappho, *Poetry of Sappho*, 22.
63 Baudelaire, *Complete Poems*, 295, 299.
64 Baudelaire, *Complete Poems*, 301.

field born of Baudelairean sapphism, in conjunction with the Sapphic oeuvre of Vivien, which becomes pertinent for reading the aesthete in *A Misalliance*.

In *The Rules of Art: Genesis and Structure in the Literary Field*, Pierre Bourdieu crowns Baudelaire as the representative figure of the 'art for art's sake' movement.[65] Bourdieu frames the 'art for art's sake' movement as a 'double refusal' of the values of the dominant bourgeois culture which 'control the instruments of legitimation' on the one hand, and the advocates of a social art who 'demand that literature fulfil a social or political function' on the other.[66] In subverting two distinct political paradigms—one organised around the market economy and the other based on regulating behaviour through good works, the aesthetes developed a strong symbolic artillery. They appropriated and mobilised the figure of the lesbian and the Greek pederastic model as symbols of resistance against the bourgeois control of family, capital, and everyday experience. Testimony to the aesthetes' defiance of bourgeois norms, Baudelaire's 'lesbian' poems in *The Flowers of Evil* (originally entitled 'The Lesbians') were among three of the six poems banned by the French courts for a 'vulgar realism offensive to decency'.[67] Ladenson maintains that Baudelaire's depictions of lesbianism were an assault on the dominant sexual morality and discursive and symbolic epistemologies of the time. Baudelaire mobilised lesbianism, Ladenson states, as 'an androgynous ideal of pure artifice that is the very opposite of a pruriently "realistic" portrayal of illicit sexuality ... his *femmes damnées* represent pure style, liberated from the shackles of mundane referentiality'.[68] The lush and luxurious settings of Baudelaire's lesbian poems signal a resistance to value defined by a utilitarian, market-based economy founded on the heterosexualised division of labour into gendered public and private spheres. Furthermore, in its backward turn, Baudelaire's antique sapphism could be said to pose a challenge to the temporal modes of chronology and precedential ordering that Jagose

---

65 Bourdieu maintains that Baudelaire 'incarnates the most extreme position of the avant-garde, that of revolt against all authorities and all institutions, beginning with literary institutions'. Bourdieu, *Rules of Art*, 65.
66 Bourdieu, *Rules of Art*, 59, 73.
67 Ladenson, *Dirt for Art's Sake*, 73. Jonathan Culler contends that the poems represent a 'transgressive eroticism' which engage a refusal 'to accept what is permitted but seek the unknown' and which also enable a language for female desire and sexuality. Culler, Introduction to *Flowers of Evil*, xiv–xv.
68 Ladenson, *Dirt for Art's Sake*, 74.

indicts as the modes of sexual sequence that produce the hierarchical heterosexual/homosexual opposition.[69] Fundamentally, the lesbian's embodiment of pure style that contests referentiality positions the figure as exerting pressure on the way in which meaning is established. In this way, the aesthetic, erotic, and temporal disposition of the figure of the aesthete constitutes a subversion of the literal, capitalist, heterochronic economy.

Writing during the belle époque, nearly 50 years after the 1857 publication of *The Flowers of Evil*, Vivien's Sapphic Baudelairean influences brought about widespread condemnation. 'Renée Vivien did not think of making herself into a thinker', scoffs French nationalist Charles Maurras, while Lillian Faderman maintains that the poet's 'infatuation with the aesthete-decadent pose' reflected her forms of self-loathing, contributed to her premature death, and made her poetry 'irrelevant to contemporary lesbians, who have long since escaped from the spell of aesthete-decadence'.[70] Yet Vivien's investment in Sappho was intellectual, bohemian, and far-sighted. Along with her lover and fellow artist Natalie Barney, Vivien studied classical Greek in order to translate Sappho into French, anonymously publishing *Sapho* in 1903, in a volume which constructs a new, more emphatically lesbian biography and context for Sappho. It includes some of Vivien's own expanded Sapphic verse as well as drawing on other major Sapphic inheritors such as Algernon Charles Swinburne.[71] Vivien wrote four poetic plays about Sappho, as well as her Sapphic novel and volumes of poetry.[72] In *The Muse of the Violets*, Vivien's 'Inscription at the base of a statue' shares a sensual landscape with Sappho and Brookner, invoking 'summer nights whose breath grazes me like a flower ... the depth of the verdure where the brook sings' and 'the rose, expiring after the harsh ravage of the heat' (*MV*, 40, 42, 42). Through a Sapphic lens, Vivien brings intimate details of lesbian eroticism to the page: 'My ingenious fingers wait when they have found / The petal flesh beneath the robe they part' (*MV*, 32). While in *A Woman Appeared to Me*, Vivien's depiction of the living room of Vally, the subject of the narrator's desire, summons

---

69 Jagose, *Inconsequence*, 1–37.
70 Lillian Faderman, *Surpassing the Love of Men: Romantic Friendships and Love between Women from the Renaissance to the Present* (New York: Morrow, 1981), 363.
71 Karla Jay, *The Amazon and the Page: Natalie Clifford Barney and Renée Vivien* (Bloomington: Indiana University Press, 1988), 63.
72 Jay, *The Amazon*, 67.

Sappho through Baudelaire—and Vivien's own living quarters: 'Inside, tiger lilies opened their great trumpets and gave off their overpowering perfume. Vally, stretched languidly on a divan covered with Persian silks, was "at home" to a few friends' (*WA*, 5). Together, Vivien and Barney were highly invested in Sapphic representation, female community, the society of nymphs and aestheticist theatrics, even owning properties on Lesbos.⁷³ 'Every being should live his private life and win, hardly, the experience which will signify nothing', Vivien articulates in *A Woman Appeared to Me*, and Vivien and Barney embody the aestheticist credo to measure all sensations through the lens of personal experience (*WA*, 3).

At the same time as working with and rereading aestheticist narratives, Vivien delivers a stunning critique of heterosexual institutions, heterosexual masculinity, the masculinist appropriation of Sappho, and the historical male aesthetic. In 'Words to a Lover', Vivien underscores the negative and compromising effects of an institution commonly presented as natural when she writes:

> I am at the age where a woman abandons herself
> To a man whom her weakness searched out but whom she dreads
> And I have never given myself like that
>
> (*MV*, 68)

In *A Woman Appeared to Me*, San Giovanni argues that 'men's actions have always had the single purpose of subjecting women to their stupid caprices, their sensuality, their unjust and cruel tyranny. And how can you not hate anyone who presents himself to you in the role of Master?' (*WA*, 36). In this way, Vivien's proto-feminist politics are remarkably progressive and her unselfconscious representational style refuses to conform to the passive female stereotype. As San Giovanni states: 'I neither love nor hate men … what I hold against them is the great wrong they have done to women. They are political adversaries' (*WA*, 8–9).⁷⁴

---

73 'Why wouldn't we assemble around ourselves a group of poetesses like those who surrounded Sappho in Mytilene and who provided mutual inspiration?' Barney asked. Natalie Barney, quoted in DeJean, *Fictions of Sappho*, 279.

74 Contrary to epitomising a submissive deferral to Romantic aestheticism, Vivien's depiction of 'the male prostitute' resembles a caricature of the male aesthete when she writes that the 'male prostitute flaunts his laziness in quarters vast as a palace. Servants liveried according to his caprice in picturesque costumes silently carry out his orders … His desires come to life in beauty. Choruses of praise echo back his pride. He passes, his forehead crowned with light, more admired than a scholar or a priest. This man has sold himself' (*WA*, 21). According to Vivien, the male prostitute's implication in the institution of marriage underlines his hypocrisy,

For Vivien, 'men are The Unesthetic par excellence', a fact which has hampered women's literary production 'because women are too often forced by convention to write about men' (WA, 34). This is in part why Vivien turns to Sappho. Sappho 'didn't deign to notice masculine existence. She celebrated the sweet speech and the adorable smile of Atthis, and not the muscled torso of the imaginary Phaon', Vivien writes in a recuperation of the myth, swerving away from Sappho's heterosexualisation and locating the women's writer firmly within Greek discourses of beauty, sensuality, and lesbianism (WA, 34).

Vivien's capacity to produce aestheticist narratives of experience about the lesbian, the women's writer, and female community, in conjunction with her radical and multifaceted critique of heterosexual patriarchy, is cause to question whether Baudelaire entirely warrants the praise of subversion lavished upon him by Bourdieu. Although Baudelaire's portrayal of Sapphic lesbians explores alternative positions of desire and identification for men, advances modes of alternative masculinity, and expands the possibilities of male homosocial desire, Morgan contests the notion that a radical sexual politics for both men and women is thereby guaranteed.[75] Likewise, Rita Felski maintains that 'the male aesthete's playful subversion of gender norms, his adoption of feminine traits, paradoxically reinforces his distance from and elevation above women, who are by nature incapable of such intellectual mobility and aesthetic sophistication'.[76] Therefore, Vivien's refusal of hetero-patriarchal values can be importantly mobilised to expand Baudelaire's 'double rupture' of bourgeois and social realist paradigms. Via Vivien, this third rupture is reinscribed herein through the hermeneutic figure of the aesthete.

>   status, and conventionality: 'marriage has sanctified the bargain made beneath the vault of a temple … This man is blessed by the church, honoured by convention, and protected by law. Only I call him "prostitute"' (WA, 21).
>
> 75 Morgan, 'Male Lesbian Bodies', 48, 40. What Morgan terms the imaginary construct of 'male lesbianism', as produced through the Sapphic intertextuality of the nineteenth-century male aesthetes, 'may be seen as an attempt on the part of an all-male avant-garde to explore an enlarged range of pleasures and subjectivities without forfeiting the sociocultural privileges long accorded to a masculinity faithful to the hegemonic model for men's gender and sexuality established by hetero-patriarchy' (41). Indeed, Morgan argues that 'Women Damned' finally expels 'Woman' from the scene of artistic creativity while abstracting and reassigning her qualities to the male subject in a strategy that is 'deeply misogynistic' (48).
> 76 Felski, 'Counterdiscourse of the Feminine', 1100.

When Blanche encounters the 'nymph-like' Sally Beamish at the local hospital, Blanche's impressions of Sally are received through a Sapphic lens regarding her appearance, behaviour, and disposition (*M*, 103). Brookner's text then proceeds to reconstitute the revolutionary discourse of Sapphic aestheticism through the relationship between Sally and Blanche. Like her radiant appearance, Sally Beamish's name casts her as a Greek figure of dancing light and heat and, moreover, as the embodiment of Blanche's heat-seeking fantasies.[77] In *A Misalliance*, Blanche regularly invokes the aphorism of J.M.W. Turner: 'The sun is God' (*M*, 7, 20, 97, 110, 165). Dinah Birch maintains that the popularity of solar mythology in the nineteenth century reflected a desire for a set of values different from those endorsed by industrial capitalism.[78] Thus, Sally Beamish is the bright sun to Blanche as the white-lit moon, just as Sally is the spark of heat that kindles Blanche's desire.[79]

In 1873, art historian Walter Pater published *The Renaissance*, an aesthetic bible, which, like much aesthetic criticism, colonises other fields with its forward-thinking, far-reaching analyses. Richard Ellmann states its controversial conclusion 'is a kind of manual of seduction of young men, somewhat masked as a manual of instruction for aesthetic critics'.[80]

---

[77] Sappho 16 praises the 'sparkling glance' of one beauty, while Sappho 58.25–26 celebrates a love that 'has made of the sun's brightness and beauty my fortune'. In 'Modern Naiad', a tribute to the modern water nymph from the Isle of Lesbos, Vivien evokes a 'vague smile', which 'flickers like the glint of sun on a foam-washed pile' (*MV*, 28); while in 'Undine', she addresses the nymph Undine with the words, 'Your laughter is light / your caress deep' (*MV*, 53).

[78] Dinah Birch, 'The Sun is God: Ruskin's Solar Mythology', in *The Sun is God: Painting, Literature and Mythology in the Nineteenth Century*, ed. J.B. Bulleen (Oxford: Clarendon Press, 1989), 58.

[79] Sally's wardrobe also takes its cues from Sappho: her sandals recall the 'intricate sandals' of Sappho 39 as well as Vivien's depiction of daybreak, from the 'Sapho' collection, as 'the dawn [which] came to me in golden sandals' (*MV*, 37). Sappho, *Poetry of Sappho*, 13. Sally's golden bracelets seem modelled on Andromache's styling in Sappho 44, 'with her many golden bracelets / and purple scented robes and intricate adornments', while Sally's red hair mimics the hair of the beloved in Vivien's 'I Love You for Being …', about whom the narrator claims: 'I love you for being a redhead and like autumn, / … / That the setting sun lights and crowns'. And Sally's 'complicated and fashionable kimono coat', like those worn by Vivien, is also emblematic of the erotic wing motif in Sappho (*MV*, 71). Sappho, *Poetry of Sappho*, 13, 14, 39. These intertextual layerings re-emphasise the particular threads between Sappho, Vivien, and Brookner.

[80] Walter Pater, *The Renaissance: Studies in Art and Poetry* (London: Macmillan, 1924); Ellmann, 'Henry James', 211.

In *The Renaissance*—the period which frames Blanche's initial interest in the nymphs of the National Gallery—Pater reinforces the connection between the heat motif, Greek culture, and male homoerotic desire. Proclaiming that Hellenism 'is the principle pre-eminently of intellectual light', Pater famously urges aesthetes to 'burn always with this hard, gemlike flame', a statement that is recalibrated in Vivien's rendering of lesbian desire as 'a love at once ardent and pure, like a white flame' (*WA*, 6).[81] Through his advice, Pater sets up an opposition between the hegemonic 'habits' of a 'stereotyped' world and the sensitivity and intelligence of an aesthetic consumer, in whom the beamish-like flame symbolises moral, intellectual, and erotic freedom.[82] For Pater, Hellenism connotes 'the care for physical beauty, the worship of the body, the breaking down of those limits which the religious system of the middle age imposed on the heart and the imagination'.[83] Citing Winckelmann (also the subject of a biography by Staël), Pater frames Hellenism as a constitutively masculine enterprise when he states: 'the beauty of Greek art will ever seem wanting, because its supreme beauty is rather male then female'.[84] Vivien, however, combats this gendering of Greek beauty with her own formulation of male and female principles. 'Everything that is ugly, unjust, fierce, base, emanates from the Male Principle. Everything unbearably lovely and desirable emanates from the Female Principle' (*WA*, 6).[85] Despite Pater's masculinist tendencies (subsequently recalibrated by Vivien), his contribution to aestheticism raises the aesthetic critic's interest beyond the art object to include the human subject, further increasing the erotic connotations of aesthetic beauty: 'The aesthetic critic, then, regards all the objects with which he has to do, all works of art, and the fairer forms of nature and human life, as powers or forces producing pleasurable sensations, each of a more

---

81 Pater, *The Renaissance*, 200, 250. In *The Renaissance*, Pater further states: 'To burn always with this hard, gemlike flame, to main this ecstasy, is success in life ... our failure is to form habits ... habit is relative to a stereotyped world, and meantime it is only the roughness of the eye that makes any two persons, things, situations, seem alike ... While all melts under our feet, we may well grasp at any exquisite passion, or any contribution to knowledge that seems by a lifted horizon to set the spirit free for a moment, or any stirring of the senses, strange dyes, strange colours, and curious odours, or work of the artist's hands, or the face of one's friend' (250).
82 Pater, *The Renaissance*; see full quote in the note above.
83 Pater, *The Renaissance*, xiii.
84 Pater, *The Renaissance*, 202.
85 DeJean, *Fictions of Sappho*, 282.

or less peculiar or unique kind'.[86] In emphasising modes of behaviour which live life as art, the aesthete's Greek turn advances a program that does not detach aesthetic values from the everyday but, as echoed by Blanche's new fascination with Sally, incorporates a new value system into the lived experience.

In addition to Sapphic and Hellenic motifs and the intersection of art and life, the process of the eroticised gaze also forms part of the signifying matrix of the aesthete. In Greek-influenced Romantic aestheticism, the gaze is imbued with the power to suspend or restore subjectivity. Sappho 31 reveals, 'For when I look at you a moment / then I have no longer the power to speak', while in Baudelaire's 'Women Damned', Delphine implores Hippolyta: 'Come, heal me with your gaze'.[87] With the emerging emphasis Romantic aestheticism places on the spectator's response to the power of art, the mechanism of the gaze triggers a process of subjectification. Given the importance placed on alternative forms of being and life experience in aestheticism, the new blueprint for subjectification offered by the aesthete is of singular importance. In *Romanticism and Its Discontents*, Brookner suggests that one of Baudelaire's most important contributions to history is his critical methodology regarding his responses to works of art:

> He is, in fact, a new type of critic, one almost entirely dependent on his own reactions, his *moi*. He believes that his reactions to painting or music or literature are as valid as the things in themselves. He is, in every context, an artist in his own right. (*RD*, 78)

For Brookner, therefore, the gaze is the vehicle through which the aesthete ascends into the being of the Romantic *moi*. The self-constituting mechanism of the gaze, in conjunction with the subversive register of the aesthete's behaviour, suggests that the performance of the aesthete constitutes an especially *contestatory* narrative of subjectification.

When Pater expands Baudelaire's response to the image to encompass a response to the historical subject—a transition which can be mapped as the shift from Blanche's interest in Renaissance art to Sally—the Platonic

---

86 Pater, *The Renaissance*, xi. Pater emphasises that the aesthete pays attention to the artistic qualities of the art object in addition to those 'of life itself, of gesture and speech, and the details of daily intercourse; these also, for the wise, being susceptible of a suavity and charm, caught from the way in which they are done, which gives them a worth in themselves' (143).

87 Sappho, in DeJean, *Fictions of Sappho*, 321; Baudelaire, *Complete Poems*, 297.

model of Pater's gaze is both homoerotic and cross-generational.[88] Underscoring the intertextuality between Sappho and Plato, Pender maintains that the strongest allusion to Sappho in Plato's *Phaedrus* concerns the sighting of the beloved.[89] In the *Phaedrus*, the gaze traces the older male lover's sighting of the beauty of the younger male beloved. Similarly, in *A Misalliance*, Blanche's gaze upon Sally Beamish's 'perfect appearance' represents a cross-generational and homoeroticised attraction to physical beauty (*M*, 61). In the *Phaedrus*, the lover's gaze upon the beloved fuels the lover's quest for self-mastery, which Plato narrates as a story about the soul's backward turn to retrieve the sacred knowledge of the philosophical forms.[90] Plato paints an image of a soul sprouting wings to symbolise the gaining of knowledge triggered upon sighting the beloved's beauty.[91] This imagery comes together in the last section of this chapter, climaxing in Blanche's pleasure-seeking flight to the sun.

In 'Theses on the Philosophy of History', Walter Benjamin draws on his own winged metaphor when he depicts history as a structure

---

88 It is not hard to see similarities between Pater and Brookner's art criticism. In *The Renaissance*, Pater encourages aesthetes to consider, '[w]hat is this song or picture, this engaging personality presented in life or in a book, to *me*? What effect does it really produce on me? Does it give me pleasure? And if so, what sort or degree of pleasure?' Pater, *The Renaissance*, x. Brookner's former student and director of the National Gallery, Neil MacGregor, recalls that '[Brookner] insisted that art historians must have the courage of their feelings as well as their convictions, that once you know David painted this picture in 1811, you must ask: What did this do to his life? What does it do to my life? And to the lives of those who have looked at it in between?' Guppy, 'The Secret Sharer', 285.

89 Pender, 'Sappho and Anacreon', 38.

90 Plato states that a 'human being must comprehend what is said universally, arising from many sensations and being collected together into one through reasoning; and this is a recollection of those things which our soul once saw when it travelled in company with god and treated with contempt the things we now say are, and when it poked its head up into what really is'. Plato, *Phaedrus*, 30.

91 Plato, *Phaedrus*, 31. The forward motion implied by the flight of wings also complements the nineteenth-century troping of lesbianism as 'the society of the future' in the work of Pierre Louÿs and Natalie Barney. Pierre Louÿs dedicated his *Les chansons de Bilitis* (1894), a literary hoax about a fictional lesbian poet of ancient Greece, who was modelled on Sappho, 'to the young ladies of the society of the future'. In turn, Natalie Barney dedicated her *Five Short Greek Dialogues* to Louÿs, stating, 'there already exist young women of the society of the future who appreciate what you have done for them and who want to thank you, however incoherently and awkwardly'. Gretchen Schultz, 'Daughters of Bilitis: Literary Genealogy and Lesbian Authenticity', *GLQ: A Journal of Lesbian and Gay Studies* 7.3 (2001): 378, 385–86.

comprised of multiple temporalities. He states that the past 'can be seized only as an image which flashes up in an instant when it can be recognised and is never seen again', and describes history as 'the subject of a structure', calling it 'a constellation which [one] era has formed with a definite earlier one'.[92] Benjamin utilises Paul Klee's painting, 'Angelus Novus'—known also as the 'Angel of History'—to formulate how historical production constitutes an ongoing negotiation and rereading of the past in the present:

> A Klee painting named 'Angelus Novus' shows an angel looking as though he is about to move away from something he is fixedly contemplating. His eyes are staring, his mouth is open, his wings are spread. This is how we picture the angel of history. His face is turned toward the past. Where we perceive a chain of events, he sees one single catastrophe which keeps piling wreckage upon wreckage and hurls it in front of his feet. The angel would like to stay, awaken the dead, and make whole what has been smashed. But a storm is blowing from Paradise; it has got caught in his wings with such violence that the angel can no longer close them. This storm irresistibly propels him into the future to which his back is turned, while the pile of debris before him grows skyward. This storm is what we call progress.[93]

In this account of historical production, Benjamin incorporates a backward turn to the past to create the possibility of a historical rereading of the present. In his reading of Benjamin, Bahti supplies the formulation of the 'metaleptic prolepsis' as the rhetorical form that produces the historical image as an effect of a backward turn from the present and a reincorporation and reconstitution of past fragments into the present (and future).[94] Bahti defines metalepsis as 'a retrospective assignation of a relationship between past and present', and prolepsis as 'an anticipation of a future event or fulfilment in and from the point of the present':[95]

> But while one can (for the sake of the present's moment argument) have prolepsis without metalepsis, one cannot have metalepsis without prolepsis. The movement connecting the past to the present—metalepsis strictly speaking—as, for example, in having the present be an effect of a past cause or an answer to a past claim or need, necessarily involves a corrective

---

92 Benjamin, 'Philosophy of History', 255, 261–63.
93 Benjamin, 'Philosophy of History', 257.
94 Bahti, 'History as Rhetorical Enactment', 189.
95 Bahti, 'History as Rhetorical Enactment', 189.

prolepsis—what I will call a metaleptic prolepsis—with which one moves from the past back to the present.[96]

Sappho's presumed suicide, by jumping from the Leucadian Cliff, is also characterised by Prins through the figure of metalepsis.[97] This movement leaves the women's writer in a state of 'authorial dispossession ... falling into an infinitely repeatable death', where '"the life story" is just another version of the "death story", then, another repetition of Sappho's leap'.[98] However, Prins suggests that 'by reading the leap rhetorically rather than thematically—as the iterability of an effect rather than the statement of a theme', in a way that complements the use of rhetorical figures in *Misreading Anita Brookner*, it is possible to read the Sapphic text as a series of reflections on the process of historical construction (as opposed to right or wrong disputes over meaning).[99] For Prins, therefore, the metalepsis inherent in Sapphic readings instantiates a new logic for literary history.[100] However, Sappho's leap can also be read thematically—as an instance of lesbian desire. In the heterosexualisation of Sappho, the poet's leap is a symbol of her despair over abandonment by Phaon. Alternatively, the Sapphic metaleptic leap can be interpreted as the instrumentalisation of the Sapphic wings and therefore as one contour in the Sapphic narrative of lesbian desire. Benjamin and Bahti's reconstitution of fragments of the past into a conception of the present, and Prins's analysis of the recursive structure of literary history as modelled by the reconstructions of Sappho, echo the aesthete's reimagining of Sapphic fragments and Hellenic forms as a subversive rereading of the image of the historical present. Additionally, the flight of Sapphic wings dramatises the reincorporation of historical homoerotic knowledge in the proleptic forward flight of subjectification.

If, on the one hand, we think of the conventional historical subject as constituted by a chronological, linear narrative, the aesthete, on the other hand, is constituted by a backwards–forwards motion. To this end, the rhetorical figure of metaleptic prolepsis (backwards forwards)

---

96 Bahti, 'History as Rhetorical Enactment', 189–90.
97 'Sappho leaps into her afterlife by metalepsis, enacting a temporal transposition that forces us to read simultaneously forward and backward in time', she states. Prins, *Victorian Sappho*, 178.
98 Prins, *Victorian Sappho*, 178–79, 190.
99 Prins, *Victorian Sappho*, 191.
100 Prins maintains that 'The moment when a "history of reception" becomes visible can itself be historicised as a recursive structure, and it requires more complex reading than straightforward sequential analysis'. Prins, *Victorian Sappho*, 246.

is effectively representative of the figure of the aesthete. In assembling the figure of the aesthete, therefore, we can superimpose the backward turn to the Greek (and its simultaneous rejection of the bourgeois heterochronic present), with the forward-bending subjectification narrative, onto the backward–forward sequence that Benjamin and Prins present as the mechanism underwriting historical production. In so doing, the rhetorical device of metaleptic prolepsis is nominated as the organising rhetorical form of the figure of the aesthete. Tracing a critical and subversive response to the present, and a backward turn to a past written through Sapphic and Hellenic motifs, the device of metaleptic prolepsis enables a new queer narrative of subjectification and desire.

To propel the metaleptic prolepsis, a narrative of metamorphosis (radical change) is offered as the narrative form for reading the performance of the aesthete. Bakhtin frames the metamorphosis narrative as 'a mythological sheath for the idea of development—but one that unfolds not so much in a straight line as spasmodically, a line with "knots" in it, one that therefore constitutes a distinctive type of *temporal sequence*'.[101] Bakhtin designates the transformative sequence of metamorphosis across the 'knots' or narrative contours of guilt, punishment, redemption, purification, and blessedness. His delineation of the non-linear metamorphosis narrative complements the backward–forward motion of the metaleptic prolepsis and provides an alternative to the progressive narratives that underwrite heterosexual privilege. Drawing on readings of Bourdieu, Jacques Lacan, Benjamin, Bahti, and Plato, the performance of the aesthete can be staged across the preconditions for a metaleptic turn, represented in the 'guilt and punishment' of Blanche's unhappy marriage breakdown; the 'redemptive flashback' as found in Blanche's encounter with the nymphs and Sally; and the prolepsis as symptomised in the 'purification and blessedness' that charts Blanche's relationship with Sally and her winged journey to the sun.

Staging the Performance of the Aesthete

I Guilt

In *The Rules of Art*, Pierre Bourdieu notes that his chief aesthete, Baudelaire, confronts a 'double bind' in the course of his revolutionary project regarding the necessity of rejecting bourgeois life, while at the

---

101 Bakhtin, 'Forms of Time', 113.

same time craving social recognition.[102] This conundrum facing the aesthete underscores the figure's problematic sense of exile or dislocation in the present. Exile was an integral part of Staël's own experience after her banishment by Napoleon in 1803, as well as a symbol of political resistance in her reading of Sappho, while Benjamin characterises the present itself as a temporal period inflected with the experience of exile.[103] Bahti explains that when Benjamin describes the present as "'the time to which the course of our own existence has once assigned [*verwiesen*] us" … *verwiesen* also means "exiled"'.[104] The aesthete's state of political exile in the present is analogous to Jacques Lacan's representation of the relationship between action and desire that constitutes guilt. Lacan depicts guilt as 'a question of the relationship between action and desire and the former's fundamental failure to catch up with the latter'.[105] Lacan claims that behaviour which is deemed 'good', which is also culturally institutionalised, nevertheless 'gives rise to a reversal that locates in the centre an incommensurable measure, an infinite measure that is called desire'.[106] He contends, 'the only thing of which one can be guilty is of having given ground relative to one's desire'.[107] For Lacan, guilt entreats the subject to discover the nature of their desire and is therefore both part of, and a precondition to, the process of self-discovery—or narrative of metamorphosis—that functions as the organising narrative of the figure of the aesthete.

In staging the performance of the aesthete across a narrative of metamorphosis in *A Misalliance*, the phase of guilt represents the subject's state of dislocation in the present prior to revelation and transformation. In this sense, the aesthete's exile can be read as a reflection of '*un moi insatiable du non-moi*', discussed by Baudelaire in *The Painter of Modern Life* (*PML*, 9). Brookner translates this as 'a self avid for non-self'; it is a state that expresses how the 'non-self' figures the space of desire that stakes a distance from the exiled 'I' of the dominant order (*GF*, 69). In *A Misalliance*, Blanche struggles between bourgeois action and contestatory desire in the conflict between her unromantic experience of the

---

102 Bourdieu, *Rules of Art*, 64, 63.
103 DeJean, *Fictions of Sappho*, 166; Benjamin, 'Philosophy of History', 254.
104 Bahti, 'History as Rhetorical Enactment', 190.
105 Jacques Lacan, *The Ethics of Psychoanalysis 1959–1960: The Seminar of Jacques Lacan Book VII*, trans. Jacques-Alain Miller, ed. Dennis Porter (London: Routledge, 2008), 385.
106 Lacan, *The Ethics of Psychoanalysis*, 388.
107 Lacan, *The Ethics of Psychoanalysis*, 392.

heterosexual romance narrative and her state of psychic discomfort after her divorce on the one hand, and her alternative queer desire for the nymphs on the other.

In the opening chapters of *A Misalliance*, we meet a protagonist split between two states: one that represents so-called good behaviour and the other state which is, as yet, unknown. Harbouring 'inner contradictions', Blanche Vernon is a woman 'schooled in good behaviour', yet someone who also suffers from 'original misunderstandings' (*M*, 6, 28, 72). These misunderstandings work to problematise Blanche's formative schooling and figure in Lacan's words, that 'ground has been given relative to one's desire' (*M*, 28, 72).[108] In 'Seminar 7', Lacan interrogates the ethical value of the good when he says, 'if one has to do things for the good, in practice one is always faced with the question: for the good of whom?'[109] In *A Misalliance*, Blanche's misunderstandings explicitly concern the lack of recognition of a certain type of desire, recalling a youthful expectation that she 'could afford to have no desires' (*M*, 70). In the absence of knowledge of her desires, Blanche's developmental process is propelled along a conventional social trajectory that originates in the domestic family and concludes in heterosexual marriage. However, none of these outcomes proves satisfactory for Blanche. Her husband Bertie is portrayed as 'the one who sprung me from that daughterly trap', a characterisation which emphasises how marriage is, by default, prefigured through the bourgeois family and how the hetero-romance narrative functions as a social escape route rather than as the denouement of natural desires (*M*, 69). In *A Misalliance*, marriage constitutes a continuation of the pedagogical process that institutionalises 'good behaviour' (the type of behaviour Lacan warns against) as heterosexual desire: 'marriage was a form of higher education' (*M*, 96). For Blanche, marriage substitutes one form of submission with another: 'It was her husband who had fashioned her into the woman she was now' (*M*, 12). Furthermore, the chasm between the action of the romance narrative and Blanche's own (supposed absence of) desire is reflected in the lack of enjoyment marriage elicits. Blanche finds herself in the unenviable state 'where one's partner, one's referent, one's *vis-à-vis*, the mirror of one's life, had turned into an acquaintance of uncertain intimacy, whose conversation, once so longed for, was, more often than not, alien, uneasy, resentful, and boring' (*M*, 2). As in

---

108 Lacan, *The Ethics of Psychoanalysis*, 392.
109 Lacan, *The Ethics of Psychoanalysis*, 392.

Vivien's *A Woman Appeared before Me*, the representation of marriage as socially and culturally enforced, pedagogical, psychologically bruising, oppressive, and unpleasant functions to denaturalise heterosexuality in *A Misalliance*. A gulf opens up between the prescribed action of the heterosexual romance narrative and a resistant, queer desire.

When Bourdieu examines Baudelaire's double bind as a revolutionary aesthete, the former situates the aesthete in a state of 'present malediction' which connotes a tension between two paradigms in the absence of knowledge of incumbent legitimation.[110] In *A Misalliance*, a cluster of Jamesian-styled signifiers about Blanche's uncertain psychic state post-divorce—her 'habitual sense of uneasiness'—are evidence of a malefic state that signifies an unresolved desire, one distant from the heterosexual romance narrative (*M*, 7). Post-divorce, Blanche is dedicated to 'keeping feelings at bay', though she experiences 'restlessness', 'an inner desolation that no one must be allowed to suspect', and a 'form of despair' and a sense of 'inactivity' (*M*, 5, 14, 47, 7, 16). Therefore, in addition to Blanche's resistance to marriage, her uneasy psychic state as a divorcée further implies the existence of a desire external to the heterosexual romance narrative, yet which has not yet become coherently articulated. Lacan states that desire 'roots us in a particular destiny, and that destiny demands insistently that the debt be paid, and desire keeps coming back, keeps returning, and situates us once again in a given track, the track of something that is specifically our business'.[111] Reading through the figure of the aesthete suggests that Blanche's desire will find articulation via the nymphs, Sally Beamish, and the Sapphic homoeroticism they imply at the point of redemption in the narrative of metamorphosis.

II Punishment
In a review of *Hotel du Lac*, Barbara Hardy noted of the main protagonist that 'Her author is cruel, arbitrarily depriving her of the good company her niceness and brightness should earn'. She adds 'This is romantic too'.[112] Brookner's depiction as punitive bears witness to the ways in which so-called cruel behaviour can enter the fictional environment. Also, as per Hardy, punishment can be a Romantic truism that elicits longing as its antidote, or it can serve as a precondition for

---

110 Bourdieu, *Rules of Art*, 65.
111 Lacan, *Ethics of Psychoanalysis*, 393.
112 Hardy, 'A Cinderella's Loneliness', 1019.

transformation or radical change. For Lacan, punishment is the price one pays when one betrays one's own desire.[113] Especially when desire remains unconscious, this punishment may be meted out socially. In this way, punishment marks the extroverted dimension of an unconscious personal desire. Lacan figures the so-called choice between action and desire as a forward–backward movement analogous to the metaleptic prolepsis that draws the aesthete to the past before propelling the figure into the future:

> One knows what it costs to go forwards in a given direction, and if one doesn't go that way, one knows why. One can even sense that if, in one's accounts with one's desire, one isn't exactly clear, it is because one couldn't do any better, for that's not a path one can take without paying a price.[114]

Invested with the social status of 'the loser', Blanche's punishment in *A Misalliance* circulates around her status as a divorcée and reflects her inability to perform the type of heterosexual femininity that underpins the heterosexual romance narrative (*M*, 30). The question marks hedging around Blanche's heterosexuality are figured both temporally and discursively, and manifest as social exclusion and public vilification. For Blanche, divorce is tantamount to an erasure of self: 'It was as if, in him, she found intimations of her own validity, as if without him that validity disappeared' (*M*, 174). Without the anchor of social legitimacy that heterosexual couples enjoy, Blanche feels that 'her life might as well be over' (*M*, 16). At the same time, this sense of erasure inevitably conditions her transformation and rebirth through a new narrative of subjectification.

Blanche's heterosexual exile is written as a challenge to chronology and to representation itself. 'Blanche thought of herself as no age at all, as dematerialized', as 'on suspension' and as 'old-fashioned … outmoded, almost obsolete' (*M*, 37, 26, 18). In Blanche's marriage, the gap between the action of the hetero-romance narrative and Blanche's desire was rendered as a failure of symbolisation: 'Over the years she had hidden her sorrows from him, and in doing so had lapsed into odd silences' (*M*, 36). Positioned with a problematic relationship to literal communication because of her exteriority to heterosexual normativity, Blanche has the burden of a secret foisted upon her. 'It was as if she herself had lost her own innocence, could think only in tortured worldly terms,

---

113 Lacan, *Ethics of Psychoanalysis*, 394.
114 Lacan, *Ethics of Psychoanalysis*, 397.

must apply her censorship to every action, every word, and was oddly fearful of revealing herself to others' (*M*, 52). In Chapter 1 of *Misreading Anita Brookner*, the secret was mobilised as a discursive form to signify same-sex possibilities through the erotic negative in the figure of the queer. This narrative returns to signal queer possibilities in *A Misalliance* prior to the revelations that spring from Blanche's encounters with the nymphs and Sally Beamish. Based on a disconnection between action and desire, punishment is staged by the social refusal of recognition: 'her odd demeanour, she knew, had worn out everybody's efforts at comprehension, for she was aware that she was seen as obstinate, unassimilable' (*M*, 50). However, other aspects of Blanche's discourse—her 'immaculate recitation of *non sequiturs*', her 'habit of arcane references', and her intertextual references to Henry James, Plato, Staël, and Rimbaud all evince a sophisticated counter-narrative fomenting under the surface of Blanche's punishment (*M*, 50, 29, 73, 18, 156).

For Blanche, punishment is registered in her feelings of invisibility and absence, but is also regulated externally as an amplification of social law. The public denouncing of Blanche's 'famous eccentricities' occurs when her ex-husband moves in with his new girlfriend: 'the legend was established and the verdict was passed: Blanche was too eccentric to be borne. She was *insupportably* eccentric. And age could only make her worse' (*M*, 30). Not only is Blanche launched on a downward spiral, her problem appears to be innate: Blanche's 'way of raising unsuitable matters at dinner parties, thus came to be seen as evidence of thin blood, of reserve, or of incapacity' (*M*, 29). In the fin-de-siècle bible of aestheticist disorder, *Degeneration* (1895), Max Nordau represents such ailments as anaemia, despondency, and an 'incapacity for action' as indicators of social and cultural disaster, partially effected by the influence of the French aesthetes (these character signifiers are explored more closely through the figure of the degenerate in Chapter 5) (*DG*, 302, 20, 21). In the performance of the aesthete, the projection of degenerate behaviour onto those outside the heterosexual matrix reflects the regulatory force of the dominant class. Accused of 'frigidity', Blanche's punishment is organised around sexual failure, reproductive failure, and heterosexual failure (*M*, 30).

III Redemption
The phases of guilt and punishment represent the aesthete's sense of exile in the present prior to breaking with bourgeois, social realist, and hetero-patriarchal values, a rupture which will go both backwards to

redemption and forwards to purification and blessedness.¹¹⁵ The stage of redemption constitutes a form of knowledge production which involves the excavation of same-sex desire through its troping in the past and a technique of 'blasting' this knowledge out of history in order for its recovery and reintegration in the present. I have argued that, in a state of exile, the gaze of the aesthete at the image of the hetero-patriarchal present triggers a subversive narrative of subjectification. In his reading of Benjamin, Bahti maps a trajectory from exile to redemption: 'referring to the present as a kind of exile, assigning it that meaning, is of one piece with the past signalling for redemption or fulfilment'.¹¹⁶ For Benjamin, then, the past holds the keys to redemption, it 'carries with it a temporal index which is always referred to redemption'.¹¹⁷ Bahti positions Benjamin's 'angel of history' as experiencing an 'awakening' or 'redemption' in its turn to the past, stating, 'the angel of history would redeem—'awaken', resurrect—the past but is instead propelled forward while nonetheless always looking back'.¹¹⁸ In differentiating between a reductive, causal historicism and a nuanced, multi-temporal historical materialism, Benjamin underscores how redemption is achieved by the materialist's 'revolutionary chance in the fight for the oppressed past', a behavioural mode that is allied to the aesthete's Sapphic practice.¹¹⁹ Benjamin writes: 'He takes cognisance of it in order to blast a specific era out of the homogenous course of history'.¹²⁰ The juxtaposition of Christian and Pagan imagery is used by both Pater and Brookner to illustrate a multivalent notion of history. Pater favours the Renaissance for the way in which the mixing of Christian and Pagan signifiers enables 'the pretext for a kind of work which carries one altogether beyond the range of its conventional associations'.¹²¹ In *A Misalliance*, Blanche's dalliance with the nymphs leads her to question the hierarchical production of chronological narratives: 'It seemed, and much against her better judgement she was being forced to think about this,

---

115 Bourdieu, *Rules of Art*, 78.
116 Bahti, 'History as Rhetorical Enactment', 190.
117 Benjamin, 'Philosophy of History', 254.
118 Bahti, 'History as Rhetorical Enactment', 188.
119 The distinction Benjamin draws is between a historicism that 'contents itself with establishing a causal connection between various moments in history' and a historical materialism that 'grasps the constellation which his own era has formed with a definite earlier one'. Benjamin, 'Philosophy of History', 263.
120 Benjamin, 'Philosophy of History', 263.
121 Pater, *The Renaissance*, 125.

a straight division between the Christian and pagan worlds, and she had supposed that the one had merely superseded the other' (*M*, 95). This drive to realign previously misleading and unrepresentative modes of perception is one of the compelling aspects of *A Misalliance*.

In staging the performance of the aesthete across a backwards turn to the Greek to reclaim fragments from the past, we reach the imperative laid out by Lacan 'to discover the desire that inhabits action'.[122] Framing desire as 'the metonymy of our being', Lacan emphasises the way in which subjectification narrates the production and formalisation of desire. Importantly, for this present study, which attempts to examine new models for subjectification and desire in the construction of narrative personae, Lacan's work reminds us how tightly conventional models of subjectification privilege reproductive sexualities.[123] Lacan tropes desire as the desire for knowledge when he states: 'the desire of man ... has quite simply taken refuge or been repressed in that most subtle and blindest of passions, as the story of Oedipus shows, the passion for knowledge'.[124] In *Misreading Anita Brookner*, the aesthete's quest for redemption through Greek knowledge creates a queer narrative of subjectification. Looking towards history, this backward-turning queer narrative also demonstrates how the heterosexual/homosexual opposition is stabilised through a 'temporal straightness' in a denial of how the past and present are constellated together in the historical image.

On one of Blanche Vernon's frequent excursions to the National Gallery, she begins to 'obsess' about 'the image of the hot day', framed herein as part of the text's Sapphic imagery. Blanche's obsessing stimulates a filtering through of past images in her mind (*M*, 7):

> What she saw was not represented on any canvas but was a kaleidoscope of fragments, possibly once seen and quite unconsciously retained. These fragments, apparently disconnected, and with little relevance to her present circumstances, seemed to possess a certain authority, since they came unbidden. She saw a window opened onto a dazzling garden; some sort of tea party, the sun glinting off a silver teapot. And then again a garden early in the morning, with water drops sparkling on the heavy heads of lilac, a cat running fastidiously through the dewy grass. (*M*, 8)

While Blanche's lush garden reveries may appear 'disconnected', alternatively they could be directly related to her chosen object of fascination in

---

122 Lacan, *Ethics of Psychoanalysis*, 385.
123 Lacan, *Ethics of Psychoanalysis*, 395.
124 Lacan, *Ethics of Psychoanalysis*, 399.

the gallery's Italian Rooms—the paintings of nymphs and deities.[125] The narrator instructs that '[t]here was even something pertinent' in a dizzy spell Blanche experienced at the British Museum, where, transported back to a holiday in Greece 'then as now she had come up against the archaic smile of the kouroi, votive figures who seemed to contain an essential secret knowledge that had always escaped her' (*M*, 8). This knowledge is supplied by the National Gallery, which represents for Blanche 'a definitive factor in her faulty education' (*M*, 8). Furthermore, given this knowledge expressly concerns the knowledge of 'love and pleasure', the knowledge of sexual desire is implied (*M*, 10). As a result there appears to be two distinct tropes for reading knowledge as the knowledge of same-sex desire in *A Misalliance*. The first, as demonstrated, concerns the matrix of Sapphic symbols, which, when read through the nineteenth-century sapphism of Baudelaire and Vivien, constitutes the knowledge of female same-sex desire. The second trope is calibrated through Blanche's contention, via Plato, that 'all knowledge is recollection' (*M*, 31). In the *Phaedrus*, knowledge is gained when the older lover is transported through the beauty of the younger boy back to the soul's understanding of the forms: 'The soul becomes winged after ten thousand years, except in the case of the soul of the man who has lived the philosophical life without guile or who has united his love of boys with philosophy'.[126] This knowledge forms part of an exchange which will then flow back to the younger boy, hence the pederastic model is also a pedagogical model insofar as the exchange of sex is also an exchange of knowledge. Both through Sapphic motifs, and through Platonic discourses of knowledge, therefore, the backwards turn to the Greek narrates historical modes of homoerotic desire. These forms of knowledge and 'turning back' effectively make the aesthete's narrative of metamorphosis a queer narrative.

In the phase of redemption, a process of absorption, transference, and the redirection of Eros is undertaken.[127] As Blanche's gaze shifts from art to life when she first catches sight of the 'spectacular' Sally Beamish,

---

125 Lilac's genus is 'Syringa' after the nymph Syrinx, who turned herself into a hollow reed when pursued by the god Pan; these 'nymphs of spring' are also remembered fondly by the narrator of Swann's Way. John L. Fiala, *Lilacs: The Genus* Syringa (Portland, Oreg.: Timber Press, 1988), 5; Proust, *Swann's Way*, 190.
126 Plato, *Phaedrus*, 29.
127 I borrow Pender's reading of 'how the force and energy of *eros* is absorbed, transferred and redirected' in his interpretation of the *Phaedrus*. Pender, 'Sappho and Anacreon', 1.

she experiences a 'slight shock of recognition' (*M*, 40).[128] In *Phaedrus*, Plato's account of the soul of the man sprouting wings is set in motion when the lover 'sees a godlike face or some form of body which imitate beauty well'.[129] Blanche's encounter with Sally sends out a sign: 'She felt as if some mild signal had been given, to which she had in some mysterious and unstated way replied' (*M*, 46). This signal is the mark of a swerve away from a temporally straight theory of historical production and towards a queer, multi-temporal structure of history.[130] Benjamin states that it is when the historical materialist 'recognises the sign of a Messianic cessation of happening' that an intervention in perception is asserted.[131] The messages that Blanche receives in sighting Sally imitate the redemptive encounter with the historical fragment which informs the aesthete's revolutionary program. 'To articulate the past historically', Benjamin states, 'means to seize hold of a memory as it flashes up in a moment of danger'.[132] Thus, For Blanche, Sally's presence becomes the embodiment of a Sapphic experience. Plato's account of the lover's beauty as 'blazing out' of life finds complement with the flame-like radiance of Sally Beamish, and with Benjamin's depiction of 'blasting a specific life out of the era or a specific work out of the lifework'.[133] In *A Misalliance*, therefore, Sally represents the 'blasting' out of knowledge from the past to the present. This 'blasting out' of the knowledge of female same-sex desire symbolises an epistemological shift from bourgeois to aestheticist paradigms to be further explored in the stages of purification and blessedness.

Blanche's reaction to Sally elicits a 'latent madness' which can be indexed as the fourth kind of madness that Plato delineates in the *Phaedrus* (*M*, 41).[134] This is 'the madness of the man who, on seeing beauty, becomes winged and, fluttering with eagerness to fly upwards … [and] in fact reveals itself as the best of all kinds of divine possession and

---

128 For Roland Barthes, the *coup de foudre* is also the moment of *ravissement* or love at first sight—'the supposedly initial episode (though it may be reconstructed after the fact) during which the amorous subject is "ravished" (captured and enchanted) by the image of the loved object'. Roland Barthes, *A Lover's Discourse: Fragments*, trans. Richard Howard (Harmondsworth: Penguin, 1990), 188.
129 Plato, *Phaedrus*, 31.
130 Bahti, 'History as Rhetorical Enactment', 195.
131 Benjamin, 'Philosophy of History', 263.
132 Benjamin, 'Philosophy of History', 255.
133 Plato, *Phaedrus*, 30; Benjamin, 'Philosophy of History', 263.
134 Plato, *Phaedrus*, 24.

from the best sources for the man who is subject to it and shares in it, and that it is when he partakes in this madness that the man who loves the beautiful is called the lover'.[135] As a signifier of Blanche's homoerotic desire, figured through the wing motif, madness connotes a break with those prescribed yet broken behaviours of sanity, relevance, and order that underwrite industrial capitalism. For Plato, the fourth form of madness stimulates the attainment of new forms of knowledge through which the lover ascends to the status of philosopher. 'Hence it is with justice that only the thought of the philosopher becomes winged … if a man uses such reminders (sensations) rightly, being continually initiated in perfect rites, he alone achieves real perfection; and standing aside from human concerns, and coming close to the divine, he is admonished by the many for being disturbed, when his real state is one of possession'.[136] For Benjamin, the redemptive 'springing out' of the present shatters the concept of historical progress.[137] Therefore, the performance of the aesthete through the stage of redemption witnesses the transference of desire on three accounts: from art to life, from past to present, and from the centrality of the heterosexual romance narrative in the stages of guilt and punishment to the queering of desire through the backwards turn to the Greek. This queering is not only accomplished through Sapphic and Hellenic tropes, but through a two-pronged temporal trope in which the metaleptic prolepsis and the synchronic juxtaposition of multiple tropes of desire conspire to break the privileging of reproductive sexuality in linear narratives of progress.

IV Purification
In her art criticism, Brookner emphasises the way in which Baudelaire's key modes of behaviour demanded a form of rigorous asceticism. This was a man who exercised a 'highly controlled mental and spiritual life' and who was 'in effect leaving no detail of one's ordinary life and behaviour to chance, practising the most obvious forms of mastery over nature' (*RD*, 65: *GF*, 67). Informed by a new set of values signified through Greek culture, the aesthete's necessary self-mastery underscores the way in which the figure both challenges the bourgeois hetero-patriarchal

---

135 Plato, *Phaedrus*, 30.
136 Plato, *Phaedrus*, 30.
137 'The awareness that they are about to make the continuum of history explode is characteristic of the revolutionary classes'. Benjamin, 'Philosophy of History', 269.

order and demands the integration of new epistemologies in the present. This chapter has examined how the metalepsis arched backwards over the stages of guilt, punishment, and redemption in the metamorphosis narrative. Now the drive of prolepsis is matched with the forward stages of purification and blessedness as it moves from the past back to the present. Therefore, where redemption is the narrative hinge reflecting the transformative power of the gaze, the phase of purification involves two forms of integration in the forwards movement of the narrative of subjectification: the reincorporation of Greek values in the present and the merging of self-control with the 'latent madness' of desire. Just as the homoerotic gaze fuels the rebirth of the aesthete, the gaze of Plato's lover stimulates the soul's narrative of incarnation along a backwards–forwards trajectory.[138] In the narrative of incarnation which traces the regrowth of the wings (a suggestively sapphic motif), self-mastery functions to balance the lover's madness: 'madness and self-control have to be balanced in the effort of recollection'.[139] In this way, purification signifies the contract between mania and control which nourishes the wings' development. In *A Misalliance*, the stages of purification follow Blanche's relationship with Sally Beamish, from her visits to Sally's cave-like, nymph-styled grotto, to her chaotic yet ultimately cleansing mission to the Dorchester, subsequent illness, and brilliant convalescence. In the stage of purification, Blanche brings her own strategies to the table to balance her curiosity with Sally before eventually unfolding her wings on a flight to the South of France.

When Blanche retrospectively reflects on her time with Sally and Elinor Beamish, she characterises them as 'An object lesson' (*M*, 127). 'They were of very great fascination to me', she says: 'I studied them as if they were a subject to which I could apply myself' (*M*, 127). Blanche implicitly frames her interest in the Beamishes as a perversion of regulatory bourgeois and moral relationship conventions: 'In some recess of her mind Blanche was aware that her friendship with Sally Beamish was not a genuine friendship but one which had been born out of her own needs', she comments; 'her motives were impure' (*M*, 75, 76). Viewed through the performance of the aesthete, Blanche's relationship with Sally Beamish is organised by a key philosophy of aestheticism, that of embracing experience for its own sake. 'Not

---

138 Pender states that 'the narrative of the myth turns from why the soul loses its wings to how it regains them'. Pender, 'Sappho and Anacreon', 28.
139 Pender, 'Sappho and Anacreon', 53.

the fruit of experience, but experience itself, is the end', Walter Pater advises in *The Renaissance*.[140] Discarding her failed commitment to 'good behaviour', Blanche's prioritisation of her experience reflects the way in which she begins to integrate her knowledge of 'love and pleasure' in the present (*M*, 28, 10). Thus, Blanche sets out to accomplish her goal to 'multiply the occasions of seeing' the Beamishes, and, in so doing, sets about using the key modes of female homosocial interaction in the domestic fiction (M, 81). Her first subversion is executed at the hospital, an institution historically associated with normative femininity through women's reproductive roles, care-giving, and service provision as mothers, nurses, and cleaners. Blanche, however, mobilises her volunteer position as a narrative vehicle to pursue the 'sudden desire' which springs up in her encounter with Sally. She muses: 'perhaps a simple interest in their situation would not come amiss, placed as she was in the unintimidating position of vague benevolence conferred on her by her duties at the hospital' (*M*, 42). Subsequently, 'falling back on trusted formulae', Blanche mobilises the family narrative to advance her cause with Sally. 'Is she your only child?' she asks (*M*, 43). Therein Blanche consciously dissimulates her desire through the discursive fabric of the family, appropriating the domestic narrative as an enabling structure for the queering of desire. In this way, Brookner's domestic narratives operate analogously to the nineteenth-century bachelor chronicle, described by Sedgwick as that which 'created or reinscribed as a personality type one possible path of response to the strangulation of homosexual panic' founded on a 'preference of atomised male individualism to the nuclear family'.[141] If, as Sedgwick maintains, a distance from the feminised domestic unit of the family created a space of resistance to male homosexual panic, then so it follows that the interiority of the unit may conversely enable female same-sex desire.

In addition to Blanche's strategic mobilisation of the domestic narrative as a vehicle to assist in the expression of her desire, her relationship with Sally Beamish is organised around three modes of generational crossings. First, Blanche's fascination with Sally recalls the cross-generational romance of the pederastic relationship in the *Phaedrus*. This integration of Hellenic sexuality that crosses generations between older and younger subjects contests the privileging of heterosexuality

---

140 Pater, *The Renaissance*, 249.
141 Sedgwick, *Epistemology of the Closet*, 192.

in the inter-generational model of reproductive sexuality. Secondly, as when Blanche gazes into the face of Elinor and is impressed by 'the idea that it was the younger of the two who was more grown-up', the mobility of generational signifiers in *A Misalliance* underscores the ongoing queer destabilisation of reproductive narratives in the novel (*M*, 42). Indeed, it is Sally's 'nymph-like' behaviour which informs Blanche's perception of shifting generational signifiers between mother and step-daughter: 'Thus the whole principle of generation would be undersold', Blanche identifies, 'for Sally would never yield her place. Her place was to be young and the centre of attention' (*M*, 103). Finally, Blanche's own identification with Elinor—her 'recognition of the child as being one like herself'—constitutes a further generational crossing. Here the shifting dynamics of triangulation between Blanche, Sally, and Elinor complement the cross-generational attention that Blanche pays to Sally (*M*, 49). Therefore, in the stage of purification, the incorporation of Sapphic desire and cross-generational Hellenism into the domestic narrative illuminates the transgressive forward movement of the performance of the aesthete in *A Misalliance*.

The generational crossings negotiated by Blanche, Sally, and Elinor are one type of movement stirred up by the performance of the aesthete. Blanche's appropriation of capital 'for experience's sake' also propels the figure's movement through her relationship with Sally. At the end of the novel, Blanche characterises her interactions with the Beamishes as a lesson in the 'laws of property' (*M*, 186). Plotting to maintain Sally's presence in her life, Blanche consciously decides that she 'must probably be prepared to pay for my entertainment' (*M*, 64). These payments materialise when Blanche regularly leaves a couple of ten-pound notes under a chipped teapot in Sally's kitchen 'to tide her over' (*M*, 82, 101, 181). In exchange, Sally deploys a self-eroticising narrative, regaling Blanche with stories of 'luxury, ease and entertainment' in her participation in an endless 'saturnalia' where she 'was used to a constant stream of favours' (*M*, 101, 80, 79). Jeff Nunokawa emphasises how capital and desire are conflated in nineteenth-century fiction when he states, 'The spectre of market society everywhere haunts the scenes of desire that everywhere haunt the Victorian novel'.[142] Contrary to the utilitarian foundations of the bourgeois market economy, however, Blanche directs

---

142 Jeff Nunokawa, 'Sexuality and the Victorian Novel', in *The Cambridge Companion to the Victorian Novel*, ed. Deidre David (Cambridge: Cambridge University Press, 2001), 134.

her commercial interests for pleasure's sake. As she advises Millie Theale from Henry James's *The Wings of the Dove*: 'she should have bought that rotter outright. What else is money for?' (*M*, 73). The erotic rewards that Blanche enjoys are demonstrated throughout the period of her investment in Sally. Sally's veiled references to the payments cause Blanche to blush and attempt 'to subdue the uncomfortable beating of her heart', figuring a response which resembles the erotic fluttering of the Sapphic and Platonic wings (*M*, 82). Similarly, Blanche's ex-husband Bertie perceives erotic undertones in Blanche's new relationship. When he visits Blanche after she has been with Sally, he 'would find her distracted, flushed, quite obviously not expecting him, and, assuming she had a lover, would become amused and rather more attentive' (*M*, 73). In this stage of purification, Blanche's erotic commodification of Sally signals her further integration of the aestheticist program. Blanche discards her previous commitment to good behaviour, progresses her (sexual) education, and uses her money to enjoy Sally's company.

Over the course of their relationship, Sally's sense of entitlement to Blanche's money becomes an obstacle to Blanche's ability to determine events. Eventually, Blanche concludes that Sally needs to assume responsibility for her own finances, and she sets about 'pulling Sally into shape' (*M*, 78). So begins a power struggle between the women which intensifies when Sally pressures Blanche to confront her husband Paul's wealthy American employer, Mr Demuth, with the purpose of gaining possession of a fur coat, 'the most primitive trophy of them all' and an iconic symbol of capitalist success (*M*, 143). Subsequently, when the Demuths come to London with Paul, Blanche finds herself in an unenviable position: 'I cannot turn up at the Dorchester and confront these strangers, making an eloquent nineteenth-century plea on behalf of widows and orphans', she despairs (*M*, 126). Blanche succumbs to Sally's demands; however, at the last moment, she purposely leaves the fur coat at the Dorchester, inevitably rejecting Sally's bid for control of the moral order. On her trip home, Blanche experiences the onset of an epic migraine, the iconic figure of feminine sexual refusal, which is nevertheless accompanied by a denouement of the Sapphic motifs of heat, damp, golden radiance, and nymphs in the text:

> The yellow sky darkened; very occasionally thick drops of rain fell and then stopped. The heated ground drank up the wetness immediately, but from the park came an occasional breath of damp air … In the quiet street, now quite dark, windows shone a golden yellow … She drifted in and out of

consciousness as if she were moving slowly down a dark passage. Past her glided the kouroi with their blind fixed smile. (*M*, 150–53)

When Blanche arrives home she is assisted by a 'beaming' neighbour, Mrs Duff, whose appropriation of the Beamish patronym witnesses a shift in power from Sally to Blanche's own circle of influence (*M*, 158). Blanche's convalescence is a revelatory experience in which she sees that 'her business with the Beamishes was at an end' and she is left feeling 'extraordinarily well' (*M*, 149, 163). In this purification stage of the aesthete's subjectification, Blanche's migraine and convalescence are located at the crossroads of an imminent choice between a return to the life of dissatisfied, bored housewife poised for her ex-husband's reappearance or an incorporation into the Sapphic 'society of the future'.

V Blessedness

In the final stage of the metamorphosis narrative, ascension to full subjectivity results in a sense of blessedness. In Plato's depiction of the soul's feathered development in love, blessedness is the crowning victory of achieving harmony between desire and self-control. Plato observes of the lover:

> [I]f the better elements of their minds get the upper hand by drawing them to a well-ordered life, and to philosophy, they pass their life here in blessedness and harmony, masters of themselves and orderly in their behaviour, having enslaved that part through which badness attempted to enter the soul and having freed that part through which goodness enters.[143]

Following the epiphanies of illness, Blanche emerges into the world feeling 'vigorous and energetic, full of rough good sense, slightly brutal' (*M*, 164). She instinctively books a holiday and is reinvigorated by hope: 'A variety of possibilities seemed to present themselves to her' (*M*, 164). With Sally's contribution to Blanche's journey of self-discovery at an end, Blanche settles some money on Elinor and discovers that 'there was no need to feel anything at all'; that the Beamishes 'were quite irrelevant to her' (*M*, 185, 186). These realisations, her impending vacation, and a new haircut all make Blanche 'feel literally weightless' and mark her independent inclusion in Sapphic culture through an identification with the 'weightless … nymphs or dryads' (*M*, 187, 117). Finally, with her journey planned, Blanche 'felt she had been granted licence to try her wings' (*M*, 189). Across the stage of blessedness, then, the performance of

---

143 Plato, *Phaedrus*, 37.

the aesthete meets with applause as Blanche prepares for the heat-seeking journey to the sun which recalibrates the erotic winged motif in a Sapphic coming-of-age narrative. At the last minute, however, Blanche's ex-husband Bertie arrives home, ready to be taken back into the fold. Thus, in *A Misalliance*, the reader is ultimately left to decide the degree to which Blanche's metamorphosis will provide a conclusive answer to this potential new obstacle.

CHAPTER THREE

The Dandy in *Brief Lives* (1990)

> Why was it impossible to enter her presence without a full quota of compliments, almost as if she were the object of some religious cult? Why did she, without doing anything for anyone, inspire such devotion, while humbler, clumsier people like myself seemed doomed to do without?
>
> Anita Brookner, Brief Lives

Introduction

In the fourth chapter of *Brief Lives*, the narrator, Fay Dodworth, recalls her first meeting with Julia Morton, the woman who becomes the focus of Fay's extended reflections. On the evening in question, Fay and her husband Owen are hosting a dinner for Charlie, Owen's boss at a city law firm, and Julia, an 'iconic' former '*diseuse*', who had been 'featured in *Vogue*' (*BL*, 44, 2, 44):

> From her first entrance into our drawing-room that evening, in ravishing black silk, with a black silk turban, it was evident that she had thrown herself body and soul into the character of a simple suburban wife. 'My darlings!' she announced, sweeping a black chiffon handkerchief from her back and draping it round her neck, 'I want you to treat me as one of yourselves. Forget about Julia. Julia is no more. Let the people have what they want. If they want ruffians there are plenty to go round. My day is done.' She put her hand to her throat and I swear there were tears in her eyes. Charlie, who must have brought unobtrusiveness to a fine art, removed the black chiffon scarf and put it in his pocket. 'What's the matter?' she said. 'Isn't that the sort of thing middle-class housewives wear? For I suppose we are all middle-class now she added, and the eyelids came down. 'What about the ruffians?' said

Owen, laughing. The eyelids were slowly and suggestively lifted. 'I dare say they are available if one knows where to look for them.' (*BL*, 39–40)

This passage illuminates the seminal themes of Brookner's ninth novel, and showcases the text as an aesthetic compendium of multiple performative modes. It reveals Julia's incomparable chic, her dramatic presence, the slightly absurd cultivation of bourgeois customs through the dinner party and the couples' sociality, but also the rejection and ridicule of suburban conventions through Julia's appropriation of the 'aristocratic' position (*BL*, 44). The scene further demonstrates the narrator's key discursive modes, which will be a focus throughout this chapter. Like Julia, Fay was a performer of some cultural renown who 'sang on the wireless' (*BL*, 8). As Fay describes it, she 'did the lighter sort of ballad, the serious spot on various comedy shows, before they all became too sophisticated' (*BL*, 8). Fay's career as a performer licenses her ability to capture and restage Julia's theatrics in a way that simultaneously underscores and effaces her own narrative skills.

Fay's intimate portrait of Julia—a woman whose 'appearance in restaurants turned heads and subdued conversations'—is enhanced throughout the novel by such touches as a glimpse into Julia's wardrobe, a review of her eating habits, a transcript of contentious soundbites, and a snapshot of her daily rituals (*BL*, 45). Figures 3–5 illustrate some of Julia's preferred designers. 'Artfully wrought', Julia's 'short sleek dark pageboy' (which is 'also old-fashioned') is her signature hairstyle; and she favours 'beautiful severe clothes by Lelong and Patou' (*BL*, 7, 7, 7, 4). The narrator delineates an iconic style of Julia's when she recalls how, in the late 1940s and early 1950s, Julia 'made her comeback, most successfully, in a white dress and turban by Mme Grès' (*BL*, 4). Grès adopted her trademark turban while in exile from the occupation of Paris. She emblematises the comeback by triumphantly reopening her boutique after the declaration of peace and 'dressed many of the most stylish women of the twentieth century', 'including Marlene Dietrich, Nan Kempner and Jacqueline Kennedy Onassis'.[1] In *Brief Lives*, Julia's 'famous presence', her 'monstrous vanity', her fabulous wardrobe, and her devastating persona combine to underline her exalted status in the text (*BL*, 44, 146).

The bourgeois conventions dramatised and demonised in Fay's recollection above are illuminated in *Brief Lives* by her domestic

---

[1] Patricia Mears, *Madame Grès: Sphinx of Fashion* (New Haven, Conn.: Yale University Press, 2007), 3.

3 1934 Lucien Lelong
silk velvet evening gown.
Illustration by Tom Tierney.
Reproduced by kind
permission of Dover Books

skills. As demonstrated in the previous chapter, food and alcohol are incorporated into the sensual signifying matrix of Brookner's aesthetes.[2] In nineteenth-century Romanticism, artists used all available commodities as part of a creative overhaul of expression and in order to rethink value. In *Brief Lives*, the main female protagonists assume both contrary and complementary relationships to food and eating. 'Food seemed a particularly uncertain commodity, owing to the extreme incompetence that prevailed', Fay recalls of the eccentric eating habits

---

2 Other critics, such as Guiliana Giobbi, identify Brookner's heroines with asceticism and anorexia. Giobbi categorises Anna Durrant from *Fraud* as an anorexic heroine; for instance: 'Anna starves herself and lives a crippled existence'. Guiliana Giobbi, '"No Bread Will Feed My Hungry Soul": Anorexic Heroines in Female Fiction—From the Example of Emily Brontë as Mirrored by Anita Brookner, Gianna Schelotto and Alessandra Arachi', *European Studies* 27 (1997): 79.

4 1936 Madame Grès draped silk jersey gown. Illustration by Tom Tierney. Reproduced by kind permission of Dover Books

at Julia's Onslow Square residence (*BL*, 141). Julia's fussy tastes stimulate Fay's skilful crafting of flavours and textures in *Brief Lives*. Fay's catering talents elevate the status of food in the novel, which at the same time remains an everyday preoccupation of the narrator.

Whether Fay is delivering rice salad from her house in Gertrude Street to Onslow Square, or fulfilling her role as audience to Julia's dramatic antics, the enmeshed acquaintanceship between the two female protagonists is intensified by their physical proximity in central London. Fay's movement throughout the metropolitan environment is offset by an attention to interiors, which complements the significance of dressing in *Brief Lives*. Fay arrives at Onslow Square to find Julia in her 'acid' living room, 'seated in her yellow chair, wearing an immaculate white suit with an orange and black blouse' (*BL*, 108, 105). Fay's location-setting and scene-construction creates the atmosphere of a stage production in *Brief Lives*, which resonates with the women's performance careers. The strong

5   1929 Patou evening ensemble.
Illustration by Tom Tierney.
Reproduced by kind permission of
Dover Books

visual and performance elements of Brookner's novel are enhanced by the existence of Julia's 'circle of acolytes', or 'entourage', which consists of a cast of minor characters—Julia's 'former dresser', Pearl Chesney; 'journalist' turned 'slave', Maureen; and the 'most perfect audience' in the form of Julia's mother—and Fay, who feels Julia sees her as 'some sort of secondary audience, a matinée audience, perhaps' (*BL*, 89, 46, 47, 48, 47, 71, 135). Fay's demotion to 'secondary audience' is the result of her potential capacity to challenge Julia's authority; unlike Maureen or Pearl, Fay was the chosen one who hosted Julia at home—and who has an affair with Julia's husband.

While Fay foregrounds Julia's famous presence, Brookner also utilises Fay's complex narrative to expose key aspects of Fay's personality and discursive modes to the reader, including her tendency to adopt an unassuming service role, whether as host, caterer, 'matinée audience', or scribe. As the introductory scene demonstrates, Fay's narrative is organised around Julia in ways which both occlude and disclose the narrator's strengths. In this chapter, Fay's self-effacing voice is advanced as a key narrative strategy in her self-representation and in the construction of her relationship with Julia. 'My activities were completely inconsequential', Fay says (*BL*, 80); 'I was too uninteresting to be eligible' (*BL*, 178); 'I did never quite meet with her approval' (*BL*, 7); 'I had failed' (*BL*, 126, 146); 'she considered me to be uninteresting, and more than uninteresting, inferior' (*BL*, 177). Fay's diffidence, by contrast, illuminates Julia's self-aggrandising pose: 'interviews were her natural mode of communication', Fay tells us (*BL*, 2). The antipathy between Fay and Julia fuels their intimacy; the tension between them is the cornerstone of an emerging mode of desire that constitutes a form of asexual sexuality and refers to an eroticised disinterest in sexual practices. 'Although I did not like her any more than she liked me, she was always in my thoughts', Fay confesses (*BL*, 119). Thus, *Brief Lives* comprises Fay's narrative of 'thraldom' to Julia, the 'cult object', who, Fay concedes, was 'enigmatic and irresistible' (*BL*, 207, 137, 145).

In part 3, *Brief Lives* is reread through the figure of the dandy. Based on intertextual readings of the *Brief Lives* compiled by seventeenth-century biographer John Aubrey, and *Imaginary Lives,* penned by the nineteenth-century Symbolist poet Marcel Schwob—in conjunction with texts by Honoré de Balzac, Jules Barbey d'Aurevilly, Charles Baudelaire, Clara Tuite, and Roland Barthes—'the detail' is nominated as the organising rhetorical device of the dandy. In particular, the dandy is produced through the detail of distinction across the everyday categories of 'talking', 'dressing', 'eating', and 'walking'. The dandy's transgressions of masculinity that reinforce negative gender stereotypes about women are examined, yet these gendered oppositions are put to the test by the cross-historical, cross-gender performance of the dandy in *Brief Lives*. Based on Tuite's contention that the dandy is an effect of a rise-and-fall narrative, the rise-and-fall narrative is advanced as the organising narrative form of the figure of the dandy.[3] In addition, boredom and transgression are presented as founding tropes in the signifying matrix of the dandy. The dandy's sexual profile is discussed as a mode of asexual sexuality which animates the relationship between the female protagonists.

In part 4, the performance of the dandy is staged across the categories of 'talking', 'dressing', 'eating' and 'walking', and along the generic contours of glamour, ruination, and ephemeral endurance that Tuite

---

3 Tuite, 'Trials of the Dandy', 155.

identifies as the markers of the rise-and-fall narrative.[4] The rise-and-fall narrative is mapped along Fay and Julia's narrative dispositions; the glamorous dressing and eroticised 'undressing' of Julia; the women's romantic exchanges through discourses of consumption; and their separation and reunion.

Plot Summary and Original Reception

Brief Lives opens with Fay Dodworth, aged 70, reading the obituary of Julia Morton (née Wilberforce, or 'will-by-force'), ten years her senior, in *The Times*. Julia's obituary precipitates the reminiscences that drive the narrative of *Brief Lives*. Fay recalls her innocent suburban childhood, in the years after the Second World War, with her father, a cinema-manager, and her shy, restless mother who insisted Fay develop a career as a singer. She recounts her first meeting with Owen and the years of their marriage, during which her intimidation by him inhibited a frank evaluation of her own feelings. She remembers feeling a sense of duty towards her mother, to her friend Millie, to Owen's mother, Vinnie, and even to Owen's career, extending to her execution of an intensive program of bourgeois hospitality. It is at one of these dinner parties, detailed in the introduction to this chapter, that Fay meets Julia, and so begins a particular form of intimacy that will span 30 years and include two holidays in Nice that the couples take together.

As the novel continues, Fay relates her grief over her mother's death and subsequently over Owen's fatal car accident in the south of France. In the aftermath, Fay moves to a flat in Drayton Gardens and begins an affair with Julia's husband Charlie. This affair signals the slow dissolution of Julia's clique, advanced by Pearl's retirement to Surrey. Fay questions the satisfaction she derives from her affair with Charlie, but when she takes a trip to see Millie in the country, Charlie has a stroke and dies. The secret nature of the relationship ordains that Fay's grief be subordinated to Julia's, and Fay consequently commits to living a more blameless existence. At a dinner party hosted by Owen's cousin, Fay is introduced to Dr Alan Carter and a friendship ensues. Although Fay's social opportunities are expanding, Julia's circle is diminishing with the announcement of Maureen's engagement. While preparing dinner for Dr Carter, Fay is summoned by Julia for domestic assistance. At the novel's denouement, Julia sustains a fall, which has disastrous

---

4 Tuite, 'Trials of the Dandy', 146.

consequences for Fay's dinner plans. Resolving to find Julia a suitable permanent arrangement, Fay, along with Julia and Pearl, arrange for Julia's relocation to Spain. The three women celebrate together before Julia takes her leave. The story closes at chapter 17, one week after narrative time commences in chapter one, and five years after Julia's expatriation to Mijas.

Brookner's increasingly negative reputation at the time of the novel's publication is compounded in the early reception of *Brief Lives*. A common complaint is that the novel's subject matter contradicts its title. In the *New Statesman*, Patricia Craig comments that '*Brief Lives* hardly seems the most appropriate title for a work in which the central characters, including the narrator, reach a ripe old age, and in which the ingredients of these lives are recounted at some length'.[5] While *Time* magazine praises Brookner's authority as an artist, the reviewer still suffers a sense of dislocation over the signification of the title, maintaining that the 'lives portrayed in this novel—the author's tenth—are hardly brief, but they radiate considerable strength and poignancy'.[6] According to the *New York Times*, the novel is 'depressing', and becomes 'steadily more painful to read' as the narrator's 'monumental gloom makes you wish certain lives in *Brief Lives* were briefer'.[7] In *Understanding Anita Brookner*, Cheryl Alexander Malcolm warns that the 'title may at first appear to be a misnomer ... The brevity to which the title refers would seem to have more to do with the periods of happiness these characters enjoy'.[8] Thus did several of the initial critics of the novel locate the title in paradoxical and incongruous opposition to the book's content. However, this confusion over how to read the title also signifies a deeper crisis regarding interpretation of the text, a problem that can be overcome by reading the novel through the figure of the dandy.

To account for the unfulfilled expectations of the title, critical scrutiny turns to the homodiegetic narrator, Fay Dodworth, and again the results are largely unflattering. Inger Björkblom brands Fay 'absurd'.[9] In the *Times Literary Supplement*, Lindsay Duguid accuses the narrator

---

5 Patricia Craig, 'An Absence of Volition', *New Statesman and Society* 3.116 (31 August 1990): 35.
6 'Brief Lives', *Time* (5 August 1991): 14.
7 Christopher Lehmann-Haupt, 'Lonely, and Then Still Lonelier', *New York Times* (22 July 1991): C16.
8 Malcolm, *Understanding Anita Brookner*, 118.
9 Inger Björkblom, *The Plane of Uncreatedness: A Phenomenological Study of Anita Brookner's Late Fiction* (Stockholm: Almqvist & Wiksell International, 2001), 48.

of duplicity. Though she describes Fay as 'an intelligent narrator', who is 'committed to being nice to people', Duguid condemns Fay's 'observations, through which we are shown their world' as 'shrewd, even spiteful'.[10] Malcolm claims that Fay's first-person narrative 'is speculative at best'.[11] She registers a range of 'wholly inconsequential and everyday scenes' in the text. Malcolm's contention is that 'understatement and the supplying of seemingly inconsequential information are common features of Brookner's writing'.[12] The general consensus is that far from being 'brief', the novel is on the contrary quite detailed, and the details of the novel are largely insignificant.

In *Reading in Detail*, Naomi Schor argues that dichotomies of the general/particular, mass/detail, and masculine/feminine result in 'the unchallenged association of woman and the particular [which] spans not only cultures, but centuries, extending from antiquity to the present day'.[13] Stating that 'the detail is gendered and doubly gendered as feminine', Schor notes that this results in the devaluation of women's writing which is associated with overblown content or form.[14] Witness the critics' dismissal of the detail in *Brief Lives* as insignificant; as Schor points out, the 'semimythical, semiscientific association' between women and detail is yet one on which 'modern-day critics have based their assessments of men's and women's respective contributions to the arts'.[15] As discussed in Chapter 2, the production of the autobiographical women's voice has been partly coterminous with its silencing. Similarly, the critical reception of *Brief Lives* shows how the rendering of the novel's details as insignificant is implicated in Brookner's construction as a women's writer. Insofar as the detail is feminised and produced through the genre of women's writing, female-indicated discursive practices are threatened with charges of irrelevance while alternative methodologies for reading the detail are left unexplored.

In the early reception of *Brief Lives*, the feminine and negative gendering of the detail weights textual epistemologies around what I have referred to as the hetero-chronic symbolic, a reading formation based on an interdependence between the production of historical context and

---

10 Duguid, 'Downward Drag', 889.
11 Malcolm, *Understanding Anita Brookner*, 118.
12 Malcolm, *Understanding Anita Brookner*, 118.
13 Schor, *Reading in Detail*, 17.
14 Schor, *Reading in Detail*, 4.
15 Schor, *Reading in Detail*, 17.

heterosexuality, and stabilised through the fantasy of literal signification. Thus, Malcolm reduces the book to 'the second of Brookner's novels about marriage'.[16] Malcolm believes that the 'friendship between Fay and Julia is largely uneventful'; as she understands it, the novel is primarily about 'the shattering of Fay's own innocence at the hands of a man'.[17] Focusing on the hetero-centric narrative, Malcolm reports on an apparent 'exclusion of historical and political events from this narrative' (thereby excluding multiple historical contexts) and, in so doing, implicitly embeds binary oppositions between the male/public/historical and the female/private/personal in the text.[18] Duguid demonstrates how *the personal* voice in women's writing becomes conflated with *autobiographical* women's writing when Brookner's first-person narration leads her to conclude that 'such close identification with the heroine's feelings produces an autobiographical feel in Brookner's novels', which work in 'forming an autobiographical curve'.[19] In this tautological reading, Duguid shapes the detail of *Brief Lives* into an autobiographical narrative and naturalises the performance of femininity and the personal voice both in the novel and in Brookner's representational strategies to effectively produce Brookner as a women's writer. Tom Wilhelmus notes that Fay is 'preoccupied with appearances, with clothing, decorating, meals, with politeness to even the most impolite people', thus his reading implicitly reconstitutes the text through a debased narrative of femininity.[20] Unable to construe an underlying theme in the text, Wilhemus thereby deems the novel 'virtually plotless'.[21] Although Wilhemus claims that 'the style seems almost a parody of itself', and thereby starts to denaturalise the relationship between femininity and the women's writing strategies, his short review does little beyond raising the notion as a possibility.[22] As with Brookner's previous novels, a wealth of critical presuppositions about gender, historical context, and the representational practice of the women's writer conspires to undermine the value of Brookner's contribution to the literary field.

16 Malcolm, *Understanding Anita* Brookner, 109.
17 Malcolm, *Understanding Anita* Brookner, 111, 117.
18 Malcolm, *Understanding Anita* Brookner, 110.
19 Duguid, 'Downward Drag', 889.
20 Tom Wilhelmus, 'Brief Lives', *Hudson Review* 45.1 (1992): 138.
21 Wilhelmus, 'Brief Lives'.
22 Wilhelmus, 'Brief Lives'.

Producing the Figure of the Dandy

In her *Times Literary Supplement* review, Duguid draws an intertextual connection between Brookner's *Brief Lives* and the identically entitled *Brief Lives* compiled by the seventeenth-century antiquarian John Aubrey, whom John Fowles labels a 'genius'.[23] But Duguid proceeds to sever ties between the texts when she fails to contest the Brookner stereotype: 'Anita Brookner's *Brief Lives* are the opposite of Aubrey's— which are public, eventful and male'.[24] On the contrary, however, the two *Brief Lives* can be seen to have much in common. Effectively, Fay herself produces Julia's biography—through the depictions of her wardrobe and dietary requirements, descriptions of her location and domestic interiors, and the recitations of backstage gossip circulated by Julia's entourage. 'I have no doubt that she would have revealed all to a biographer, had one been forthcoming', she states of Julia (*BL*, 145). Both *Brief Lives* tend towards the deconstruction of the public/ private, eventful/banal, male/female oppositions that Duguid insists upon. And both texts mobilise the use of seemingly inconsequential and scandalous detail to produce biographical characters, resulting in common accusations of 'plotlessness'.

Popularly credited with being the first biography, Aubrey's *Brief Lives* are a collection of manuscripts containing biographical sketches and paraphernalia detailing extraordinary, banal, and sensitive information from over 400 lives of 'famous and ordinary people' and are notorious for their staging of 'idiosyncratic detail'.[25] Aubrey scholar Kate Bennett emphasises the ornamental nature of the manuscripts and the materiality of the *Lives* when she describes them as 'paper museums, cabinets of curiosities as well as literary texts'.[26] John James Purdon invokes the unique physicality of the manuscripts in his depiction of their 'rough line drawings, printed pages, epitaph transcriptions and holograph letters from correspondents, all of which are frequently pasted or sewn

---

23 Duguid, 'Downward Drag', 889; John Aubrey, *Monumenta Britannica; or, A Miscellany of British Antiquities*, ed. John Fowles (Boston: Little, Brown, 1980), x.
24 Duguid, 'Downward Drag', 889.
25 Alison Woollard, 'Review: Brief Lives', *BBC* (12 February 2008): www.bbc.co.uk/ essex/content/articles/2008/02/12/review_brief_lives_feature.shtml; Jon Bruce Kite, *A Study of the Works and Reputation of John Aubrey (1626–1697): With Emphasis on His 'Brief Lives'* (New York: Edwin Mellen Press, 1993), 133.
26 Bennett, 'John Aubrey's Collections', 220.

into them'.²⁷ The manuscripts constitute a collage of different types of media—a material object of 'intertextual inserts', which reference other texts and physical objects such as portraits of their subjects (mostly housed with the manuscripts in the Bodleian Library, Oxford), coins, collectables, and other artefacts.²⁸ They act as a canvas for a range of notation styles, marginalia, and ellipses; Aubrey marked pages with '...' and '—' and '[]' to signal an omission, memory lapse, or pending information, and blank pages were reserved for text that never materialised.²⁹ Notes and symbols decorate the margins as a reminder of absent information, to seek further information, or to expand on aspects in or beyond the text.³⁰ Drawing a comparison between the two *Brief Lives*, Fay's descriptions of wardrobe choices, menu plans, walking routes, and domestic interiors can be said similarly to constitute an aesthetic compendium of intertextual inserts that transforms 'insignificant' detail into something more significant.

Owing to its 'scandalous' content, Aubrey's *Lives* was never intended for publication in his lifetime.³¹ In compiling the *Lives* for use by fellow antiquarian and biographer, Anthony Wood—a man whom John Fowles will characterise as difficult, jealous, and paranoic—Aubrey warns Wood that 'these arcana are not fitt to lett flie abroad, till about thirty years hence; for the author and the persons (like medlars) ought to be first rotten'.³² The potential inclusion of material so scandalous that Fowles will deem it 'private or scandalous' centuries later prompts Aubrey to request that when using the *Lives*, Wood 'make a Castration ... and ... sowe-on some Figge-leaves'.³³ The propagation of scandalous detail is also a feature of Brookner's *Brief Lives*. Fay notes Julia's desire to procure 'unseemly detail' from everyday conversation while Tom Wilhemus remarks that Fay's 'tone' throughout the text manages 'to hide everything—including some very scandalous activity' (*BL*, 184).³⁴ Anthony Wood's refusal to heed Aubrey's warning about the *Lives*'s transgressive content results in Wood's conviction for libel, expulsion

27 Purdon, 'Aubrey's "Discourse"', 227.
28 Purdon, 'Aubrey's "Discourse"', 232.
29 Purdon, 'Aubrey's "Discourse"', 235.
30 Purdon, 'Aubrey's "Discourse"', 235.
31 Kite, *A Study*, 95.
32 Aubrey, quoted in Purdon, 'Aubrey's "Discourse"', 239.
33 Fowles, Introduction to *Monumenta Britannica*, xv; Aubrey, quoted in Purdon, 'Aubrey's "Discourse"', 239.
34 Wilhemus, 'Brief Lives', 138.

from Oxford, and the offending parts of contentious publication, *Athenae Oxoniensis* (1691–92) being burned.[35]

Subsequently, Wood brands Aubrey 'a shiftless person, roving and maggoty-headed, and sometimes little better than crazed', responsible for material which was 'exceedingly credulous … with fooleries, and misinformation's, which sometimes would guide him [Wood] into paths of error'.[36] This negative stereotype of John Aubrey has persisted and characterises the representation of John Aubrey in Patrick Garland's stage production of *Brief Lives*, performed in March 2008. 'The character dodders about his musty, chaotic rooms, rambles from anecdote to anecdote, and hurls the contents of his chamber pot out of the window, wiping his hands on a curtain', reports Benedict Nightingale in *The Times*.[37] As such, literal impressions of the boring and scandalous persist in dominating critical reflection of both Brookner's and Aubrey's *Brief Lives*.

The chaotic nature of Aubrey's manuscripts and their resistance to the conventions of mainstream publishing mean that, throughout the centuries, Aubrey's rangy *Lives* have been subject to historically contingent editorial ideologies.[38] As with Brookner's *Brief Lives*, the interpretation of Aubrey's *Lives* hangs on the question of how to read its vast amounts of 'idiosyncratic detail'.[39] In 2005, John James Purdon's discovery of an ancient Greek inscription printed in front of the title 'Brief Lives' on Aubrey's MS1 raises new possibilities for Aubreyan interpretation. Purdon claims that despite the fact that this was 'Aubrey's first title … scholarship has tended to treat the word as at best a curiosity', a practice he deems 'inappropriate … given Aubrey's clear record of careful titling'.[40] Purdon mobilises the Greek text to arbitrate the 'latent ambiguity' attending Aubrey interpretation. He examines Anthony Powell's 1948 translation of the Greek word as 'pieces written on the spur of the moment'.[41] In this analysis, the 'brief' of

---

35 Fowles, Introduction to *Monumenta Britannica*, xv–xvi.
36 Fowles, Introduction to *Monumenta Britannica*, xv–xvi.
37 Benedict Nightingale, '*Brief Lives* at the Theatre Royal, Windsor', *The Times* online (21 March 2008): www.thetimes.co.uk/article/brief-lives-at-the-theatre-royal-windsor-00qqgg6ssxd (subscription required).
38 Kite, *A Study*, 170. Thus, Kite contends that 'the reception of the *Lives* as a historical document ought to be discussed, for the degrees to which it has been accepted are also central to gauging Aubrey's reception'.
39 Kite, *A Study*, 133.
40 Purdon, 'Aubrey's "Discourse"', 230.
41 Purdon, 'Aubrey's "Discourse"', 229.

the title is interpreted as a reference 'to the style and circumstances of writing, but not ... to the content of the *Lives*', making a distinction between the narration of the text and the text's narrative.[42] Moving further back, Purdon traces the meaning of the Greek inscription to a source contemporaneous with Aubrey, Blount's *Glossographia* (first published 1656), in which it is translated as 'schediasm', meaning 'a sudden invention or a work extempore', or 'schedical', meaning 'hasty, sudden, extemporary, not labored'.[43] This translation describes Aubrey's methodology in compiling the *Lives*: the way in which information came to him and subsequently the way in which he documented it. Further back-crossing the intertextual network, Purdon extends his investigation to Greek sources. In Cicero's letters to Atticus (which Aubrey possessed), 'extempore' was used 'in the expectation of the fading of rash words ... and acknowledges ... the tendency of speech to vanish into thin air'.[44] In Plutarch, historical and biographical narrative was the appropriate medium for capturing the 'fading and momentary' nature of oral discourse, a culture Purdon claims is visually represented in Aubrey's otherwise-lawless manuscripts. An epigraph on the title page of MS8 elaborates further:

> The trouble is that the spoken word dies even as it is born, and leaves nothing behind it to take bodily shape and to survive. Words have wings: you know the phrase Homer uses about them, and a Syrian poet makes them into a species of bird. If one doesn't capture these fugitives in writing, they quickly flee the memory.[45]

Purdon reads the epigraph as 'richly suggestive of the relation between the fleeting, spoken word and the word as an object on paper'.[46] In this passage, Aubrey represents brevity as a temporal signifier of the ephemeral oral narrative and a reflection of the oral transmission of biographical material. The conversational and anecdotal way in which Aubrey's *Lives* are narrated, including their emendations and absences, are historical effects of a culture in which oral narrative was privileged over the written text. In this sense, the brevity documented in the title symbolises the recognition that the form of the *Lives* constitutes a textual composition that navigates the dichotomy between oral and

---

42 Purdon, 'Aubrey's "Discourse"', 230.
43 Purdon, 'Aubrey's "Discourse"', 230.
44 Purdon, 'Aubrey's "Discourse"', 230.
45 Purdon, 'Aubrey's "Discourse"', 228.
46 Purdon, 'Aubrey's "Discourse"', 228.

written texts. Based on the intertextual indications between Brookner and Aubrey's identically titled texts, and the reading of the signification of brevity to imply orality, Purdon's discovery also illuminates new possibilities for the interpretation of Brookner's novel.

In 1813, Phillip Bliss was the first to publish extensive sections of Aubrey's manuscript.[47] The nineteenth-century publication of *Brief Lives* made the text's primary reception historically contemporaneous with the emergence of French Romanticism. In 1896, the French aestheticist Marcel Schwob (1867–1905) published *Imaginary Lives*, a collection of fictionalised biographies of historical personalities. Like Aubrey and Brookner, Schwob was a prolific journalist, writer, critic, essayist, scholar, and translator.[48] Celebrated as a 'manifesto of Decadent aesthetics', Schwob's preface to *Imaginary Lives* is also a homage to John Aubrey.[49] Schwob contends that, contrary to what we now call the 'grand narratives' of history, Aubrey's talent as a biographer is derived from his practice of documenting the small pieces of eccentric personal detail from the lives of his subjects.[50] In his reading of Aubrey's *Brief Lives*, Schwob contrasts 'the imprint of a raindrop; the tiny mark left by an insect' with the archival philosophy of Aubrey's manuscripts and the narrative sweep of his precursor.[51] Such detail corresponds to Fay's observational detail in *Brief Lives*: 'Through the window a tiny silver plane was a point of brilliance in a cloudless light blue sky', Fay notes (BL, 133). For Schwob,

47 Kite, *A Study*, 105.
48 Herberto Fernández reports that Schwob is depicted as 'an avant-garde writer who paved the way for new narrative techniques in the 20th century' in his review of María José Hernández Guerrero's 2002 book, *Marcel Schwob: escritor y traductor*. Herberto Fernández, 'Compte rendus', *Meta: Translators' Journal* 48.4 (2003): 588. Schwob was also honoured by his Symbolist friends. Oscar Wilde dedicated 'Les Sphinx' (1894) to Schwob; Paul Valéry dedicated *Monsieur Teste* (1896) to him; Edmond de Goncourt lauded Schwob as a 'hallucinatory resurrector of the past', and, later, Jorge Luis Borges affirmed that his own *A Universal History of Infamy* (1936) was inspired by Schwob. See Alex Szogyi, 'Fiction: In Short', *New York Times Book Review* (21 April 1985): 24.
49 Kite, *A Study*, 133.
50 Schwob, *Imaginary Lives*, 7–16.
51 Schwob, *Imaginary Lives*, 7. Schwob celebrates the way Aubrey records how Milton 'pronounced the letter R very hard'; how Spencer was a 'little man with his hair cut short, wearing a little collarette and little cuffs'; how, for Bacon, 'none of his servants dared appear before him in any boots but those made of Spanish leather, for his nose was sure to detect the smell of calf skin, which he detested'; and how Hobbes 'grew very bald in his old age' and 'was very much annoyed by the flies lighting on his bald head'. Schwob, *Imaginary Lives*, 11.

detail adds distinction to the everyday: '[s]tatesman, poet or clockmaker, each subject finds, under his pen, some unique trait distinguishing that man forever among all men'.[52] Schwob's rendering of the detail also flags the scandalous and banal: 'Sores and wounds he knew, and his greatest regret was that his body was not supple like a dog's so that he might lick them', he muses in his imaginary life of the egalitarian philosopher, Crates of Thebes.[53] Shifting the status of the detail from history to aesthetics, Schwob argues that Aubrey's ability to render character through idiosyncratic detail is constitutive of an art form: 'Contrary to history, art describes individuals, desires only the unique. It does not classify, it unclassifies'.[54] At the fin de siècle, Schwob's privileging of the detail reflects a process that gathers momentum throughout the nineteenth century—a period Naomi Schor describes as 'the Golden Age of the Detail'.[55] Conjoining the scandalous, biographical, idiosyncratic, and aestheticised material from Aubrey, Schwob, and Brookner, the detail can be situated as the organising rhetorical form for producing the figure of the dandy.

In the nineteenth century, the pace of industrialisation and historical change enabled new forms of mobility between the classes and genders, but also elicited anxieties over an inability to perceive radical differences in social and sexual status. Roland Barthes states that 'clothing had to cheat, as it were, the theoretical uniformity that the Revolution and the Empire had bequeathed it; and within a universal type of clothing there was now a need to maintain a certain number of formal differences which could exhibit the difference between social classes'.[56] In 1830, Honoré de Balzac published *Treatise on Elegant Living*, asserting that 'The exterior life is a sort of organised system that represents a man as accurately as a snail's colours recur on its shell', a comment that recalls Marcel Schwob's reading of John Aubrey and Fay's observation of the minutiae in *Brief Lives*.[57] Described as an 'attempt to determine the general laws that govern the details', *Treatise on Elegant Living* is nominated by Napoleon Jeffries as among the three 'essential and defining texts of French dandyism', along with Jules Barbey d'Aurevilly's *On Dandyism and*

---

52 Schwob, *Imaginary Lives*, 9.
53 Schwob, *Imaginary Lives*, 28.
54 Schwob, *Imaginary Lives*, 7.
55 Schwob, *Imaginary Lives*, 66.
56 Barthes, 'Dandyism and Fashion', 66.
57 Balzac, *Treatise on Elegant Living*, 44.

George Brummell (1845) and Charles Baudelaire's *The Painter of Modern Life* (1863), all of which inform the intertextual network that produces the figure of the dandy.[58] Linking the specification of the detail or the *je ne sais quoi* to the function of a status-marker, Balzac comments:

> differences have vanished in our society: all that remain are nuances. Consequently, good breeding, elegant manners, the *je ne sais quoi*, the fruits of a complete education—these form the only barrier separating the man of leisure from the busy man ... Hence the high price that the majority places on education, on the purity of language, on the grace of deportment, on the relatively easy manner in which an outfit is worn, on the careful choice of living quarters: in short, on the perfection of everything proceeding from the person. Do we not imprint our manners and thought on everything that surrounds us and belongs to us? 'Speak, walk, eat or dress yourself, and I will tell you what you are'.[59]

For Balzac, the apparent collapse in social differences intensifies public scrutiny over an individual's social performance, domestic practices, knowledge, and narrative and thereby gives rise to the production of the detail as a distinguishing marker between subjects. Balzac expounds an ideal of perfection and exclusivity—signified through the detail—across the generic categories of talking, dressing, eating, and walking. Insofar as walking constitutes the public mode of the dandy's movement from place to place, it conversely connotes the new value attributed to domestic interiors in aestheticism and the complementary 'commodity fetishism' of the nineteenth century.[60] The very particularity of the production of the detail in the nineteenth century leads Barthes to describe the phenomenon as the emergence of a new aesthetic category imbued with the purpose of circulating 'a new value: *taste*, or better still, as the word is appropriately ambiguous, *distinction*'.[61]

Contending that 'dandyism reconstitutes ornament as detail', Clara Tuite maintains that the production of the detail as a mark of distinction in the nineteenth century supersedes the macaronic excesses of the 1770s.[62] Tuite argues that '[d]etail is the sign of distinction

---

58 Balzac, *Treatise on Elegant Living*, 55; Jeffries, Introduction to Balzac, *Treatise on Elegant Living*, xiv.
59 Balzac, *Treatise on Elegant Living*, 23.
60 Rosalind H. Williams, *Dream Worlds: Mass Consumption in Late Nineteenth-Century France* (Berkeley: University of California Press, 1982), 148.
61 Barthes, 'Dandyism and Fashion', 66.
62 Tuite, 'Trials of the Dandy', 147.

and singularity, but it is not—and this is where it differs from the ornament—conspicuous'.⁶³ The elegant subtleties that inform how the detail underwrites the production of the dandy are illuminated in Barbey's depiction of dandyism as comprised of multiple chords: '[w]hat might be called the chord of Dandyism, one of the thirty-six thousand chords that compose that devilish instrument, so complex and sometimes so deranged'.⁶⁴ The chords of everyday distinction harmonise throughout the *Brief Lives* intertextual network between Aubrey, nineteenth-century Romantic aestheticism, and Brookner's novel in a symbiotic relationship between brevity and the detail. In assembling the narrative fabric for the dandy, the figure appears through multiple chords of distinction, based on the way in which the rhetorical form of the detail is extrapolated across the categories of walk, talk, eat, and dress. In addition, boredom and transgression act as foundational chords of dandyism, and underwrite the figure's contested modes of gender, sexual, and temporal subversion. To complete the narrative complex of the figure, Tuite's rise-and-fall narrative operates as the organising narrative form of the dandy.

In the nineteenth century, the dandy's foray into the realm of the everyday detail and the figure's immersion in multiple forms of consumption enact forms of gender crossing into the private sphere historically associated with women. Barbey concedes, 'the dandy has something of the woman about him'.⁶⁵ However, Charles Baudelaire's insistence that '*la femme est le contraire du dandy*' reflects anxieties in a male-dominated Romantic aestheticism about the threat of being over-identified with the female sphere.⁶⁶ These anxieties could be said to align with Thais E. Morgan's analysis of the way in which the male aesthetes' 'male lesbianism' fail to significantly break with male heterosexual codes, as outlined in the discussion of the aesthete in Chapter 2.⁶⁷ Dandies were keen to fend off the perceived dangers of a usurping femininity. In this way, their impetus to demonstrate exclusivity and distinction in the realm of the everyday was caught up in strategies which simultaneously delegitimised women's work

---

63 Tuite, 'Trials of the Dandy', 147.
64 Barbey, 'On Dandyism', 151.
65 Barbey, 'On Dandyism', 137.
66 Charles Baudelaire, quoted in Philip G. Hadlock, 'The *Other* Other: Baudelaire, Melancholia, and the Dandy', *Nineteenth-Century French Studies* 30.1–2 (2001): 64.
67 Morgan, 'Male Lesbian Bodies', 48, 40.

and female performativity.⁶⁸ Yet the dandy's masculine performance of femininity (or aesthetic masculinity) can also be leveraged against bourgeois masculinity with its ideological foundations in utilitarian capitalism and narratives of progress and reproduction. Napoleon Jeffries frames the dandy's gender-crossing as an act which 'broke down the barriers between aesthetics and the everyday' and potentially liberates women from a naturalised identification with the private sphere.⁶⁹ However, Roland Barthes's description of dandyism as an 'essentially masculine phenomenon' is testimony to the way in which, specifically in the French canon, the dandy's temperament is profiled around modes of behaviour which reinforce the figure's typically masculine control, fearlessness, and detachment.⁷⁰ Barbey lists the unpredictable, impertinent, capricious, haughty, and audacious as behaviours which are characteristic of the dandy and which therefore reinforce the dandy's masculinised authority.⁷¹

It is interesting to consider how the reluctance of critics to read Brookner's novels through Romantic aestheticism is a continuation of nineteenth-century gender binaries which devalue the transgressive potential of female performativity. However, in *Misreading Anita Brookner*, the production of the dandy as a figure of transgression is intent on bringing together both nineteenth-century masculine and contemporary feminine modes of gender-crossing and performativity.

In *Brief Lives*, Julia embodies the dandy's ideal of masculine authority. 'There was a distinctly masculine side to her, in her refusal to entertain weak hopes and fears, her judicial appraisal of her gifts and attributes, her professional competence and objectivity, her hardy egotism', Fay states (*BL*, 146). Julia is portrayed as 'alarming', 'sardonic, hieratic, heartless', 'capricious', 'speculative', 'mocking', 'watchful … acute … dangerous' (The Caprice is also the name of the restaurant Julia nominates to lunch with Fay and Pearl Chesney before her exile to Spain), and therefore her behaviour reconstitutes the attributes of masculinist dandyism as framed by Barbey (*BL*, 3, 7, 41, 49, 50, 57, 206). Many of Fay's descriptions of Julia resound of Barbey's insistence that 'confidence … does the work

---

68 Rita Felski argues that 'the dandy, in pursuit of uniqueness through the narcissistic cult of self, sees women as exemplifying the uniformity and standardisation of modern life that he most abhors'. Felski, 'Counterdiscourse of the Feminine', 1100.
69 Jeffries, Introduction to *Treastise on Elegant Living*, vii.
70 Barthes, 'Dandyism and Fashion', 67.
71 Barbey, 'On Dandyism', 114, 115, 119, 120, 106.

of a conscience' for the dandy.⁷² Fay muses, 'I never knew a woman so little given to self-doubt or self-questioning. If she thought a thing she said it, and if she wanted to do something she did it. She was impervious to remorse, for in her eyes her desires were always justified' and she depicts Julia as someone whose 'feelings were so far from the surface, so deeply buried, that they gave her no information' (*BL*, 132). In mobilising Baudelaire's dandy as embodying 'opposition and revolt' and Barbey's assertion that 'Dandyism follows its law, or rather, it is a deviation from the law which makes it a law unto itself', the production of the figure across masculine and feminine performances and historical contexts functions to bring the subversive potential of Brookner's female-identified contemporary oeuvre to light (*PML*, 28).⁷³ The spinning of the dandy as a hermeneutic figure to read *Brief Lives* is based on the way in which the contemporary female performance of nineteenth-century aesthetic masculinity recasts the transgressive potential of the dandy through the genre of women's writing and challenges the stereotype of the passive, conservative, and unawakened Brooknerine. As with the other Romantic personae cast in this project, the delineation of intertextual figures across historical context disrupts the way in which gender identity is grounded in historical periodisation and literal symbolisation, and, in so doing, destabilises the hetero/homosexual opposition.

In 'Trials of the Dandy', Tuite uncovers a seminal dandy text which she contends has been neglected in favour of the French canon of dandy literature—Captain William Jesse's *Life of George Brummell* (1844).⁷⁴ In classifying Jesse's *Life* as a 'scandalous memoir', a genre descriptor recalling the work of John Aubrey and Marcel Schwob, Tuite argues that the figure of the dandy is produced through a rise-and-fall narrative.⁷⁵ By restoring to the dandy the 'breakdown, abjections, effeminacy and corporeality that Jesse traces', and illuminating the dandy's characteristics of femininity and recessed homosexuality, Tuite redresses the sanitised, masculinist imbalance of French literary dandyism through a rhetorical intervention.⁷⁶ Her excavation of the rise-and-fall narrative from the dandy's rhetorical armature supplies an organising narrative form for the figure. Insofar as the rise-and-fall narrative combines French

---

72 Barbey, 'On Dandyism', 100.
73 Barbey, 'On Dandyism', 87.
74 Tuite, 'Trials of the Dandy', 44.
75 Tuite, 'Trials of the Dandy', 145.
76 Tuite, 'Trials of the Dandy', 161.

and British representations of social and literary dandyism, masculine and feminine dispositions, and effeminate and homosexual signifiers, this narrative form regenerates the organising absences of the French canon in ways which complement the historical and gender crossings which in turn inform the intertextual production of the dandy in Brookner's *Brief Lives*.

Tuite pitches the rise-and-fall narrative across the generic contours of glamour, ruination, and ephemeral endurance.[77] Her interpretation demonstrates how the plotting of the detail of distinction across the categories of the everyday is shaped into a narrative which emphasises a journey from 'a glamorous form of scandalous celebrity to a scandalous celebrity of abjection'.[78] With the dandy as his muse, Jesse's *Life* of George Brummell recuperates further intertextual connections between the biographical *Lives* authored by John Aubrey, Fay's biographical portrait of Julia in *Brief Lives*, and the production of scandalous and inconsequential detail into a rise-and-fall narrative. These intertextual crossings mark Aubrey's *Brief Lives* as a precursor dandy text and Aubrey and Brookner's texts as precursor modes of the celebrity genre.[79] Seizing the rise-and-fall narrative for the organising form of the dandy, the movement of the figure can be propelled across the categories of walk, talk, eat, and dress and along the contours of glamour, ruination, and ephemeral endurance, as they are realised in Brookner's *Brief Lives*.

In *On Dandyism and George Brummell*, Barbey maintains that 'Dandyism is the product of a bored society, and boredom makes you bad'.[80] Boredom acts to 'produce the unexpected' and the capricious: 'Caprice will inevitably assert itself and break through positions that seemed impregnable, yet had long been undermined by boredom', Barbey explains.[81] In *Brief Lives*, Fay's identification as dull and boring is a key component of her self-effacing narrative—examined through the category of 'talk' in the following section—and emerges as an inter-subjective response to Julia's performative presence and

---

77 Tuite, 'Trials of the Dandy', 146.
78 Tuite, 'Trials of the Dandy', 146.
79 According to Tuite, the delineation of these genre modes is useful for mapping the protocols for 'transforming contemporary celebrity into posthumous, textualised fame' and for reading the ways in which contemporary media operate to produce privileged and abjected historical subjectivity. Tuite, 'Trials of the Dandy', 146.
80 Barbey, 'On Dandyism', 113.
81 Barbey, 'On Dandyism', 79, 94.

her voracious need for entertainment. In casting the dandy across the relationship between Fay and Julia, the performance of the figure in *Brief Lives* crosses the modes of identification and disidentification that Tuite engages as key affects of the rise-and-fall narrative.[82] This interrelational mode of boredom as a discourse of exchange is evident in Fay's reflections on her relationship with Julia: '[s]he was a fascinating but difficult woman whose affections were beyond me: I took it entirely for granted that she found me dull. I fell into a hazy receptive mood when I was with her, not quite knowing the right responses, my own identity in abeyance'; 'I, on the contrary, found myself eager to please, but as usual I disappointed her. She found me dull' (*BL*, 106). On the other hand, Julia might frequently exclaim, 'did you ever meet such a boring woman?' (*BL*, 7). Thus, Julia 'found me boring', Fay maintains: 'I bore her'; 'she strikes me as a woman with an enormous capacity for boredom' (*BL*, 92, 106, 114).

In crossing historical and gender contexts, and as a configuration of the relationship between the two female main protagonists, the performance of the dandy in *Brief Lives* writes back to the annexation of boredom and *ennui* as transgressive masculinity in the French canon and provides an alternative interpretation to the prevailing reading of boredom in Brookner's oeuvre. Within the literary field, the signification of boredom in Brookner's fiction fuels criticism that Brookner's novels are boring: 'there is much to bore a listener here', ran one reviewer's analysis of the audio book of *The Next Big Thing*.[83] In *Boredom*, Patricia Meyer Spacks classifies Brookner's fiction, including *Brief Lives*, as characteristic of a 'postmodern imaginative use of boredom'.[84] Despite contextualising Brookner's representations of boredom as a literary strategy, Spacks reads boredom literally when she claims that Brookner 'conveys no glimmer of hope' and that 'Boredom marks the powerless in Brookner's imagined world'.[85] In contrast to the critics who dismiss Brookner for being boring, or who, like Spacks, maintain that boredom has been naturalised, in *Misreading Anita Brookner* it is sequestered into the intertextual signifying matrix which produces the figure of the dandy.[86] Boredom is recuperated

---

82 Tuite, 'Trials of the Dandy', 145.
83 Ratner, 'The Next Big Thing', 145.
84 Patricia Meyer Spacks, *Boredom: The Literary History of a State of Mind* (Chicago: University of Chicago Press, 1995), 265.
85 Spacks, *Boredom*, 268, 270.
86 Spacks, *Boredom*, 272.

as a motif for the subversion of both utilitarian capitalist and gender-normative paradigms.

In the nineteenth century, the dandy's belief that 'every day is a holiday', as articulated by Balzac, and the figure's commitment to 'the permanent pursuit of happiness', as expressed by Baudelaire, constitutes a subversion of a masculinist allegiance to a regime of discipline, structure, and order which signified values of success and productivity in emerging industrialist Europe (*PML*, 26).[87] Rosalind H. Williams deduces that 'In a society where the bourgeois loudly proclaimed the virtues of thrift, utility and work, the dandy rejected all these values as vulgar and sordid, and, increasingly, as irrelevant besides'.[88] In the present reconfiguration of the dandy, the 'rich and idle' cast of the *Brief Lives* are recruited into an anti-utilitarian resistance movement (*BL*, 35). Julia's famous career as a *diseuse*, for example, and her cultivation of the aristocratic position, protect her from assimilation into the bourgeoisie: 'She had the fearlessness of the true aristocrat: her announced intention of becoming middle-class was in fact a jeer at those who already were' (*BL*, 44).

In *Romanticism and Its Discontents*, Brookner reinforces the connection between aristocracy and dandyism when she suggests that 'Dandyism is the mark of the aristocrat' (*RD*, 65). In *Brief Lives*, Julia's entourage, partially financed by Charlie, her 'usual lament about the demise of staff', and her lack of knowledge about the subsequently endangered origins of her upkeep, all reflect the dandy's imperviousness to money and the figure's propensity to accrue debt (*BL*, 89, 140). In heralding the dandy as a subversion of capitalist utilitarianism, the figure can be marshalled against the criticism that Brookner's heroines live privileged and meaningless lives.[89] Rejecting the reductive interpretation of female privilege in Brookner's novels, it is possible to suggest that Fay's income—partially funded by her own singing and radio career and partially by the legal and nefarious business dealings of her husband—enables

---

87 Balzac, *Treatise on Elegant Living*, 49. Baudelaire celebrates the 'rich, idle' attributes of the dandy as vocational characteristics of the figure's resistance to the horrors of modernity (*PML*, 26).

88 Williams, *Dream Worlds*, 116.

89 'There is no real mystery in a Brookner novel. People (usually women) in good clothes, with civilised manners and quaint ways of speaking, inhabit a contained world of exquisitely decorated rooms and quiet libraries, constantly examining their emotional landscapes'. Barbara Love, 'Falling Slowly', *Library Journal* 123.30 (1998): 152; 'Brookner's characters always live above the purses of most of her readers'. Seymour, 'Mistress of Gloom', 107.

her to participate in the elite and aesthetic cultivation of a dandified self through the crafting of her own entertainment, performance, beauty, and gourmet living. This delineation of the dandy shifts the figure's nineteenth-century transgression of bourgeois masculinity to the contemporary female domain to deconstruct the opposition between nineteenth-century Romantic aestheticism and femininity and to reconstruct the strategic and ironic performance of femininity in Brookner's contemporary novel.

Barbey explicitly deploys the dandy against narratives of progress.[90] In *Brief Lives*, Fay explains that 'Julia was always out of date' (*BL*, 4). Both female protagonists boast names which figure a resistance to progress narratives: 'Julia Morton' signifies a 'youthful death' while Fay Dodworth, or 'faded worth', connotes a flashback to a past era (*BL*, 45). The dandy's anti-progress strategies include the embracing of what Barbey calls 'an antique calm'.[91] As Fay documents, Julia commands the anachronistic broken clock as an emblematic figure: 'She would sometimes go out to take one of her many defunct clocks and watches to the jeweller's near South Kensington station, but these were occasions for getting into character' (*BL*, 45). Julia is also associated with anachronism through her signature forms of dress. She possesses an 'archaic' habit 'of placing her underclothes on a chair in her bedroom and covering them with a square of silk reserved for this purpose' (*BL*, 4). Fay documents that 'She looked anachronistic in her long dresses, with the chiffon handkerchief tied to the little finger of her left hand' (*BL*, 2).

Julia's patronage of Mme Grès also invokes the anachronistic. In *Madame Grès: Sphinx of Fashion*, Patricia Mears frames Grès's legacy around three central elements: the incorporation of Grecian components into her gowns, ethnic influences, and sculptural qualities. In Chapter 2, we saw how the backwards turn to the Greek is a defining characteristic of Romantic aestheticism, where it operates as a form of homosexual coding. Grès herself was seen as anachronistic after delaying her transition from couture to ready-to-wear until 1980, even though Patou, Lelong, and Chanel had all launched their more accessible lines in the 1920s. Anachronism—as a temporal trope in Brookner's work and a figure for the lesbian—represents a challenge to normative constructions of gender,

---

90 'Progress, with its political economy and territorial divisions, is in the process of turning humankind into a race of vermin'. Barbey, 'On Dandyism', 173.
91 Barbey, 'On Dandyism', 93.

sexuality, and representation which depend on contemporaneity as a core legitimising principle.⁹² In 'Dandyism and Fashion', Barthes's sole clause for allowing the possibility of contemporary dandyism rests on the strategic utility of anachronism.⁹³ Barthes's critique exemplifies how the motif of the 'old-fashioned' in *Brief Lives* functions as a rejection of progress narratives and a mode of distinction in a world saturated by fashionable objects. Furthermore, by associating the anachronistic with the perverse, Barthes aligns the dandy's temporal profile to a queer disavowal of the normative enforcement of sexuality.

Where anachronism registers a resistance to capitalist ideology encoded in progress narratives, it also rejects the modes of gender and sexual normativity that are figured through narratives of generation and reproduction. In the French dandy texts, the sexual profile of the dandy emphasises the figure's asexual, anti-reproductive, and non-familial registration. Despite the fact the dandy represents 'an attack on Puritanism', Barbey also maintains that 'Historically speaking celibacy appears to have been the general rule for dandies ... the true dandy throws off all the constraints and duties of sex, whether of monogamy, paternity, or thraldom to the hearth. If there is an opposite of the family man, it is he'.⁹⁴ The French dandy opposes the apparatus which produces sexuality as natural, while at the same time disdains the open flaunting of regulations. 'He was not what is known as a libertine', Barbey states, he was free from the 'slavery' of desire.⁹⁵ Yet the dandy's disinterest in accruing the conquests of a conventional heterosexual masculinity informs what Barbey defines as an 'undecided intellectual sexuality'.⁹⁶ This sexual control and detachment is symbolised in the

---

92 Jagose's claims that 'derivation and secondariness ... mark the emergence of lesbianism as a culturally available category' and that 'our modern sex/gender system ... produces the contemporary figure of the lesbian precisely as a problem of visibility' both underscore how the lesbian's constructed deviation from the original and the contemporary effect her production through the trope of anachronism. Jagose, *Inconsequence*, 5, 12.

93 Discussing how the rise of the fashion industry shifts the signifying potential of the detail of distinction in the twentieth century, Barthes states: 'Fashion is an institution and today nobody believes anymore that it *distinguishes*, only *unfashionable* is a notion of distinction ... Fashion is health, it is a moral code of which the unfashionable is nothing but illness or perversion'. Barthes, 'Dandyism and Fashion', 68.

94 Barbey, 'On Dandyism', 90, 43.

95 Barbey, 'On Dandyism', 100–01.

96 Barbey, 'On Dandyism', 148.

element of coldness. 'The distinguishing characteristic of the dandy's beauty consists above all in an air of coldness which comes from an unshakeable determination not to be moved', Barbey maintains; the dandy is 'pale and lymphatic, cold as the sea'.[97] While failing to address any of the stigmatising modes of femininity or anality that Tuite illuminates in Jesse's biography of George Brummell, the French texts deploy an anti-progress, anti-utilitarian, and anti-reproductive narrative which nevertheless calibrates a queer profile for the figure of the dandy.

In *Brief Lives*, the dandy's asexual sexuality is patterned across the relationship between Fay and Julia. An 'aquiline beauty', 'devoid of softness', with a 'wintry heart', Julia possesses the coldness and masculine rigidity which underscore her rejection of discourses of bourgeois reproductive femininity which reinforce woman's fecundity (*BL*, 2, 3, 200). When Fay visits Julia after Charlie's death, she finds the older woman in bed, much to her interest:

> There was, to me, something shocking in the expanse of white shoulder and arms, left on view for visitors: her flesh looked cold, preserved in its marble chill from unwonted surges of the blood, ageless, in its way perfect, remarkable by any standards. (*BL*, 132)

Fay's fascination with Julia's 'hard sexy mannerisms' restages the way in which the dandy's intellectual sexuality is nevertheless the subject of eroticisation (*BL*, 3). The dandy 'redoubled his attraction', Barbey notes, because 'he never became giddy'.[98] Fay's attraction to Julia persists in spite of Julia's emotional and sexual detachment. 'There was an essential sterility about Julia, who accepted love, but could not bestow it', Fay states (*BL*, 178). Julia's negation of reproductive heterosexuality is shared by the dandy and mirrored by Fay, who, like the majority of Brookner's heroines, is also childless. By producing an asexual, non-reproductive sexuality through the performance of the dandy, and as the dominant narrative of desire between the two female protagonists, the figure's sexual profile is rendered outside of the reproductive imperative of capitalist ideology and as a queer problematisation of the heterosexual family as the dominant mode for representing desire. Barbey's representation of dandies as 'Hermaphrodites of History' suggests the figure crosses masculine, feminine, and temporal boundaries and therefore has the capacity to intervene in the production of historical context which underwrites

---

97 Barbey, 'On Dandyism', 28, 74.
98 Barbey, 'On Dandyism', 101, 102.

heterosexual privilege.[99] In this sense, the intertextual performance of the dandy in *Brief Lives* constitutes an exemplary configuration of Barbey's hermaphrodites. When Tuite reveals the rise-and-fall narrative as the organising narrative form of the dandy, thereby illuminating the feminine and homosexual signifying possibilities of the figure, she emphasises the dandy's 'capacity for scandalous corporeality as well as for fashionable glamour'.[100] In the final section of this chapter, the rise-and-fall narrative guides the performance of the dandy across the categories of 'talk', 'dress', 'eat', and 'walk', as they are found in *Brief Lives*, and along the narrative contours of glamour, ruination, and ephemeral endurance. In the category of 'talk', the construction of glamour is examined before staking the rise-and-fall narrative around Fay's asexually eroticised dressing and undressing of Julia in the category of 'dress'. Subsequently, glamour, fall, ruination, and ephemeral endurance are plotted in the undulating tenors of Julia's voice, the changing fortunes of Fay's exquisite acts of service, Julia's exile to Spain, and her celebrated re-imagining.

Staging the Performance of the Dandy

I Talking

In *On Dandyism and George Brummell*, Barbey emphasises the ephemeral or 'brief life' of the dandy's oral narrative. 'God has compensated for the brevity of life by its intensity, in order that the love of perishable things should not be lost to our hearts', Barbey states: 'So Brummell's witticisms will not be quoted. They would not live up to his reputation, even though they deserve to do so. The circumstances in which they shot forth, which gave them their electric charge so to speak, no longer exist'.[101] Barbey's focus on the transient life of oral discourse echoes Aubrey's concern with the 'fugitive' life of the oral narrative and is restaged in the multiple oral and ephemeral narrative conventions associated with Fay and Julia. In underlining the cultural status of both female protagonists, the performance of the dandy across the oral category of 'talk' is implicated in the construction of glamour which marks the first contour in the rise-and-fall narrative.

---

99 Barbey, 'On Dandyism', 148.
100 Tuite, 'Trials of the Dandy', 146. Tuite also notes the figure's contextual lability, stating, 'The dandy is a lever of ambiguity, generating a series of often opposing meanings that are radically dependent upon context' (162).
101 Barbey, 'On Dandyism', 117.

Fay's self-conscious, first-person narrative invokes the classic properties of the extempore, oral narrative form. Ruth Scodel explains that extempore techniques were a feature of oral conventions in Greek poetry, a genre which informs narrative organisation in both Aubrey's *Brief Lives* and Romantic aestheticism.[102] Greek narratives imply an extemporaneous situation of 'spontaneous speech' in two ways. Scodel maintains that first '[t]he "I" of the personal lyric generates an impression of spontaneity because the poem seems properly carried along by the speaker's thoughts and especially prominent. The poet's personality as a poet, on the other hand, is not especially prominent'.[103] Secondly, a spontaneous narrative is underscored by 'self-correction' which involves 'having the speaker change his mind, stop himself or announce that he had spoken inappropriately'.[104] Scodel concludes that 'there is an obvious connection between self-correction and the presentation of character'.[105] Extempore or 'spontaneous' narrative, therefore, is the primary formal mode for a character like Fay Dodworth, who self-identifies as uncertain and inadequate.

Both spontaneous and self-correcting forms of extempore discourse manifest in Fay's narrative. As a professional singer and radio performer, the narrator, Fay Dodworth, has an oral vocation. Throughout the text, Fay slips into song: 'Arcady, Arcady is always young', she intones (*BL*, 9). The fading of the oral text is lamented in Fay's wistful recall, while the lists of songs she cites with quotation marks emphasise the belatedness of the written against the oral text. At the same time, the age of the songs themselves (and the gesture to a prelapsarian time in the case of 'Arcady') complicates the association of orality and performance with immediacy. This conflict between the oral and written—which traverses the opposition between the British social dandy and the French literary dandy—is similarly re-enacted by the way in which Fay meticulously restages Julia's speech acts through quotation, and, in so doing inserts the primary oral text into the belated, secondary text of *Brief Lives*.

The extempore narrative organisation enables the way in which Fay's self-narration is inflected by the inconsequential, boring, uncertain, and

---

102 Ruth Scodel, 'Self-Correction, Spontaneity, and Orality in Archaic Poetry', in *Voice into Text: Orality and Literacy in Ancient Greece*, ed. Ian Worthington (Leiden: E.J. Brill, 1996).
103 Scodel, 'Self-Correction, Spontaneity, and Orality', 65.
104 Scodel, 'Self-Correction, Spontaneity, and Orality', 62.
105 Scodel, 'Self-Correction, Spontaneity, and Orality', 64.

repetitive. 'I remember at the time I went to the hairdresser's' the narrator recalls, or, 'I did nothing else for a couple of days', she informs us (*BL*, 69, 118). Uncertainties, omissions, and absences underscore the textual strategies of Brookner, Aubrey, and the nineteenth-century aesthetes in their challenges to mark the brief life of the oral narrative. 'There was the time when he took Julia away to the sun, Majorca, I think it was', Fay says, straining for the detail: 'Memory begins to falter here, as if in anticipation of darker times ahead' (*BL*, 108, 52). Orality is also implied by the way in which rhetorical questions are addressed to the reader. 'How could it hurt? Whom could it hurt?' Fay invites us to moralise: 'How could I deny her something to read?'; 'how does one close the door on feeling, when there is still time to use it?' (*BL*, 103, 116, 129). The use of ellipses in the text mimic the 'trailing off' of the oral voice: 'I was a pretty girl, I married well … It all seems a long time ago' (*BL*, 10). Repetition is another formal device which operates to make the written text appear unedited and authentic. Fay repeats the phrase 'of course' 48 times in the 217-page novel. Fay's vigorous 'of course' narrative buffers the text with signifiers of spoken speech, making her focalisation appear spontaneous and intimate. The 'of course' speaking form creates effects of spontaneity and self-correction. It acts as an interrupting mechanism which punctures the novel with Fay's presence and imposes a mode of self-aggrandising authority on the text.

In Brookner's early reception, the novelist is frequently conflated with her 'inadequate' heroines in what underwrites the autobiographical production of the Brookner text. However, in framing the dandy's performance across an array of extempore forms, Brookner's novel is illuminated more so as a series of literary devices. In *Brief Lives*, for example, the narrator's self-deprecating voice is challenged by other characters in the text. Julia's dresser, Pearl Chesney, reveals the narrator's conversation is less boring than we are led to believe when she tells Fay, 'you always did have a way with words' (*BL*, 194). Similarly, the narrator's reputation as a performer is enough to bring her recognition at a dinner party where she divines her host to be 'offering me as a sort of attraction' (*BL*, 156). Fay muses, 'I was a relic to them, almost a celebrity', recalling her warm farewell: 'You must come again soon, Fay. You've been a tremendous hit' (*BL*, 157). Even the 'monstrous' Julia commends Fay's performance on 'Woman's Hour': 'I thought your diction quite good, surprisingly good' (*BL*, 194). Thus, following the conventions of the unreliable narrator, Fay's extempore self-effacing narrative cannot be entirely conflated with a self-effacing reality. By staging the performance of the dandy across the category of 'talk', Fay's acts of self-curtailment and self-negation can be framed as part of the glamorisation and eroticisation of Julia's discursive performance.

Through Fay's focalisation, Julia's theatrical behaviour can be seen to employ multiple aspects of the dandy's provocative performative mode. 'Her pauses, her irony, her nervelessness gave her full command, while her inflection gave her utterances a scurrility of which she seemed innocently unaware', Fay states of Julia, channelling Barbey's comment that Brummell 'did not throw out witticisms, he let them drop' (*BL*, 136).[106] Julia intimidates Fay largely with an unspoken power. 'Over the pale blue eyes the eyelids were heavy and capable of conveying multiple innuendos of an unvaryingly derogatory nature', Fay remembers, summoning Barbey's proposition that Brummell 'was so intellectual a force that he ruled more by his aura than by his words' (*BL*, 3).[107] Fay explains that Julia 'was by nature a miniaturist who excelled at drawing into her field of activity nuances, intimations, unspoken thought, the most tenuous of personal statements. She was better at the glancing criticism than at spontaneous magnanimity … Julia was essentially a creature of insinuation, the eyelids lowered and then flying open, request and accusation mingling, retribution to follow'. In her specifying of the 'glancing criticism', Fay conjures the brevity of the dandy's epigrammatic style, itself a recalibration of the extempore techniques of the improvisatrice or *diseuse*. Despite the strength of Julia's ephemeral oral narrative, it relies for its aura on Fay's additional contextualising descriptions of her behaviour and 'hard sexy mannerisms' (*BL*, 3). Moving from the public stage to the domestic interior, Julia's 'dangerous' and 'alarming' temperament is directed toward her entourage. On one occasion, 'Maureen, during one of her absences at Peter Jones, was convicted of gracelessness (difficult to deny) and Mrs Chesney was adjured to her face to lose some weight' (*BL*, 50). On another occasion, Pearl's contribution to the group is undermined through reading habits sutured to a class hierarchy: 'No earthly use asking Pearl', said Julia. 'She's never read a book in her life' (*BL*, 112). Therefore, whether through self-negation, self-exaltation, or scandalous commentary, the performance of the dandy across the category of 'talk' constructs the glamorous heights of the two female performers at the centre of the text.

---

106 Barbey, 'On Dandyism', 114.
107 Barbey, 'On Dandyism', 115.

II Dressing

Balzac instructs that '[c]lothing governs opinions, it determines them, it reigns'.[108] In *Brief Lives*, Julia attaches a similar significance to clothing: '[g]etting dressed was the main event of Julia's day', Fay states: 'Julia liked the artificial climate of her dressing-room rather than anything more natural or variable' (*BL*, 105, 46). Tuite pitches the heights of George Brummell's glamour around his London days, 'when he would be openly on display at his immaculate and elaborate *toilette* to a large group of fashionable young men known as the "Dandiacal Body", who would attend his levees to observe him performing intimate acts of grooming and ablution'.[109] The customs and rituals which construct the dandy's glamour are restaged in *Brief Lives* around Julia's well-attended toilette, the signifiers of exclusivity and detail in her garments and her social performance. Fay remembers Julia:

> sweeping one into her bedroom, flinging open her many wardrobes and demanding to be told what to wear. She had already made up her mind on this point, and she was never wrong, but she liked to deplore one's own lack of taste in hazarding what was to be a laughable suggestion. This exchange, which was frequently repeated, was one of a number of rituals by which she reinforced her ascendancy. (*BL*, 4–5)

Thus Julia's backstage circle act as the 'Dandiacal Body' around her toilette and collaborate in her glamorous appearance and persona. Years after Julia's public career is over, Julia's dresser, Pearl Chesney, remains a faithful member of the Body, 'for the touch of glamour conferred by Julia's superb appearance' (*BL*, 112). But just as Julia's 'perfect' appearance assists in the construction of glamour in the text, the staging of the performance of the dandy through a rise-and-fall narrative insists that Julia's fall and ruination will also be enacted across the category of 'dress' (*BL*, 132).

In 'Trials of the Dandy', Tuite nominates Brummell's cravat as 'a vital accessory to his vocational dandyism, so much so that Jesse's *Life of Brummell* can also be said to offer a life of Brummell's cravat'.[110] Barthes underscores the significance of Brummell's tie when he represents the Brummellian 'knot' (or cravat) as a primary signifier of nineteenth-century dandyism.[111] The cravat emblematises the performance of glamorous

---

108 Balzac, *Treatise on Elegant Living*, 68.
109 Tuite, 'Trials of the Dandy', 156.
110 Tuite, 'Trials of the Dandy', 147.
111 Barthes, 'Dandyism and Fashion', 66.

detail through which the dandy is produced. 'Confined to clothing', Balzac states: 'elegance consists in an extreme refinement in the details of the outfit'.[112] In *Brief Lives*, the knot resurfaces in Julia's signature affectation and mode of dress. Barbey claims the dandy maintains a 'refined affectation', and in *Brief Lives* this effect is reproduced in the signature chiffon handkerchief knotted to Julia's little finger:

> the chiffon handkerchief tied to the little finger of her left hand: this was an affectation of hers, but it did not go down well when the fashion was for sausage curls shoved under a turban and overalls that tied around the waist. (*BL*, 2)[113]

Additionally, the 'knot' of Mme Grès's turban and the Grecian drapery of the gown act as homage to the detail of the dandy. Mears lauds Grès's sense of detail when she says 'Grès was a *couturière* in the traditional sense of the word. She did not sketch or leave the technical process to assistants. Every garment from her atelier was crafted by hand, by her, using either inexpensive muslin to create a prototype or the action ground fabric itself'.[114] In staging the performance of the dandy in *Brief Lives*, the knot is reconstituted as an intertextual object which forms part of the figure's attention to glamorous and scandalous detail. Tuite maps Brummell's rise-and-fall from the social heights symbolised by his impeccable cravat and social toilette to humiliation in the degeneration of his clean, white linen, his imprisonment and abjection, and finally to his death from syphilitic dementia 'in a state of sartorial, psychic and corporeal ruination'.[115] By mapping the rise-and-fall of Brummell in the degeneration of his dress codes, from the heights of his impeccable cravat to the disintegration of standards of cleanliness and the adoption of the formerly unthinkable—a black silk handkerchief—Brummell's rise-and-fall is dramatised most definitively in the category of dress.[116] Analogously, the dandy's rise-and-fall in *Brief Lives* can be staged through the undressing (or 'unknotting') of Julia's signature style. In this reading, the figurative fall propelled by the dandy—across the relationship between Fay and Julia—also stages an erotic fall which engages the dandy's queer forms of asexual and erotic display.

112 Balzac, *Treatise on Elegant Living*, 72.
113 Barbey, 'On Dandyism', 101.
114 Mears, *Madame Grès*, 4.
115 Tuite, 'Trials of the Dandy', 145.
116 Tuite, 'Trials of the Dandy', 160.

The first stage in Julia's undressing manifests with the departure of her dresser, Pearl Chesney, who is also responsible for Julia's laundry. Laundry plays a central role in the narrative of misfortunes that Tuite sketches around Brummell's fall and ruination. The importance Brummell places on clean laundry fuels his avoidance of literal marks on clothing and the cultivation of extreme cleanliness, but also informs his incarceration in a Caen prison for debts to the laundry-woman responsible for his immaculate white linen.[117] In *Brief Lives*, Julia's debts to her laundry woman are largely emotional: Pearl's departure signals the imminent dissolution of Julia's backstage clan, foreshadowing Maureen's surprise engagement to the unprepossessing Mr Smallwood. When Julia's entourage holds a small gathering to say farewell to Pearl, a certain type of ending is figured for Julia which begins a downward spiral along the rise-and-fall narrative. 'It was as if Julia were taking a curtain call with her accompanist, summoned from her obscure position behind the piano' (*BL*, 161). Julia's theatricalised finale connotes the advent of closure around all modes of talk, dress, eat, and walk. When Fay notes 'there was something wrong with Julia', she charts a downward trajectory in Julia's drawn features, reinforcing the degeneration of her dress code. Fay registers an alteration in Julia's voice, newly hearing 'the bass voice of old women', which constitutes a perversion of Julia's 'ageless' masculinity in the category of talk (*BL*, 161). The narrator tracks an intensification of Julia's lack of appetite in her 'untouched' whisky, an effect of decline in the category of 'eat' (*BL*, 161). All these dramatic moments occur at Julia's Onslow Square flat, because, as Fay reports 'Nowadays [Julia] rarely went out' (*BL*, 44). The retardation of Julia's movements equate to a declension in the category of 'walk'.

Following the loss of her 'Pearl', the second stage of Julia's undressing witnesses the loss and destruction of another type of jewel. Fay arrives at Onslow Square and is 'disproportionately shocked' to find Julia wearing only one earring:

> 'Why, Julia,' I said. 'You've lost an earring.' 'I dropped it somewhere,' she replied indifferently. Later that morning I saw a gleam beside her narrow left foot. 'There it is!' I said. 'Beside your left foot. Don't tread on it.' But as I bent down to pick it up the slow foot brushed over it and crushed it. This incident disturbed me. Julia said nothing, pretended not to notice. Mrs Wheeler, arriving with a tray of coffee, pursed her lips and nodded meaningfully in my direction behind Julia's rigid back. (*BL*, 184)

117 Tuite, 'Trials of the Dandy', 153.

Just as Tuite plots Brummell's loss of control of bodily functions as part of the rise-and-fall narrative, Fay observes of Julia that 'It was the first sign that her control was not what it once had been' (*BL*, 184). At this stage of the performance of the dandy across the rise-and-fall narrative, the crushed jewel beneath the foot of the crushing Julia traces a further dereliction of Julia's formerly unassailable standards. The phonetic correlation between 'jewel' and 'Julia' is suggestive of the degree to which both 'dress' and 'talk' discourses are intricately interwoven in the dandy's identity. It follows that the degeneration of Julia's dressing marks a similar decline in her discourse and person.

In the final stage of undressing through the rise-and-fall narrative, Julia summons Fay for help bathing. Mobilising a voice 'low and cold, less the voice of an old woman than of an old man' (*BL*, 188), Julia again appropriates the male register in a crossing which is commensurate with the gender-transgressive performance of the dandy. Here the further fall in Julia's speech register reflects decline in the once-glamorous category of 'talk'. From her flat in Drayton Gardens, Fay is unable to resist her friend's request for assistance. She hastily completes her cooking preparations—examined in the category of 'eating'— and departs for Onslow Square where she finds the 'dishevelled' Julia:

> making her way slowly into the bedroom. She undressed equally slowly, revealing the lingerie of a *cocotte* on limbs which were beginning to look wasted. The whiteness of her body shocked me: I didn't think I should be witnessing it. I lowered her into the sweet-smelling water of the bath, and turned my back. By this time I was trembling, although I did not quite know why. (*BL*, 189)

Together, Julia's striptease and Fay's reactions activate the modes of asexual sexuality and the complementary forms of eroticisation that Barbey reveres in Brummell, as well as modes of recessed homosexuality that Clara Tuite excavates in Jesse's *Life of George Brummell*. Julia's performance is both detached and sexualised, whereas Fay's response echoes an experience of sexual arousal. 'Shocked', 'trembling', as well as unknowing, Fay's physical and psychological states suggest the 'fey' attraction and denial of attraction that Eve Kosofsky Sedgwick defines as the Jamesian homoerotic negative (*BL*, 189).[118] By illuminating a cluster of nineteenth-century sexual and homoerotic narratives in Brookner's

---

118 Sedgwick, *Epistemology of the Closet*, 202.

contemporary text, the performance of the dandy stages a queering of the central female relationship in *Brief Lives*.

Fay's presence fails to deflect Julia's scrutiny. On the contrary, Julia's uncanny ability to divine the subtext forces Fay to reveal her dinner plans with Dr Alan Carter. In response, Fay battles Julia's impetus to locate her relationship with Carter on an erotic register. 'We might go away for a few days, that's all', she says (*BL*, 190). The sexual discourse between the women intensifies the erotic tenor of the bathing scene:

> Julia laid a heavy wet arm around my neck, disarranging my hair in the process. 'Going away?' she said. 'Well done.' She pretended to fall, or maybe she did fall, I no longer know, and in her effort to hold onto me tore the stitches from the shoulder of my blouse. I could feel the slow uncoiling of my hair as it fell down my back. Her body, a dead weight, supported itself on my shoulders as I staggered back; she had renounced all responsibility for her movements, either that or she was more incapacitated than I knew. Horrified, I managed to get her into the bedroom. (*BL*, 190)

At the denouement of the rise-and-fall narrative, Julia's fall and undressing climaxes with a simultaneous undressing of Fay. Thus, Julia's fall and undressing constitutes an erotic fall and mutual undressing between the female protagonists. In Tuite's rendering of the rise-and-fall narrative, she argues that Brummell's experience of being observed at the prison latrine, and his resulting constipation, produces 'the "dandiacal body" … as a marked male body, made for display yet abjected and effeminised by anality'.[119] Reconstituting the performance of the dandy in *Brief Lives* across the historical and gendered intertextual network, the spectacle of abjection resurfaces in Fay's horror at the women's mutual dishabille and the figure's recessed homosexuality morphs into a queer performance enacted by ageing female bodies. The dandy's slow dance across Julia's dressing and undressing illuminates how the female body of *Brief Lives* acts as a signifier of both asexual sexuality and homoerotic desire.

III Eating

In the nineteenth century, rapid industrialisation impacted on the eating habits and social customs of the middle classes. The dinner party itself became a site for the patterning of status between hosts and guests.[120] So

---

[119] Tuite, 'Trials of the Dandy', 155.
[120] 'The arriving guests would see the spacious and well-kept house, the elegant reception rooms, the well-trained staff, the luxurious table appointments, in particular the display of silver; good wine and food would put them in good

too in *Brief Lives*, where specialised modes of consumption are integral to the practice of elegant living and adumbrate the construction of glamour. 'You're so clever with food', Fay recalls Julia telling her (*BL*, 41). Discreetly yet consistently throughout the novel, Fay's elegant menus catalogue a delicate combination of flavours, textures, and colours crafted to effect an aesthetic experience. In the mode of exchange mobilised by their relationship to eating, Fay provides the supply for Julia's demand. Thus, Julia's authority over the means of production ensures that Fay's menus index her value to Julia. Fay's hand-wrought delicacies include a 'careful' casserole of chicken and peppers, followed by lemon mousse and coconut *tuiles* (*BL*, 35); little parcels of cold salmon, of tongue, of fruit tart and hothouse peach and madeira cake (*BL*, 64, 107); vegetable terrine, baked chicken and rice, fresh rolls and a sliver of Stilton (*BL*, 188); cold veal with a tunny sauce and strawberry tart (*BL*, 78); a simple salad of tomatoes and olives, with oil and basil dribbled over them (*BL*, 54), cold curried chicken and fruit salad (*BL*, 198); rice salad (*BL*, 146); and sherry and seed cake (*BL*, 67).

The behavioural modes of hosting and catering are integral to the construction of femininity through the roles of food management and service in the domestic space, in opposition to the production of masculinity in roles of power and authority in the public space. In *Aesthetic Pleasure in Twentieth-Century Women's Food Writing*, Alice L. McLean contrasts proscriptive women's food writing with the nineteenth-century development of gastronomic literature, 'a genre primarily concerned with honing the sensual and intellectual pleasure of gastronomy' and tightly linked to 'a well-educated, cosmopolitan, witty, and articulate masculinity', also known as the dandy.[121]

Framing the nineteenth-century male dandy through elite modes of gastronomy and consumption reinforces the double dichotomy in which

---

humour and would show their host's taste and knowledge and the liberality of his expenditure'. Elizabeth Ayrton, *The Cookery of England* (London: André Deutsch, 1974), 7.

121 McLean notes how qualities of duty, practical instruction, self-effacement, and economy of style characterise domestic cookbooks written for and by women from the late eighteenth century. Alice L. McLean, *Aesthetic Pleasure in Twentieth-Century Women's Food Writing: The Innovative Appetites of M.F.K. Fisher, Alice B. Toklas, and Elizabeth David* (New York: Routledge, 2012), 1, 2–3. 'His taste for good food, as delicate as a flavour and as exacting as a passion, had always been one of the most pronounced aspects of his hedonism', Barbey states of Brummell. Barbey, 'On Dandyism', 134.

women are removed from social power by their association with food in the domestic space, only to be divorced from cultural status through food by their association with utilitarian aspects of their role in the domestic space. However, the transhistorical production of the dandy in *Brief Lives* across male and female modes of performance complicates traditional associations, on the one hand, between food and femininity and, on the other hand, between masculinity and aestheticism. In *Brief Lives*, Julia's performance of masculine control resists the historical annexation of the female reproductive body in the category of 'eat'. A 'strikingly tall and slim' woman, Julia survives primarily on omelettes and whisky (*BL*, 3). '"Plenty of calories in whisky," she would say, and Mummy would give a delighted laugh' (*BL*, 91). Julia's mythic lack of appetite stimulates Fay's acts of culinary artistry and the provision of sensual pleasure and therefore food becomes both a signifier of glamour in *Brief Lives* and a mode of eroticised exchange between the two women.

In the early stages of the narrative of Julia's undressing, Fay's apprehension of Julia's decline occurs simultaneously with Julia 'tormenting' Fay about her relationship with Dr Alan Carter (*BL*, 184). '"How's that man of yours?" she would say, "What's he like in bed?"' (*BL*, 184–85). Julia's behaviour pressures Fay into confecting a dinner date with Carter, a man she finds 'rude… inattentive, critical, disappointing, and cruel' (*BL*, 164, 164, 174). 'In my boiling discomfort I resolved to go straight home, ring Carter, and invite him to dinner. I was not happy about this; it was all wrong', Fay states (*BL*, 162). In the denouement of the narrative of Julia's undressing, Julia connects Fay's dinner plans with Dr Alan Carter to prospective marriage plans and a sexual relationship. '"Coming to dinner is he?" she said, making her way slowly into the bedroom … "Are you going to marry him?" … "But you're having an affair with him, aren't you?"' (*BL*, 189–90). This metonymical shift reveals how Fay's catering is imbued with erotic content in *Brief Lives*. Discourses of consumption are transferred onto erotic discourses and aestheticised as avant-gardist representational forms through the performance of the dandy. In this way, combined with Fay's passionate interest in Julia and her dedication to an aestheticised and pleasurable servicing of Julia, Fay's delicate menus can be read as small love poems to Julia.

Having installed Dr Carter in a triangulated relationship with Fay and herself, Julia subsequently usurps his position in the climax of the rise-and-fall narrative in the category of 'eat'. On the day of the dinner party, Fay meticulously attends to her preparations, putting the finishing touches on a vegetable terrine. With her hands sticky with aspic, a gelatinous signifier of sexual fluids, Fay takes a phone call from Julia: 'I might have a bath and go straight to bed', Julia says, 'Perhaps you could bring some fruit or something' (*BL*, 188). This is the summons to the final fall and undressing, discursively produced as a request for fruit, the biblical symbol of the fall. After engineering the Carter dinner, Julia subsequently arrests Fay's preparations and hijacks her afternoon. Following the undressing at Onslow Square, Fay arrives home with her appetite sated. She botches her remaining kitchen duties, knocking the vegetable terrine off the bench and 'sending a spray of carrot mousse' over her shoes (*BL*, 191). In this image, the conjunction of the eroticised spray and wastage figures the dandy's sexual profile outside the narrative of heterosexual reproduction. The subtextual heterosexual romance between Fay and Carter is turned into a farce: Carter declares the 'deranged' Fay 'hysterical' before quickly retreating from the scene of destruction (*BL*, 191, 192). The dandy's performance across the narrative of ruination and fall is nearly complete. 'Behind my own ruin lay Julia', Fay concludes as she surveys a 'ruined dish and a ruined evening' and a 'ruined kitchen' (*BL*, 193, 192, 193). Through the performance of the dandy, the rise-and-fall narrative propels Julia back to the central focus of Fay's attentions.

IV Walking

Balzac intended *Treatise on Elegant Living* to be part of a broader study entitled the *Pathology of Social Life*, along with a volume called *Theory of Walking*.[122] The production of the dandy through the category of walking plays upon three important chords of the figure. First, walking is a mode of display for the dandy, both in gait and dress. Secondly, it is a mode of behaviour which enacts the 'brief life' temporality of the dandy. In *The Painter of Modern Life*, Baudelaire praises the ability of painter Constantin Guys to capture 'the passing moment' as he moves through the maze of the modern metropolis (*PML*, 5). Brookner underscores Baudelaire's status as a dandy in *Romanticism and Its Discontents* when she observes that he 'aspired to the form of distinction, emblem of a highly controlled mental and spiritual life, worn by that curious type of moral pilgrim and sartorial perfectionist whom he calls the dandy' (*RD*, 65). Complementing Aubrey's recognition of the fugitive passing of the oral text, Baudelaire defines modernity as 'the ephemeral, the fugitive, the contingent, the half of art whose other half is the eternal and the

---

122 Jeffries, Introduction to *Treatise on Elegant Living*, xx.

mutable' (*PML*, 13). In this sense, walking stages the temporality of the detail through which the dandy is produced. Finally, in constituting the public display of the dandy's social persona, walking conversely illuminates the private side of the dandy's appearance in the form of the domestic interior. 'The article of clothing, the bed, the coupe are all shelters for the person, the way a house is the great article of clothing that covers man and the things he uses', states Balzac.[123] Not only does the performance of the dandy in the category of 'walk' traverse the generic contours of rise, ruination, and fall, the dandy's resurrection—what Tuite denotes as the dandy's 'ephemeral endurance'—can be reassembled as part of this classification of movement and presence.[124]

In *Brief Lives*, Fay's movement through the local environment is mapped in the street names, tube stations, galleries, museums, restaurants, and entertainment venues which surface in the text. Fay's movement past these trace names collaborate in the production of glamour around the figure of the dandy. Her walks reflect the privileged environs of Kensington and Chelsea, Marylebone, Belgravia, Mayfair, and Soho—west and central London—by referencing the residences of major and minor characters in Onslow Square, Sloane Square, Swan Court, Chelsea Manor Street, Gertrude Street, Egerton Crescent, Drayton Gardens, Hanover Square, Great Portland Street, Foubert's Place, and Lowndes Square. In naming sites such as South Kensington Station, the Kensington Library, Harrods, Peter Jones, Selfridges, the Fulham Road, the Victoria and Albert Museum, the Science Museum, Regent Street, Harley Street, the Soane Museum, and holidays in the French Riviera or the British countryside, Fay's narrative registers the leisure-class contexts of *Brief Lives*. The socio-economic privilege of the milieu is indicated by the way in which Fay's narrative, by comparison, contextualises the suburbs of London, a spatial delineation which denotes Fay's less-privileged origins and the homes of the novel's minor characters. In this case, street names fade into suburbs, and include Camberwell Grove, Ealing, Golders Green, Finchley, and Acton. While Fay remains active throughout the novel, in the opening chapter she apprehends a premature decline in Julia's movements: 'it struck me as odd', Fay reveals: 'Julia was not infirm, although she was very stiff, and she was only in her sixties. It was simply that she felt more in control in Onslow Square than she would have done in the street, where she would have been just another widow' (*BL*, 7). By the

---

123 Balzac, *Treatise on Elegant Living*, 55.
124 Tuite, 'Trials of the Dandy', 144.

time Julia is 74, Fay remarks that she is 'immobile and bitter' (*BL*, 175). This declension narrative later manifests in Julia's literal fall when her immobility progresses to collapse in the category of 'walk'.

'In playing the dandy', Balzac notes, 'a man becomes a piece of furniture for the boudoir'.[125] Julia's increasing confinement shifts attention from public spaces to the dressing room, living room, and bedroom at Onslow Square. In the nineteenth century, the growing prosperity of the bourgeoisie, falling prices, and debates about style and taste 'created a market for instruction in the art of decoration'.[126] In 1882, the iconic British dandy, Oscar Wilde, spoke on house decoration and handicrafts during his lecture tour of America.[127] Paraphrasing pre-Raphaelite painter William Morris, and invoking the philosophy of the art-for-art's-sake movement, Wilde asserts: '[h]ave nothing in your house that has not given pleasure to the man who made it and is not a pleasure to those who use it'.[128] Gore states that 'the public took to aesthetic domestic decoration with enthusiasm. Favoured colours were drab olive green and peacock blue and gold'.[129] The upswing in public attention towards interior decoration, however, was accompanied by the need to discriminate on the grounds of the detail of distinction, the organising rhetorical form of the dandy. Indeed, as Gore points out, Wilde's own 'search for originality caused him to break a number of the decorative conventions which he was still publicly and emphatically peddling in his lectures'.[130] The ongoing challenge for the dandy was to be both the apotheosis and antithesis of the cause célèbre.

In *Brief Lives*, the opposition between popular and elite modes of taste which produce the figure of the dandy are connoted in Fay's alternative descriptions of her own living arrangements vis-à-vis Julia's more glamorous abode. Over the course of her relationship with Julia, Fay lives in Gertrude Street, Chelsea, in the house decorated by her husband's first wife Hermione, and later in a flat in Drayton Gardens, South Kensington. Fay's dislike of the Gertrude Street residence brings about an opportunity to demonstrate her own superior tastes and registers a resistance to her marital home. Furthermore, Fay rejects the

---

125 Balzac, *Treatise on Elegant Living*, 58.
126 Charlotte Gere with Lesley Hoskins, *The House Beautiful: Oscar Wilde and the Aesthetic Interior* (London: Lund Humphries/Geffrye Museum, 2000), 77.
127 Gere and Hoskins, *The House Beautiful*, 88.
128 Oscar Wilde, quoted in Gore and Hoskins, *The House Beautiful*, 88.
129 Gore and Hoskins, *The House Beautiful*, 95.
130 Gore and Hoskins, *The House Beautiful*, 102.

house precisely for the colours that Gore names as the popular shades of the decorating movement:

> When I first visited Owen's house I had felt my eyes watering: she had done out the rooms in dark harsh colours, indigo, sage green, and the brooding red of claret. There was a large chandelier in each of the two rooms of the first floor, which opened out into each other. Everything was so spotless, excessive, and chilly. Owen's bed, which seemed to me twice the normal size, had a white satin coverlet with sculptured edges to match the white satin padded and buttoned bedhead ... when I saw that bed I realised that Owen was not—could not be—for me. (*BL*, 25)

But Fay's horror of 'the terrible bed' in fact fuels her relationship with Julia: 'It was a relief to go to Onslow Square', she reports, tracing a change in preference from the environment of compulsory heterosexuality to the site of her erotic scenes with Julia (*BL*, 155, 46). Despite the fact that Fay finds Julia's flat 'almost equally unwelcoming', her descriptions of Onslow Square by contrast operate to illuminate Julia's glamour, most significantly by invoking the palette which Wilde mobilises in his residence in Tite Street, Chelsea (*BL*, 46). Gore states that Wilde wanted 'a predominately pale scheme carried right through the house'.[131] This consisted of yellow walls, white woodwork and fittings, white-and-blue curtains, and a white-and-yellow silk coverlet.[132] Fay remarks of Julia that she 'liked colours which contained no warmth, and the white carpet and the white and yellow lilies in the enormous vases of clear glass seemed to reduce the temperature, which was always chilly, even further' (*BL*, 46). Thus, Fay's polemic against the 'absurd appurtenances' of Gertrude Street function to underscore her own more aristocratic tastes and therefore her similarity with Julia, whose 'ultramarine' bedroom and 'ultramarine satin nightgown' similarly project the dandy's chilly erotic appeal (*BL*, 132. 132).

Towards the end of the novel, however, the dandy's movement across the stages of ruination and fall inform Fay's desire to remove Julia from the local environment. 'I can't look after her, Pearl', Fay states. 'There's no reason why I shouldn't, but I'm not going to do it' (*BL*, 201). With that, Fay organises Julia's relocation to her brother's house in Spain. 'I saw the two of them in the sun, endlessly reminiscing about their childhood, while the companion made himself useful with drinks', Fay fantasises as she makes plans to relieve herself of the burden of Julia.

---

131 Gore and Hoskins, *The House Beautiful*, 98.
132 Gore and Hoskins, *The House Beautiful*, 103.

This exile is situated at the climax of the rise-and-fall narrative in the category of 'walking'.

In staking out the rise-and-fall narrative, Tuite characterises its final stage as the place of 'ephemeral endurance'.[133] Implicitly surviving 'the fall', the dandy's capacity for ephemeral endurance is mirrored in the search for the 'brief life' of the oral form.[134] As underscored by Tuite, the significance of framing both the fleeting and the continuous in the rise-and-fall narrative is testimony to the way in which the written undertakes to commemorate the oral, whether in Jesse's necessarily written account of the oral and the abject or Barbey's imagination.

In *Brief Lives*, the dandy's performance across the marker of ephemeral endurance is staged in each of the categories of walk, talk, eat, and dress. In 'dress', Julia's signature designer, Mme Grès is famous for her enduring appeal; having trained as a sculptor, Grès's work is more emphatically associated with the realm of high art in contrast to the increasingly commercial prerogatives of the fashion industry.[135] While Julia's fall is executed most dramatically through her 'undressing', her power is nevertheless restored in ways that restage her glamorous heights. Following the bathing scene, the narrator is forced to question her own account of the incident. 'I thought I saw signs of neglect in Julia herself, but a closer look told me that I had been imagining a decay of which there was no trace' (*BL*, 203). Subsequently, on the day of Julia's departure, Fay arrives at Onslow Square to find 'Julia looking exceedingly pale and exceedingly chic' (*BL*, 210). In 'eating', the loss of Julia means that Fay has no outlet for her romantic culinary ministrations. Julia, however, returns to the table through the symbol of her iconic dish—the omelette. 'I try to take things slowly', Fay concedes after Julia's departure, 'but am always ahead of myself, and frequently sit down to lunch—an omelette—at midday' (*BL*, 214). In 'walking',

---

133 Tuite, 'Trials of the Dandy', 160.
134 Tuite states that '[t]he relative absence of textual deposits left by Brummell sends Jesse looking for whatever pieces of testimony and oral history anyone formerly connected with Brummell might care to give him. Barbey, on the other hand, is confident that such things are lost—remoter than classical ruins—and draws comfort from the idea that they can only be recreated through fantasy ... The absence of textual deposits is for Barbey an opportunity for invention and the consecration of ephemerality'. Tuite, 'Trials of the Dandy', 161.
135 Mears notes that 'Because Grès was not a fashion trendsetter in the obvious sense and did not create novel, thematic collections, she and her work are often considered to exist outside the realm of changing fashion'. Mears, *Madame Grès*, 5.

Julia revisits South Kensington via the two postcards she sends to Fay and Pearl Chesney, reminding them of her enduring presence. Fay states: 'Mine, which was more mysterious but more affecting, stated, "Should auld acquaintance ... Regards, Julia"' (*BL*, 213). Finally, in the category of 'talking', the dandy's passage across the point of ephemeral endurance links the beginning and ending of the novel through the trope of the obituary, the quintessential 'brief life'.

The novel opens with Fay reading Julia's 'substantial obituary' in *The Times*, a narrative consecrated to preserving the biographical life (*BL*, 1). The novel concludes a week later in Julia's voice, shifting narrative authority from Fay to Julia through the citation of the oral text:

> So irrelevant did her death seem that I almost looked forward to discussing it with her, felt something like a quickening of interest. 'What was it like?' I should have asked. The eyelids would have come down again as she considered. 'Not all that bad,' I can hear her say, in her most famously throw-away tone. 'You might give it a try one of these days.' (*BL*, 217)

Thus, the closing line of the text represents Julia's unceasing authority, both through the 'brief life' text and through her incubation in Fay's psyche. In exemplifying the way in which the figure of the dandy is produced and performed across the relationship between the two women, the dandy's ephemeral endurance is staged through the figure's enigmatic resurrection in Brookner's contemporary women's fiction.

CHAPTER FOUR

The *Flâneur* in *Undue Influence* (1998)

> I was aware that I had not behaved well, had, ever since we had met, exerted undue influence.
>
> Anita Brookner, *Undue Influence*

Introduction

Claire Pitt, the 29-year-old narrator of *Undue Influence*, has an 'odd habit of making up people's lives for them' (*UI*, 176). Claire's imagination is so prominent a characteristic that her best friend, Wiggy, also 'an artist of a sort', suggests that Claire 'should write a novel' (*UI*, 9, 13). Claire's imagination is most commonly triggered by her other great passion, walking. Every day, Claire walks from her home at Montagu Mansions to her work—a Gower Street bookshop named Ex Libris—where she first encounters Martin Gibson, an 'extraordinarily desirable' former London University academic who specialises in the German Romantics (*UI*, 126). The 'golden' Martin Gibson is also identified as a walker (*UI*, 111). Martin's dying wife, Cynthia, somewhat disingenuously encourages Martin's independence through walking. 'He is quite free in the daytime. In fact I make him go out; I know he likes to walk. I insist that he does so, though I suspect he doesn't always enjoy it', Cynthia informs Claire (*UI*, 40). Claire and Martin make acquaintance when Martin feigns immersion in a volume of Heinrich Heine's poems in the Ex Libris basement while looking for a copy of Theodor Fontane's *Jenny Treibel* (1892).

The Ex Libris bookshop is owned by Hester and Muriel Collier, elderly sisters whose residence in nearby Marchmont Street mark them as spiritual neighbours of Virginia Woolf. Published in 1925, Woolf's *Mrs*

Dalloway is a canonical walker's text whose characters traverse the paths of central London also walked by Brookner's characters. At first, Claire is sceptical about the similarities between the Collier sisters and Woolf, and puzzles over the 'accident of geography' that places them in the same vicinity (*UI*, 59). But Claire's professional duties expand to include the editing of notes penned by St John Collier, 'a minor belletrist', into a manuscript that was to be entitled 'Walks with Myself' (*UI*, 14). Its author had set out to 'explore different areas of London, Putney, Kennington, Southwark [and] Bloomsbury', Muriel Collier tells Claire; the book 'was to be a companion for the solitary walker' (*UI*, 61).

In 'Walking in the City', Michel de Certeau distinguishes between the state-defined desire to control our experience of space in city planning and the experience of the *Wandersmänner*—the walkers whose 'intertwined paths give shape to spaces'.[1] For de Certeau, the city represents 'a contradiction between the collective mode of administration and an individual mode of appropriation'.[2] He contends that walkers' spatial practices constitute a 'poetic and mythic experience of space' resulting in an outcome whereby a '*migrational*, or metaphorical, city thus slips into the clear text of the planned and readable city'.[3] According to de Certeau, if 'one admits that spatial practices in fact secretly structure the determining conditions of social life', then the act of walking 'is a process of *appropriation* of the topographical system on the part of the pedestrian'.[4] Because de Certeau apprehends a 'parallelism between linguistic and pedestrian enunciation', where the walker's operative use of the city creates 'intertwining, unrecognised poems' that anarchically transform the functionalist grid in a similar way to how the poet appropriates language in the Symbolic, his insights into the bold appropriations of the walker can also be extrapolated to the level of text.[5]

Reading Brookner's nineteenth novel in this light, therefore, Claire's walking can be interpreted as an act of resistance against the regulation of contemporary behaviour that instructs when and how particular identities may use public space. Additionally, the narrator's narratives of imagination can be seen as parallel to her journeying through the city and as potential acts of poetic subversion. However, while de Certeau

1 De Certeau, 'Walking in the City', 106.
2 De Certeau, 'Walking in the City', 96.
3 De Certeau, 'Walking in the City', 93.
4 De Certeau, 'Walking in the City', 97.
5 De Certeau, 'Walking in the City', 99, 93.

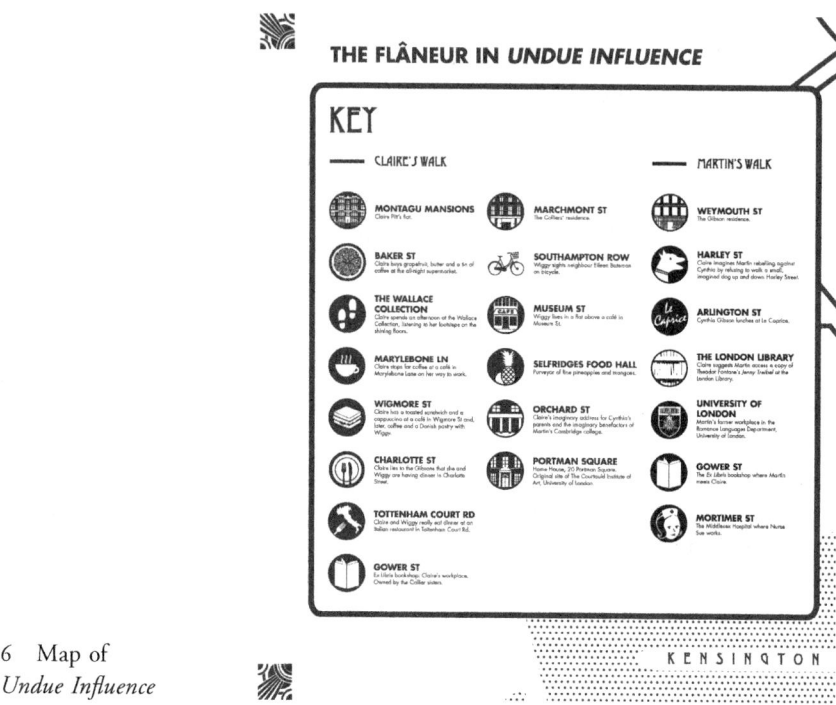

6   Map of *Undue Influence*

privileges the anarchical proclivities of walkers, he maintains that maps of walking routes miss 'the act itself of passing by'.[6]

> It is true that the operations of walking can be traced on city maps in such a way as to transcribe their paths ... [but maps] allow us to grasp only a relic set in the nowhen of a surface of projection. Itself visible, it has the effect of making invisible the operation that made it possible. These fixations constitute procedures for forgetting.[7]

According to de Certeau, unlike walking, maps are invariant and reject the reality of lived experience.

However, an argument can be pitched against this contention, and here I enlist the support of a map to do so. 'The *Flâneur* in *Undue Influence*' is a walking map that illustrates two imagined walks for Claire Pitt and Martin Gibson, divined from *Undue Influence*, which can help to trace their daily experiences. Claire's walk begins at her home at Montagu Mansions (1). From there, she journeys down Baker Street (2), where

6 De Certeau, 'Walking in the City', 97.
7 De Certeau, 'Walking in the City', 97.

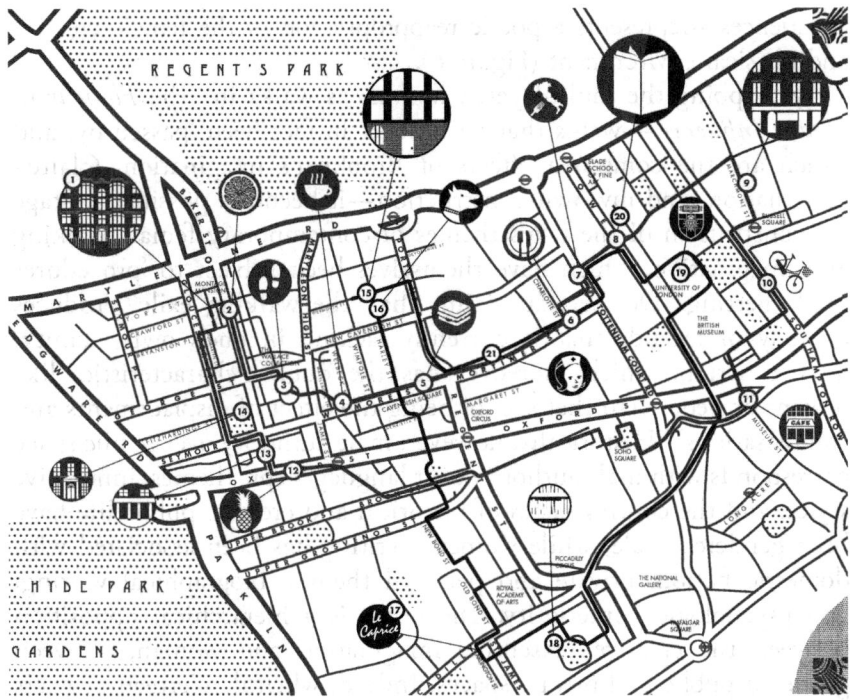

she occasionally shops at the late-night supermarket, past the Wallace Collection (3), where, like many Brooknerines, she sometimes passes idle hours, to a café in Marylebone Lane (4), where she imagines the life story of another patron before heading to a different café in Wigmore Street (5), where she eats with Wiggy. Next comes a restaurant Claire invents, to impress Martin and Cynthia, in Charlotte Street (6), followed by a more conventional Italian diner in Tottenham Court Road (7), where she actually eats dinner. The proximity of Gower Street (8), home to Ex Libris, to Marchmont Street (9) enables Claire to visit the Colliers at home, with an offering of grapes from a local fruit barrow, when Hester Collier is injured. From Marchmont Street, Claire's passage is followed back home via Southampton Row (10), Wiggy's flat in Museum Street (11), and Selfridges Food Hall (12), where Claire fulfils her needs for exotic fruit, to Orchard Street (13), the address Claire imagines for Cynthia Gibsons's parents, and, finally, past Portman Square (14), the original site of the Courtauld Institute of Art, where Brookner studied and lectured in the field of French Romantic art history from 1977 to 1989. Specifically to mark these sites on a map—literally to map the fictional world of Brookner's text by tracing Claire's real and imagined experiences—represents a poetic reappropriation of the female creative and physical environment (Figure 6).

By mapping the multi-layered fictions as walks in 'The *Flâneur* in *Undue Influence*'—walks that have never in fact been 'passed by' and which are the combined effects of Brookner's imagination, Claire's imagination, and my own construction—it becomes possible to stage a reconstitution of the text's themes of contemporary female walking and imagination, which have themselves been subject to 'procedures for forgetting'. De Certeau claims that 'the walking exile' produces a 'body of legends that is currently lacking in one's own vicinity; it is a fiction, which moreover has the double characteristic, like dreams or pedestrian rhetoric, of being the effect of displacements and condensations'.[8] Historically, however, male authority over public space corresponds with male authority over language: epic themes, innovative styles, and the contingencies of historical and creative public life have been gendered male, while women's writing has been associated with domestic fiction, private and personal themes, biographical writing, and psychological interiority. The result is a hierarchical opposition between the creative masculine imagination and woman, between gendered public and private spaces. Indeed, when de Certeau neglects to name the gendered distribution of material and symbolic space, he implicitly recodes his 'procedures for forgetting' as a patriarchal strategy.

A central theme of *Misreading Anita Brookner* is to consider ways in which an organising dichotomy between 'woman' and 'artist' has impacted on Brookner's interpretation. Chapter 2 linked the silencing of the first-person voice of the Sapphic female poet to discourses of absence which helped produce Brookner as an autobiographical women's writer. Chapter 3 examined how Baudelaire fortified an opposition between 'woman' and 'the dandy', preserving cultural authority around aesthetic masculinity while undermining women's representational practices. This chapter engages directly with two themes of the broader project, misreading and intertextuality, to emphasise the female creative imagination and its relationship to aestheticism, literary status, and avant-garde or postmodernist literary practice—in distinction to its relationship to romance narratives.

De Certeau claims that the functionalist city attempts to erase 'the stories and legends that haunt urban space like superfluous or additional

---

8 De Certeau, 'Walking in the City', 106.

inhabitants'.[9] These stories 'are the object of a witch-hunt, by the very logic of the techno-structure', he says.[10] But has not Brookner's intertextual women's writing been something of the object of a cultural 'witch-hunt'? In which case, the aim here is to restore the ghosted subtext of Brookner's novel by producing the figure of the *flâneur*—an archetype of the artist—through a signifying matrix of walking, imagination, and misreading, as well as the narrative of influence and the rhetorical figure of peripeteia as queer reversal. This mission mobilises nineteenth-century notions of masculine creativity in the narration of contemporary female performativity. In presenting the walking map entitled 'The *Flâneur* in *Undue Influence*', we adopt 'procedures for remembering' by underscoring a 'body of legends' about creative imagination and public life that are focalised in Brookner's female oeuvre.

In part 2, after a plot summary of *Undue Influence*, the novel's early reception is reviewed. According to critics, the standout problem of the novel is the unwieldy imagination of the female protagonist. The text's themes of walking are almost completely ignored and Claire's tendency to imagine stories about the people around her is blamed for her unmarried state and childless existence.

In part 3, texts by Charles Baudelaire and Harold Bloom's *The Anxiety of Influence* are marshalled to produce the figure of the *flâneur* in *Undue Influence*. Common themes of *The Anxiety of Influence* and *Undue Influence* are illuminated, with special regard paid to how the signifier of 'influence' operates. Bloom contends that '"influence" is a metaphor, one that implicates a matrix of relationships—imagistic, temporal, spiritual, psychological—all of them ultimately defensive in their nature' (*AI*, xxiii). To Bloom, then, influence is a 'menace', the cause of anxiety and a malign yet enabling force which is fought and transformed by imagination: 'the poet, in writing his poem, is forced to see the assertion against influence as being a ritualised quest for identity' (*AI*, 70, 65). In Brookner's work, influence also connotes the use of power to achieve a necessarily subjective result. 'I was aware that I had not behaved well, had, ever since we had met, exerted undue influence', states Claire about her relationship with Martin (*UI*, 198). Drawing on Bloom's depiction of intersubjective relationships between artists, Claire's imagination can be seen as an exercise of power which enables her to confront personal challenges while rejecting conventional relationship outcomes.

9 De Certeau, 'Walking in the City', 106.
10 De Certeau, 'Walking in the City', 106.

In part 4, the performance of the *flâneur* is staged, using what Bloom delineates as the six 'revisionary ratios' that inform the narrative of influence. The performance of the *flâneur* in *Undue Influence* offers an alternative way to narrate intersubjective gender relations that both values female creativity and refuses to reproduce the heterosexual romance as the main story to be told about Brookner's fiction.

Plot Summary and Original Reception

Narrative time in *Undue Influence* commences shortly after the death of Claire's mother and traces a period of personal and professional upheaval for the protagonist. Following a period of grief spent at home in Montagu Mansions, Claire is relieved to return to work in Gower Street. When she encounters a new customer, Martin Gibson, he strikes her as 'remote in time ... visiting from another world' (*UI*, 35). She reveals: 'I wanted to know his story, which I was quite capable of inventing for myself' (*UI*, 32). Claire personally delivers a copy of *Jenny Treibel* to Martin's home in Weymouth Street, where she meets his sick wife Cynthia—'the sort of woman who would have whispered confidences into the dog's ear' (*UI*, 85). Later, Claire and her friend Wiggy return to visit Cynthia, according to Wiggy, 'in the spirit of nineteenth-century ladies visiting stricken cottages' (*UI*, 73). Martin and Cynthia, both individually and as a couple, become the focus of Claire's extensive speculations.

After Cynthia dies, Claire and Martin's relationship accelerates. They embark on a brief sexual relationship, though one marked by the lack of personal and emotional rapport between them. At the same time, Claire faces difficulties at work; while struggling to edit the oblique manuscript of St John Collier's 'Walks with Myself', Hester Collier sustains a fall and the sisters decide to sell the bookshop. The death of Wiggy's neighbour, Eileen Bateman, compounds the mounting sense of tragedy in the novel. Following Martin's successful holiday to Italy and the consequent resurgence in his confidence, Claire plans her own trip to Europe. But, as Claire prepares to leave, Wiggy sights Martin on an evidently romantic shopping trip with Cynthia's former nurse Sue. Claire is shocked by the one romantic outcome she had never imagined.

In the initial reception of *Undue Influence*, critics appear confounded by the text. Eluned Summers-Bremner intuits 'a palpable absence of meaning that is never given form', condemning what she regards as the 'seemingly senseless', 'inexpressible', 'unincorporable', and 'inarticulate' aspects of *Undue Influence*.¹¹ Inger Björkblom is unable to fully parse the significance of Claire's walking, although she broaches an interesting possibility when she notes that 'Claire often spends time walking in parks just to make time pass—could this be a resistance to bourgeois utilitarianism?'¹² Cheryl Alexander Malcolm concedes that the way Claire narrates her walks around the cathedral cities of France 'indicates a significance beyond what may be obvious' but neglects to elucidate further.¹³ Some critics suggest the text's vigorous intertextuality may imply alternative meanings. Wendy Steiner claims that Claire 'affects the brave independence of the Baudelairean *flâneuse*', but is unable to expand on the hermeneutic possibilities that such an insight could entail.¹⁴ Eileen Williams-Wanquet details a number of intertextual references in *Undue Influence*, but her conclusion that all these references merely function to 'teach a moral lesson through their poetic justice' anchors Brookner's representational strategy to a moral didacticism.¹⁵ Thus does Williams-Wanquet's criticism restage the nineteenth-century clash between female conventional moral didacticism and male experimental avant-garde practice that informs the way in which Brookner is designated a personal, women's writer, and therefore not an aestheticist.

Despite the text's ambiguity, many commentators fall back on old habits of analysis that inexorably reduce the plot to one of a failed heterosexual romance. As such, Malcolm concludes that '*Undue Influence* is the story of a twenty-nine-year-old shop clerk who falls in love with one of her customers'.¹⁶ In *World Literature Today*, Mary Kaiser similarly asserts that 'the novel revolves around Claire's gradual recognition that her sexual liberation has made her more a victim than a predator'.¹⁷ In *Booklist*, Donna Seaman claims the text is 'about the ongoing battle of the sexes'.¹⁸ As becomes habitual in Brookner's reception, where her particular identification as a women's writer prioritises heterosexual romance over creative experimentation, critics frame the text through

11 Eluned Summers-Bremner, 'Love's Pleasure, Love's Pain', *Dalhousie Review* 84.3 (August 2004): 455.
12 Björkblom, *Plane of Uncreatedness*, 131.
13 Malcolm, *Understanding Anita Brookner*, 196.
14 Steiner, 'She Who Won't Be Obeyed', 34.
15 Williams-Wanquet, *Art and Life in the Novels of Anita Brookner*, 162.
16 Malcolm, *Understanding Anita Brookner*, 191.
17 Mary Kaiser, 'Undue Influence', *World Literature Today* 74.3 (2000): 592.
18 Donna Seaman, 'Undue Influence', *Booklist* (15 October 1999): 394.

the heterosexual romance narrative, decry the behaviour of the female protagonist, and subsequently puzzle over the relevance of Brookner's contribution to the literary field.

In failing the expectations of the heterosexual romance narrative, Claire bears the burden of critical outrage. Across various reviews, she is condemned as 'repellently mean-spirited', 'chilly, distant and self-deluded', and 'deeply flawed'.[19] Claire's performance of femininity conflicts with the type of gender behaviour that critics perceive as appropriate within the moment of the text's production in the late 1990s: 'how can this still be the way of the world at the end of the twentieth century?' asks Steiner.[20] Criticism of Claire's evidently non-normative gender performance effectively generates a contrasting portrait of desirable and normative contemporary femininity. Assumptions about the significance of Claire's female gender presuppose an analogous emphasis on the importance of Martin Gibson as a potential male partner in the novel. For Malcolm, for instance, Claire's attitude towards Martin is tantamount to an 'adoration [as] all-consuming as religious ecstasy'.[21] As a result, Claire's gendered first-person narrative is co-opted into the representational structure of the heterosexual romance that produces its successful female and male protagonists along a before-and-after, chronological, and developmental sequence of coupling and reproduction.

In the absence of a successful conclusion to the heterosexual romance narrative, the critical consensus is that the chief factor sabotaging Claire's heterosexual performance is her imagination. Malcolm states that Claire 'lives surreptitiously through other people, as if their lives were as accessible as the books that surround her ... she treats people as she does books ... people are only known to this protagonist on a surface level'.[22] Steiner maintains that both Brookner and Claire are 'cynical

---

19 Steiner, 'She Who Won't Be Obeyed', 34; Melody A. Moxley, 'Undue Influence', *Library Journal* 125.13 (2000): 182; Malcolm, *Understanding Anita Brookner*, 191.
20 Steiner, 'She Who Won't Be Obeyed', 34; similarly, Kaiser (wrongly) concludes that, though the novel 'seems contemporary, it must be set in the 1960s'. Kaiser, 'Undue Influence', 592; and, further, Williams-Wanquet states that in both *Undue Influence* and *The Bay of Angels*, 'the heroines Claire and Zoë are liberated young women belonging to later generations, yet both react like older women and have a panoramic vision of the second half of the century'. Williams-Wanquet, *Art and Life in the Novels of Anita Brookner*, 55.
21 Malcolm, *Understanding Anita Brookner*, 194.
22 Malcolm, *Understanding Anita Brookner*, 191–95.

women with overstrained imaginations'.[23] And Williams-Wanquet laments that Claire's narrative 'has little relation to reality'.[24] Deemed 'tragic', 'depressing', 'odd', and 'strange', Claire courts disapproval precisely because her imagination is held to prevent the attainment of heterosexual romance, which is conflated with reality for contemporary women.[25] 'Claire has no one', Malcolm explains.[26] By representing Claire's imagination as a threat to her femininity and, therefore, her chance at heterosexual coupling, critics implicitly construct contemporary femininity as that which prioritises heterosexual reproduction over imagination and creativity. In this way, at the very time when the female imagination becomes a subject for direct appraisal, critics once again revert to the organising dichotomies between woman and artist and the feminised romance and the masculinised aesthetic culture that disavows and trivialises women's representational practices and results in Brookner's devaluation in the literary field, all the while creating a generic authority around the practices of the male writer–artist.

Producing the Figure of the *Flâneur*

In *The Genius of the Future*, Brookner emphasises the significance of the imagination to Baudelaire. She quotes from his *Salon of 1859*.

> How mysterious is imagination, that Queen of the Faculties! It touches all the others; it rouses them and sends them into combat. At times it resembles them to the point of confusion, and yet it is always itself, and those men who are not quickened by it are easily recognisable by some strange curse which withers their productions like the fig-tree in the Gospel. It is both analysis and synthesis ... It is Imagination that first taught man the moral meaning of colour, of contour, of sound and of scent. In the beginning of the world it created analogy and metaphor. It decomposes all creation, and with the raw materials accumulated and disposed in accordance with rules whose origins one cannot find save in the furthest depths of the soul, it creates a new world, it produces the sensation of newness. Since it has created the world (so much can be said, I think, even in a religious sense), it is proper that it should govern it. (*GF*, 68–69)

---

23 Steiner, 'She Who Won't Be Obeyed', 34.
24 Williams-Wanquet, *Art and Life in the Novels of Anita Brookner*, 186.
25 Seaman, 'Undue Influence', 394; Ron Charles, 'Undue Influence', *Christian Science Monitor* (27 January 2000): 17; Williams-Wanquet, *Art and Life in the Novels of Anita Brookner*, 186; Summers-Bremner, 'Love's Pleasure, Love's Pain', 443.
26 Malcolm, *Understanding Anita Brookner*, 195.

For Baudelaire, then, imagination is the core component of creative subjectivity. Imagination distinguishes artists from mortals; it is the very substance of creative existence and artistic practice; it enables the charting of new worlds; and, indeed, is responsible for the creation and control of the world. Analogous to his opposition between woman and the dandy, Baudelaire's imaginative subject is also implicitly male, and antithetical to the female 'creature', whom he says 'is perhaps only incomprehensible because it has nothing to communicate' (*PML*, 30). In this way, Baudelaire's proselytising of the imagination is implicated more broadly in the nineteenth-century specification of creative genius around the figure of the male artist.

In his chapter on modernity in *The Painter of Modern Life*, Baudelaire characterises the archetype of the zeitgeist as a 'solitary, gifted with an active imagination, ceaselessly journeying across this great human desert' (*PML*, 12). In *Romanticism and Its Discontents*, Brookner frames imagination as the salient feature of *The Painter of Modern Life*:

> undoubtedly Baudelaire's most memorable utterance on the business of creative imagination is *Le Peintre de la Vie Moderne*, in which painting is hardly mentioned at all. This is nominally a report on the work of Constantin Guys, referred to throughout as 'MG', out of deference to Guys's desire for anonymity. It is a device that serves him well, for it enables him to take over Guys's work in a way that he was never quite permitted to do with regard to Delacroix. (*RD*, 73)

To organise his philosophy of the contemporary, enacted by the 'solitary with an active imagination', Baudelaire mobilises two key male figures who merge in *The Painter of Modern Life*. First is the painter Constantin Guys, or MG, a man whose work suggests a 'pure poetic hypothesis, conjecture, a labour of the imagination' (*PML*, 6). Guys's impressionistic sketches of contemporary scenes satisfy Baudelaire's desire to capture the modern in the historical, while, as Brookner notes, Guys himself primarily operates as a Baudelairean rhetorical device. The other figure is the *flâneur*—the peripatetic poet who can creatively evoke the zeitgeist through portraits produced by his urban journeying:

> Observer, philosopher, *flâneur*—call him what you will; but whatever words you use in trying to define this kind of artist, you will certainly be led to bestow upon him some adjective which you could not apply to the painter of the eternal, or at least more lasting things, of heroic or religious subjects. Sometimes he is a poet; more often he comes closer to the novelist or the

moralist; he is the painter of the passing moment and all of the suggestions of eternity that it contains. (*PML*, 4–5)

In Baudelaire's representation, the *flâneur* is constituted both through the imagination—the creative drive which transmutes the historical moment into an aesthetic object—and through the peripatetic energy that fuels the way knowledge is creatively produced in the metropolis. In embodying the symbiosis between walking and writing, Baudelaire's peripatetic poet pre-empts de Certeau's apprehension of a homology between walking and imagination in 'Walking in the City'.[27]

Bloom reaffirms the status of the male imagination in nineteenth-century Romanticism in *The Anxiety of Influence*. Producing a 'genealogy of imagination', Bloom pitches his theory about the fight for cultural supremacy—between artists and texts—as a 'battle between strong equals, father and son as mighty opposites, Laius and Oedipus at the crossroads' (*AI*, 117, 11). Contending that every poet suffers an anxiety or 'fear that no proper work remains for him to perform', Bloom frames imagination as the saving vice of the Romantic poet and an antidote to the threatened cultural invisibility (*AI*, 148). Bloom plots a 'narrative of influence' that unfolds as the story of a power struggle between the reputation of an established strong poet (the precursor) and the imagination of an upcoming new poet (the ephebe). As a narrative about how meaning is negotiated between texts, Bloom's narrative of influence is also a theory of intertextuality. His contention that 'the meaning of a poem can only be a poem, but *another poem—a poem not itself*' recalls Michael Riffaterre's instruction that intertextuality constitute 'a reference to meaning elsewhere' (*AI*, 70).[28] However, foreshadowing Brookner's general exclusion from an identification with Romantic aestheticism, no female poets appear in Bloom's narrative and his intertextual battle is officially sketched as a relationship between generations of men. 'We remember how for so many centuries, from the sons of Homer to the sons of Ben Johnson, poetic influence has been described as a filial relationship', Bloom pronounces, outlining the tussle between 'the strong poet and the Poetic Father' (*AI*, 11, 28, 44). For Bloom, imagination is serious, important, esteemed, relevant—a signifier of masculine strength and authority. 'Poets write through enthusiasm and imagination. Poets strike out the seeds of knowledge through imagination, and then they shine more bright',

27 De Certeau, 'Walking in the City', 100.
28 Michael Riffaterre, 'Syllepsis', *Critical Inquiry* 6.4 (1980), 627.

Bloom proclaims (*AI*, 40). 'Weaker talents idealise; figures of capable imagination appropriate for themselves'; and: 'To be in imaginative need is to be in poverty' (*AI*, 5, 141). As such, the male creative imagination absolves behaviour that would otherwise be deemed morally questionable: 'Strong poets ... should always be condemned by a humanist morality'. 'The more delusive, the stronger the imagination, the stronger the poem', Bloom asserts. 'What the strong poet, like the solipsist, *means* is right, for this egocentricity is itself a major training in imagination. Every narrowing of the circumference is compensated for by the poetic illusion (a delusion, and yet a strong poem) that the centre therefore will hold better' (*AI*, 85, 121).

In *Undue Influence*, Brookner portrays her young, contemporary, female protagonist, Claire Pitt, in the manner previously evoked by Baudelaire—as 'a solitary walker' gifted with an active 'imagination' (*UI*, 9, 91). Claire's imagination is triggered by her vocational walking. 'Mostly I walked, speculating on the people I passed, on the conversations I overheard. These are the consolations of the solitary walker, and the habit has stayed with me', as Claire puts it (*UI*, 9).[29] She self-identifies as a 'mental stalker' who engages in the 'construction' of stories about those around her (*UI*, 13, 71). Described as 'a resource, an endowment, even a gift', Claire's 'aberrant imagination' is galvanised by random strangers, casual acquaintances, her employers, her family, and, once, the owner of a pair of abandoned men's shoes in the street (*UI*, 176, 91).[30] Invoking a spectrum of artist–signifiers that reconstitute the performance of nineteenth-century creative and subversive masculinity delineated in Baudelaire and Bloom, Claire describes herself as on 'the outer margin' with a 'hazardous world view', an 'unreliable witness' who 'from time to time, courted danger' and has a 'bad character' (*UI*, 47, 47, 9, 90, 97). Claire's 'unclassifiability' likewise complements Bloom's

---

29 In addition to *The Painter of Modern Life*, a great Romantic walker precursor text is Jean-Jacques Rousseau's *Reveries of the Solitary Walker* (1782). In *Romanticism and Its Discontents*, Brookner refers to Rousseau as 'often invoked almost automatically as the patron saint of the [Romantic] movement' (*RD*, 8). See Jean-Jacques Rousseau, *Reveries of the Solitary Walker*, trans. Peter France (Harmondsworth: Penguin, 1979).

30 Claire's ability to use fragments of information to piece together stories about strangers also suggests that James's 1898 novella, *In the Cage*, featuring a London telegraphist who reconstructs the lives of service-users from the sensitive details to which she is exposed, might be useful for an intertextual study of *Undue Influence*. See Henry James, *The Turn of the Screw* (Harmondsworth: Penguin, 1946).

insistence that, 'a poet's stance, his Word, his imaginative identity, his whole being, *must* be unique, or he will perish, as a poet' (*AI*, 71). She also possesses that 'dangerously unhealthy attitude' which Bloom praises as conditioning the ephebe's rebellion against the precursor: 'heath is stasis' (*UI*, 24; *AI*, 95). Bloom's insistence that 'Great poetry necessarily tells lies, fictions essential to literary art' complements Claire's own self-appraisal: 'I knew my character was poor, that I could lay claim to few moral qualities' (*AI*, xix; *UI*, 37). In conceding that she has 'left simple rationality quite a long way behind' and remarking 'I had little experience of normal work' (*UI*, 46, 95), Claire possesses the attributes of dysfunction and non-normative behaviour that condition the poetic character. Claire also rejects an association with normative femininity as embodied by Cynthia Gibson and nurse Sue. 'Both she and her patient were in some sense female and more female than I was', Claire observes (*UI*, 83). Like Bloom's casting of the strong poet in the role of Satan, where he states that 'there is the state called Satan, and in that hardness poets must appropriate for themselves', Brookner's practice of totemistic naming costumes 'Claire Pitt' in a similar guise to connote the burning pits of hell (*AI*, 32). Across a spectrum of transgressive signifiers, Claire's bad behaviour contradicts the stereotype of Brooknerines as polite, passive creatures. Indeed, Claire's behaviour, along with many other Brooknerines, including Rachel from *A Friend from England* and Julia from *Brief Lives*, can be seen to fit within Bloom's definition of the artistic temperament which incorporates 'a complex critical matrix in which the notions of indolence, solitude, originality, imitation and invention are most strangely mixed' (*AI*, 37).

In *The Painter of Modern Life*, Baudelaire installs a reversal at the heart of the *flâneur*'s ascension to subjectivity. In the first instance, he frames a practice of self-obfuscation as a key component in the production of an aesthetic identity by praising the way in which M.G. signs his work without a signature: 'Not a single one of his drawings is signed, if by signature you mean that string of easily forgeable characters which spell a name and which so many other artists affix ostentatiously at the foot of their least important trifles' (*PML*, 5). Next, Baudelaire celebrates the way in which M.G. ostensibly desires anonymity. He claims that 'when he learnt that I had it in mind to write an appreciation of his mind and his talent, he begged me ... to suppress his name, and if I must speak of his works, to speak of them as if they were those of an anonymous artist' (*PML*, 5). Thus Baudelaire promises to 'humbly comply with this singular request. The reader and I will preserve the fiction that Monsieur

G. does not exist' (*PML*, 5). In this rhetorical reversal, Baudelaire's undertaking to remove M.G. from the scene of identity is the very action that performs M.G.'s identity. Subsequently, Baudelaire profiles the *flâneur* as an '"I" with an insatiable appetite for the "non-I"' (*PML*, 9). In this case, the dissimulating dispersal of the ego is the action which, by a reverse movement, effectively produces the poetic subject. This reverse narrative of subjectification functions analogously to the metaleptic prolepsis underwriting the construction of the aesthete in Chapter 2. These anti-chronological movements provide alternatives to the developmental narrative that prepares hetero-chronic subjectivity.

In Bloom, the narrative of intertextual influence always comprises a mode of reversal that he describes as a misreading. Maintaining that 'to imagine is to misinterpret', Bloom states that '[p]oetic Influence … always proceeds by a misreading of the prior poet, an act of creative correction that is actually and necessarily a misinterpretation' (*AI*, 30). Detailing what constitutes an epistemological shift between texts, Bloom uses the motif of the swerve to characterise the way in which poetic reversal functions. He argues that the poet 'swerves away from his precursor … This appears as a corrective movement in his own poem, which implies that the precursor poem went accurately up to a certain point, but then should have swerved, precisely in the direction that the new poem moves' (*AI*, 14). For Bloom, this 'upwards fall' constitutes a type of 'repetition both undone and dialectically affirmed' (*AI*, 104, 83). The poetic reversal designates a movement between artists and texts that is rendered on both biographical and historical planes. On the biographical level, Bloom commands the poet to 'quest antithetically enough, and live to beget yourself' (*AI*, 79). He echoes Baudelaire's formulation of the 'self avid for non-self' when he maintains that: '"Be me but not me" is the paradox of the precursor's implicit charge to the ephebe. Less intensely, his poem says to its descendent poem: "Be like me but unlike"' (*AI*, 70). On the historical plane, poetic reversal enacts a paradigm shift in which the strength of the new poet's misreading gives the impression that the precursor poem has actually been influenced by him. '[W]here it, the precursor's poem, is there let my poem be', Bloom instructs (*AI*, 80). When this is the outcome, Bloom maintains 'all of them achieve a style that captures and oddly retains priority over their precursors, so that the tyranny of time almost is overturned, and one can believe, for startled moments, that they are being *imitated by their ancestors*' dramatically characterising the misreading as a chronological and familial reversal (*AI*, 140). As the privileged mechanism of the intertextual relationship,

Bloom's theory of misreading and reversal reflects the potential of the figure of the *flâneur* to be a source of transgression, even against its originating male precursors.

In *Undue Influence*, the fictional dimension of Claire's imagination means that her speculations are constantly the source of misreadings. As she herself acknowledges, her narratives are 'fantasies', 'illusory', and 'inaccurate' (*UI*, 20, 27, 32). 'Naturally it was likely that none of this was true' is a common refrain in the text (*UI*, 3). Claire's imagined narratives therefore encompass a belated qualification, retraction, or reversal. 'I was forced to abandon the story I had told myself about her. Sometimes connections are misleading', she says (*UI*, 3). 'It was not the first time I had been guilty of a misapprehension' (*UI*, 5). 'Misconceptions are inevitable' (*UI*, 9), she further reflects. Mapping the reverse direction of her imagination from a projected point of origin, as well as transmutations of movement, plot, and interpretation, Claire's literal and figurative wanderings reconstitute the reversals designated by Baudelaire and Bloom. On the level of story events in *Undue Influence*, reversals characterise Claire's reading of Martin Gibson, as well as her walks to work and back from Montagu Mansions to Gower Street, and their suspension after her employment ends, and the failure of the 'Walks with Myself' project. On the level of interpretation, reversals characterise the way in which the figure of the *flâneur* in *Undue Influence* writes back to the masculinist appropriation of imagination, influence, and intertextuality.

The Goncourt brothers, Brookner's precursors in Romantic aestheticism, describe Constantin Guys's movement through the streets as a type of 'zigzagging' that complements the artist's narrative style (*PML*, 10 n. 1). In a passage that visually and discursively invokes the move of swerve and reversal, the Goncourts portray Guys as

> A little man with an animated face, a grey moustache, looking like an old soldier; hobbling along, constantly hitching up his sleeves on his bony arms with a sharp slap of the hand, diffuse, exuberant with parentheses, zigzagging from idea to idea, going off at tangents and getting lost, but retrieving himself and regaining your attention with a metaphor from the gutter, a word from the vocabulary of the German philosophers, a technical term from art or industry, and always holding you under the thrall of his highly-coloured, almost *visible* utterance. (*PML*, 10 n. 1)

As a tracking of the backward–forward motion in both form and content, the zigzagging swerve also underscores how the figure of reversal constitutes what de Certeau explains as 'a homology between verbal figures and the figures of walking'.[31] Therefore, in delineating reversal as the organising rhetorical mode of misreading and influence, the figure of peripeteia is nominated as the representative rhetorical term for the peripatetic *flâneur*. Gerald Prince defines peripeteia as:

> The inversion (REVERSAL) from one state of affairs to its opposite. For example, an action seems destined for success but suddenly moves toward failure, or vice versa. According to Aristotle, peripety (PERIPETEIA) is, along with RECOGNITION (ANAGNORISIS) the most potent means of ensuring the tragic effect.[32]

On the symbolic plane, the peripeteiac reversal traces the peripatetic tracks of the *flâneur*'s movement through the imaginary plane of the text's city and the city's text.

In Bloom's text, the reversals staged through the narrative of influence contest the regulation of subjectivity through normative behavioural codes, familial affiliation, and chronological determinism to implicitly figure the narrative of influence as a queer narrative.[33] Specifically, Bloom links the discourse of perversion historically used to trope homosexuality to the peripeteiac reversals of the narrative of influence. In a move that valorises perversion as a necessary component of the poet's artillery, Bloom states:

> strong poets necessarily are perverse, 'necessarily' here meaning as if obsessed, as if manifesting repetition compulsion. 'Perverse' literally means 'to be turned the wrong way' but to be turned the right way in regard to the precursor means not to swerve at all, so any bias or inclination perforce must be perverse in *relation to the precursor*, unless context itself (such as one's own surrounding literary orthodoxy) allows one to be *an avatar of the perverse*, as the French line Baudelaire–Mallarmé–Valery was of Poe, or Frost of Emerson. To swerve (Anglo-Saxon *sweorfan*) has a root meaning of 'to wipe off, file down, or polish', and, in usage, 'to deviate, to leave the straight line, to turn aside (from law, duty, custom)'. (*AI*, 85)

---

31 De Certeau, 'Walking in the City', 100.
32 Gerald Prince, *A Dictionary of Narratology* (Lincoln: University of Nebraska Press, 1987), 70.
33 Tuite asserts that Bloom's 'anxiety of influence is strictly masculine, Oedipal, and homosocial'. Clara Tuite, 'Decadent Austen Entails: Forster, James, Firbank, and the "Queer Tale" of *Sanditon* (comp. 1817, publ. 1925)', in *Janeites: Austen's Disciples and Devotees*, ed. Deidre Lynch (Princeton, NJ: Princeton University Press, 2000), 121.

In tying the swerve to perversion, and deviation to the zig-zag patterning, Bloom annexes tropes of successful creative behaviour to queer performativity. And, in classifying Baudelaire as 'an avatar of the perverse', Bloom underscores the French poet's location in the queer canon.

For Bloom, the narrative of influence leverages the perverse mentality of the poet against the Freudian family romance. 'Poetry is the anxiety of influence, is misprision, is a disciplined perverseness. Poetry is misunderstanding, misinterpretation, misalliance. Poetry (Romance) is Family Romance' (*AI*, 95). Where 'Romantic Love' is the ideological presentation of the heterosexual romance narrative, Bloom's narrative of influence reverses the direction of the heterosexual romance. He contends: 'Romantic Love is the closest analogue of Poetic Influence, another splendid perversity of the spirit, though it moves precisely in the opposite direction' (*AI*, 31). In sketching his influence narrative, Bloom entreats 'to centre upon intra-poetic relationships as parallels of family romance' (*AI*, 7). The intertextual genealogy that Bloom delineates as the substantive content of the narrative of influence provides an alternative narrative to the hetero-chronic bias of the Freudian family romance. In this way, the production of the *flâneur* through a narrative of influence renders the figure's movement through the text as an act of queer performativity.

In *Undue Influence*, discourses of walking and imagination that produce the figure of the *flâneur* also operate as tropes for modes of non-normative or queer sexual desire. Claire's walking holidays in Chartres, Amiens, Bourges, Strasbourg, Vienne, Autun, Troyes, Le Mans, Dijon, Coutances, and Rouen are occasions where 'minor adventures may or may not take place' (*UI*, 13). She refers to her 'not quite innocent holidays in cathedral cities, making opportunities for myself which now seemed to me equally shameful' and later admits to being 'tired of those buccaneering excursions, tired of ecclesiastical details and then less than ecclesiastical behaviour in which I indulged' (*UI*, 21, 130).[34] Likewise, Claire is disappointed by 'the increasing

---

34 In *Romanticism and Its Discontents*, Brookner outlines how the Romantic philosophers, led by Rousseau, provided an alternative to Christian doctrine. 'The attempt to codify a new morality free from orthodox Christian dogma was pursued by a number of men who gradually took on the allure of lay preachers, and of these the greatest and most famous was Jean-Jacques Rousseau' (*RD*, 9). Through the vernacular of a Rousseauan walker, then, Claire's adventures in cathedral cities further signify a detour from the gender roles and reproductive narratives as defined by the Christian church.

wordlessness, or decreasing wordiness' of St John Collier's signature text 'Walks with Myself'—a state that is subsequently explained when she discovers a secret sexual tryst. After finding the last page of Collier's manuscript glued to the back cover of the notebook, Claire steams the leaves apart to uncover '[i]n tiny writing, on the ultimate page ... the words, "I cannot go on", and a name, Agnes' (*UI*, 96). The revelation that Collier's walks were part of a dissimulation strategy to cover an illicit sexual affair further dramatises walking as an eroticised pursuit in *Undue Influence*. In *Fortune in Men's Eyes*, Dewey Ganzel points out that 'John Collier' was also the name of a notorious nineteenth-century Shakespearean forger.[35] As such, intertextual indications between the nineteenth-century Collier and Brookner's Collier suggest the two men have a common investment in dissimulating fictional texts that underscore the contingent nature of meaning. The trope of walking as an erotic and symbolic pursuit in *Undue Influence* suggests alternative forms for thinking about desire in the text and challenges the wisdom of mobilising the heterosexual romance narrative as the methodological tool for interpreting Brookner's novel.

The fantasising aspect of Claire's imagination also imbues her narrative with sexual content. 'I indulged in a little make-believe, of which I was mildly ashamed', Claire confesses (*UI*, 130). After an evening speculating on the relationship between Cynthia and Martin Gibson, she reveals: 'Then I went to bed, determined to put the evening out of my mind. In this I partly succeeded' (*UI*, 45). The narrator's allusions to the erotic function of her imagination suggests that it fulfils auto-erotic goals. The text's associations between the eroticised walk and masturbation is reaffirmed in the figure of the glue which binds the pages of Collier's signature text. The auto-erotic tropes of *Undue Influence* coexist alongside Claire's explicit rejection of the heterosexual romance narrative. 'I did not want, had not ever wanted, what is smugly defined as a long term relationship. I had other appetites, other plans', she states (*UI*, 126). In addition to her sexually adventurous walking, Claire's gender-crossing, her masculine ethics, and her unsentimental view of marriage problematises any impetus to neatly resolve the text through the heterosexual romance narrative.

As an alternative methodology, Bloom's narrative of influence provides a developmental plot which traces 'the passing of Individuals through

---

35 Dewey Ganzel, *Fortune in Men's Eyes: The Career of John Payne Collier* (Oxford: Oxford University Press, 1982).

States' and 'the life-cycle of the poet-as-poet'; yet it is simultaneously a narrative of reversal: 'he who lives with continuity cannot be a poet'; and it is also a story about relationships (*AI*, 44, 7, 78). Invoking a walking metaphor to argue that 'Good poets are powerful striders' whose skills necessarily include 'wandering beyond limits', Bloom narrates his theory of 'poetic development' across six 'revisionary ratios' which take their names from Greek and ancient sources: *clinamen*, *tessera*, *kinosis*, *daemonisation*, *askesis*, and *apophrades* (*AI*, 36, 104, 147, 7). As a queer alternative to the heterosexual romance narrative, complete with its own developmental contours, Bloom's narrative of influence also constructs character roles which map an intersubjective relationship between the ephebe and precursor poet. He claims that 'Modern poets are necessarily miserable dualists' and that poetry 'is learned first through the young poet's or ephebe's experience of another poet' (*AI*, 35). Bloom's delineation of actors' roles complements Claire's personality in *Undue Influence*. Over the course of the text, Claire already underscores the constructed dimension of her actions when she describes herself as playing a 'role' (*UI*, 38, 56, 73, 82, 122, 195).

Therefore, based on the production of the *flâneur* around signifiers of imagination, the peripatetic, misreading, peripeteia, and the narrative of influence, Claire is cast in the role of the 'anti-natural' ephebe and Martin as the precursor poet (*AI*, 10). Bloom positions the precursor as the old vanguard elite whose reputation is to be misread and reread in the assault launched by the upcoming strong poet. Like Bloom's strong artist imbued with 'godhood', Claire's early impressions of Martin emphasise his transcendent status (*AI*, 87). Claire imbues Martin with an 'iconic presence' and as representative of the type of outsider and beautiful tragedy embodied by the Romantic artist: 'He was a man torn between achievement and frustration', impeccably groomed but in possession of a 'psychic injury' and available for annexation (*UI*, 31, 36). However, throughout the text, Claire also subjects Martin to an effeminising eroticisation which undermines his 'strong poet' status. Martin is 'A man who was not quite a man … The idea had a perverse appeal', Claire reflects (*UI*, 34). 'Although he looked like a man, and an exceptionally graceful man, he was as sensitive as a girl', she notes (*UI*, 107). Martin's appeal to Claire is enhanced through her perception of him as 'emptied of manhood' (*UI*, 38), 'deprived of manliness' (*UI*, 56), 'subject to coercion' (*UI*, 69), and 'impotent' (*UI*, 38, 72, 107). Rendered through the figure of the *flâneur*, the casting of Claire as ephebe and Martin as precursor poet licenses a range of crossings between nineteenth-century and contemporary modes of temporal and gender normativity which destabilises the narrative of fixed, binary sexual difference underwriting the heterosexual romance and narratives of reproduction. In offering an alternative narrative for thinking about the relationships between subjects, the *flâneur*'s passage along the narrative of influence constitutes a queer intertextual romance.

In *Undue Influence*, there are two occasions when Claire's first-person narrative transfers the authority of self-representation to Martin Gibson. Both times, Martin represents himself through the sign 'M.G.': the signature through which Baudelaire produces the *flâneur* in a movement of reversal in *The Painter of Modern Life*. On the first occasion, Martin leaves a note for Claire on her typewriter at work: 'We should be very happy to see you both on Saturday, if convenient. Kind regards. M.G. Please forgive note' (*UI*, 76). On the second occasion, he sends a card to Claire informing her of his imminent return to London: 'I will be with you on the 15th. Regards M.G.' (*UI*, 183). Bloom emphasises the prestige of the signature when he claims the revisionary ratios comprise 'a unified meditation of the melancholy of the creative mind's desperate insistence upon priority' (*AI*, 13). In rendering the *flâneur* as a hermeneutic figure, 'M.G.' is framed as an intertextual signifier between Baudelaire, Bloom, and Brookner which swerves priority from the masculine imagination connoted in the proper name signifier to appropriate priority through the performance of the feminine in Brookner's oeuvre. In this sense, the production of the *flâneur* across texts by Baudelaire, Bloom, and Brookner can be used to reverse Baudelaire and Bloom *through* Brookner. As the emblematic personae of the narratives of intertextual relations and misreading which negotiate status in the literary field, the *flâneur* represents a key persona for the intertextual project 'Misreading Anita Brookner'. Crossing gendered historical representational practices, and swerving away from a masculinised Romantic aestheticism at the same time as revaluing Brookner's nineteenth-century intertextual practice in the genre of women's writing, the *flâneur* constitutes a metatextual figure who seeks transparency of construction at the same time as reimagining new possibilities for the Brookner text.

Staging the Performance of the *Flâneur*

I Clinamen *or Poetic Misprision*

Harold Bloom frames the first stage of his six revisionary ratios, *clinamen*, as 'poetic misreading or misprision proper' (*AI*, 14). He takes the word '*clinamen*' from Lucretius, 'where it means a "swerve" of the atoms so as to make change possible in the universe' (*AI*, 14). Maintaining that 'strong poets make poetic history by misreading one another, so as to clear imaginative space for themselves', Bloom states:

> The poet so stations his precursor, so swerves his context, that the visionary objects, with their higher intensity, fade into the continuum. The poet has, in regard to the precursor's heterocosm, a shuddering sense of the arbitrary— of the equality, or equal haphazardness, of all objects. This sense is not reductive, for it is the continuum, the stationing context, that is reseen, and shaped into the visionary; it is brought up to the intensity of the crucial objects, which then 'fade' into it. (*AI*, 42)

Responding to the aura of the precursor's legacy, the subjectivisation of the new poet begins only after he swerves the pre-existing context of the precursor's oeuvre. The swerve conditions the misreading which generates the poetic text or imaginative narrative of the ephebe. According to Bloom, this original misreading is a liberating gesture constitutive of the birth of Art.

In *Undue Influence*, Martin Gibson's appearance at the Ex Libris bookshop radiates the 'iconic presence' which Bloom associates with the precursor poet (*UI*, 31). 'He gave an impression of almost futile luxury ... He implied an army of servants ... He was obviously rich, certainly idle. I imagined his empty day, every gesture aiming at sublimity', Claire observes (*UI*, 31). Bloom contends that 'The strong misreading comes first; there must be a profound act of reading that is a *kind of falling in love* with a literary work. That reading is likely to be idiosyncratic, and it is almost certain to be ambivalent, though the ambivalence may be veiled' (*AI*, xix). After Claire's admiring yet conflicted appraisal of Martin, her imaginative misreading gathers pace:

> I wanted to know his story, which I was quite capable of inventing for myself. ... I thought I detected an unhappy home background, an invalid sister to whom he was deeply attached. This selfless sister ... would urge him to go out and enjoy himself. But the poor fellow would be half-hearted in this pursuit, would seek refuges, indeed basements, where his presence would impress but would remain unchallenged. (*UI*, 32)

Therefore, with no knowledge of Martin's life and only her observations to fuel her imagination, Claire begins to create a narrative about Martin which she fills with family characters, psychic dispositions, and plot structure. Read as a performance of *clinamen*, Claire's initial imaginative misreading of Martin constitutes a visionary construction of the objects around him and enables Claire to establish a (poetic) dialogue with him. The imaginary status of Claire's narrative ensures she is constantly able to adjust the details as she desires: 'I altered my estimate of him. He was a dilettante, a caste I had always admired' (*UI*, 32). Her portrait of Martin stimulates further imaginary conversations she holds with him. 'Your sympathy is quite adequate, I should have said; do not allow it to become excessive. Vulnerability is commendable; masochism is not', she imagines herself saying (*UI*, 36). The interdependence between Claire's imagination and her misreadings emphasise the poetic status of Claire's narrative. 'I had no way of knowing how accurate or inaccurate this picture was', Claire admits, while the subsequent unveiling of Martin's reality both underscores the extent of Claire's swerve and conditions further opportunities for her misreadings throughout the text.

II Tessera *or Completion and Antithesis*

Bloom names the second phase of the poetic quest '*tessera*': 'from the ancient mystery cults, where it meant a token of recognition, the fragment say of a small pot, which with the other fragments would reconstitute the vessel' (*AI*, 14). Invoking a process of reconstitution via fragmentation, Bloom's *tessera* describes misreading as a form of bricolage in which different components of historical texts are brought together to reconstitute a new textual object. Therefore, *tessera* also defines the methodological process deployed throughout this book, where narrative fragments of nineteenth-century Romantic aestheticism are reconstituted in the vessel of Brookner's twentieth-century fictions. Rendered as a process of completion and antithesis, Bloom states that 'in the *tessera*, the later poet provides what his imagination tells him would complete the otherwise "truncated" precursor poem and poet, a "completion" that is as much misprision as a revisionary swerve is' (*AI*, 66). The *tessera* is thus a further form of misreading, which, in developing the momentum established in the *clinamen*, simultaneously enhances the authority of the ephebe.

When Claire visits Martin at Weymouth Street, she discovers the truth about one of her early misreadings: '[i]t was not his sister who was the invalid. It was his wife' (*UI*, 37). Claire's penetration of Martin's domestic realm, and, through this, the introduction of Martin's sick wife Cynthia to the story, provide further material for Claire's imagination. Claire imbues Cynthia with the qualities of the *femme fatale*: she is malicious, manipulative, infantile, precocious, and deceitful. As Claire develops her tale about Cynthia, she invents for the other woman a rich and spoilt background, a powerful philanthropic family, and a self-involved, insecure, jealous, and predatory character which is deployed in the destruction of Martin's career. 'I was making this up, of course, but it struck me as entirely feasible', Claire reveals. 'I doubt this had ever taken place' (*UI*, 44, 70).

Claire's imaginative misreading of Cynthia and the Gibsons stimulates a new round of speculation about Martin. In this particular narrative, Claire intensifies her effeminising of Martin. Formerly having admired Martin in the bookshop, 'he seemed now to be reduced to a sort of servant' (*UI*, 38). In fact, Claire begins to view him as 'deprived of manliness' and 'a man subject to coercion', asking herself, '[w]hat demons did he exorcize by constant service to others? What self-denial, what self-abnegation did he consider to be required of him?' (*UI*, 56, 69, 66). Claire supplies the answer herself: '[t]his was my construction, and it pleased me' (*UI*, 71). Propelling Martin along a gender-crossing, Claire's effeminising of him draws on a language of cultural taboos which complements Bloom's *tessera*. Bloom insists that, 'The quester, who finds all space filled with his precursor's vision, resorts to the language of taboo, so as to clear a mental space for himself' (*AI*, 66). Diminished by disappointment, Martin and Cynthia become, in Claire's eyes, 'tragic figures, whose pleas must be heard at a higher court. They were not simply solipsists, they were soliloquists, drawn together in a fateful bond which demanded witnesses. There was no room, there was no *place*, for outsiders ... This was truly a remarkable union' (*UI*, 73). The fact that Cynthia's death not long afterwards leaves Claire so 'enormously, even disproportionately shocked' is testament to the degree of her misreading of the Gibsons (*UI*, 83).

In *Undue Influence*, Claire's extended misreading of Martin and Cynthia produces a bigger story about the Gibsons, which is also wrong. Imbuing Martin with weakness, Claire assumes an obverse position of authority which brings with it the need 'to impose the realities of life' on him (*UI*, 36). For Bloom, the *tessera* enacts a 'reductiveness', which is 'a kind of misprision that is a radical misinterpretation in which the precursor is regarded as an over-idealiser' (*AI*, 69). The new dynamic involves a type of 'correcting', Bloom states: '[a]s the poets swerve downwards in time, they deceive themselves into believing they are tougher-minded than their precursors' (*AI*, 69). The antithetical relationship created between weakness and strength enables the narrator to confidently forge ahead with her poetic quest.

III Kenosis *or Repetition and Discontinuity*

The ephebe's misreading swerve aims to rupture an over-determining dialectic between past and present, thus *kenosis* constitutes 'a movement towards discontinuity with the precursor' (*AI*, 14). Bloom takes the term from St Paul, 'where it means the humbling or emptying-out of Jesus by himself' (*AI*, 14). The *kenosis* performs a reversal which moves away from the epistemological authority of the precursor poet.

> *Kenosis* or 'emptying', [is] at once an 'undoing' and an 'isolating' movement of the imagination … In strong poets, the *kenosis* is a revisionary act in which an 'emptying' or 'ebbing' takes place *in relation to the precursor*. This 'emptying' is a liberating discontinuity, and makes possible a kind of poem that a simple repetition of the precursor's afflatus or godhood could not allow.

The stage of *kenosis*, then, mobilises discontinuity as a method for resisting the hegemonic reproduction of epistemological formations. De Certeau similarly references a form of *kenosis* when he describes the effect of walking practices on the street's proper names. 'Linking acts and footsteps, opening meanings and directions, these words operate in the name of an emptying-out and wearing-away of their primary role'.[36] The emptying of *kenosis* pre-empts the constitution of a new cultural authority.

Multiple scenes in *Undue Influence* follow a similar trajectory in which Claire and Martin converse at the same time as which Claire's internal dialogue creates another, secondary, narrative. The overall effect is that two different and disconnected narratives occur simultaneously. Following Cynthia's death, Martin emerges at Ex Libris where he bombards Claire with his memories about his wife: 'When I met her I thought I had never really looked at a woman before. She was so feminine, had such an awareness of me!' he tells the narrator (*UI*, 106). While audience to Martin's reminiscing, Claire holds a separate discussion in her head in which she imagines how Cynthia's insecure and competitive nature would have had an emasculating effect on

---

36 De Certeau, 'Walking in the City', 105.

Martin and derailed his academic career. The moral scope of Claire's speculations are unlimited, just as Bloom maintains that the 'strong imagination comes to its painful birth through savagery and misinterpretation' (*AI*, 86). Thus, Claire decides that Martin 'no longer had the resources of his work to comfort him, for like the clever creature that she was and remained to the end Cynthia would have seen that his work was her enemy'; thus, Claire concludes, 'they had both been unhappy' (*UI*, 108, 109). Claire acknowledges the role of her imagination in her narrativising: 'I told myself that I knew nothing of his life, that my own construction had entirely taken over from facts' (*UI*, 109).

However, in addition to the misreading, discontinuity is also enforced by the degree to which Claire withholds her own version of events from Martin. 'Naturally I said none of this', Claire reports. 'I was there to help him to rearrange his story' (*UI*, 111, 111). The process is repeated in the following chapter when Martin is overcome by 'relentless nostalgia' at a Covent Garden restaurant (*UI*, 126). Martin's self-absorption leaves Claire picking at various facts to reanimate her imagination. '"What was Cynthia's background?" I inquired, anxious to define this matter' (*UI*, 125). The disconnection between the couple prevents Claire from discussing Wiggy's neighbour's death and fuels further internal dialogue: 'I was feeling extraordinarily unhappy', Claire admits, as she recognises that 'the idea of exchange was what was noticeably absent' (*UI*, 123, 123). 'This evening was a palpable failure', she eventually determines (*UI*, 124). This disconnection is maintained at a subsequent dinner at Claire's flat when Martin acknowledges, '"I've been very selfish, talking about myself. Now, what about you? I know hardly anything about you"' (*UI*, 147). However, Claire refuses the opportunity to re-establish a connection, instead musing to herself how '[t]his was a little failing he had shared with Cynthia, but now was hardly the time to tell him so. In fact it was the one thing I should never remark upon' (*UI*, 147). In stereotyping Martin and letting him continue undeterred, Claire manages to intensify the state of *kenosis*.

Bloom states that in *kenosis* 'the poet falls or ebbs into a space and time that confine him, even as he undoes the precursor's pattern by a deliberate, willed loss in continuity. His stance *appears* to be that of his precursor … but the meaning of the stance is undone; the stance is emptied of its priority, which is a kind of godhood, and the poet holding it becomes more isolated, not only from his fellows, but from the continuity of his own self' (*AI*, 90). For their final dinner at Montagu Mansions, Martin oppresses Claire with stories of his holiday while Claire supplies the conventional responses. 'It sounds marvellous', she says. 'Good weather?' (*UI*, 184, 184). In this scene, Claire is trapped in the details of Martin's representations while her comments reinforce his reality: she is confined in time and space and her stance reflects his stance. However, Claire's internal narrative tells another story and runs for over three pages. She reveals, '[o]ur exchanges were not half so fascinating as the conversation I was having with him in my head' (*UI*, 185).

> Listen, Martin, I was saying. Let me tell you about yourself. ... You lack empathy. ... Everything you say—are saying—is of an extreme banality. ... You find it more comfortable to operate under restraint. When Cynthia was alive you were dutiful ... I will not ask you how you feel, because you would not tell me. Your masochism, or perhaps it would be kinder to call it your impermeability, supplied your psychic needs. ...
>
> What I am saying is politically incorrect in the highest degree. ... Your apparent virginity is your strongest suit. The more untouched a man appears to be the stronger the temptation to touch him, not only physically but emotionally. ...
>
> It might also surprise you to know that when you are with me I feel lonely. Are we not two civilized grown-ups? Perhaps only one of us is civilized, and I can't yet decide which of us it is. You dismiss my complicity as unwomanly, not quite up to your cloudy standards. This gives you permission to be quite ruthless, in a way that once surprised me, but no longer does. No doubt you see me as a fallen creature: as I say, my transactions are simple. What I perhaps understand, as you do not, is that it is your behaviour that is aberrant, rather than mine. ... I am left with the feeling that I have comprehensively failed ...
>
> Naturally I said none of this. (*UI*, 185–87)

Both in form and content, therefore, Claire's imaginary narrative overwhelms and undermines Martin's holiday tales, emptying him of priority and making him appear increasingly irrelevant. By engaging in communication with Martin at the same time as which she conceals her own dialogue, Claire both fakes and breaks a dialectic with him. She invisibly relieves herself of the role his narrative demands of her, instead channelling her authentic narrative and imagination into an internal dialogue. By refusing to share herself as an imaginative subject, and by maintaining separation between her dialogue and Martin's, Claire prioritises discontinuity over the social conventions of reciprocity and intimacy romanticised in the heterosexual romance.

IV Daemonisation *or the Counter-Sublime*
Daemonisation describes a process in which the ephebe so stations himself in relation to the precursor 'as to generalise away the uniqueness of the earlier work' (*AI*, 15). Referencing 'a movement towards a personalised Counter-Sublime', Bloom borrows the term '*daemonisation*' from Neo-Platonic usage where an intermediary being enters into the adept and assists in denaturalising the aura of exclusivity that the precursor previously commands. 'Turning against the precursor's Sublime, the newly strong poet undergoes *daemonisation*, a Counter-Sublime whose function suggests the *precursor's relative weakness*. When the ephebe is daemonised, his precursor is necessarily humanised' (*AI*, 100). In this stage of the inter-subjective developmental narrative, *daemonisation* deromanticises the precursor and conversely enhances the new talents of the ephebe.

The revisionist stance of *daemonisation*, in which the ephebe revokes the previously exalted status of the precursor, thereby traverses two planes. At the outset of their acquaintance, therefore, Claire characterises Martin as a 'spotless hero' with a 'golden legend', in 'the Arthurian or Burne-Jones category' (*UI*, 36, 111, 142). However, as Claire both begins to know Martin's story and to invent it, she develops a portrait of him in which he is debased by 'his mother's neglect and his wife's affectionate mockery' (*UI*, 88). She deduces that he was 'the loser on both accounts ... He expressed desire, but it was desire for admittance to a world from which he felt excluded' (*UI*, 88). After Cynthia's death, Martin's appeal is further tarnished by his fall into a conventional bourgeois existence. Martin contemplates returning to work, he exudes an aura of social participation, friends and holidays compete for his time and he acquires a patina of everyday normality. The fashionable restaurants favoured by Martin leave Claire unimpressed. Dinner was, she regrets, 'not to my taste. It was the sort of formal meaningless place that gets written about, largely on account of the people who can be seen there' (*UI*, 120). Likewise, Martin's narrative becomes tediously familiar: '[h]is confessions were like press releases: utterly predictable, and available to all' (*UI*, 155). Bloom asserts that in *daemonisation* 'the Great Original remains great but loses his originality' (*AI*, 101). Martin's changed status in the mainstream leaves Claire feeling more isolated. 'This new confidence puzzled me', she remarks (*UI*, 189). 'I wished that I could feel the same. I wished that I could find the words to put us both at our ease, for although he seemed comfortable enough I was not' (*UI*, 189). 'He had outdistanced me', Claire concludes, realising that she was 'no longer that disinterested friend but was newly revealed as an adversary' (*UI*, 192, 193). *Daemonisation* thus dramatises another power shift in the intersubjective relation: 'This division brings order, confers knowledge, disorders where it knows, blesses with ignorance to create another order' (*AI*, 100). As Martin's appeal is distributed more widely, his absorption into daily life reduces his unique qualities. Similarly, the loss of a feigned simpatico between Claire and Martin illuminates Claire's solitary state in preparation for her ascension to strong poet status.

V Askesis *or Purgation and Solipsism*
In *askesis*, the new poet 'yields up part of his own human and imaginative endowment, so as to separate himself from others, including the precursor' (*AI*, 15). Taking the terms from the practice of pre-Socratic shamans, Bloom states: 'Askesis is a movement of self-purgation which intends the attainment of a state of solitude' (*AI*, 15). Bloom marks *askesis* as a 'self-curtailment' won at 'a terrible cost', a form of temporary reduction which pre-empts the development of 'a new style of harshness' (*AI*, 115–121). After the protracted and exhaustive process of negotiation and exchange between the two poets, *askesis* now sees the ephebe retreat into a meditative state.

From the start of *Undue Influence*, Claire represents herself as a 'solitary character' *(UI,* 9). In one sense, her solipsism is a family legacy. Referring to her mother, Claire states: 'this hidden life, or rather those private lives, mine and hers, explained why I was so much alone and had remained so, why I made up so much in default of direct contact with others, why I kept my own counsel, which was some compensation for the isolation I sometimes felt' (*UI*, 110). In another sense, when read through the figure of the *flâneur*, Claire's solipsism invokes the legacy of the Romantic artist. In the novel, Claire values her professional life and her friendship with Wiggy as protection against her Romantic alienation. So when she loses her job and Wiggy goes on holiday, the main protagonist is left in an increasingly vulnerable state. In addition, Martin's absence and his new sociability disarm Claire of diversions. She worries: 'It was clear that for all my sympathy, no, my pity for him, I had nothing to set in the balance. My lonely wanderings did not stand comparison with evenings on the terrace. … the idea of exchange was what was noticeably absent' (*UI*, 123). Increasingly, Claire finds it difficult to occupy herself. 'I felt in a sense illegitimate, even shameful', she says, adding that 'a lethargy was beginning to envelop me' (*UI*, 172, 174). She becomes highly self-critical.

> It was only natural that I seemed uninteresting; I was even uninteresting to myself. The proof of this was my new inability to speculate. This had always been such a resource, an endowment, even a gift, that its disappearance, however temporary, however ephemeral, however rationally explained—my change of circumstances—left me desolate. (*UI*, 176)

Stripped of the usual distractions, Claire plummets into a psychic abyss where she begins to doubt herself and her contribution. A sense of failure envelops the narrator: 'I was so preoccupied by my own failure—my inactivity, my solitude—that I accepted this particular failure of right' (*UI*, 198). Devoid of resources, the narrator endures a period of suffering. She disappears into the parks, necessarily removing social contact and spending all day in places where she cannot be found. On a strained date with Martin, Claire repeatedly notes her distress: '[s]o strong was my wish to be alone that I even stood at the window, looking out, until the scrape of a match told me that Martin was lighting a cigarette, and that the main business of the night was still to come' (*UI*, 188). Both alone or in company, Claire's intensified solitude climaxes immediately prior to the novel's denouement.

VI Apophrades *or the Return of the Dead*

In the final stage of the revisionary ratios, *apophrades* represents 'the ultimate placing and reduction of ancestors' (*AI*, 147). *Apophrades*, Bloom explains, comes from 'the Athenian dismal or unlucky days upon which the dead returned to reinhabit the house in which they live' (*AI*, 15). The apophradian reversal effects a situation both 'drastic and (presumably) absurd' which demonstrates the ascendant position of the ephebe. The new strong poet assumes a crown which reflects

> the triumph of having so stationed the precursor, in his own work, that particular passages in *his* work seem to be not presages of one's own advent, but rather to be indebted to one's own achievement, and even (necessarily) to be lessened by one's greatest splendour. The mighty dead return, but they return in our colours, and speaking in our voices, at least in part, at least in moments, moments that testify to our persistence, and not to their own. (*AI*, 140)

The final ratio articulates Bloom's central thesis that creative influence appears to flow backwards not forwards. According to Bloom, the status of the artist is won by a movement of historical revisionism in which our reading of the past is filtered by our reading of the present.

The preparations for Claire's appropriation of the strong poet status witness a period of time which oversees a 'necessary apprenticeship for a kind of reinstatement' (*UI*, 208). Claire's solipsistic recovery alters the power dynamic between herself and Martin, such that she creates a more equivocal split between them. '[I]t was true that I now wanted to goad him, to wring some sort of confession out of him, to have all his weakness for myself, rather than see it so lightly displayed', she maintains (*UI*, 193). The narrator confesses to withholding approval from Martin, represents herself as a 'transitional object or system' in a proleptic anticipation of a converted relationship and notes that while 'Martin had remained in character I had somehow slipped out of mine' (*UI*, 195, 194, 198). During her period of enforced confinement, Claire contrives a small holiday, 'a calculated absence, undertaken merely in relation to a convincing return' (*UI*, 207). De Certeau's contention that 'travel (like walking)' produces 'by a sort of reversal ... the "discovery" of relics and legends ... in short, something like an "uprooting in one's origins"'—combined with the sexual connotations of Claire's walking holidays—suggests that Claire's travel plans indicate a rejection of Martin, which further underscores a change in emphasis from the hetero-romance narrative to the narrative of influence.[37] Finally, as de Certeau affirms, this shift is dramatised in the terms of 'uprooting' the narrative of origins or executing a reversal of conventional family narratives. Bloom clarifies his reversal of familial narratives with a citation from Nietzsche—'when one hasn't a good father, it is necessary to invent one' and from Kierkegaard—'He who is willing to work gives birth to his own father' (*AI*, 56, 26). Likewise, Claire decides it was 'as if my antecedents had failed in some genetic task' (*UI*, 180). Rendered through the performance of the *flâneur*, these subjective, erotic, and familial shifts signal imminent changes in the power dynamic between the ephebe Claire and precursor Martin. In the lead-up to her holiday, Claire has a 'disquieting' dream.

> I was in a wide street which I could not identify. Some paces in front of me was Martin, but a Martin whom I did not know. Martin was a much younger man, with dishevelled hair and a livelier step. I could see him quite clearly: he wore an open-necked shirt, which was out of character, and he appeared to be skipping along and humming to himself ... Do you remember so-and-so? I said, but he looked at me as if I were a stranger, before taking off again, with that curiously insouciant step. He soon outdistanced me but I kept him within my sights, so that we both made our discordant way down that broad street, Martin ahead, myself following vainly behind. (*UI*, 210)

37 De Certeau, 'Walking in the City', 107.

In this penultimate scene, Claire apprehends a shift in character roles which pre-empts the ephebe's ascension to strong poet. Furthermore, this shift is rendered through the figure of generational slippage that Bloom mobilises to define the operative effects of the narrative of influence: 'the tyranny of time almost is overturned, and one can believe, for startled moments, that they are being *imitated by their ancestors*' (*AI*, 140). Thus, Claire reads her dream as presenting Martin 'as if he were a boy again, while I had grown older, older than the age I was now, in the present' (*UI*, 210). Recasting Martin as an innocent boy and herself as the knowing stranger, Claire's dream licenses a generational switch in which she appropriates the space of the strong poet and substitutes Martin in the place of the ephebe.

Throughout *Undue Influence*, Claire battles with Martin in various ways, attempting to gain subjective, aesthetic, and intellectual authority. She invents a character for Martin, continually misreads his reality, refuses to expose herself to him, relinquishes him to a normal life, and removes herself from the world. Bloom contends that 'detachment from one's own imagination … destroys any individual imagination' and it follows that Claire's highly invested imagination continually reiterates her autonomy and poetic strength. When Wiggy unearths Martin's secret by catching Martin and Sue in an intimate Selfridges shopping spree, Claire's aesthetic independence is complete. 'All I knew was that now, as never before, I should find it easy to leave', she states (*UI*, 220).

Like the aesthete and the dandy, the *flâneur* provides an insight into the disposition of the creative personality we now know as the artist. These three personae have intersecting, but quite distinct, aesthetic personalities and behaviours. The production of the *flâneur* in *Undue Influence* involves remixing nineteenth-century discourses of male artistic genius with contemporary female subjectivity (in conjunction with queer erotic, familial, and temporal narratives) to rearrange and reconstitute the relationship between Claire and Martin. In so doing, the figure of the *flâneur* reappropriates female imagination as an authentic creative and technical practice, and provides a new way to think about gender relations outside the heterosexual romance narrative.

CHAPTER FIVE

The Degenerate in *Falling Slowly* (1998)

> She shrugged: people read novels superficially, invariably remembered the wrong parts: why should she not be superficial too?
>
> Anita Brookner, Falling Slowly

Introduction

In *Falling Slowly*, Miriam and Beatrice Sharpe are Brookner's first and only sister protagonists in an oeuvre that uses and remodels the conventions of domestic fiction. The Sharpe sisters are survivors of a family where the parents 'hated each other' (FS, 16). Through a close third-person point of view, Miriam remembers:

> her mother threatening illness, collapse, even death, if not humoured, her father all tearful resentment, hardly a man at all, or at least not a man as dreamed of by two wistful girls. And further back, even beyond this, there were memories of an embittered grandmother berating her daughter for marrying such a man, while the two girls ran up to their bedrooms and refused to come down, thus prolonging the dissatisfaction that was the very climate of their home. (FS, 9)

In this warring environment, Mr Sharpe attempts to recuperate authority by silencing his family. '"Silence is golden," had been their father's favourite maxim' (FS, 185). That mandated silence becomes an organising discursive mode for Miriam and Beatrice. Miriam remembers that 'in effect they had all been barred from communication, not only in that silent house, which she now saw with surprise as the home they had both lost, but later, throughout their lives' (FS, 185). Miriam's 'wordlessness' throughout her relationship with Beatrice's former agent, Simon Haggard, a man who bears the same patronymic as nineteenth-century masculine adventure novelist H. Rider Haggard, in addition to Beatrice's 'absences' and 'invisibility', all restage the original forms of silence that are part of the Sharpe family discourse (*FS*, 51, 72, 113, 171).

In *The History of Sexuality*, Michel Foucault frames silence as a form of discourse:

> Silence itself—the things one declines to say, or is forbidden to name, the discretion that is required between different speakers—is less the absolute limit of discourse, the other side from which it is separated by a strict boundary, than an element that functions alongside other things said, with them and in relation to them within over-all strategies.[1]

In Foucault's formulation, silence is a part of the signifying order and one of multiple forms of symbolic expression. Silence, then, is a type of figurative discourse with strong connotative characteristics that coexist with other forms of articulation in any given context. Living under a paternal decree of silence, Miriam and Beatrice turn to books for remedial purposes. Miriam remembers that, 'As girls, she and Beatrice had read voraciously, seeking alternatives to their restricted lives' (*FS*, 131).

Miriam Sharpe, like many Brooknerines, is a reader of Henry James. Eric Haralson underscores how 'Henry James' has become a queer signifier when he states, '"Henry James" is a construction of the narratives that have grown up around him. James and the possible sexualities that his ornate manner—on the page as in life—either conceals or reveals (or reveals by concealing) have continued to prove provocative to authors throughout the twentieth century and down to the present day'.[2] Haralson notes how the queerness of James emerges partly through the 'suggestive juxtapositions and contexts of usage' in which 'Henry James', and Jamesian themes of aesthetic masculinity and circumlocutionary meaning are culturally recirculated—and I emphasised this particular queerness of Henry James in the figures of the queer in Chapter 1 and the aesthete in Chapter 2.[3] In *Falling Slowly*, the sisters' reading practices coexist with and are enabled by their silence, marking the way in which silence itself is not a void of expression. The discursive modes of the

---

1 Foucault, *History of Sexuality*, 1: 27.
2 Haralson, *Henry James and Queer Modernity*, 22.
3 Haralson, *Henry James and Queer Modernity*, 6.

Sharpe sisters are adumbrated by the textual environments and practices that constitute the signifying order of *Falling Slowly*.

Beatrice Sharpe is identified as a rereader. The narrator describes Beatrice on one occasion, when she was tiring of her circumstances, as feeling like she would be 'better off in bed, reading *Jane Eyre* for the eighth or ninth time' (*FS*, 117). In Brookner's interviews, rereading surfaces as an important practice of hers. In the *Paris Review*, Brookner speaks of rereading Proust. 'He kept himself in a state of mind so hypnotic and dangerous that one approaches rereading him almost with fear'.[4] And, when asked by Nigel Ford whether she considers rereading to be more important than reading a book for the first time, Brookner responds emphatically, 'I think it is, I think it is'.[5] Along with intertextuality and misreading, rereading is a central concern of this book, especially through a methodology that incorporates close reading and narrative reversals.

For Duc Jean des Esseintes, the decadent aesthete of Huysmans's *Against Nature*, finding a book that bears rereading is a prerogative. 'My God! How few books there are that are worth rereading', he laments (*AN*, 158). Like Miriam and Beatrice after him, the duke suffers a 'dismal childhood', with indifferent parents (*AN*, 3). 'The only memory of his parents that he retained was one of fear, he knew no feeling of gratitude or affection' (*AN*, 4). And, like the Sharpe sisters, the duke turns to books: 'reading or dreaming, he would soak himself in solitude' (*AN*, 5). As an adult, des Esseintes's despair with the state of reading in general, and fin-de-siècle cultural production in particular, is both cause and effect of his rigorous practice of rereading (*RD*, 163). The duke describes his nineteenth-century rereading practice as a process:

> similar to that whereby metal strips are passed through a steel drawing plate, from which they emerge as very thin and light in weight, reduced almost to invisible threads ... only books which could survive that kind of treatment ... were sufficiently tough to withstand the additional test of rereading. (*AN*, 145)

The aesthetic conditions to which des Esseintes subjects a text, in which meaning is contingently constructed and remade, reflect how meaning is produced in relation to other signifiers in a signifying chain. Des

---

4 Brookner, in Guppy, 'Art of Fiction', 157.
5 Anita Brookner, interview by Nigel Forde, *Bookshelf*, BBC Radio 4 (31 January 1991).

Esseintes's respect for textual plurality is illustrated by his predilection for a certain type of artwork: 'he wanted a work of art both for what it intrinsically was and for what it potentially allowed him to impart to it', thereby evincing the collaborative aspect of meaning-making (*AN*, 127). As indicated by Huysmans's work, the sense that language is malleable and multifaceted is an underlying value of the Symbolist movement. In Théophile Gautier's preface to Baudelaire's *The Flowers of Evil*, for instance, Gautier champions 'a style that is ingenious, complicated, learned, full of shades of meaning and research, always pushing further the limits of language ... [and which] expresses new ideas with new forms and words'.[6] Dramatised by the trope of rereading, the Symbolists' semantic and aesthetic theories underscore the open-ended nature of signification in which meaning is contextually contingent and continually reinscribed through a hermeneutic process. In a Derridean cultural context where nothing is outside the text, the trope of rereading names the way the reader is already navigating an archive of cultural narratives when producing knowledge about a text. In this sense, every reading is a form of rereading, in that all readings are discursive framings pre-recorded by embedded cultural practices.

In *Degeneration*, Max Nordau's 500-page diatribe on the nineteenth-century fin-de-siècle condition, the author represents the French aesthetes and Romantics, including Baudelaire, Stéphane Mallarmé, Huysmans, and the fictional des Esseintes, as iconoclastic degenerate figures—for the most part because of their use of figurative symbolic practices that include textual multiplicity and ambiguity.[7] According to Nordau, Huysmans represents 'the classical type of the hysterical mind without originality, who is the predestined victim of every literary suggestion', while des Esseintes is 'an arrant scoundrel ... an unspeakable idiot ... [a] Decadent with all his instincts perverted' (*DGN*, 302, 308–09). One of Nordau's most relentless critiques of the degenerates is levelled at the discursive modes that match key discursive characteristics of the Sharpe sisters. The French aesthetes and Romantics, Nordau proclaims, are exemplary of 'the senseless stammering and babbling of deranged minds, and ... the

---

6 R.K.R. Thornton, *The Decadent Dilemma* (London: Edward Arnold, 1983), 19.

7 A German citizen, Nordau re-enacted historical national rivalries between Germany and France to argue that France hosted the worst effects of the century due to revolution and violent upheaval. 'This explains why hysteria and neurasthenia are much more frequent in France, and appear under such a greater variety of forms, and why they can be studied far more closely in this country than anywhere else' (*DGN*, 42).

convulsions and spasms of exhaustion' which constitute the degenerate subject (*DGN*, 42). Against Huysmans's celebration of polymorphous meaning in rereading, Nordau is offended by the implied ambiguity of language. 'Clear speech serves the purpose of the communication of the actual … It has, therefore, no value in the eyes of a degenerate subject', Nordau maintains (*DGN*, 118). He claims that 'Degenerates lisp and stammer, instead of speaking. They utter monosyllabic cries, instead of constructing grammatically and syntactically articulated sentences' (*DGN*, 554). The degenerates' perceptions are 'disturbed and obscured' and 'vague often to the point of being unintelligible' (*DGN*, 69, 104), while their habit of repetition is condemned as a mark of 'intellectual debility' (124).

> They cannot make use of definite words of clear import, for their own consciousness holds no clearly-defined univocal ideas which could be embodied in such words. They choose, therefore, vague equivocal words, because these best conform to their ambiguous and equivocal ideas. The more indefinite, the more obscure a word is, so much better does it suit the purpose of the imbecile, and it is notorious that among the insane this habit goes so far that, to express their ideas, which have become quite formless, they invent new words, which are no longer merely obscure, but devoid of all meaning. We have already seen that, for the typical degenerate, reality has no significance. (*DGN*, 118)

Nordau's tirade against the Symbolists' degenerate discourses functions to create a regulatory narrative that privileges literal and linear representation as normal, natural, healthy, and real. By mobilising the aesthetes and Romantics to represent, on the one hand, what is 'evanescent, floating, cloudy … [and] emotional' and, on the other, what is real, linear, and normal, Nordau's profiling of the degenerate is strategically invested in representing ideal and non-ideal forms of behaviour that are inextricably linked to producing an opposition between literal and figurative discursive modes (*DGN*, 118). In this chapter, the literal/figurative opposition is deployed to produce the figure of the degenerate in *Falling Slowly*. It is through this figure of the degenerate that a battle is waged—a battle over the right to designate what is real or normal and what is perverse or fictive, based on an opposition between the literal and the figurative. The value and status of the literal and the figurative, and their capacity to discount or reflect historical identities and interpretative possibilities, is reproduced in tensions around the practice of rereading.

In *No Future*, Lee Edelman illuminates how the opposition between literal/figurative discourse is mapped onto the heterosexual/homosexual opposition, and ultimately deconstructed by queer analytical practices. In a theoretical move which functions to indict Nordau's investment in the possibility of literal representation, Edelman argues that literal signification is based on an unstable fantasy, given that the Symbolic is 'built on a self-constituting negation—which it denies in the hope of reaching meaning through signification'.[8] The instability of the signifying chain can be likened to the degeneration of the sign per se, and its symbolic alignment with figurative discourse. Constantly subject to a process of decay and renewal, the sign attains meaning contingently through a process of rereading and figuration. The notion that all signs are subject to a process of construction in which meaning is defined contextually leads Edelman to conclude that even literalisation is the effect of a figurative economy when he condemns 'the literalisation of the figural logics that various social subjects are made to inhabit and enact'.[9] Thus does Edelman determine that the opposition between literal and figurative discourse is one built on a false presupposition that is invested in the propagation of certain ideological positions. He connects the impossibility of affixing meaning in the signifying chain to reactionary attempts to organise social reality according to the imaginary identifications of heterosexual reproduction.[10] Edelman endows the queer with the project of 'imagining an oppositional political stance exempt from the imperative to reproduce the politics of signification (the politics aimed at closing the gap opened up by the signifier itself)', a process that can be executed through queer textual analysis.[11] Central to this project would be acknowledging the relevance of the figure of the lesbian to debates on discursivity. Failing to do so risks reproducing the same politics of signification which effaces the lesbian from the heterocentric symbolic order.

In this chapter, therefore, the stance of queer oppositionality is related to the practice of a lesbian rereading, reaffirming the indeterminacy of the sign, whether literal or figurative. The innate degeneracy of the sign in the symbolic order is connected to the figure of the degenerate, and the degenerate and the lesbian are framed as exemplary figures of the

8 Edelman, *No Future*, 5.
9 Edelman, *No Future*, 14.
10 Edelman, *No Future*, 13.
11 Edelman, *No Future*, 7.

practice of queer rereading. The sister relationship of *Falling Slowly*'s Miriam and Beatrice becomes the stage on which a queer deconstructive process unfolds. The resultant performance of the degenerate in the domestic fiction exposes the figurative process behind supposedly literal and natural formations of heterosexual reproduction, while recasting signs into new narrative formations.

Following the now established template, part 2 of this chapter provides a plot summary of *Falling Slowly* and a critique of the novel's initial critical reception and analysis. In part 3, the figure of the degenerate is assembled from Nordau's *Degeneration,* Huysmans's *Against Nature,* and Brookner's *Falling Slowly,* as well as queer analytical texts by Terry Castle, Annamarie Jagose, and Edelman. The degenerate emerges through a spectrum of behavioural signifiers that are grafted onto an opposition between the literal and the figurative, signifiers that enable the figurative to reread the literal. Next we consider the rhetorical figure of syllepsis, which mediates between the literal and the figurative, as well as the 'no future' narrative, which tracks against hetero-chronic tropes. Based on the signifiers of absence, invisibility, and backwardness that are staged in the familial symbolic and which inform lesbian discursivity and temporality, the figure of the degenerate can also be seen to manifest as lesbian sisters in the queer family matrix. In turn, the production of the degenerate assists in deconstructing narratives of heterosexual marriage and reproduction and repurposing transgressive signs in the text for a queer rereading. Based on the idea that the narrative disposition of the degenerate favours a synchronic (rather than diachronic) performance, in part 4 the performance of the degenerate is staged in three palimpsestic tableaux in the text. In these three different scenes, the shifts between literal and figurative readings demonstrate the mutable nature of so-called rigid designators and the life-affirming properties of degenerate signs.

Plot Summary and Original Reception

Falling Slowly tells the story of two sisters who are 'outside the norm' (*FS,* 187). The novel opens with a close third-person narration of Miriam's experience in the aftermath of Beatrice's premature death. Miriam makes her way to the London Library, to work on 'translating contemporary novels of no particular merit into English', a profession which emphasises the practice of rereading as a cultural and commercial form (*FS,* 4). En route, Miriam is diverted by Eugène Laloue's painting, *Place du Châtelet under Snow*, hanging in a Duke Street gallery window (*FS*, 1). The image conjures a sense of homecoming and triggers Miriam's memories of Beatrice from their unhappy childhood and adolescence.

As the narrative starts to focus on an earlier time, it suggests that we use memories to reread and produce our own biographical narratives. In their early years, the sisters identify as opposites to each other: Beatrice, a piano accompanist, is 'romantic and unpredictable' while Miriam is considered to be the realist (*FS*, 12). These dispositions filter through the private lives of the two women. Beatrice staunchly opposes any form of 'routine coupling' whereas pragmatism informs Miriam's decision to marry Jonathan Eldon, whom she divorces five years later (*FS*, 114). As the novel progresses, however, the dichotomy between the sisters is destabilised. In her affair with Simon Haggard, Miriam's realism is eroded by fantasy and obsession, while Beatrice makes alarming personal decisions about life and death matters. Similarly, the sisters' identification within a high culture/pop culture divide is deconstructed when Beatrice forces herself to make an uncharacteristic visit to the Tate Gallery and Miriam finds herself reading Beatrice's tabloid newspapers.

Despite some early success, Beatrice's career as an accompanist falters and she is beset by health problems. Beatrice's booking agent, Max, sends the 'golden' Simon Haggard to inform Beatrice that her contract will not be renewed, and a chance encounter between Miriam and Simon fuels a secret love affair between them (*FS*, 41). Haggard's ingress into Miriam and Beatrice's relationship precipitates the sisters' decision to settle into separate living arrangements. Beatrice feels 'too ashamed at her fall from grace … to bear another's eyes watching her', and Miriam is preoccupied with her 'refulgent' partner (*FS*, 60, 46). While Miriam obsesses over her relationship with Haggard, she is befriended by journalist Tom Rivers, whose name (and role) recalls *Jane Eyre*'s austere clergyman St John Rivers, the man Jane almost marries before she returns to Thornfield Hall. Meanwhile, Beatrice is momentarily diverted by the reappearance of Max, though he is 'not a suitor, [but] a courtier' (*FS*, 159). However, her health continues to deteriorate, and Miriam's affair comes to an end.

The sisters' changing circumstances reunite them, and they once again live under the same roof. They re-establish a tradition of Sunday walks, although now when Beatrice takes Miriam's arm it is 'no longer out of inclination but from necessity' (*FS*, 163). As Miriam curtails her other activities in order to be with Beatrice, Beatrice makes a difficult decision. 'Her own life, she knew, was finished … She would prefer to die at home, or even to linger on indefinitely, but she knew that this would be too hard on Miriam' (*FS*, 172). Soon after, Beatrice is hit by a car and dies in hospital. Miriam is left to grieve her absent sister. A friendship slowly develops with Tom Rivers until he dies suddenly and unexpectedly. This final period of bereavement proves revelatory for Miriam.

The 1998 reception of *Falling Slowly* was accompanied by declarations that Brookner's oeuvre had entered a period of decline. In 1998, Gillian Tindall opined:

> Once, Brookner knew that people didn't actually talk like that. Indeed, the perceptible space between the realities of life and the words used to dissemble them was one of the many wry delights of her early novels. Somewhere along the avenue to the eighteenth novel, *Falling Slowly*, this sharpness of vision has blurred.[12]

Organised around a narrative of degeneration, which maps a devolution from sharpness to blurriness, Tindall's review romanticises a past popularity for the novelist which nevertheless remains committed to perpetuating the Brookner stereotype. The attribution of blurriness to Brookner likewise gestures to a preferable clarity presumably attainable elsewhere. In this way, reporting the failure of Brookner and her heroines is invested within the implicit hierarchical specification of a field of phantom writers who represent superior forms of literary practice and gender performance.

The degeneration narrative proves to be a particularly useful weapon in the arsenals of Brookner's critics. Brookner's 'impeccable craftsmanship and worldly irony make each of her novels memorable, but here her heroines' passivity becomes exasperating', complains *Publisher's Weekly*, implicitly harking back to an imaginary era to emphasise the Brooknerine's historical incongruity.[13] Merle Rubin agrees that the characters of Miriam and Beatrice represent a whole new degree of difficulty in the Brookner canon. 'Readers who've found many of Ms Brookner's characters downright maddening in their capacity for hitting upon ways to stay lonely, depressed and miserable may very well lose patience with this novel', she states.[14] Cheryl Alexander Malcolm's classic response to Miriam's reverie as audience to Eugène Laloue's *Place du Châtelet under Snow* in Chapter 1 provides an awkward account of what

12 Tindall, 'Safe Sorrow', 23.
13 'Falling Slowly', *Publishers Weekly* (26 October 1998): 42.
14 Merle Rubin, 'The Search for a Suitable Suitor', *Wall Street Journal* (20 January 1999).

otherwise might be thought of as symbolic content. 'None of Brookner's protagonists is ever short of a pound', Alexander remarks: 'Why not buy the picture?'[15] Such comments do, however, reflect the consumer-oriented, late-capitalist historical context of Brookner's novel.

Accusations of plotlessness, repetition, and excessive detail surface yet again in the critical reaction to *Falling Slowly*. 'This is a short novel in which not very much happens', Ron Charles relays in his review of *Falling Slowly* in the *Christian Science Monitor*.[16] 'There is no real mystery in a Brookner novel ... Brookner offers no surprises', writes Barbara Love in *Library Journal*.[17] Lack of action is also suggested in Heather Mallick's comment that *Falling Slowly* constitutes 'literary dawdling', a representation that implicitly invokes the minutiae of detail and proliferations of signs in what Naomi Schor defends as decadent literary and critical practices in *Reading in Detail*.[18] The suggestion that 'nothing happens' in *Falling Slowly* is such a habitual response to Brookner's novels that they cry out to be contextualised differently. As it stands, the criticism that has the effect of conflating the heterosexual romance with narrative progress, effectively ghosts alternative modes of expression and relating.

As with her previous novels, Brookner is not spared from personal criticism. Claire Messud views Brookner's themes as part of the author's unfortunate egotism. 'Brookner, in her repeated tracing of this trajectory of negation, seems smugly to condone it, and in so doing deprives her characters of tragedy'.[19] Here, the critique of repetition levelled at Brookner connotes a creative—and, beyond that, sexual—sterility which binds themes of negation to childlessness, reproductive failure, and queerness without also engaging the historical, figurative, elected, and subversive modes of these discourses.

For Barbara Fisher, Brookner's attention to detail is potentially detrimental to the reader's health. 'The novel is all dissection, examination,

---

15 Malcolm, *Understanding Anita Brookner*, 184.
16 Ron Charles, 'Loneliness Dissected with Stunning Precision', *Christian Science Monitor* (7 January 1999): 20.
17 Love, 'Falling Slowly', 152.
18 Mallick, 'Depressive Tale Lacks Substance'; 'Decadence in literature signifies a disintegration of the textual whole, the increasing autonomy of the parts, and in the end a generalised synecdoche. The decadent style is inherently ornamental. Decadence is a pathology of the detail'. Schor, *Reading in Detail*, 43.
19 Claire Messud, 'The Stifled Life', *New York Times Book Review* (31 January 1999): 7.

and analysis; there is little action. At the end, the reader is relieved to be released from the scrutiny of these arid lives', Fisher states.[20] Fisher's criticism implicitly panders to the physical and contagious properties of the degeneration narrative. *Publishers Weekly* mobilises Brookner's detail to effectively stigmatise loneliness. Contending that Brookner's mode of characterisation has her 'minutely dissecting the particular state of suspended loneliness in which they dwell', the *Weekly* depicts a tragic union between form and content which reflects badly on the uncoupled.[21]

Across Brookner's early reception, the use of euphemism to infer rather than name heterosexual arrangements is indicative of how heterosexuality is constructed as self-evident. In 'Depressive Tale Lacks Substance', Mallick asserts that '*Falling Slowly* is about two women depressed by the onset of middle age and wondering if they will spend the rest of their lives alone'.[22] In this review, 'alone' connotes the absence of men; the 'substance' found 'lacking' is presumably heterosexuality; and the lack of heterosexuality implies a 'depressive tale'—a narrative pathology about which readers are necessarily warned. Reviews like Mallick's accrue symbolic authority by implying the existence of an unmediated relationship between signifier and signified that supposedly secures literal representation, at the same time as they build on established reading conventions to figure historical meaning around compulsory heterosexuality. In figuring heterosexuality through a literal signifying network, Mallick's review exemplifies Edelman's contention that literal signification is an effect of a figurative economy.[23] Ostensibly referencing the Brookner text, but simultaneously framing social reality, the authority of the literal is accomplished by mobilising and denying a figurative economy.

A similar slippage between the literal and the figurative is evidenced in Rubin's review of *Falling Slowly*. She describes Miriam and Beatrice Sharpe as 'middle-aged women whose prospects for happy endings are, alas "falling slowly"'.[24] Rubin's reference to 'happy endings' gestures to the generic (and phallic) conclusion of the heterosexual romance narrative. In Rubin's review, Miriam and Beatrice are the degenerate figures whose

---

20 Barbara Fisher, 'Falling Slowly', *Boston Globe* (3 January 1999): M2.
21 'Falling Slowly', *Publishers Weekly*, 42.
22 Mallick, 'Depressive Tale Lacks Substance'.
23 Edelman, *No Future*, 15.
24 Rubin, 'The Search for a Suitable Suitor'.

tragic lives bear witness to the primary, natural, and pre-eminent status of heterosexuality. By weaving her reading of degeneration from an implied heterosexual norm, to the book's title, Rubin naturalises the connection between title and content—or signifier and signified—concealing the narrative mechanisms through which heterosexuality is figured. As Rubin's quotation marks prove, however, her reading of 'falling slowly' is in fact metaphorical. Rubin appropriates a figure of speech in which heterosexuality is performed by using colloquial language to invoke the historical conventions of the heterosexual romance in a phrase that—as is demonstrated in part 4—can nonetheless refer to other tropes and discourses of the text and context.

Producing the Figure of the Degenerate

Throughout the nineteenth century, the infrastructure of the new consumer society develops, imperialist policies expand western influence throughout the world, and a wealth of new professions emerge, including those which meld the identity of the subject with sexuality, such as psychoanalysis and sexology. At the fin de siècle, anxieties associated with rapid development intensify. Narratives of cultural change become linked to narratives of degeneration, with political, social, and aesthetic implications. Claiming that 'contemporary civilisation' has brought about widespread 'fatigue and exhaustion', Max Nordau's *Degeneration* exemplifies mainstream responses to historical change that circulate a moral panic (*DGN*, 42, 40).[25] 'We stand now in the midst of a severe mental epidemic', Nordau states in a study he describes as a 'long and sorrowful wandering through the hospital' (*DGN*, 537, 536). Against Nordau's dismissal of 'loafing aestheticism', Brookner links social and political upheaval in nineteenth-century France, and Romantic aestheticism, with the emergence of 'an organically connected number of resounding masterpieces in a relatively short space of time' (*DGN*, 337; *RD*, 3). In their own challenges to narratives of progress, the aesthetes and Romantics constitute a subversive and contestatory subculture who objectify the central nodes of institutional authority and critique attempts to claim moral and political ascendancy.

---

25 In *Fictions of Loss*, Stephen Arata maintains that *Degeneration* presents a 'clear articulation of the "common sense" view of degeneration'. Stephen Arata, *Fictions of Loss in the Victorian Fin de Siècle: Identity and Europe* (Cambridge: Cambridge University Press, 1996), 32.

The delineation of two opposing sides to the degeneration narrative is a crucial part of the mechanism for producing the degenerate. The degenerate, asserts Nordau, represents 'a morbid deviation from an original type' (*DGN*, 16). Through the mechanism of degeneration, Nordau establishes an asymmetrical dichotomy that can be identified primarily through an opposition between the literal and the figurative, the unequal status of which is restaged across a class of behavioural modes. A consummate figure of duality, the degenerate is produced through the specification of sets of negative behaviours, including absence, invisibility, and backwardness, that are simultaneously mobilised to infer modes of conduct deemed to be normal, natural, healthy, and primary. 'In order to understand how the consciousness of the "I" (morbidly exaggerated and frequently increasing to megalomania) originates, we must recall how the healthy consciousness of the "I" is formed', Nordau argues, concealing the degree to which the process of recalling itself constitutes the mechanism of a dynamic production in his logic (*DGN*, 244). The active mechanism that creates the figure of the degenerate engages a metonymical function which threads signifiers across both negative (degenerate) and positive (normal) planes. The classification of non-degenerate behaviours as normal, healthy, and part of a signifying system in which there is no gap between the signifier and signified, continually function to attribute illness and perversion to those characteristics which Nordau labels as degenerate, that fail to rank in the signifying order, and that constitute part of a derivative and figurative system of signification.

Despite the normative impetus of Nordau's degenerate, the figure is also imbued with a self-reflexive mechanism that informs the layered practice of rereading. Indeed, Nordau emphasises a contestatory nature as characteristic of the degenerate. 'The ordinary man always seeks to think, to feel, and to do the same as the multitude; the decadent seeks exactly the contrary', he states (*DGN*, 305). The degenerate's refusal to assimilate makes the figure a force of originality. 'He ... seeks for the basis of all phenomena, especially those whose first causes are completely inaccessible to us ... He is ever supplying new recruits to the army of system-inventing, metaphysicians, profound expositors of the riddle of the universe, seekers for the philosophers stone, the squaring of the circle and perpetual motion' (*DGN*, 20–21). To this end, Nordau classifies degenerates as revolutionaries: 'the writings and acts of revolutionists and anarchists are also attributable to degeneracy' who are implicated in the evil task of trying to improve the world (*DGN*, 21). 'Thus he becomes an improver of the world, and devises plans for making mankind happy', Nordau states (*DGN*, 31). Contradicting his representation of the degenerate's inadequacies, Nordau also maintains that 'It must not for that matter be supposed that degeneration is synonymous with absence of talent' (*DGN*, 22). He cites Legrain to contend that the 'degenerate may be a genius' (*DGN*, 31). In traversing a deviation from an implied point of origin, the figure's capacity to address its own shift from the original to the secondary or derivative exposes the original itself to be none other than a construction. In revealing the original to be not in fact an original, but a secondary level of representation like that of the degenerate itself, the self-reflexive logic of the figure challenges and rereads the way in which forms of historical authority are produced. In this way, the degenerate is an exemplary metatextual figure of deconstruction. It is this productive and deconstructive capacity of the figure which is emphasised here in the casting of the degenerate.

Nordau generates the degenerate subject across a continuum of physical, mental, empirical, sexual, and discursive behaviours.[26] In addition to Nordau's indictment of the figure's speech, degenerate behaviours also include: emotionalism, mental weakness, despondency, pessimism, moral insanity, a vague fear of all men and of the entire phenomenon of the universe, self-abhorrence, repetition, ennui, melancholy, sombreness, despair of himself and the world, dejectedness, a disinclination to action of any kind, powerlessness to will, self-deception, the unfortunate capacity to be tormented by doubts, unbalanced, petty, impressionable (*DGN*, 19–25). To his list of qualities identified as symptomatic of degenerate behaviour, Nordau adds mysticism, which he defines as 'the inaptitude for attention, for clear thought and control of the emotions'; egomania, which he frames as an effect 'of obtuseness in the centres of perception, of aberration of instincts from a craving for sufficiently strong impressions, and of the great predominance of organic sensations over representative consciousness'; and 'false Realism', which 'proceeds from confused aesthetic theories, and characterises itself by pessimism and the irresistible tendency to licentious ideas, and the most vulgar and unclean modes of expression' (*DGN*, 536). The degenerate, Nordau states 'makes things far more difficult for himself than the ordinary man' (*DGN*, 307). The result is that Nordau calls on society to 'mercilessly crush under his thumb the anti-social vermin', which he names the degenerates

---

26 According to Arata, Nordau's attribution of degeneracy ranges across 'diverse topics as sexual deviance, national character, class, literary style, interpretation, professionalism and modernity'. Arata, *Fictions of Loss*.

(*DGN*, 556). Embodying the worst characteristics of the time, the degenerate is, according to Nordau, an obstacle to true evolutionary progress and civilisation.

Published in 1998, *Falling Slowly* is a fin-de-siècle text which emerges a hundred years after the English translation of Nordau's text was published. Nevertheless, the sweep of behaviours Nordau invokes in *Degeneration* reappear in the performance of the Sharpe sisters. These behaviours include: dullness (*FS*, 7), a delirium of ennui (*FS*, 8), decline (*FS*, 9), discomfiture (*FS*, 11), a strange absence of practicality (*FS*, 13), unreformed childishness (*FS*, 19), boredom (*FS*, 20), fatigue (*FS*, 25), inactivity (*FS*, 31), depression (*FS*, 31), indolence (*FS*, 31), a smiling negation of a more energetic life, alarm (*FS*, 31), invisibility (*FS*, 51), inability (*FS*, 58), anxiety (*FS*, 59), vacancy (*FS*, 61), disorientation (*FS*, 62), instability (*FS*, 63), dematerialis(ation) (*FS*, 80), disorder (*FS*, 81), vast inadequacies (*FS*, 96), deterioration (*FS*, 96), restlessness (*FS*, 97), lawlessness (*FS*, 98), deception (*FS*, 98), solitude (*FS*, 98), singularity (*FS*, 102), dispossession (*FS*, 105), frightening absences (*FS*, 113), artifice (*FS*, 130), exile (*FS*, 133), illness (*FS*, 135), collapse (*FS*, 135), fear (*FS*, 144), idleness, worthlessness, loss of meaning (*FS*, 144), wordlessness (*FS*, 153), and panic (*FS*, 170). Where Nordau states the degenerate is 'an invalid who does not see things as they are, does not understand the world, and cannot take up a right attitude towards it', Brookner represents Beatrice Sharpe with a 'ruinous ability to understand what was being enacted' (*DGN*, 243; *FS*, 58). Where Nordau implicates the profile of the degenerate in a 'predilection for inane reverie', Miriam Sharpe confronts 'a day on which concentration would not be possible, a day on which images would give way to words' (*DGN*, 24; *FS*, 4). And, in *Falling Slowly*, the narrator states that 'Beatrice had been well named'—and the name of 'B Sharpe', for Beatrice as a pianist, evokes a musical note that does not exist (*FS*, 9).

The intertextual indications of degeneracy between *Degeneration* and *Falling Slowly* are repeated between *Against Nature* and Brookner's novel. In *Against Nature*, the degenerate anti-hero, Duc des Esseintes, plans a trip to London only to be waylaid by the sensorial impressions on offer in an English tavern which quench his desire for any real travel. 'What was the point of moving, when one could travel so splendidly just sitting in a chair? Wasn't he in London now, surrounded by London's smells, atmosphere, inhabitants, food, utensils? … I would be insane to risk losing, by an ill-advised journey, these unforgettable impressions', des Esseintes decides, before returning back to his country estate (*AN*, 114). In *Falling Slowly*, Beatrice drafts an alternative life for herself in Nice with her former agent Max, yet later deduces that the 'beauty of certain fantasies was that they needed no reality to structure them. Her future life in the south of France was already perfect, complete. Why run the risk of translating it into the stuff of every day?' (*FS*, 144) This continuum of degenerate signifiers in *Falling Slowly* can be seen to more broadly symptomise illness, absence, invisibility, and backwardness. In particular, these behaviours operate as indicators of the degenerate's contestatory relationship to literal naming in the symbolic order. In bringing together a host of behaviours which connote a figurative signifying system, my contention is that the behaviours that Nordau, Huysmans, and Brookner mark as degenerate are reconstituted in the performance of the Sharpe sisters through a signifying matrix which produces the figure of the degenerate in *Falling Slowly*.

In generating sets of contrary and opposing qualities, Nordau's regulatory hierarchy of behaviours include behaviours which are gendered and sexualised. He states:

> Sexual psychopathy of every nature has become so general and so imperious that manners and laws have adapted themselves accordingly. They appear already in the fashions. Masochists or passivists, who form the majority of men, clothe themselves in a costume which recalls, by colour and cut, feminine apparel. Women who wish to please men of this kind wear men's dress, an eyeglass, boots with spurs and riding-whip, and only show themselves in the street with a large cigar in their mouths. (*DGN*, 538)

Here, Nordau's delineation of cross-dressing as degenerate behaviour conversely reconstitutes gender-appropriate behaviour through the heterosexual matrix. Nordau classifies women and youths as 'those components of the race in whom the unconscious outweighs consciousness' and, in so doing, he constructs masculinity as the epitome of historical subjectivity (*DGN*, 332). In his discussion of Paul Verlaine, Nordau maintains that 'the special characteristic of his degeneration is a madly inordinate eroticism', thereby gesturing to the existence of a natural and self-evident performance of sexuality (*DGN*, 120). Nordau frames homosexuality as degenerate per se, arguing that 'vice looks to Sodom and Lesbos' (*DGN*, 12). In his notes on Baudelaire, Nordau claims that 'Women Damned' is 'a piece dedicated to the worst aberration of degenerate women, [which] terminates with this ecstatic apostrophe to the heroines of unnatural vice' (*DGN*, 291). Arata underscores the specifically symbolic and punitive status of homosexuality in narratives of degeneration when he states that '[t]hough homosexuality was but one of the many spurious forms of criminal degeneracy identified by late-Victorian pathologists, by the 1890s it was frequently used to stand for the rest'.[27] According to Nordau's law of hierarchical oppositions, and the metonymical function of his logic along signifiers of illness, absence, invisibility, anachronism, and backwardness, the privileged historical subject is a reproductive heterosexual male who emphasises the abjection of the figure of the lesbian as the most degenerate subject of all.

Nordau's offering anticipates Castle and Jagose's analyses of the figurative status of the lesbian in the symbolic order.[28] Like the thematic associations bridging Castle's account of the lesbian and Nordau's degenerate, the mechanisms of sexual hierarchisation that Jagose indicts as the fundamental 'strategy of representation in the maintenance of the ideological bulwark of gendered and sexual hierarchy' function to restage the active asymmetrical dichotomy through which the figure of the degenerate is produced.[29] Based on the symbiotic thematic and temporal switches underwriting the production of the lesbian and the degenerate, lesbianism is thereby nominated as the representative erotic mode of the degenerate. Tuite's contention that 'the practice and privilege of decadence is a male prerogative. Ill health is a privileged category only in the male homosexual aesthetic economy' is a reminder of the challenge of recognising a type of female decadence.[30] Therefore, in producing the degenerate across a spectrum of behaviours that underscore a figurative relationship to signification as a type of illness, Brookner's appropriation and rereading of decadent ill health in a female homosexual aesthetic economy is particularly valued as an act of performative Romanticism.

The analysis presented here suggests the relevance of the institution of the family to the figure of the degenerate, both insofar as nineteenth-century anxiety circulated around gender, sexuality, and family, and due to the status of *Falling Slowly* as domestic fiction. In *Against Nature*, Des Esseintes's ill health is partly attributed to aristocratic 'interbreeding', a symptom of the breakdown or implosion of heterosexual reproduction (*AN*, 3). Des Esseintes's familial debility reflects the way in which the domestic narratives of nineteenth-century literature problematise the familial positions of reproductive heterosexuality. Examining nineteenth-century literary devices in the domestic fiction, Sarah Annes Brown coins

27 Arata, *Fictions of Loss*, 54.
28 Castle, *The Apparitional Lesbian*, 45; Jagose, *Inconsequence*, x.
29 Jagose, *Inconsequence*, 3.
30 Tuite, 'Decadent Austen Entails', 127.

the term 'lesbian incest effect' to evaluate how nineteenth-century tropes lend 'a particular quasi-sexual charge to the way sisterly relations are represented in texts of the period'.[31] Likewise, then, Brookner's representation of the sister relationship, calibrated through her nineteenth-century intertextual strategies, functions to create an intimate relationship which provides an alternative to the heterosexual romance narrative.

In *Falling Slowly*, for Miriam, 'all considerations of love merely served to revive memories of her sister Beatrice' (*FS*, 5). Miriam and Beatrice are 'inescapably joined' and 'each hankered for the closeness of the other' (*FS*, 60, 10). The sisters are further viewed as 'devoted' to each other; it is a word used to describe their parents too—a 'devoted couple', as Miriam used to 'hear said of [them]'—and it also forms the basis for Brown's framing of the lesbian sister incest-effect (*FS*, 9, 9, 9). Indeed, the erotic potential of familial relationships is emphasised in *Falling Slowly* while the erotic stereotype of heterosexual relationships is undermined. Thus, Miriam sees Simon Haggard and his wife 'as part of the same family, in more ways than one, as if they were siblings, and incest the most natural thing in the world'. And Max confesses that he 'wanted a woman like his mother, his sister, but where to find her?' (*FS*, 106, 65). On the other hand, Miriam's real husband, Jon, is downgraded: '[s]he had loved him as a brother, or as an old friend' (*FS*, 10). When Nordau attempts to secure the law of the father in *Degeneration*, privileging the male heterosexual subject and abjectifying the lesbian, he produces an analogous logic across both the symbolic order and the familial symbolic. Insofar as the law of the father and the paternal code secure authority through the rejection of the lesbian from the symbolic order, it necessarily reconfigures the figure of the lesbian sisters as the most transgressive of all. Therefore, in addition to the thematic and temporal indications between Nordau, Brookner, Castle, and Jagose, the intertextual formulations of the sororal trope combine to produce the figure of the degenerate across the sister relationship in *Falling Slowly*.

In spinning the degenerate across the sister relationship in *Falling Slowly*, it is the degenerate's queer contestatory mode, particularly in the

---

31 Sarah Annes Brown, *Devoted Sisters: Representations of the Sister Relationship in Nineteenth-Century British and American Literature* (Aldershot: Ashgate, 2003), 135. Brown argues that Christina Rossetti's *Goblin Market*, for example, 'creates a sense of incestuous closeness between the sisters … the poem's goal might be seen to be the creation of a female sexual and familial matrix which excludes the masculine'. Brown, *Devoted Sisters*, 145.

context of the heterosexual romance narrative of the domestic fiction, that is underscored. In *Degeneration*, Nordau glosses his selection of prized behaviours as constitutive of the pursuit of the ideal (*DGN*, 334). In a trans-historical symbiosis, the Sharpe sisters' negatively valued attributes are inscribed alongside the category of the ideal. The plotting of the ideal in *Falling Slowly* tracks the heterosexual romance along the generic contours of gender-normative development: coupling and reproduction. Thus, Miriam says to Beatrice, '[y]ou too want an ideal man, to give you that ideal life you fantasize about' (*FS*, 17). Lying in bed, Beatrice would 'arrange herself for her ideal lover, even if he never came' (*FS*, 20). She fantasises about 'the ideal family' and 'the ideal man' with 'an ideal appearance. That was how she would know he was ideal' (*FS*, 57, 57, 57). For Miriam, the ideal becomes discursive through her attraction to Simon Haggard. Miriam's desires focus on the 'ideal image' of the 'ideal home' with the 'ideal family' (*FS*, 180, 34, 47).

Judith Butler explains how the ideal is a symbolic category:

> Ideality of being ... belongs to symbolic positions. The symbolic is secured precisely through an evacuation or negation of the living person; thus a symbolic position is never commensurate with any individual who happens to occupy it; it assumes its status as symbolic precisely as a function of that incommensurability.[32]

Butler's framing of the ideal as an imaginary category with which subjects are never commensurate is recast through the production of the degenerate as a figure of deconstruction. In producing the degenerate across categories of the non-ideal and the ideal, and through the emplotment of the heterosexual romance, the deconstructive and contestatory modes of the figure nevertheless question the authority of the heterosexual romance narrative in the text.

In *Falling Slowly*, the propagation of the ideal heterosexual romance is simultaneously plotted and challenged through Beatrice's reading of romance fiction and through a narrative subtext in which the sisters' behaviour problematises marriage and heterosexual authenticity. Much to Miriam's consternation, Beatrice is a fan of popular romance fiction.

> Between her favoured covers men were always handsome, dashing, and articulate, while women were altogether charming, as was Beatrice herself, never more so than when choosing her books, so rapt in contemplation of

---

32 Judith Butler, *Antigone's Claim: Kinship between Life and Death*, Wellek Library Lectures (New York: Columbia University Press, 2000), 14.

this ideal conjunction that she hardly had time to notice the real if imperfect men who favoured her with a speculative glance. (*FS*, 12–13)

Based around gender-normative stereotypes and a developmental narrative, the romance fiction maps out a heterosexual ideal. However, in her seminal appropriation of the romance text, Janice Radway argues that readers bring different experiences to their reading of the romance narrative.[33] For Beatrice, the romance text has value as artifice. 'In the books she favoured, but wistfully, women were unmasked, laid bare by a man who finally understood them. She knew that this was rubbish' (*FS*, 59). The propagation of the heterosexual romance as artifice absolves Beatrice from heterosexual consummation. Thus Beatrice participates in 'radiant pantomimes of affection' for 'men who had meant nothing to her' (*FS*, 57, 57). She exudes a distinct 'lack of curiosity' in potential male partners, who leave her 'untouched' and whose variety of failings altogether undermine the authority of the heterosexual romance as the privileged narrative of desire in the text (*FS*, 56, 13, 111). For Beatrice, men are either 'too old' or 'too young', 'too beautiful', too 'inexperienced', or possess too much 'sexual curiosity', 'Not you ... but someone like you could have been the answer' (*FS*, 12, 165, 17, 66, 66). Beatrice's resistance to any type of 'routine coupling' is therefore protected by the romance text (*FS*, 114). Additionally, the romance text marks the production of Beatrice's erotic desire within a homosocial environment. Beatrice 'sought to ally herself with the heroines of novels rather than with the practical business of finding a partner' (*FS*, 114). Beatrice's obsession with the woman 'laid bare', in books usually written by women, functions to produce and maintain her desire within a female homoerotic economy (*FS*, 59). Therefore, despite her predilection for the heterosexual romance narrative, Beatrice's real-life choices prevent heterosexual practices, circulate her desire in a homosocial economy, and deconstruct the authority of the heterosexual ideal.

Beatrice's sister Miriam reads her own parents' romance narrative as 'a revenge tragedy, in which each partner was exculpated, blaming the other. Hideous to witness' (*FS*, 19). Miriam's own contrived and unpleasant marriage to Jonathan exposes the illusion of naturalised heterosexuality. She 'had married not out of love but out of impatience ... and even then she had to work hard' (*FS*, 29). Miriam remembers her husband as 'a small compendium of irritating habits' and recalls her five-year

---

33 Janice Radway, *Reading the Romance: Women, Patriarchy, and Popular Literature* (Chapel Hill: University of North Carolina Press, 1991).

marriage 'with shame, with irritation' (*FS*, 35, 24). During her affair with Simon Haggard, Miriam's perception of Simon's 'ideal family' is framed through a trope of reading, which (like Beatrice's reading of romance fiction) denaturalises the heterosexual romance narrative: Miriam 'felt as if she were reading a book, a masterpiece containing all the best fictional ingredients, written in a language she had not known she understood' (*FS*, 57, 46). 'His real life, his life away from her, she discounted, preferring to relegate it to the pages she had not yet read, in the same beloved book' (*FS*, 47). Miriam's understanding of heterosexuality as a literary trope emphasises its status as a constructed narrative, contrary to its mainstream representation as an organic social formation.

Miriam's marriage 'occasioned enormous surprise, even outrage, largely on aesthetic grounds' in Beatrice (*FS*, 30). And when Miriam's friend Suzanne marries a man she met at a dating agency, Beatrice is similarly 'uncomprehending, almost stricken', as Miriam recalls (*FS*, 39). Nordau frames Huysmans's *Against Nature* as a degenerate perversion; however, Beatrice's response to others' marriages mobilises comparable terminology, this time against heterosexual coupling: 'Miriam could see that Beatrice was hurt, not only aesthetically, but morally as well, as if to surrender part of oneself, even the most expendable part, were an offence *against nature*' (*FS*, 39; italics mine). Against Nordau, in *Falling Slowly*, French literature is set in opposition to the realities of married life. When Suzanne and her mother-in-law visit the Sharpe sisters, Suzanne's new wifely consumer practices signal a rejection of the French canon. 'This is my new endowment, said Suzanne's laugh; it goes with realism, and also with status. French literature? I used to be fascinated, but now we are off to the Harrods sale; Mother loves Harrods' (*FS*, 38). The heterosexual romance narrative is plotted as a developmental ideal, but the production of the degenerate across the ideal and non-ideal facilitates that narrative's deconstruction.

One way in which *Misreading Anita Brookner* illuminates challenges to the heterosexual narrative is through narrative reversals such as the aesthete's metaleptic prolepsis, the dandy's rise-and-fall narrative and the *flâneur*'s peripeteia. In *Falling Slowly*, the degenerate is constituted through a no-future narrative. Towards the end of *Degeneration*, Nordau predicts that 'the feeble, the degenerate, will perish … The aberrations of art have no future' (*DGN*, 550). Nordau's characterisation of the degenerate through a narrative of no future reflects the way in which the figure is organised by a profile which traverses, on the one hand, narratives of generation, reproduction, chronology, and linearity that consolidate the heterosexual romance in the domestic fiction, and, on the other hand, narratives of decline, backwardness, and multi-temporal forms. In *Against Nature*, Duc des Esseintes's aversion to the contemporary world fuels a backwards turn against narratives of generation and futurity. 'When the period in which a man of talent is condemned to live is dull and stupid, the artist is haunted, unknowingly perhaps, by a yearning for a different era', Duc des Esseintes muses (*AN*, 147). Brookner harnesses the trope of no future in her reading of *Against Nature*, endorsing Zola's position when she comments that his 'prediction was in fact correct. À Rebours [*Against Nature*] contained no future. It was a work that exhausted its own idiom' (*RD*, 164). Here, Brookner characterises the no-future narrative of *Against Nature* as emblematic of the degeneration of the sign, a motif that marks the open-endedness of meaning—the sign has no future. In *Falling Slowly*, Miriam mobilises the no-future narrative against the heterosexual romance as a symbol of agency and authority in declaring that she has 'no future' with Jonathan: 'She knew that she had no future with Jon, for as she grew older, he would grow uncannily younger' (*FS*, 36). The trope of no future also reappears in the narrator's representation of Miriam's relationship to reproductive narratives. That Miriam is 'grieved to realize that there was no future in her way of life' reflects the way in which narratives of futurity are tethered to framing social reality around modes of heterosexual reproduction (*FS*, 102).

In *No Future*, Edelman mobilises the no-future narrative as a queer resistance to the hetero-normative logic of the political field organised around what he terms 'reproductive futurism'.[34] Edelman argues that in contemporary Western democracies, social reality is shaped by a political consensus, spanning from the right to the left, and organised around the figure of the child.[35] Based on privileged narratives of generation, the child enacts 'a logic of repetition that fixes identity through identification with the future of the social order'.[36] The effect is that our political and social reality, and their ongoing future iterations, are preconditioned on heteronormativity.

> This means not only that politics conforms to the temporality of desire, to what we might call the inevitable historicity of desire ... but also that politics

---

34 Edelman, *No Future*, 2.
35 'The Child has come to embody the telos of the social order and come to be seen as the one for whom that order is held in perpetual trust', Edelman contends. Edelman, *No Future*, 11.
36 Edelman, *No Future*, 25.

is a name for the temporalisation of desire, for its translation into a narrative, for its teleological determination.[37]

Edelman's analysis of the political temporalisation of desire is useful in explaining how the narrative personae cast in this book can either normalise or contest certain ideological readings of a text. His evocation of the child as a collocating figure for a set of social, temporal, and representative behaviours evinces similarities to the hermeneutic figures I mobilise, although mine are presented as contestatory, whereas for Edelman the child is innately conservative.[38] To intervene in the continuous revaluation of social reality around heteronormative practices, Edelman supplies the death drive as the energetic form that represents a queer oppositionality: 'the death drive names what the queer, in the order of the social, is called forth to figure: the negativity opposed to every form of social viability'.[39] Just as Jagose refuses to validate tropes of visibility, Edelman contends that the work of queer oppositionality is 'a refusal of every substantialisation of identity, which is always oppositionally defined and by extension of history as linear narrative (the poor man's teleology) in which meaning succeeds in revealing itself—as itself—through time'.[40] Indeed, the cast of Romantic personae engaged thus far demonstrate that it is possible to use methodological identity forms that are constituted through a variety of non-linear narratives.

Pitched against the figure of the child, and organised by a narrative of no future, the degenerate can be thought of as the figure who incarnates the queer oppositional practice of the death drive. In the previous chapter, the *flâneur* surfaced as the exemplary figure for the epistemological work of this book, insofar as the figure dramatises the potential of intertextual recombination, misreading, and women's creative practice. In this chapter, the degenerate appears as the exemplary figure of the methodological work of *Misreading Anita Brookner* who addresses the naturalised epistemological constructs that dictate how cultural debates are discursively mandated. Edelman celebrates queer theory as 'a particular story of why storytelling fails'.[41] In refusing a synchronic,

---

37 Edelman, *No Future*, 9.
38 Edelman's child can be compared to the figure we know as 'the historical subject': both are considered to be representatives of the historical context in which they are produced and therefore prioritise heterosexual identification.
39 Edelman, *No Future*, 9.
40 Edelman, *No Future*, 4.
41 Edelman, *No Future*, 6.

linear reading of *Falling Slowly*, the no-future narrative enables the diachronic staging of the performance of the degenerate in part 4.

In his broad opposition to figurative expression, Nordau names Symbolist poet Stéphane Mallarmé as a key perpetrator of a 'language which does not aim at the communication of definite thought', citing a statement of Mallarmé's that he finds particularly offensive (*DGN*, 118). 'To name an object means to suppress three quarters of the pleasure ... Our dream should be to suggest the object', Mallarmé had written, implicitly referencing the contingent operation of the signifying chain (*DGN*, 118). In 'Syllepsis', however, Michael Riffaterre affirms Derrida's stance to praise Mallarmé for his expert manipulation of the type of 'undecidable' narrative that underscores how the epistemological onus is always on readers to create their own version of the text. Derrida defines this undecidability through the rhetorical figure of syllepsis. In Riffaterre's words, syllepsis is 'the trope that consists in understanding the same word in two different ways at the same time, one meaning being literal or primary, the other figurative'.[42] In Riffaterre's definition, syllepsis is the rhetorical figure that governs the shift between the literal and the figurative. Therefore, complementing the way in which the degenerate is produced across the shift between the literal and the figurative, syllepsis is nominated as the organising rhetorical form for the figure of the degenerate. Like Nordau's specification of the degenerate, syllepsis governs the way in which meaning is produced and naturalised through a hierarchy of the literal and figurative.

In 'Syllepsis', Riffaterre distinguishes between the literal and the figurative through different classifications of meaning on the one hand, and significance on the other.[43] Riffaterre's definition of meaning as 'when words signify through their one-on-one relationship with nonverbal referents, that is, their reference to what we know as reality', parallels the construction of literal signification as unmediated and self-evident, as in Nordau.[44] Conversely, Riffaterre defines significance as when 'words signify through their relationship with structural invariants ... by presupposing an intertext either potential in language or already actualised in literature'.[45] Here, his understanding of significance corresponds to the definition of figurative signification as a second-order symbolising

---

42 Riffaterre, 'Syllepsis', 629.
43 Riffaterre, 'Syllepsis', 625.
44 Riffaterre, 'Syllepsis', 627.
45 Riffaterre, 'Syllepsis', 627.

system. For Riffaterre, however, this figurative signification is a more evolved and avant-garde practice; in this way, he deviates from Nordau. Via Mallarmé and Derrida, Riffaterre draws on Mallarmé's discussion of the hymen to make his point. Mallarmé states that 'the scene [a drama, or rather a pantomime] bodies forth only an idea, not an action: it is like a hymen between desire and its realisation, or between an act committed and the memory of it'.[46]

According to Mallarmé, a sign's inability to inscribe meaning in the world makes it a static object that is yet contingent on context to activate its meaning. Inspiring Riffaterre's distinction between meaning and significance, Derrida argues that Mallarmé's grammar prevents the reader from choosing between 'hymen' as 'marriage', a symbolic union or fusion, and 'hymen' as a 'vaginal membrane', the barrier to be broken through if desire is to reach what it desires.[47] In representing the undecidability of the hymen around a literal/figurative dichotomy defined by choices of either marriage or membrane, Riffaterre negates the hymen's role as a signifier of female sexuality. In this way, Riffaterre's ascription of signifying possibilities around either (cultural) marriage or (biological) tissue appropriates the hymen for either patronymic heterosexuality or the masculinist avant-garde and ignores the representational possibilities of an economy of female same-sex desire. Even in privileging figurative signification, Riffaterre re-enacts the logic that both Terry Castle and Annamarie Jagose indict in their analyses of the historical construction of lesbian invisibility (mirrored in the creation of the degenerate). In producing the degenerate across a shift between the literal and figurative and through the lesbian sister relationship in *Falling Slowly*, the sylleptic hymen can be reclaimed for female-centric queer readings.

Staging the Performance of the Degenerate

I Proper-Name Titling

In the original reception of *Falling Slowly*, the title of the book is taken to refer to the degeneration of the Sharpe sisters, revealed by their unmarried, childless state, their failures in the realm of heterosexual romance. However, the text itself reveals another way in which the syntagm 'falling slowly' can be read. Before a dinner appointment with former beau Jacob, Beatrice lies down while listening to the radio.

---

46 Riffaterre, 'Syllepsis', 628.
47 Riffaterre, 'Syllepsis', 628.

> She rested on her bed in the afternoon, and must have slept, for the next thing she heard was the end of the shipping forecast: 'And finally Malin Head.' Then a very brief instant of confusion until the somehow soothing last words, '... falling very slowly.' (*FS*, 64)

Broadcast four times a day on BBC Radio 4, the shipping forecast is a British institution.[48] In 1995, Michael Green, Controller of Radio 4, commented that many listeners 'testify to the soothing, not to say soporific effect the forecast has on them'.[49] In the forecast, the quantifier 'falling slowly' refers to a classification of atmospheric pressure changes between sea and air, measured in hectopascals, and recorded every three hours on the synoptic scale. As a rigid designator, therefore, the forecast 'falling slowly' is part of an empirical signifying system in which scientific codes are figured as literal discourse. This literal rendering of 'falling slowly' as weather forecast reveals the hetero-chronic reading of 'falling slowly' to be, in fact, a highly figurative reading. In its literal capacity to identify weather trends, the syntagm 'falling slowly' contests the authority of the title signifier 'falling slowly' to connote the text's primary subject as the heterosexual romance, exposes the figurative production of the seemingly self-evident presuppositions that circulate around Brookner's novels, and underscores other hermeneutic possibilities cited in the proper noun.

Like other forms of media, the shipping forecast is appropriated and reproduced by listeners according to the requirements of context. The capacity of users to circulate texts according to their own organising regimes reflects the way in which all signifiers are implicated in figurative representational systems. In *Falling Slowly*, the radio is an object the sisters associate with their mother, as Miriam recalls:

> I think of Mother whiling away the afternoons, with nothing to do, in that room in which nothing ever seems to have been disarranged, so tightly was it packed together, all chintz curtains and covers, repressively creating a false impression of comfort. I once came home earlier than usual and found her sitting on that overstuffed sofa, with the *Radio Times* on her lap, just staring into space. (*FS*, 16)

Miriam's recollection of her mother with the *Radio Times* suggests that the radio is part of the family's communication economy. Mrs Sharpe's

---

48 Peter Jefferson, *And Now The Shipping Forecast: A Tide of History Around Our Shores* (Cambridge: UIT Cambridge, 2011).
49 'Dropping off before Malin Head', *Independent* (2 August 1995): www.independent.co.uk/voices/dropping-off-before-malin-head-1594380.html.

appropriation of the radio waves can be seen both as resistance to Mr Sharpe's patriarchal decree that 'silence is golden' and as recourse to an alternative communication strategy. Towards the end of Beatrice's life, verbal dialogue between the sisters entirely gives way to the shipping forecast: '"Malin Head rising today," was sometimes the only comment that passed between them' (*FS*, 164). As such, in the figurative discursive coda of the Sharpe family, where the radio carries resistant meaning through the maternal line, the shipping forecast connotes a private mode of communication between the sisters which circumvents the authority of the literal.

Analogous to its intermittent radio presence, the refrain of the shipping forecast reappears throughout *Falling Slowly* as a type of generic contour in the text. As a weather predictor, the forecast is a warning of an imminent change in environmental conditions. In this way, it alerts us to the significance of Beatrice's visit to the Tate Gallery, where the conditions at sea in J.M.W. Turner's *A Ship between Two Headlands* and Beatrice's apprehension of a 'ghost ship' coming through the canvas combine to effect an erotic transformation in the relationship between the sisters (*FS*, 145).[50]

II Proper-Name Subjects
Prior to the fall which leads to her death, Beatrice Sharpe forces herself to the Tate Gallery, ostensibly to please her sister. Wandering aimlessly through the gallery, Beatrice eventually feigns interest in J.M.W. Turner's *A Ship between Two Headlands*. The painting ranks among the undated canvases controversially classified as 'late Turner' and has a special significance in nineteenth-century fin-de-siècle narratives of genius and degeneration.[51] On the one hand, the painting was acclaimed by the French aesthetes and Romantics, and noted for establishing the critical significance of Turner in the movement from representation to abstraction (which is visual language for the shift from literal to figurative).[52] 'At first he stuns you', Huysmans enthused of Turner. 'What land, what Eldorado, what Eden flames with this wild brilliance, these floods

---

50 The director of the Tate galleries, Sir Nicholas Serota, wrote his master's thesis on J.M.W. Turner under the supervision of Anita Brookner and Michael Kitson.
51 William Vaughn, 'Turnabouts in Taste: The Case of the Late Turner', in *Romanticism and Postmodernism*, ed. Edward Larrissy (Cambridge: Cambridge University Press, 1999), 29–46.
52 Vaughn, 'Turnabouts in Taste', 29.

of light refracted by milky clouds, flecked with fiery red and slashed with violet, like the precious depths of opal?'[53] On the other hand, the blurriness of the late Turners was decried by nineteenth-century critics as a reflection of the artist's degeneration and decline.[54] Presenting a haze of golden mist and vapour, through which the indistinct indication of a 'ghost ship' shears the horizon between two headlands; the painting's abstraction manifests all the 'blurriness' that Nordau despised about symbolic form and for which Brookner was condemned in her early reception (*FS*, 145; *DGN*, 20).[55]

At first Beatrice is soothed by the Turner, which exudes a sense of 'majesty', 'serenity', and 'magical' 'incorporation' (*FS*, 144). This initial sense of belonging is followed by a disturbing awareness of transience and the ephemeral nature of experience. Stumbling backwards, Beatrice perceives a 'swirling rhythm that her eyes had not appreciated, for a moment dizzily apprehended that there was no solid ground, no place for rest' (*FS*, 144). At this point, Beatrice becomes aware of the subject's submission to an external authority and the division of the world into a series of known objects with their accompanying systems of classification and status. The 'vaporisation' of objects for which Turner's abstraction is iconoclastic also reveals that what Beatrice has experienced as social reality is nevertheless subject to its own structural laws and conditions. Beatrice's perception, 'that ships nor headlands were neither real nor relevant', references the arbitrary nature of this knowledge (*FS*, 146). The revelation accompanies a recognition that the objects produced through the dominant narrative can 'evaporate' and therefore be deconstructed and reformulated according to historically contingent conditions of perception.

Finally, the blurry canvas elicits a type of despair that forces Beatrice to question the lives that the sisters have adopted as their reality: 'what she had seen drew her eyes again, and again her eyes misted with tears. If this was paradise, this golden light, this ship becalmed on an immaterial sea, then she saw quite clearly her pitiful fallen condition' (*FS*, 146). Beatrice senses that the arbitrary laws to which she and Miriam have held

---

53 Joris-Karl Huysmans, 'Goya et Turner', in *Écrits sur l'art, 1867–1905* (Paris: Bartillat, 2006). Translation in Bart Johnson, 'JK Huysmans on Turner', *True Outsider* (blog), 21 February 2011: wordpress.com/2011/02/21/51/ (subscription required).
54 Vaughn, 'Turnabouts in Taste', 29.
55 Tindall, 'Safe Sorrow', 23.

themselves accountable have been at the expense of their own 'paradise'. Her 'agonizing' revelations intensify further when the Turner appears to become unhinged (*FS*, 146). 'The picture now seemed to her to have lost its immobility, to be involved in some surreptitious circular rotation. For a moment—but she had lost track of time—the void represented was the exact embodiment of the void inside her own head' (*FS*, 146). At this stage, the ideological foundations propping up social reality have degenerated until degeneration finally becomes embodied in Beatrice herself. 'Are you all right, Madam?' a gallery warder asks Beatrice after 'seeing her haggard face' (*FS*, 146). The performance of the degenerate is thereby engaged by Beatrice's turn at the Turner, and the sylleptic switch is 'turned' at the trope (where trope literally means 'to turn') of Beatrice's 'haggard' degeneration. Subsequently, Beatrice's slide into the signifier 'haggard' activates her appropriation of the masculine patronym of Miriam's lover, Simon Haggard and that of nineteenth-century masculine adventure novelist, H. Rider Haggard, whose 1890 novella *Beatrice* describes the experiences of a woman who 'has lost everything, and found nothing, and loves nobody'.[56] In assuming the signifier of Miriam's lover and the masculine adventurer, Beatrice's turn away from her familial subjection to the law of the father coincides with her enlightened understanding of her predicament. At this moment, fuelled by the gap in the signifying chain, the performance of the degenerate deconstructs institutionalised heterosexuality through the patronym to produce a queering of the sister relationship in the proper-name signifier.

III Death and Figuration

Beatrice characterises her experience at the Turner as reaching 'the abyss'; her rapprochement with 'the ghost ship, gliding … towards her' pre-empts her death months later when she falls in front of a car (*FS*, 147, 145). In this sense, the falling slowly shipping forecast predicts Beatrice's falling as a figurative death that is followed by a literal death. In Roland Barthes's *Lover's Discourse*, 'the ghost ship' refers to the end of romantic love: 'the love which is over and done with passes into another world like a ship into space, lights no longer winking'.[57] For Barthes, the 'errantry' that is an effect of recognising the state of the ghost ship 'produces iridescence: what results is the nuance'.[58] In claiming that 'the

---

56 H. Rider Haggard, *Beatrice* (London: Reader's Library, 1927), 16.
57 Barthes, *A Lover's Discourse*, 101.
58 Barthes, *A Lover's Discourse*, 103.

nuance is the last state of a colour which can be named', Barthes aligns the state of the ghost ship to Turner's blurred abstraction.[59] Nevertheless, in *Falling Slowly*, Beatrice's death fails to erase her from the text; rather, through Miriam's memory and recollection, Beatrice's death animates her life. As Miriam observes, 'Beatrice, dead, had more of a life even now than her insouciant husband' (*FS*, 23). In *The Apparitional Lesbian*, Castle laments the way in which 'the lesbian has been ghosted or made to seem invisible by culture itself'.[60] However, Castle also argues that the spectral metaphor commands a subversive power.

> The dead are indeed brought back to life; the absent loved one returns. For the spectral vernacular, it turns out, contains its own powerful and perverse magic. Used imaginatively—repossessed, so to speak—the very trope that evaporates can also solidify.[61]

Aligning the lesbian with the spectral, Castle illustrates the way in which 'life'—or what Edelman calls 'social reality'—corresponds to a historical context in which the historical subject is presupposed as heterosexual through his/her construction in a world where literal signification is privileged. In this schematic, 'death' constitutes the time/space context that underscores the natural authority of those granted historical status through a literal signifying regime.

In propelling the sylleptic shift between the literal and the figurative, it becomes possible to refuse the reduction of interpretive possibilities to a literal order. This refusal stakes a claim against making queerness stand for death in order to frame life around the heterosexual romance. Henceforth, the degenerate's intervention in the symbolic order impacts on our reading of Beatrice's death. Animated by discourses of life, Beatrice's can thus be seen as part of a self-reflexive signifying order that confronts the figurative nature of literal symbolisation. In this way, the performance of the degenerate traverses the site where 'narrative realisation and derealisation overlap' that Lee Edelman frames as queer theory's place of origin in order to celebrate the intrinsically queer nature of meaning-making.

Following Beatrice's appropriation of the haggard signifier, and Miriam's protracted period of grief after the deaths of her sister and Tom Rivers, Miriam enters a state of relative peace and begins to embrace a

---

59 Barthes, *A Lover's Discourse*, 103.
60 Castle, *The Apparitional Lesbian*, 4.
61 Castle, *The Apparitional Lesbian*, 46.

new perspective. The formerly golden Simon Haggard loses all brilliance in Miriam's eyes. 'The only surprise was that she felt no curiosity about him. His physical splendour was no longer a memory; it was as if he had become a dead star, a random fragment of astronomical matter, beyond usefulness' (*FS*, 206). Haggard's figurative death matches Tom Rivers's literal death. Although Miriam notes the 'ephemeral' nature of Tom's character, marking his significance in death, she envisions him 'striding away from her' (*FS*, 206, 205). A type of psychic resolution occurs for Miriam where Simon and Tom attain parity in this literal/figurative death. 'She saw the faces of Simon and of Tom Rivers quite distinctly, as if both were dead and had appeared to her in a dream. That Tom was dead she did not doubt, and Simon living, yet now they seemed to have come together in some mysterious conjunction' (*FS*, 212). With life shifting into death and death animating life, distinctions between the literal and the figurative are indistinguishable and await full determination within a transparent economy of production.

Miriam compares the renegotiation of status that death enables to the process of rereading. 'There were to be no more inequalities, no more inadequacies: praise and blame were irrelevant. The stories were not unfinished. On the contrary: they were still potent, like books so important that one read them over and over again' (*FS*, 212). Framing death as the filter through which perception is readdressed, death figures the contingent life of the sign along the signifying chain and imbues the practice of rereading with the ultimate power to determine life as value. Linking rereading with the narrative strategy of syllepsis, in which the switch between the literal and the figurative deconstructs the authority of the literal, Miriam's revelations function to restage death as a life form. Emphasising that she has 'no faith', Miriam's 'more unexpected' feelings elicit revelations about endings and beginnings (*FS*, 204, 205).

> In a state of Edenic honesty, but with all their worldly experiences still to inform them, the dead would at last confess as they had never done in life, could at last bestow praise, affection, love, not for some absent Deity but for one another. ... Simply she knew that the dead were composed of the same material, that there were no more differences between them, and that had these differences not been perceived earlier, in life, as it were, it was because the living were so frequently in error. (*FS*, 205)

Staging death as the site where subjects have the power to articulate a love that was denied in life, Miriam apprehends death as imbued with possibilities that life could never facilitate.

Miriam's new awareness accompanies further revelations about Beatrice: 'Miriam now sensed that she was united with her sister as never before' (*FS*, 204). While Miriam once sensed Tom 'striding off into regions with no geographical boundaries', her experience of her sister is different:

> Beatrice was always turned towards her, smiling discreetly from behind her piano, with none of the disappointment that had clouded her gaze as life let her down. This Beatrice, she could see, was possessed of some secret knowledge she had not formerly apprehended; there had been some sort of reconciliation. (*FS*, 205)

Here, in death, Beatrice is in full possession of the Jamesian secret knowledge that partly informs the text's queer rereading. Simultaneously, Miriam proposes that the type of knowledge brought on by death rationalises the process of rereading. In this way, Miriam's promotion of rereading to incorporate the secret knowledge that unites her and Beatrice 'as never before' finally claims the sylleptic hymen for Brookner's queer female oeuvre.

In the final passages in the book, Miriam wakes early with her radio as companion:

> All seemed to be in order. She would make her tea, take it back to bed, until the shipping forecast released her into the day's activity. A blessed pause ensued. 'Ronaldsway,' she heard. That meant the bulletin was nearly over. 'And finally Malin Head,' said the careful voice. 'Falling very slowly.' (*FS*, 215)

This final forecast in the text marks Miriam and Beatrice's familial discursive mode, recalibrated through the figure of the degenerate as a queer mode of communication. In light of the new possibilities enabled by rereading, Miriam realises that 'at last, she was ready to proceed' (*FS*, 216). Possessed with a new accountability, she makes her way forward with the undying love of her sister Beatrice.

Epilogue

The Storyteller Returns: *Hotel du Lac* (1984)

> But, after a moment, she thought that this was not entirely accurate and, crossing out the words 'Coming home,' wrote simply, 'Returning.'
>
> Anita Brookner, *Hotel du Lac*

Introduction

How does Brookner work with words? What kind of storyteller is she?

In *Misreading Anita Brookner*, I have drawn on the adventure narrative, the metamorphosis narrative, the rise-and-fall narrative, the narrative of influence, and the no-future narrative, as well as a slate of rhetorical devices and textual behaviours, to show how literary criticism can act on what it sees. As we have witnessed, most of these narrative modes embrace forms of repetition, backward turns, reversals, and secondariness in ways that are queer—for how they historically conjure the figure of the lesbian, for how they formally resist what I have termed hetero-chronic figuration, and for the sort of queer content these turns invoke, such as Blanche Vernon's immersion within a Sapphic domain in *A Misalliance*. Along the way, I have argued against multiple criticisms of Brookner—including that she is too repetitive—not only by showing that repetition has different types of meaning, such as in the a + A hendiadys of *A Friend from England*, but by embracing cross-historical intertextual epistemologies to interpret a variety of tropes and discourses. In their backward turns to history and away from linearity, many of the rhetorical modes I have engaged throughout the book are also variations on narratives of return.

In this final chapter I therefore want to return to Brookner's formal arrival in the literary field and her 1984 Booker Prize winner, *Hotel du Lac*, which is itself organised by a narrative of exile and return. The narrative of return in *Hotel du Lac* introduces the figure of the storyteller as a genius female narrative technician, proleptically predicting the novelistic interventions of Anita Brookner. *Hotel du Lac* begins with the extradiegetic narrator framing a view through the hotel window by which romance novelist, Edith Hope, stands at the start of her 'brief exile' in Vevey (*HL*, 8). It introduces a cast of characters at the hotel, and slowly reveals their secrets and scandals, including Edith's. It closes with Edith signalling her return to David, her lover, in London. In 'The Storyteller—Reflections on the Works of Nikolai Leskov', Walter Benjamin conjures a dual nature for the figure of the storyteller who embodies 'two archaic types ... the resident master craftsman and the traveling journeyman'.[1] Benjamin cites the German adage, 'When someone goes on a trip, he has something to tell about', marking the way in which a 'brief exile' might be narratively productive for Edith as a romance writer.[2] In sketching a signifying matrix for the figure of the storyteller, Benjamin asserts that the 'first true storyteller is, and will continue to be, the teller of fairy tales', a vocation which complements Edith's romance writing and her revival of Aesop.[3] As Edith tells her agent, in the most famous scene of Brookner's oeuvre, 'it is my contention that Aesop was writing for the tortoise market' (*HL*, 27–28). Benjamin also emphasises the storyteller as a figure of oral transmission, a person whose job is first to listen, and then retell what they have heard. Benjamin's contention that 'the gift for listening is lost and the community of listeners disappears' partly informs his belief that 'the art of storytelling is coming to an end'.[4] But the oral focus of *Hotel du Lac* (the only one of Brookner's novels to be adapted for television), calibrated through the female voice, challenges many of Benjamin's assumptions about gender, narrative, and temporality.

Despite Benjamin's masculinist focus in 'The Storyteller', the prototypical storytelling figure is Scheherazade in *The Arabian Nights*.

---

1 Benjamin, 'The Storyteller', 84.
2 Benjamin, 'The Storyteller', 84.
3 Benjamin, 'The Storyteller', 102.
4 Benjamin, 'The Storyteller', 91, 83.

Indeed, Benjamin characterises *The Arabian Nights* as replete with narrative 'tricks with which the attention of the listener was captured'.[5] Like *Arabian Nights*, *Hotel du Lac* consists of a frame narrative in which voice shifts between an extradiegetic and (Edith as the) intradiegetic narrator, as well as embracing repeated analepses and occasional focalisation through minor characters. In 'Lesbian Intertextuality', Elaine Marks claims the frame narrative model 'is frequent in writing about lesbians' and she cites Colette's *The Pure and the Impure* (1933)—Edith's choice of reading matter at the Hotel du Lac—as an iconic example (*HL*, 67).[6] Calling Colette 'the foremother' of a type of lesbian writing, Marks states she 'occupies a privileged place and therefore takes up most space in a study of lesbian intertextuality'.[7] Anne Freadman inserts Colette into the storytelling tradition when she states that 'Colette is above all a storyteller. I mean this precisely in the sense used in Walter Benjamin's famous article, "The Storyteller: Observations on the Works of Nikolai Leslov"'.[8] Describing *The Pure and the Impure* as 'an investigation into the nature and laws of the erotic life', Judith Thurman notes that it features a 'sympathetic listener' to a class of 'restless ghosts'.[9] A prior model of the storyteller is Germaine de Staël, whom Marks includes in her list of French women writing lesbianism.[10] We previously encountered Staël (a woman Brookner describes as 'at the centre of all lives, except perhaps her own') in *A Misalliance*, as the subject of Blanche Vernon's abandoned dissertation.[11] In 1809, Staël published *Corinne ou l'Italie*, a romantic saga which features the storytelling persona in the figure of the genius woman writer, about whom Staël writes, she 'combined too many talents; she was too remarkable in every way'.[12] Corinne's vocation as an improvisatrice connects Staël's novel both to the figure of the storyteller and to the canon of women's writing, interweaving

---

5 Benjamin, 'The Storyteller', 101.
6 Elaine Marks, 'Lesbian Intertextuality', in Stambolian and Marks, *Homosexualities and French Literature*, 348; Colette, *The Pure and the Impure*, trans. Herma Briffault (New York: New York Review of Books, 2000).
7 Marks, 'Lesbian Intertextuality', 362.
8 Anne Freadman, *The Livres–Souvenirs of Colette: Genre and the Telling of Time* (Leeds: Modern Humanities Research Association/Maney Publishing, 2012), 7.
9 Judith Thurman, 'Introduction', in Colette, *The Pure and the Impure*, xv.
10 Marks, 'Lesbian Intertextuality', 354, 373.
11 Brookner, *Soundings*, 164.
12 Madame de Staël, *Corinne, or Italy*, trans. Sylvia Raphael (Oxford: Oxford University Press, 2008), 122.

traditions of women's writing, orality, lesbianism, and genius. In *Hotel du Lac*, a series of narrative tools, tricks, and techniques, including silence and orality, misreadings and reversals, satire, anagnorisis, and paraprosdokian, transform the novel into a melting pot of anticipation, suspense, and revelation, implicitly recasting the figure of the storyteller, and prophesying Brookner's performative romanticism. Throughout the novel, these narrative tricks control how information is filtered to the reader in a way that underscores the authority of the writer, while, through a series of misreadings and reversals, casts doubt on that very same authority.

As a traveller returning home, the storyteller has a vested interest in souvenirs, or memories. Enduring 'probation' at the Hotel du Lac, Edith is unsettled by memories of home, by family memories, and, in dream-like liminal states, by the sound of a door closing (*HL*, 36, 78, 137, 141). 'Somewhere, at some level of consciousness, she heard a door close' (*HL*, 65). Marcel Proust's À *la recherche du temps perdu*—the iconic text for involuntary memory, which is itself a form of return—is a key satellite in Brookner's intertextual universe. Linking Proust to the figure of the storyteller, Christopher Prendergast states that 'probably no book haunted [Proust's] imagination more' than *Arabian Nights*.[13] Of particular interest to Proust was the 'open sesame' trope of the Ali Baba story that he recasts in *La recherche* through an emphasis on the 'door that suddenly and unexpectedly opens to save us'.[14] In Chapter 3 of *The Pure and the Impure*, when Colette speaks of Damien, the Don Juan styled lover, she observes that 'Between Damien and the woman there was not the slightest hint of diplomacy. It was rather a question of merely pronouncing the magic word, 'Open sesame!''[15] In this case, 'open sesame' refers to the doors of the female genitalia.

These analyses are interesting for how they help to position Edith's decision-making at the denouement of *Hotel du Lac*. In the fifth of five letters she pens to David over the course of her sojourn, Edith indicates that she will (once again) break off their relationship, this time to marry the 'heartless' Mr Philip Neville (*HL*, 97). Edith enlists Proust in her cause. 'I know, you see, that whatever you feel for me, or perhaps I should say, once felt for me, I am, as Swann said of Odette, not your

---

13 Christopher Prendergast, *Mirages and Mad Beliefs: Proust the Skeptic* (Princeton, NJ: Princeton University Press, 2013), 74.
14 Christopher Prendergast, *Mirages and Mad Beliefs*, 74.
15 Colette, *The Pure and the Impure*, 45.

type', she writes to David (*HL*, 180). But the following morning Edith revises her decision when she finally pieces together the secret behind the closing doors that have echoed through her consciousness at the hotel:

> Making her way silently along the thick carpet, anxious not to awaken or alarm the sleeping guests, she was just in time to see Jennifer's door open and Mr Neville, in his dressing gown, emerge. With a caution equal to her own, he concentrated on making no noise, and pulled the door to very slowly. In the dim light left burning overnight she could quite clearly make out his controlled and ambiguous smile.
> Of course, she thought. Of course. (*HL*, 183)

This anagnorisis precipitates Edith's return from exile to London and ostensibly her return to David. If we interpret Edith's recognition via Proust and through the *Arabian Nights*, we can also make sense of this final 'open sesame' as a form of homoerotic salvation.

At the close of the novel, Edith sends one final message to David: '"Coming home." But, after a moment, she thought that this was not entirely accurate and, crossing out the words "Coming home," wrote simply, "Returning."' (*HL*, 184). In an effort to explain Edith's decision to change 'coming home' to 'returning', Brookner told John Haffenden: '"Coming home" would be coming back to domestic propriety: "home" implies husband, children, order, regular meals, but "Returning" is more her honest view of the situation'.[16] Like Odysseus, Edith returns to a Penelope, her neighbour (Penelope Milne) at the creative bunker where she can be most productive. Brookner draws a dichotomy between the type of domestic life that Edith has repeatedly disavowed in her rejection of marriage and an unspecified alternative that might represent Edith's storytelling vocation, her profession as a women's writer, and a lesbian eroticism that is suggested through the figure of the doors and an intertextual association with Colette. In this way, the figure of the storyteller in *Hotel du Lac* bespeaks an emphasis on technical prowess that is proleptic of the aestheticist themes of *A Misalliance* (and their engagement with nineteenth-century Sapphic eroticism), Brookner's fascination with detail, orality, and performance in *Brief Lives*, and with imagination and influence in *Undue Influence*.

---

16 Brookner, in Haffenden, *Novelists in Interview*, 71.

EPILOGUE

The Storyteller's Toolbox

While at the Hotel du Lac, Edith Hope twice steps out with fellow hotel guest, the 'sadistic' Philip Neville, a man with an 'eighteenth-century face' whose appearance resembles the figure in Francisco Goya's 'Portrait of the Duke of Wellington' (1812–14) (*HL*, 101, 97, 81). Serving time at the hotel for scandalous behaviour, Edith cherishes her relative anonymity among the hotel '[i]nmates' (*HL*, 106). Mr Neville, however, breaks Edith's 'cover', much to her amusement, and she initially finds herself drawn to his wry offer to 'deconstruct the signifiers of [her] discourse' (*HL*, 79, 76). But insult and intrigue conspire to corrode Mr Neville's potential influence over Edith. After a lunch outing, 'furious' with his unsolicited advice on love and marriage, Edith summons a writer's strategy (*HL*, 102):

> To contain her anger—for she could not find her way down to the lake unaided—she tried various distancing procedures, familiar to her from long use. The most productive was to convert the incident into a scene in one of her novels. 'The evening came on stealthily,' she muttered to herself. 'The sun, a glowing ball ...'. (*HL*, 102)

Despite failing in her immediate enterprise, Edith's narrating is an innate part of her writer's practice. When her officious neighbour Penelope styles herself as the perfect candidate for characterisation in Edith's romance fiction—'I'm the one with all the stories ... I wonder she doesn't put me in a book'—Edith is left to consider, 'I have ... You did not recognise yourself' (*HL*, 127, 127). In both these examples, Brookner foregrounds Edith's writing practice through a narrative orality in which Edith either speaks out loud, listens to another person speaking, or talks to herself. Recurrent throughout *Hotel du Lac*, these forms of narrative orality bridge Edith's writing practice to the figure of the storyteller, reshaping it through the persona of the women's writer.

A typical Brooknerine, Edith Hope is a literary heroine. Like the other Brookner heroines under investigation in this study—booksellers, performers, a student, and a translator—Edith is both an outsider and insider in ways that are linked to her status as a women's writer. She is 'out of place'; '[o]ut of phase with the world'; 'at fault'; 'a stranger to the very act of celebration' (*HL*, 10, 93, 146, 115). In addition to citing Proust, Edith is intertextually aligned with the modernists, whose post-Romantic lessons included an emphasis on technical self-awareness, and immersion within the queer and lesbian canons. Edith claims to look like Virginia Woolf and her editor describes her appearance as 'remarkably Bloomsburian' (*HL*, 63, 27). When Edith reflects on having 'unworthy thoughts' about the female guests at the hotel, she thinks: 'I have taken the name of Virginia Woolf in vain' (*HL*, 88, 88.) Edith's pseudonym, Vanessa Wilde, invokes Woolf through her sister's name, Vanessa Bell, which Edith combines with Wilde in a reference to the queer nineteenth-century aesthetes. At the Hotel du Lac, Edith 'regretfully' disqualifies reading Henry James and chooses instead Colette's 'beautifully named *Ces plaisirs, qu'on nomme, à la légère, physiques*' (also known as *The Pure and the Impure*) in which Colette points out that 'le plaisir' is a euphemism for orgasm.[17] In *The Pure and the Impure*, the narrator 'Colette' urges an acquaintance, Charlotte, who fakes orgasms with her younger lover, to 'try to find the thing you "really and truly" lack'.[18] Colette's figuring of the orgasm as lack, has interesting connotations for interpreting the 'lack' of Brookner's *Hotel du Lac[k]*. Edith's focus on Colette's title implies that its own significance in *Hotel du Lac* is one of a pleasurable and erotic nature, while Sherry A. Dranch points out that Colette's cast in *The Pure and the Impure* are 'anti heroines'.[19] A text contested across multiple planes, *The Pure and the Impure* is detailed by Kadji Amin as a 'multivocal, fragmentary text [that] resolutely refuses a unitary, objective vision, frustrating the demand for overarching theories and classificatory schemas through which to understand the queer genders and sexualities it describes'.[20] With multiple chapters recording female (and male) same-sex relationships in both a journalistic and judgemental mode, *The Pure and the Impure* takes a queer scopophilic pleasure in the subjects it records.[21] Connecting queer female modernists, Helen

---

17 Both Skinner and Williams-Wanquet compare *Hotel du Lac* to *The Portrait of a Lady*, while *Hotel du Lac* and *Daisy Miller* share the location setting of Vevey. Skinner, *The Fictions of Anita Brookner*, 68. Williams-Wanquet, *Art and Life in the Novels of Anita Brookner*, 236. Colette, *The Pure and the Impure*, 38.
18 Colette, *The Pure and the Impure*, 23.
19 Sherry A. Dranch, 'Reading through the Veiled Text: Colette's "The Pure and the Impure"', *Contemporary Literature* 28.2 (1983): 177.
20 Kadji Amin, 'Ghosting Transgender Historicity in Colette's *The Pure and the Impure*', *L'Esprit Créateur* 53.1 (2013): 114. Elizabeth Ladenson states that the text 'presents exceptional difficulties … *Le pur et l'impur* cannot be ignored; neither, however, does anyone seem to know quite what to make of it'. Elisabeth Ladenson, 'Colette for Export Only', *Same Sex/Different Text? Gay and Lesbian Writing in French*, Yale French Studies 90 (1996): 27.
21 Ladenson emphasises that Colette and Proust were held under the unsympathetic sway of sexology when she states that both of them 'are chronologically

Southworth emphasises numerous biographical, stylistic, textual, and thematic ties between Woolf and Colette, and reads *A Room of One's Own* and *The Pure and the Impure* together to suggest 'a reciprocity or dialogue between the two writers'.²² *Hotel du Lac*'s interest in the queer modernists and the differences they present to the literary context of Edith's 1980's romance novels suggest once again the potential value of looking outside a singular historical period to read the text.

In her *Paris Review* interview, Brookner herself asserted the temporal hybridity of Edith's character, anticipating the performative Romanticism of Rachel Kennedy, Blanche Vernon, Fay Dodworth, Claire Pitt, and Miriam Sharpe when she said, 'Edith Hope is not a twentieth-century heroine, she belongs to the nineteenth century'.²³ And when *Hotel du Lac* won the Booker Prize in 1984, the chairperson of the judges, Professor Richard Cobb, praised the novel for being 'almost eighteenth-century'.²⁴ Like other Brooknerines, Edith's outsider status is also cultural and ethnic. Reviewing Edith's arrival at the Hotel du Lac, the hotelier, M. Huber, muses, 'Hope, Edith Johanna. An unusual name for an English lady. Perhaps not entirely English. Perhaps not entirely a lady' (*HL*, 23). Edith's exile to the Hotel du Lac is merely one instance of a more fundamental exile that is personal and professional and also connotes Edith's Jewishness. Thus, Edith is dispossessed of the carelessness that Brookner elsewhere identifies with the English. 'People say that I am always serious and depressing, but it seems to me that the English are *never* serious—they are flippant, complacent, ineffable, but never serious, which is sometimes maddening'.²⁵ So Edith is 'a householder, a ratepayer … a deliverer of typescripts well before the deadline' (*HL*, 8). Her quiet discipline, her 'five novels, of some length, there to prove she had not spent her time gazing out of the window', and her relative acceptance that her 'profile was deemed to be low' all conspire to make her an assimilated insider within the social and professional milieu of her historical context (*HL*, 30, 9).

> and theoretically situated at the crossroads of nineteenth- and twentieth-century sexologies, inversion, and homosexuality'. Ladenson, 'Colette for Export Only', 41.
> 22 Helen Southworth, *The Intersecting Realities and Fictions of Virginia Woolf and Colette* (Columbus: Ohio State University Press, 2004), 70.
> 23 Brookner, in Guppy, 'Art of Fiction', 161.
> 24 Professor Richard Cobb, interview by R. Mayne, 'Kaleidoscope', BBC Radio 4 (18 October 1984).
> 25 Brookner, in Shusha Guppy, 'The Art of Fiction XCVIII: Anita Brookner', 150.

By making her author protagonist a female romance fiction writer with queer literary tastes, Brookner complicates the insider/outside dichotomy. Edith is a successful writer, but her success is contested from multiple angles. As witnessed by Miriam Sharpe's despair over Beatrice's reading material in *Falling Slowly*, romance fiction is a female, mass-market, pop-cultural form devalued as an unartistic and conservative encoding of the heterosexual romance narrative with its stereotypical gender identities. Reflecting the beleaguered status of the romance genre, two of Edith's suitors easily disparage her occupation. Jilted fiancé Geoffrey Long does not 'approve of women working, and he teased her about the amount of time she gave to her books' (*HL*, 119). Mr Neville, on the other hand, lobbies for an identity change. He seemingly bolsters his marriage proposal by insisting that Edith 'may begin to write rather better' than she had thought possible, adding that 'Edith Neville is a fine name for an author' (*HL*, 165, 165). Were Edith to remain an unmarried romance novelist, she would, he tells her, 'look a bit of a fool' (*HL*, 165). Brookner also satirises the romance genre in *Hotel du Lac*, revealing that her heroine writes 'under a more thrusting name' and making hyperbole innate to Edith's craft: 'the evening came on stealthily' (*HL*, 8, 102).[26] This critique of the romance genre is re-enacted in the criticism of *Hotel du Lac*, a novel described by Martha Bayles as 'a Harlequin romance for highbrows'.[27] Skinner's claim that '*Hotel du Lac* is the most original and innovative of Brookner's novels, even as it also remains the one most intimately linked to the world of popular romance' reflects how qualities associated with the avant-garde male canon are implicitly privileged over genres associated with women's writing.[28] The persistence of these hierarchies have been a contributing factor in the original misreading and devaluation of Brookner's oeuvre.

26 In the *Paris Review*, Brookner distinguishes between romance novels and the Romantic novel: 'Romance novels are formula novels. I have read some and they seem to be writing about a different species. The true Romantic novel is about delayed happiness, and the pilgrimage to go through to get that imagined happiness. In the genuine Romantic novel there is a confrontation with truth and in the "romance" novel a similar confrontation with a surrogate, plastic version of the truth.' Romantic writers are characterised by absolute longing—perhaps for something that is not there and cannot be there. And they go along with all the hurt and embarrassment of identifying the real thing and wanting it'. Anita Brookner, interview by Shusha Guppy, 'The Art of Fiction XCVIII: Anita Brookner', 161.
27 Martha Bayles, 'Romance à la Mode', *New Republic* 192.12 (25 March 1985): 37–38. Williams-Wanquet, *Art and Life in the Novels of Anita Brookner*, 8.
28 Skinner, *The Fictions of Anita Brookner*, 66.

EPILOGUE

In view of this dichotomy, Brookner's drafting of Edith into a gendered practice, with contested status in a literary field organised around the male canon, signifies the potential subversiveness of a range of genres of women's writing, including romance. Brookner also signals that, in *Hotel du Lac*, questions of writing practice will be tied to themes of gender, love, marriage, and the heterosexual romance narrative, and that these themes will be dealt with satirically.

While at the hotel, Edith plans to transform her 'curious hiatus' into an opportunity to work on her sixth novel, *Beneath the Visiting Moon*, whose title invokes *Antony and Cleopatra* (*HL*, 9). But Edith spends less time nutting out the finer details of her book than she had anticipated. Instead, she is absorbed by the backstage elements of the storyteller's craft: honing the senses (a vocation associated with the aesthete in Chapter 2 of *Misreading Anita Brookner*), sorting ephemeral impressions, observing the minutiae of detail (a narrative form associated with of the dandy in Chapter 3), listening to other people's stories, and turning raw material into narrative. On her first evening, Edith encounters 'a rosy scent' in the hotel corridor, attributing it (wrongly) to Monica, only later to align it with Iris and Jennifer Pusey (*HL*, 24, 34). In *The Pure and the Impure*, the narrator describes the olfactory as 'the most aristocratic of our five senses'.[29] In the salon, Edith apprehends a crumpled newspaper yet to be cleared away, observes Mme de Bonneuil's ring 'crested, but with the indentations worn away', and later observes quite fetishistically of Jennifer that 'from her teeth a tiny thread of saliva hung glistening' (*HL*, 25, 31, 115). Descending into the salon on her first afternoon (in the wake of a urinary misdemeanour by Monica's dog Kiki, whose name is also a 1940s signifier for androgynous lesbianism), Edith is introduced to the 'delightful spectacle' of the Puseys, whom she studies 'as if under hypnosis' (*HL*, 18, 18). As per their tacit contract, Edith submits to Iris Pusey's will to dominate. When Edith tells Mrs Pusey her room number, Iris replies with a barely coded reading of Edith's sexual status: 'That little room at the end. Of course, there are very few single rooms in a place like this' (*HL*, 42). And when Edith is collectively pushed by the Puseys, Monica, and Mr Neville into renovating her appearance, she is nevertheless punished for straying from her bookishness.

---

29 Colette, *The Pure and the Impure*, 59. Colette hoped the book would detail 'my personal contribution to the sum total of our knowledge of the senses'. Colette, *The Pure and the Impure*, 58.

'Why, Edith,' cried Mrs Pusey, with her usual vivacity. 'What on earth have you done to your hair? Come and join us, dear. Let me have a proper look at you.'

...

'Oh, but I think I liked it better the other way,' said Mrs Pusey. (*HL*, 156, 156)

As the target of Mrs Pusey's self-aggrandisement, Edith appears to conform to the stereotype of the passive Brooknerine that is doggedly stamped onto Brookner's original reception. Thus, Robert E. Hosmer comments that '[u]nease, uncertainty, and introspection combine to make Edith Hope one of the most guilt-ridden figures in contemporary literature; this woman blames herself for the rudeness of others and assumes responsibility for the offensive behaviour of others'.[30] Skinner claims that 'the external narrator's foregrounding of Edith's anxiety assumes almost obsessive proportions', which he relates to an 'emphasis on silence' in the novel.[31] Yet among the lessons that *Hotel du Lac* can take from *A Friend from England*, *A Misalliance*, *Brief Lives*, *Undue Influence*, and *Falling Slowly* is that deviations from normative femininity most frequently announce the presence of an artistic persona.

After all, Edith is not completely innocent; nor is she always silent. The narrator tells us that Edith 'lied well', she uses a 'disguised voice', she is an adulterer and a polyamorist, she 'prided herself on giving nothing away', she is at times 'loquacious' and 'entertaining', and she eavesdrops on, gossips about, satirises, and mimics her fellow guests (*HL*, 85, 62, 61, 10, 10). Like the narrator of *The Pure and the Impure*, who states 'mine is the very human pleasure of witnessing catastrophes', Edith is not one to avert her face.[32] Ladenson states that the title Colette originally gave to *The Pure and the Impure* was *Le fourbe* ('the deceiver'), underscoring the duality of the speculative storyteller.[33] Ladenson also notes that, like many of the texts in the Brookner intertextual archive, *The Pure and the Impure* has a scandalous history: 'Colette's first attempt to publish the text in serial form in the journal *Gringoire* in 1931 came to a bad end, with the fourth installment literally cut off in the middle of a sentence because of the scandalous nature of its contents'.[34] While these

---

30 Robert E. Hosmer Jr, 'Paradigm and Passage: The Fiction of Anita Brookner', in *Contemporary British Women Writers: Texts and Strategies*, ed. Robert E. Hosmer Jr (London: Palgrave Macmillan, 1993), 37.
31 Skinner, *The Fictions of Anita Brookner*, 78, 78.
32 Colette, *The Pure and the Impure*, 28.
33 Ladenson, 'Colette for Export Only', 26.
34 Ladenson, 'Colette for Export Only', 26.

subversive characteristics conflict with the Brooknerine stereotype, they are integral to the development of Edith's skill as a storyteller and her investment in a lesbian homoerotic. They are most clearly evidenced in the letters she writes to David.

Arriving at the hotel, Edith extracts two folders from her bag, swiftly rejecting work on *Beneath the Visiting Moon* in favour of letter-writing. Over the course of her stay, Edith's five letters to David, through which she wrests narrative authority from the extradiegetic narrator, constitute the bulk of her writing practice. As Liana Piehler notes, 'throughout her stay, the most vivid examples of her writing come in the form of letters addressed to her lover David'.[35] And so Edith abandons Monica and the cakes at Haffenegger's café, saying, 'I think I'll go back ... I've got some letters to write' (*HL*, 149). Embedded within the frame narrative but authored by Edith, the letters represent the most unmediated access the reader is given to Edith as writer.

In contrast to her more restrained personal style, Edith's letters are captivating and engaging, eliciting Anne Tyler's observation that 'Edith's chatty, affected letters to her lover, reproduced verbatim, seem highly unlike her'.[36] In 'The Storyteller', Benjamin underscores how the intrinsic orality of the storyteller is foundational to its theatrical nature:

> In genuine storytelling the hand plays a part which supports what is expressed in a hundred ways with its gestures trained by work ... In fact, we can go on and ask oneself whether the relationship of the storyteller to his material, human life, is not in itself a craftsman's relationship, whether it is not his very task to fashion the raw material of experience, his own and that of others, in a solid, useful, and unique way.[37]

Edith's letters are the sites where we witness the craftsperson shaping the raw material of life in unique ways. In Peter Brooks's rereading of Benjamin, he emphasises how nineteenth-century writers such as Henry James, Balzac, and Barbey d'Aurevilly obsessively explore 'a fictive situation of oral communication'.[38] According to Brooks, such tales generally rely on a structure of embedded narrative (like *Hotel du*

---

35 Liana F. Piehler, *Spatial Dynamics and Female Development in Victorian Art and Novels: Creating a Woman's Space* (New York: Peter Lang, 2003), 134.
36 Anne Tyler, 'A Solitary Life is Still Worth Living', *New York Times* online (3 February 1985): www.nytimes.com/1985/02/03/books/a-solitary-life-is-still-worth-living.html (subscription required).
37 Benjamin, 'The Storyteller', 108.
38 Peter Brooks, 'The Storyteller', *Yale Journal of Criticism* 1.1 (1987): 21.

Lac) and depend upon a situation 'where the exchange and transmission of narrative is at issue'.[39] Similarly, in *Hotel du Lac*, Edith's impetus to 'write up' the astonishing and trivial behaviour of the Puseys, as well as report on Monica's eating disorder (Edith tells David that the 'story behind this is interesting' [*HL*, 80]), also makes the epistolary site the central place where listening is transmuted to storytelling in the novel (*HL*, 48). Against Skinner's contention that Edith's silence is a resistance to language, her letters capture the way that listening cultivates a silence that later metamorphoses into language. In this way, Edith's letters function as a medium for the storyteller's improvisational style that embraces oral modes, satire, mimicry, and rhetorical questioning, as well as multiple forms of imaginative misreading.

In Chapter 3 of *Misreading Anita Brookner*, we saw how the nineteenth-century dandy's aphoristic style, along with elements of narrative self-correction, was part of the oral narrative of *Brief Lives*. In *Hotel du Lac*, Edith is also prone to aphoristic flourishes: 'It is not true that Satan makes work for idle hands to do; that is just what he doesn't', she reflects, for example (*HL*, 158). But the most emphatically oral components of *Hotel du Lac* surface in Edith's letters. In her second letter to David, Edith satirically appropriates Iris Pusey's persona, posing a series of questions:

> When my husband was moved to Head Office, occasioning that tragic departure from Haslemere, where exactly did he go? What was his Head Office Head Office of? There is a nuance in Mrs Pusey's behaviour, and even something, dare I say it, about the cut of Jennifer's jib, that leads me to suspect that my husband might have been the kind of man who calls a shop a retail outlet. ... Did he slip off from time to time for a solitary spree at the tables? Was he a closet member of the Marbella Club? I rather hope so, but there is no evidence to support this. (*HL*, 47)

Framed through the storyteller's dynamic of listening and retelling, Edith's oral epistolary style emphasises her artistry and authority. Contrary to the perceived 'tortoisedom' supposedly integral to her practice as a romantic novelist, the personal performance of Edith in her letters is theatrical, dramatic, and technical (*HL*, 30). In this storytelling performance, Edith joins the tradition of the genius women's writer and the figure of the lesbian that is styled through Sappho, Staël, Woolf, and Colette.

---

39 Brooks, 'The Storyteller', 22.

The novel's epistolary scenes also evidence Edith's frequent imaginative misreadings. In the performance of the *flâneur* in *Undue Influence* in Chapter 4 of *Misreading Anita Brookner*, imagination and misreading were shown to be specialised tools of the Romantic artist. Claire Pitt's prized speculations also helped to swerve the interpretation of Brookner's novel away from the heterosexual romance and towards the narrative of influence. In *Hotel du Lac*, Edith is similarly possessed of a boundless capacity for reverie. An early statement by David—'I must be getting back to the Rooms'—transports Edith into a scene akin to that of the *Arabian Nights* (*HL*, 56).

> She turned the amazing sentence over in her mind, conjuring up vistas of courtyards with fountains trickling and silent servants in gauze trousers bringing sherbet. Or possibly large divans in whitewashed houses shuttered against the heat of the afternoon, a dreaming, glowing idleness, inspired by Delacroix. Or of grave merchants, with clicking amber beads, in coffee houses below pavement level. Opium dens. Turkish baths. A tiled hammam, its walls bright with coins of light reflected from the water. Peace. (*HL*, 56)

Powered by words, Edith's imaginative flight reveals her creative, Romantic nature. And, as Piehler notes, 'David's words inspire the fantasy—and, yet, they do not involve imaginings of *him*!'[40] Such creative speculations contradict Edith's apparent dismissal of imagination in the early parts of the novel. 'So much for the novelist's famed powers of imagination', she writes to David (twice) in reference to herself; she had first fancied that a fellow aeroplane passenger was a specialist in tropical diseases only later to find he worked with tungsten, and she had then conceptualised Mme de Bonneuil as a confectioner's widow only later to discover she was a countess (*HL*, 11). Not only are Edith's misreadings a very symptom of her imagination, her repudiation of imagination constitutes a reversal of its own. Brooknerian peripeteia proliferate throughout *Hotel du Lac*, and manifest in Edith's return from Switzerland to London, both her decisions not to get married, and her efforts to write letters but not send them. Reversals are evident even in small instances, such as when Edith orders coffee, and decides no she will have tea (*HL*, 99). They are perceptible in Edith's psychology, such as when she appraises Jennifer's character by first deciding she must have a boyfriend, then later retracting that impression (*HL*, 103). Reversals have physical resonance in Kiki's vomiting, poetic significance in the

---

40 Piehler, *Spatial Dynamics and Female Development in Victorian Art and Novels*, 135.

trope of the closing doors, and more formal force in the shift of voices between extradiegetic and intradiegetic narrator. Reversals are also indicated in the types of negations and denials to which Edith is prone. She tells herself that 'of course none of those people would fit into the sort of fiction I write', and yet it turns out that the Puseys are readers of Vanessa Wilde, and her fellow hotel guests slip easily into material for her letters to David (*HL*, 21).

In *The Pure and the Impure*, the narrator 'Colette' talks to her celebrity friend X about the sexual conquests of his friend Maasen. X, however, wants to know where Colette got her information. 'On this source of information, all sources are suspect', Colette replies.[41] Ladenson nominates this response as a 'fitting epigraph to the entire volume'.[42] Ladenson's contention—that the (sexual) knowledge offered up in *The Pure and the Impure* is partial, contingent, contextual, and can be applied 'to representations of sexuality in general'—finds resonance in *Hotel du Lac* through the operation of misreading.[43] Misreading and reversal are patterned throughout the narrative in Edith's fascination with the Puseys' floating ages. First, Edith predicts Jennifer Pusey is 25 years old, only to revise the Puseys' ages 'to the upper 60s and the early 30s' a mere page later (*HL*, 19, 20). Subsequently, incriminating language used by Iris Pusey means that 'Edith realized that ages would have to be revised once more' (*HL*, 34). This reconsideration is repeated twice more when Iris physically steadies herself against Jennifer (*HL*, 43, 63). And, listening to Iris lament the disappearance of the local expert in drawn-thread blouses, Edith speculates that Jennifer is now only 'a few years younger' than herself (*HL*, 55). 'Thirty-two? Thirty-three? Possibly thirty-four?' (*HL*, 55). Three-quarters of the way through the book, Iris's birthday brings about the final revelations. 'Astounding news!', Edith writes to David, 'Mrs Pusey, that pinnacle of feminine chic, that arbiter of taste, that relentless seeker after luxury goods, that charmer of multitudes, is *seventy-nine!*' (*HL*, 103). Even more arresting is the discovery that 'Jennifer, like me, is thirty-nine, although her curious combination of plump body and expressionless face makes her seem no older than fourteen' (*HL*, 112). As revealed in *Undue Influence*, the ensemble of imagination, misreading, and reversal are creative techniques that underscore the presence of the artist persona. For Edith, as for Claire Pitt, the facts are not as important

---

41 Colette, *The Pure and the Impure*, 36.
42 Ladenson, 'Colette for Export Only', 25.
43 Ladenson, 'Colette for Export Only', 26.

as the stories themselves; indeed, facts are primarily useful for how they enable a story to evolve and climax. And, as a storytelling technique, imaginative misreading creates a deferral that keeps readers in suspense as the supposed facts are always liable to change. Such a technique underscores the authority of the artist in charge of the narrative flow, while at the same time casting doubt over an authority that is seemingly unsustainable. Benjamin states that 'every real story … contains, openly or covertly, something useful. The usefulness may, in one case, consist in a moral; in another, in some practical advice; in a third, in a proverb or maxim. In every case the storyteller is a man who has counsel for his readers'.[44] In *Hotel du Lac*, the lesson for readers is that attempts to seal off meaning will create a narrative excess in the form of memories and reflections that are triggered through the writing process, and therefore expectations about a narrative may need to be revised.

Those Pleasures Which Are Lightly Called Physical

For Edith, the inability to contain a text is an unsettling revelation, as it was for Max Nordau in *Degeneration* in his fight against the instability of meaning. This information comes to Edith primarily over the course of her letter-writing to David. Stranded at the homosocial 'gynaceum' of the hotel, Edith laments 'women, women, only women, and I do so love the conversation of men' (*HL*, 61, 21). Thus her letters initially appear to be a bridge to David. As Edith acknowledges, the letters are intended 'to amuse, to divert, to relax—these had been her functions, and indeed her dedicated aim' (*HL*, 114). However, as Marks notes, 'the gynaceum … has become, since the eighteenth century, the preferred locus for most fictions about women loving women', and Edith's letters are unable to maintain closure in the heterosexual circuit between Edith and David.[45] In her reading of Colette, Ladenson notes that Colette's storytelling is impure for its sexual caricaturing, which attempts to shape a spectacle for consumption.[46] Similarly, in Edith's letters, her attempts to contain the text as heterosexual performance conversely functions

---

44 Benjamin, 'The Storyteller', 86.
45 Marks, 'Lesbian Intertextuality', 357.
46 Ladenson reads Colette's Orientalism in *The Pure and the Impure*, in which the east markets itself to the west's desires, as the text's own declaration of impurity. '[O]ur tour guide deliberately obfuscates her own credential as expert, as well as the authenticity of what she reveals', Ladenson states. Ladenson, 'Colette for Export Only', 27.

to arrest them at significant points. This impurity—or storytelling inauthenticity—subsequently produces a queer narrative excess outside the letter-text; as Edith concedes, 'something had gone wrong or was slipping out of control' (*HL*, 114). Instead of containing the text, Edith's writing precipitates a series of returns and slippages which become keys to reading Edith's scopophilic fascination with the mother/daughter pairing of Iris and Jennifer Pusey. Ladenson reads the 'impurity' of *The Pure and the Impure* as indicative of Colette's own bisexuality, also shared by Virginia Woolf.[47] Thurman states that the cast of *The Pure and the Impure* 'have been forced to deny or renounce the forbidden aspects of themselves—which are, put simply, their impure true feelings'.[48] For Dranch, Colette's occupation of the text also evidences a struggle for self-mastery: 'as pleasure is suppressed, power begins to sustain Colette's discourse on sexuality', she states.[49] In a comparable fashion, Edith's decision not to send her letters, as well as her ability to sustain reflection outside them, are implicated in a critical stage of the self-constitution of the artist, an *askesis* that informs part of the narrative of influence that we visited in Chapter 4. As evidenced throughout *Misreading Anita Brookner*, Brookner draws on aestheticised and historicised intertextual familial tropes to figure homoerotic desire, from the erotic mother figure through Stendhal and Giorgione and the Platonic father/son model in *A Friend from England* to the Sapphic mother/daughter duo of *A Misalliance* and the devoted sisters of *Falling Slowly*. In *Hotel du Lac*, Iris and Jennifer Pusey constitute a formative example of the lesbian erotic model we encounter in later Brookner texts, a model which is given particular resonance through the intertextual key of Colette.

In her first letter, Edith's text is arrested the moment she addresses David with the words her father used to address her mother: 'My dear life, as my father used to call my mother, I miss you so much' (*HL*, 12). As Edith positions the figure of the mother as the object of her desire, the homoerotic mother–daughter duo is forged, and Edith's heterosexual love object is eclipsed. 'She remained seated at the table for a few minutes, then took a long breath, and put the cap back on her pen' (*HL*, 12). The significance of writing love letters as a familial practice is illuminated during the second letter. Breaking away from the text, Edith has an extended memory in which she recalls finding a fragment

---

47 Ladenson, 'Colette for Export Only', 31.
48 Judith Thurman, 'Introduction', in Colette, *The Pure and the Impure*, ix.
49 Dranch, 'Reading through the Veiled Text', 179.

of a letter written from her father to her mother, 'its purpose now lost, and only its opening sentence hinting at earlier, happier times' (*HL*, 49).

Edith's homoerotic scopophilia is also given context as she stops writing her second letter to recall her father rescuing her from her mother's '[a]nnoyance and frustration' by taking her to the Kunsthistorisches Museum: 'And when he stopped longingly before a picture of men lying splayed in a cornfield under a hot sun she burst into further tears' (*HL*, 49, 49). In this case, Edith's father's homoerotic longing functions as a queer return that illuminates how the pleasure of looking functions within the familial context that Edith scans to make sense of her experience.

Edith's memory of the sight of two women's bodies entwined at the bedroom doorway further hijacks her ability to complete her second letter: 'Edith laid down her pen. It was all very well to write up Mrs Pusey and Jennifer, but she was still left with that memory of the two women lovingly entwined as they saw her to the door to say goodnight' (*HL*, 47–48). Ladenson states that in 'a number of places [Colette] depicts erotic relations between women as based on a model of maternal tenderness', engaging the mother figure as trope of lesbian eroticism in Colette's work.[50] Marks's comment that in *The Pure and the Impure*, the 'spectrum of female homosexuality is sanctified by comparison to the mother–daughter relationship' provides some insight into the Pusey mother/daughter relationship as consumed and produced by Edith.[51] In multiple ways, Edith styles Iris as the sexual figure *par exemple*; Marks states that 'the female figure who dominates Colette's female hierarchy is the mother figure'.[52] And, following what Marks labels Colette's 'voyeurism', most of Edith's celebration of the Puseys emerges through a scopophilic pleasure, a female homoerotic pleasure that is signified through the title of Colette's 'beautifully named' book, which Edith first invokes in French and only later in English: 'those pleasures which are lightly called physical' (*HL*, 67, 184). According to Edith, Iris Pusey (whose surname figures the female genitalia) is 'an enchantress' with a 'disposition to flirt, even when there was no one around to flirt with' (*HL*, 39, 83). Iris's self-eroticisation is exemplified at her birthday party when she describes the 'twelve years of selfless and dedicated "trying"' to conceive Jennifer (*HL*, 113). Edith's eroticising of the Puseys is also

---

50 Ladenson, 'Colette for Export Only', 34–35.
51 Marks, 'Lesbian Intertextuality', 364.
52 Marks, 'Lesbian Intertextuality', 364–65.

indicated in her speculations, in letter four, on 'Jennifer's married life as being an extension of her present one; simply, there will be three of them instead of two' (*HL*, 110). In the period of reverie prompted by writing the third letter, Edith claims her own mother and aunt would have branded Mrs Pusey '[t]rès portée sur la chose' (*HL*, 84). Deflected through her mother's words in French, Edith's branding of Iris Pusey as a sex addict infuses the Puseys with an erotic aura that fuels Edith's obsession and simultaneously conceals her participation in the eroticisation. Edith's constant recourse to the familial to express desire represents a homoerotic recuperation of the mother figure.

In the third letter, Edith's narrative is interrupted when she finds herself on the threshold of revealing too much about Mr Neville: 'Edith laid down her pen, for it would have been inappropriate to continue' (*HL*, 81). However, it is not Mr Neville who sustains her interest. Instead, Edith again drifts into reflections about the Puseys, recalling 'that glimpse, that Edith had had, in [Jennifer's] bedroom, of those exotic *déshabillés*, not all of them in the quietest of taste' (*HL*, 83). Again the target of Edith's scopophilic tendencies, Jennifer is perceived as 'an eye-opener, if you will permit the vulgarity' in her 'pink harem pants ... with an off the shoulder blouse' (*HL*, 106, 106–07). For Edith, Jennifer is a disembodied erotic spectacle: 'a girl wearing rather tight white trousers (rather too tight, thought Edith) which outlined a bottom shaped like a large Victoria plum' (*HL*, 18). Edith locates Jennifer in the same realm of *Arabian Nights* fantasyland in which she had formerly placed David, enabling a slippage between her male lover and her female erotic object. Thus Jennifer incarnates 'a stolidity which verged on opulence' and evokes an 'odalisque ... revealing quite a lot of very grown-up flesh' (*HL*, 40, 78). Throughout the novel, Edith's focus on Jennifer's body, appearance, age, mannerisms, and psychology result in an objectification in which Edith fails to apprehend Jennifer as a subject in her own right. Edith's refusal of mutuality between Jennifer and herself explains her shock at discovering that she and Jennifer are the same age, and underlies Edith's inability to apprehend Jennifer's affair with Mr Neville.

Edith's reluctance to complete a single letter to David is given context when she breaks away from the text of letter four after 'hidden areas, dangerous shoals, erupted into her consciousness' (*HL*, 116). At this point, the text returns to the reason for Edith's 'tiny exile': her real-life rejection of the heterosexual marriage narrative (*HL*, 117). As each previous letter follows a similar pattern of textual arrest and familial return that refigures the homoerotic mother/daughter spectacle, they all restage the rejection of the conventional romance narrative (*HL*, 8). And, if the letters are indeed love letters, they are also love letters about women. Once Edith acknowledges her rejection of the heterosexual romance in letter four, she is able to complete her first letter to David, in which she informs him of her intention to marry Mr Neville. However this letter, too, is aborted once Edith discovers that Mr Neville—or is it Jennifer?—is otherwise occupied.

The Heterosexual Romance Satire

The sham marriage of Heather and Michael in *A Friend from England*, Blanche Vernon's uneasy marriage in *A Misalliance*, the adulterous union between Fay and Charlie in *Brief Lives*, the marriage trials of Martin and Cynthia in *Undue Influence*, and the distasteful spectacle of marriage in *Falling Slowly* are all ways in which Brookner explores how the ideal of marriage conflicts with its reality. In *Hotel du Lac*, satire represents the most effective way to capture this chasm: Janet Giltrow describes the novel as an 'ironic romance' that presents a highly regulated social order at the same time as it employs a tone that enables more subversive meanings to exist below the surface.[53] Reversing the typical romance structure that climaxes in marriage, *Hotel du Lac* instead hosts a series of revelations that climax in two marriage refusals. Indeed, Giltrow calls Edith's time at the hotel her 'reverse honeymoon'.[54] In Chapter 9, Edith finally remembers how she was propelled to her marriage as if to the guillotine; en route to the registry office she is newly struck by the 'extraordinary charm' of her neighbourhood including 'the funeral parlour' and 'the newsagent, with his discreet display of adult magazines' (*HL*, 129, 129, 129). Sighting the 'mouse-like seemliness' of her future husband awaiting her arrival, Edith quietly requests her driver—who surmises 'she was one of the guests'—to pass the gathered onlookers and continue on around the park (*HL*, 129, 130). Returning home unmarried and condemned, Edith is still pleased to note her publisher sipping champagne in the garden, and later arranges to meet her lover. As is repeatedly demonstrated in the novels, Brookner's take on marriage and the happy-ever-after fairy-tale is unconventional.

---

53 Janet Giltrow, 'Ironies of Politeness in Anita Brookner's *Hotel du Lac*', in *Ambiguous Discourse: Feminist Narratology and British Women Writers*, ed. Kathy Mezei (Chapel Hill and London: University of North Carolina Press, 1996), 215.
54 Giltrow, 'Ironies of Politeness', 222.

But, even in exile, Edith's escape is not complete. At the Hotel du Lac, she is courted by Mr Neville, whose romancing involves threats of physical violence ('I cannot bear to see a woman cry; it makes me want to hit her' [*HL*, 168]); undermining commentary ('Whoever told you that you looked like Virginia Woolf did you a grave disservice' [*HL*, 158]); coldness (in response to hearing about his *famille rose* dishes Edith retorts: 'You are wrong ... I do not love *things* at all' [*HL*, 164]); and multiple attempts to dissuade Edith of her belief in love.[55] As Maroula Joannou states in her reading of *Hotel du Lac* as both deployment and subversion of the romance genre, Neville's 'proposal is predicated on a fundamental misreading of Edith's character ... It is, of course, precisely such indiscreet behaviour, the jilting of her dull but kindly and attentive suitor on her wedding day, that has precipitated Edith's exile in Switzerland'.[56] If Edith doubts the appeal of marriage, then it is not hard to see why.

And it is not only Edith's experience that puts marriage to the test in *Hotel du Lac*—the novel's main cast of players similarly conspire to disabuse readers of the social fantasy surrounding the institution. Reversing the traditional gender stereotype, Neville's first wife left him for a man ten years his junior. David cheats on '[s]exy' Priscilla with Edith (*HL*, 86). Iris Pusey styles herself as a romantic icon and yet her dead and unnamed husband is valued primarily for the financial benefits he bestowed, including property, luxury goods, and travel. The individualistic nature of Iris's dialogue on marriage, which fundamentally serves to highlight her superiority to other women, is circulated at the expense of those guests who have not managed to procure such adoration, including her own daughter, childless Monica, and the widowed Mme de Bonneuil. Iris's idealised marriage fantasy effectively forces Jennifer to exist in an adolescent time warp, where she retreats into psychological absence and uses the hotel busboy as a foil to cover up sexual behaviour that conflicts with her mother's mythologising. Monica's marriage is in abeyance, blamed on fertility problems and held aloft with an eating disorder. Mme de Bonneuil is the collateral damage of her son's second marriage, evicted by her daughter-in-law to serve time alone at the hotel.

Critics of *Hotel du Lac* draw attention to the irony that while Edith

---

55 Skinner, *The Fictions of Anita Brookner*, 164.
56 Maroula Joannou, 'Essentially Virtuous? Anita Brookner's *Hotel du Lac* as Generic Subversion', in *Fatal Attractions: Re-scripting Romance in Contemporary Literature and Film*, ed. Lynne Pearce and Gina Whisker (London and Sterling, Va.: Pluto Press, 1998), 88.

is a romance novelist, she herself rejects marriage, even as she claims, 'I believed every word I wrote' in her novels (*HL*, 181).⁵⁷ But Edith's return home enacts another choice: the decision to tell stories. For, unlike Edith's two other male suitors, David inspires Edith to create:

> 'Well, darling, what news from Cranford?' David used to say, stretching out his long arm to gather her to him as they sat on her big sofa. And that had always been her cue to present him with her gentle observations, always skilfully edited, and to watch the lines of fatigue on his lean and foxy face dissolve into a smile. (*HL*, 114)⁵⁸

The narrative orality of Edith's letters, their tricks and techniques, misreadings, reversals, and anagnorisis all freight value around the significance *Hotel du Lac* places on Edith as a women's writer. In her fourth letter to David, Edith sheds further light on her occupation when she tells him that her mother 'comforted herself … by reading love stories, simple romances with happy endings. Perhaps that is why I write them' (*HL*, 104). Based on the novel's queer intertextual associations, Edith's statement suggests that romance writing is a practice that aims to give pleasure to the eroticised mother figure.

Conclusion

The year after Brookner won the Booker Prize for *Hotel du Lac*, and was roundly condemned for it, the novelist spoke about the gendered context of the prize.

> The interesting thing about this year's Booker Prize—and I can speak about this quite dispassionately—is that in recent years the prize has gone to a very masculine type of novel. And there seems to have been a slight reaction against that tradition. I say 'a slight reaction' advisedly, because it is felt, I think subliminally, that the big money should be on the male yarn and should stay there. But I think there's room for another kind of novel.⁵⁹

In *Misreading Anita Brookner*, I have tried to show that Brookner does indeed write a different kind of novel. In *Hotel du Lac*, Brookner's concern with technique, aesthetics, and narrative form is proleptic of her later

---

57 Giltrow, 'Ironies of Politeness', 215. Williams-Wanquet, *Art and Life in the Novels of Anita Brookner*, 236.
58 Dranch notes that '"foxy" … was always an item in the lexicon that Colette employed to describe her own features'. Dranch, 'Reading through the Veiled Text', 178.
59 Brookner, in *Publishers Weekly*, 68.

novels in which her cross-historical, intertextual technique becomes more pronounced. And once the multi-temporal nature of Brookner's texts are brought into the frame, the possibilities for interpretation are multiplied. Spanning several historical contexts, the Brooknerine's performative Romanticism combines male and female behaviours and produces what Judith Butler calls 'unpredictable and inadvertent convergences' in the subject.[60] The Brooknerine's transgressive performance of gender, against the backdrop of nineteenth-century tropes and motifs for male and female homoerotic desire, enables her to bypass regulatory forms of heterosexuality. The queerness of the Brookner protagonist and of her intimate relationships with other female subjects in Brookner's feminocentric oeuvre foreground the importance of the figure of the lesbian in Brookner's fiction.

This significance is further enhanced by the historical reading of tropes of invisibility, anachronism, absence, secondariness, and belatedness, all of which conjure the figure of the lesbian and the women's writer and are thematically associated with the Brookner text. The expansion of the Brookner text across historical periods and intertexts signals the efficacy of using figurative interpretive models when reading Brookner. The cross-generational Brookner subject, her queer relationships, her station in familial narratives—and how these key features of Brookner's world intermingle—all license the genre of the domestic fiction to develop beyond the preoccupations of the heterosexual romance narrative.

The broad historical, discursive, and temporal reach of Brookner's novels has therefore inspired new forms of interpretation in *Misreading Anita Brookner*. By summoning a cast of Romantic hermeneutic figures to read Brookner, I hope to have revealed multiple connections between symbolic practices, historical context, and sexual identities. By producing intertextual figures, conjured from a combination of behavioural modes, narrative devices, and rhetorical forms, I aim to have illustrated how subjects function as discursive effects within the textual environment, unveiling the movements and relationships of these subjects as non-normative, or queer.

Above all, through an immersion in the codings and decodings of the tricks and the layers and the irony and the playfulness of the Brookner text, I hope to communicate the consummate joy in discovering the brilliance of Brookner as women's writer, supreme technician, and transcendent storyteller.

---

60 Butler, *Gender Trouble*, 145.

Bibliography

Albert, Nicole. 'Sappho Mythified, Sappho Mystified or the Metamorphoses of Sappho in Fin-de-Siècle France'. *Journal of Homosexuality* 25.1/2 (1993): 87–104.
Allen, David. 'Lovers and Other Dangers'. Review of Anita Brookner's *Altered States*. *The Australian* (19 October 1996).
Amin, Kadji. 'Ghosting Transgender Historicity in Colette's *The Pure and the Impure*'. *L'Esprit Créateur* 53.1 (2013): 114–30.
Appignanesi, Lisa and John Forrester. *Freud's Women*. London: Virago, 1993.
Arata, Stephen. *Fictions of Loss in the Victorian Fin de Siècle: Identity and Europe*. Cambridge: Cambridge University Press, 1996.
Armstrong, Nancy. *Desire and Domestic Fiction: A Political History of the Novel*. New York: Oxford University Press, 1987.
Aubrey, John. *Monumenta Britannica; or, A Miscellany of British Antiquities*. Edited by John Fowles. Boston: Little, Brown, 1980.
Ayrton, Elizabeth. *The Cookery of England*. London: André Deutsch, 1974.
Bahti, Timothy. 'History as Rhetorical Enactment: Walter Benjamin's Theses "On the Concept of History"'. In *Allegories of History: Literary Historiography after Hegel*. Baltimore, Md.: Johns Hopkins University Press, 1992: 183–204.
Bakhtin, M.M. *The Dialogic Imagination*. Edited by Michael Holquist. Translated by Caryl Emerson and Michael Holquist. Austin: University of Texas Press, 1981.
—— *Problems of Dostoevsky's Poetics*. Edited and translated by Caryl Emerson. Minneapolis: University of Minnesota Press, 1984.
Balzac, Honoré de. *A Start in Life*. Translated by Katharine Prescott Wormeley. Adelaide: University of Adelaide Library, 2007: ebooks. adelaide.edu.au/b/balzac/start/.
—— *Treatise on Elegant Living*. Translated by Napoleon Jeffries. Cambridge, Mass.: Wakefield Press, 2010.
Barbey d'Aurevilly, Jules. 'On Dandyism and George Brummell'. Translated by George Walden. In George Walden, *Who is a Dandy?* London: Gibson Square Books, 2002: 62–175.

Barthes, Roland. *The Fashion System*. Translated by Matthew Ward and Richard Howard. New York: Hill & Wang, 1983.
—— *The Language of Fashion*. Translated by Andy Stafford. Edited by Andy Stafford and Michael Carter. Oxford: Berg, 2006.
—— *A Lover's Discourse: Fragments*. Translated by Richard Howard. Harmondsworth: Penguin, 1990.
—— *S/Z: An Essay*. Translated by Richard Miller. New York: Hill & Wang, 1974.
Baudelaire, Charles. *Complete Poems*. Translated by Walter Martin. Manchester: Carcenet, 1997.
—— *The Painter of Modern Life and Other Essays*. Edited and translated by Jonathan Mayne. London: Phaidon Press, 1964.
Bayles, Martha. 'Romance à la Mode', *New Republic* 192.12 (25 March 1985): 37–38.
Bayley, John. 'Ladies'. Review of Anita Brookner's *A Misalliance*. *London Review of Books* (4 September 1986): 20.
Benjamin, Walter. *Charles Baudelaire: A Lyric Poet in the Era of High Capitalism*. Translated by Harry Zohn. London: Verso, 1997.
—— *Illuminations: Essays and Reflections*. Translated by Harry Zohn. New York: Schocken Books, 1968.
Bennett, Kate. 'John Aubrey's Collections and the Early Modern Museum'. *Bodleian Library Record* 17.3–4 (2001): 213–45.
Bennett, Tony. 'Texts in History: The Determinations of Readers and their Texts'. In *Reception Study: From Literary Theory to Cultural Studies*. Edited by James L. Machor and Philip Goldstein. New York: Routledge, 2001: 61–74.
Birch, Dinah. 'The Sun is God: Ruskin's Solar Mythology'. In *The Sun is God: Painting, Literature and Mythology in the Nineteenth Century*. Edited by J.B. Bulleen. Oxford: Clarendon Press, 1989.
Birkerts, Sven. 'Private View'. Review of Anita Brookner's *A Private View*. *New Republic* (24 April 1995): 41.
Björkblom, Inger. *The Plane of Uncreatedness: A Phenomenological Study of Anita Brookner's Late Fiction*. Stockholm: Almqvist & Wiksell, 2001.
Blakeney, Sally. 'Failing Females'. Review of Anita Brookner's *Falling Slowly*. *The Australian* (26 September 1998).
Bloom, Alice. 'A Friend from England'. Review of Anita Brookner's *A Friend from England*. *Hudson Review* 41 (1988–89): 544.
Bloom, Harold. *The Anxiety of Influence: A Theory of Poetry*. 2nd edn. New York: Oxford University Press, 1973.
Bourdieu, Pierre. *The Rules of Art: Genesis and Structure of the Literary Field*. Translated by Susan Emanuel. Stanford, Calif.: Stanford University Press, 1992.

Bowen, Deborah. 'Preserving Appearances: Photography and the Postmodern Realism of Anita Brookner'. *Mosaic* 28.2 (June 1995): 123–48.

Brookner, Anita. 'Anita Brookner'. Interview by Amanda Smith. *Publishers Weekly* (6 September 1985): 67–68.

—— 'The Art of Fiction XCVIII: Anita Brookner'. Interview by Shusha Guppy. *Paris Review* 104 (Fall 1987): 147–69.

—— *Brief Lives*. Harmondsworth: Penguin, 1991.

—— *Falling Slowly*. London: Viking, 1998.

—— *A Friend from England*. London: Grafton Books, 1988.

—— *The Genius of the Future; Studies in French Art Criticism: Diderot, Stendhal, Baudelaire, Zola, the Brothers Goncourt, Huysmans*. London: Phaidon, 1971.

—— *Greuze: The Rise and Fall of an Eighteenth-Century Phenomenon*. London: Elek, 1972.

—— Interview by Gail Caldwell. *Boston Globe* (5 June 1985): 31.

—— Interview by Hermione Lee. *Book Four*. Channel 4 (8 September 1985). VHS cassette accessed at British Film Institute National Archive (9 May 2006). No. 131309.

—— Interview by John Haffenden. In John Haffenden, *Novelists in Interview*. London: Methuen, 1985: 57–75.

—— Interview by Nigel Forde. *Bookshelf*. BBC Radio 4 (31 January 1991).

—— Interview by Sue MacGregor. 'Woman's Hour'. BBC Radio 4 (13 January 1982).

—— 'Just Don't Mention Jane Austen'. Interview by Robert McCrum. *Observer* (28 January 2001): www.theguardian.com/books/2001/jan/28/fiction.janeausten.

—— *A Misalliance*. London: Grafton Books, 1987.

—— *Providence*. Harmondsworth: Penguin, 1991.

—— *Romanticism and Its Discontents*. London: Viking, 2000.

—— 'The Secret Sharer: An Interview and Profile of Anita Brookner'. Interview by Shusha Guppy. *World and I* 13.7 (July 1998): 282–88.

—— 'Self Reflecting'. Interview by Sheila Hale. *Saturday Review* 11.3 (1985): 35–38.

—— 'A Singular Woman'. Interview by Mick Brown. *Telegraph* online (19 February 2009): www.telegraph.co.uk/culture/books/authorinterviews/4639980/A-singular-woman.html (subscription required).

—— *Soundings*. London: Harvill Press, 1997.

—— *A Start in Life*. Harmondsworth: Penguin, 1991.

—— *Strangers*. London: Fig Tree, 2009.

—— *Undue Influence*. London: Viking, 1999.

Brooks, Peter. 'The Storyteller', *Yale Journal of Criticism* 1.1 (1987): 21–38.

Brown, Sarah Annes. *Devoted Sisters: Representations of the Sister Relationship in Nineteenth-Century British and American Literature*. Aldershot: Ashgate, 2003.

Bruzelius, Margaret. *Romancing the Novel: Adventure from Scott to Sebald*. Lewisburg, Pa.: Bucknell University Press, 2007.

Butler, Judith. *Antigone's Claim: Kinship between Life and Death*. New York: Columbia University Press, 2000.

—— *Gender Trouble: Feminism and the Subversion of Identity*. New York: Routledge, 1990.

Byron, George Gordon, Thomas Moore, Walter Scott, and Thomas Campbell. *The Life, Letters and Journals of Lord Byron*, vol. 4. rev. edn, 1830; repr. London: J. Murray, 1932 (page references are to the 1932 edition).

Castle, Terry. *The Apparitional Lesbian: Female Homosexuality and Modern Culture*. New York: Columbia University Press, 1993.

Charles, Ron. 'Loneliness Dissected with Stunning Precision'. Review of Anita Brookner's *Falling Slowly*. Christian Science Monitor (7 January 1999): 20.

—— 'Undue Influence'. Review of Anita Brookner's *Undue Influence*. Christian Science Monitor (27 January 2000): 17.

Clemens, Justin. *The Romanticism of Contemporary Theory: Institution, Aesthetics, Nihilism*. Aldershot: Ashgate, 2003.

Colette. *The Pure and the Impure*. Translated by Herma Briffaut. New York: New York Review of Books, 2000.

Craig, Patricia. 'An Absence of Volition'. Review of Anita Brookner's *Brief Lives*. New Statesman and Society 3.116 (31 August 1990): 35.

—— 'On Not Being Overwhelmed'. Review of Anita Brookner's *A Misalliance*. Times Literary Supplement (29 August 1986): 932.

Culler, Jonathan. Introduction to Charles Baudelaire, *The Flowers of Evil*. Translated by James N. McGowan. Oxford: Oxford University Press, 1998.

Dalley, Jan. 'Sympathy for the Bedevilled: Fraud'. Review of Anita Brookner's *Fraud*. Independent on Sunday online (23 August 1992): www.independent.co.uk/arts-entertainment/book-reivew--sympathy-for-the-bedevilled-fraud--anita-brookner-cape-1499-1542086.html.

De Certeau, Michel. 'Walking in the City'. In *The Practice of Everyday Life*. Translated by Steven Rendall. Berkeley: University of California Press, 1984.

DeJean, Joan. *Fictions of Sappho, 1546–1937*. Chicago: Chicago University Press, 1989.

Dellamora, Richard. Introduction to *Victorian Sexual Dissidence*. Edited by Richard Dellamora. Chicago: Chicago University Press, 1999: 1–20.

Dranch, Sherry A. 'Reading through the Veiled Text: Colette's "The Pure and the Impure"', *Contemporary Literature* 28.2 (1983): 176–89.
Duguid, Lindsay. 'The Downward Drag and the Loss of Allure'. Review of Anita Brookner's *Brief Lives*. *Times Literary Supplement* (24 August 1990): 889.
Eberstadt, Fernanda. 'Good Works and Bad Lovers'. Review of Anita Brookner's *A Misalliance*. *New York Times Book Review* (29 March 1987): 10.
Edelman, Lee. *No Future: Queer Theory and the Death Drive*. Durham, NC: Duke University Press, 2004.
Ellmann, Richard. 'Henry James among the Aesthetes'. *Proceedings of the British Academy* 69 (1983): 209–28.
Emerson, Sally. 'Recent Fiction'. Review of Anita Brookner's *A Start in Life*. *Illustrated London News* (August 1981): 76.
Faderman, Lillian. *Surpassing the Love of Men: Romantic Friendships and Love between Women from the Renaissance to the Present*. New York: Morrow, 1981.
Felski, Rita. 'The Counterdiscourse of the Feminine in Three Texts by Wilde, Huysmans, and Sacher-Masoch'. *PMLA* 106.5 (1991): 1094–105.
Fernández, Herberto. 'Compte Rendus'. *Meta: Translators' Journal* 48.4 (2003): 588.
Fiala, John L. *Lilacs: The Genus Syringa*. Portland, Oreg.: Timber Press, 1988.
Fisher, Barbara. 'Falling Slowly'. Review of Anita Brookner's *Falling Slowly*. *Boston Globe* (3 January 1999): M2.
Fisher-Wirth, Ann. 'Hunger Art: The Novels of Anita Brookner', *Twentieth-Century Literature* 41.1 (1995): 1–15.
Foucault, Michel. *The History of Sexuality*, vol. 1, *An Introduction*. Translated by Robert Hurley. Harmondsworth: Penguin, 1981.
Freadman, Anne. *The Livres–Souvenirs of Colette: Genre and the Telling of Time*. Leeds: Modern Humanities Research Association/Maney Publishing, 2012.
Freeman, Elizabeth. 'Packing History, Count(er)ing Generations'. *New Literary History* 31 (2000): 727–44.
Freud, Sigmund. 'Fragment of an Analysis of a Case of Hysteria ("Dora") (1905 [1901])'. In *Case Histories, 1, 'Dora' and 'Little Hans'*. Penguin Freud Library, 8. Edited by Angela Richards. Translated by Alix Strachey and James Strachey. Harmondsworth: Penguin, 1990: 31–164.
Friedell, Deborah. 'Disengagement'. Review of Anita Brookner's *The Rules of Engagement*. *New Republic* (9 February 2004): 32.
Fullbrook, Kate. 'Anita Brookner: On Reaching for the Sun'. In *British Women Writing Fiction*. Edited by Abby H.P. Werlock. Tuscaloosa and London: University of Alabama Press, 2000.

Ganzel, Dewey. *Fortune in Men's Eyes: The Career of John Payne Collier.* Oxford: Oxford University Press, 1982.

Genette, Gérard. *Palimpsests: Literature in the Second Degree.* Translated by Channa Newman and Claude Doubinsky. Lincoln: University of Nebraska Press, 1977.

—— *Paratexts: Thresholds of Interpretation.* Translated by Jane E. Lewin. Cambridge: Cambridge University Press, 1997.

Gere, Charlotte with Lesley Hoskins. *The House Beautiful: Oscar Wilde and the Aesthetic Interior.* London: Lund Humphries/Geffrye Museum, 2000.

Giltrow, Janet. 'Ironies of Politeness in Anita Brookner's *Hotel du Lac*'. In *Ambiguous Discourse: Feminist Narratology and British Women Writers.* Edited by Kathy Mezei. Chapel Hill and London: University of North Carolina Press, 1996: 215–37.

Giobbi, Guiliana. '"No Bread Will Feed My Hungry Soul": Anorexic Heroines in Female Fiction—From the Example of Emily Brontë as Mirrored by Anita Brookner, Gianna Schelotto and Alessandra Arachi', *European Studies* 27 (1997): 73–92.

Gray, Paul. 'Understated Outrage at Growing Old'. Review of Anita Brookner's *Making Things Better (The Next Big Thing). New Leader* 85.6 (2002): 44.

Greene, Thomas. *The Vulnerable Text: Essays on Renaissance Literature.* New York: Columbia University Press, 1986.

Grover, Jan Zita. 'Small Expectations: Anita Brookner's Novels', *Women's Review of Books* 11.10–11 (1994): 38–40.

Hadlock, Philip G. 'The *Other* Other: Baudelaire, Melancholia, and the Dandy'. *Nineteenth-Century French Studies* 30.1–2 (2001): 58–67.

Haggard, H. Rider. *Beatrice.* London: Reader's Library, 1927.

Haralson, Eric. *Henry James and Queer Modernity.* Cambridge: Cambridge University Press, 2003.

Hardy, Barbara. 'A Cinderella's Loneliness'. Review of Anita Brookner's *Hotel du Lac. Times Literary Supplement* (14 September 1984): 1019.

Higonnet, Patrice. 'Artists of Indefinite Longing'. Review of Anita Brookner's *Romanticism and Its Discontents. Times Literary Supplement* (3 November 2000): 16.

Hosmer, Robert E. Jr. 'Paradigm and Passage: The Fiction of Anita Brookner'. In *Contemporary British Women Writers: Texts and Strategies.* Edited by Robert E. Hosmer Jr. London: Palgrave Macmillan, 1993: 26–54.

Howard, Deborah. 'Giorgione's *Tempesta* and Titian's *Assunta* in the Context of the Combrai Wars'. *Art History* 8.3 (1985): 271–89.

Huysmans, Joris-Karl. *Against Nature.* Translated by Margaret Mauldon. Oxford: Oxford University Press, 1998.

—— 'Goya et Turner'. In *Écrits sur l'art, 1867–1905*. Paris: Bartillat, 2006. Translation in Bart Johnson, 'JK Huysmans on Turner', *True Outsider* (blog), 21 February 2011: wordpress.com/2011/02/21/51/ (subscription required).

Independent. 'Dropping off before Malin Head' (2 August 1995): www.independent.co.uk/voices/dropping-off-before-malin-head-1594380.html.

Ingres, Jean-Auguste-Dominique and Anita Brookner. *J.A. Dominique Ingres, 1780–1867*. Masters, 16. London: Knowledge Publications, 1965.

Jagose, Annamarie. *Inconsequence: Lesbian Representation and the Logic of Sexual Sequence*. Ithaca, NY: Cornell University Press, 2002.

James, Henry. 'The Author of "Beltraffio"'. In *The Novels and Tales of Henry James*, vol. 16. New York: Charles Scribner's Sons, 1907–09.

—— *The Beast in the Jungle.* In *Complete Stories, 1898–1910*. New York: Library of America, 1966: 496–541.

—— 'The Portrait of a Lady'. In *The Novels and Tales of Henry James*, vols 3–4. New York: Charles Scribner's Sons, 1907–09.

—— *The Tragic Muse.* In *The Novels and Tales of Henry James*, vols 7–8. New York: Charles Scribner's Sons, 1907–09.

—— *The Turn of the Screw.* Harmondsworth: Penguin, 1946.

Jay, Karla. *The Amazon and the Page: Natalie Clifford Barney and Renée Vivien*. Bloomington: Indiana University Press, 1988.

Jefferson, Peter. *And Now the Shipping Forecast: A Tide of History around Our Shores*. Cambridge: UIT Cambridge, 2011.

Jenny, Laurent. 'The Strategy of Form'. In *French Literary Theory Today*. Edited by Tzvetan Todorov. Translated by R. Carter. Cambridge: Cambridge University Press, 1982.

Joannou, Maroula. 'Essentially Virtuous? Anita Brookner's *Hotel du Lac* as Generic Subversion'. In *Fatal Attractions: Re-scripting Romance in Contemporary Literature and Film*. Edited by Lynne Pearce and Gina Whisker. London and Sterling, Va.: Pluto Press, 1998: 84–97.

Judd, Elizabeth. 'Plotless Wonder'. Review of Anita Brookner's *Making Things Better*. *Atlantic Monthly* (April 2003): 109.

Kaiser, Mary. 'Undue Influence'. Review of Anita Brookner's *Undue Influence*. *World Literature Today* 74.3 (2000): 592.

Kelly, Frances. *The Illustrated Language of Flowers: Meaning, Magic and Lore*. Illustrated by Amanda Cunliffe. Victoria: Penguin, 1992.

Kenyon, Olga. *Women Writers Talk: Interviews with 10 Women Writers*. Oxford: Lennard Publishing, 1989.

Kermode, Frank. 'The Obedient and the Free'. Review of Anita Brookner's *A Misalliance*. *Guardian* (29 September 1986): 21.

Kite, Jon Bruce. *A Study of the Works and Reputation of John Aubrey (1626–1697): With Emphasis on His 'Brief Lives'*. New York: Edwin Mellen Press, 1993.

Kliebenstein, Georges. *Figures du destin stendhalien*. Nancy: Presses Sorbonne Nouvelle, 2004.
Kristeva, Julia. *The Kristeva Reader*. Edited by Toril Moi. Oxford: Basil Blackwood, 1986.
—— *Tales of Love*. Translated by Leon S. Roudiez. New York: Columbia University Press, 1987.
Lacan, Jacques. *The Ethics of Psychoanalysis 1959–1960: The Seminar of Jacques Lacan Book VII*. Translated by Jacques-Alain Miller. Edited by Dennis Porter. London: Routledge, 2008.
Ladenson, Elisabeth. 'Colette for Export Only', *Same Sex/Different Text? Gay and Lesbian Writing in French*, Yale French Studies 90 (1996): 25–46.
—— *Dirt for Art's Sake: Books on Trial from 'Madame Bovary' to 'Lolita'*. Ithaca, NY: Cornell University Press, 2007.
Lanham, Richard. *A Handlist of Rhetorical Terms*. 2nd edn. Berkeley: University of California Press, 1991.
Larson, Jennifer. *Greek Nymphs: Myth, Cult, Lore*. New York: Oxford University Press, 2001.
Lassner, Phyllis, Ann V. Norton, and Margaret D. Stetz. 'Introduction: Anita Brookner in the World'. *Tulsa Studies in Women's Literature* 29.1 (2010): 15–18.
Lee, Hermione. 'Melancholia in Maida Vale'. Review of Anita Brookner's *Look at Me*. *Observer* (27 March 1983): 32.
Lehmann-Haupt, Christopher. 'Lonely, and Then Still Lonelier'. Review of Brookner, *Brief Live*. *New York Times* (22 July 1991): C16.
Light, Alison. 'A Family Romance'. Review of Anita Brookner's *A Family Romance*. *New Statesman and Society* 6.260 (9 July 1993): 33.
Love, Barbara. 'Falling Slowly'. Review of Anita Brookner's *Falling Slowly*. *Library Journal* 123.30 (December 1998): 152.
Love, Heather. *Feeling Backward: Loss and the Politics of Queer History*. Cambridge, Mass.: Harvard University Press, 2007.
Lucco, Mauro. *Giorgione*. Milan: Electa, 1995.
Lucey, Michael. *The Misfit of the Family: Balzac and the Social Forms of Sexuality*. Durham, NC: Duke University Press, 2003.
McClellan, Ann K. *How British Women Writers Transformed the Campus Novel: Virginia Woolf, Dorothy L. Sayers, Margaret Drabble, Anita Brookner, Jeanette Winterson*. Lewiston, NY: Edwin Mellon Press, 2012.
McFarlane, Brian. 'A Small, Tenacious Addiction to Life'. Review of Anita Brookner's *The Bay of Angels*. *Saturday Age* (7 April 2001): E11.
McLean, Alice L. *Aesthetic Pleasure in Twentieth-Century Women's Food Writing: The Innovative Appetites of M.F.K. Fisher, Alice B. Toklas, and Elizabeth David*. New York: Routledge, 2012.

McRae Amoss, Benjamin. 'Figures du destin stendhalien'. Review of Georges Kliebenstein's *Figures du destin stendhalien*. *Nineteenth-Century French Studies* 35.2 (2007): 498.

Malcolm, Cheryl Alexander. *Understanding Anita Brookner*. Columbia: University of South Carolina Press, 2002.

Mallick, Heather. 'Depressive Tale Lacks Substance'. Review of Anita Brookner's *Falling Slowly*. *Toronto Sun* (6 September 1998).

Manzini, Francesco. 'Figures du destin stendhalien'. *French Studies: A Quarterly Review* 60.1 (2006): 128.

Marks, Elaine. *Marrano as Metaphor: The Jewish Presence in French Writing*. New York: Columbia University Press, 1996.

Marmo, Arianna. 'Purity and Perversion: Renée Vivien's Ophelia Poetry'. *New Readings* 12 (2012): 64–72.

Mayer, Peta. 'The Paratextual Construction of Anita Brookner: Chronotopic Conflict in the Book Review and Author Interview', *Women: A Cultural Review* 19.1 (2008): 49–68.

Mayne, R. 'Kaleidoscope', BBC Radio 4 (18 October 1984).

Mears, Patricia. *Madame Grès: Sphinx of Fashion*. New Haven, Conn.: Yale University Press, 2007.

Merck, Mandy. 'The Train of Thought in Freud's "Case of Homosexuality in a Woman"'. In *Perversions: Deviant Readings by Mandy Merck*. London: Virago, 1993: 13–32.

Messud, Claire. 'The Stifled Life'. *New York Times Book Review* (31 January 1999): 7.

Miller, D.A. *Narrative and its Discontents: Problems of Closure in the Traditional Novel*. Princeton, NJ: Princeton University Press, 1981.

Moers, Ellen, 'Mme de Staël and the Woman of Genius', *American Scholar* 44.2 (1975): 225–41.

Moi, Toril. 'Representation of Patriarchy: Sexuality and Epistemology in Freud's "Dora"'. In *In Dora's Case: Freud—Hysteria—Feminism*. Edited by Charles Bernheimer and Claire Kahane. New York: Columbia University Press, 1985.

Moore, Caroline. 'Baby, It's Cold Outside'. Review of Anita Brookner's *Leaving Home*. *Spectator* (19 February 2005): 38.

Morgan, Thaïs E. 'Male Lesbian Bodies: The Construction of Alternative Masculinities in Courbet, Baudelaire, and Swinburne'. *Genders* 15 (1992): 37–57.

Morris, Meaghan. *The Pirate's Fiancée: Feminism, Reading, Postmodernism*. London: Verso, 1988.

Moxley, Melody A. 'Undue Influence'. Review of Anita Brookner's *Undue Influence*. *Library Journal* 125.13 (2000): 182.

Niall, Brenda. 'Alone Again, Naturally'. Review of Anita Brookner's *The Bay of Angels*. *Weekend Australian* (7–8 April 2001): R15.

Nightingale, Benedict. '*Brief Lives* at the Theatre Royal, Windsor'. Review of performance of *Brief Lives* (written and directed by Patrick Garland). *The Times* online (21 March 2008): www.thetimes.co.uk/article/brief-lives-at-the-theatre-royal-windsor-00qqgg6ssxd (subscription required).

Nordau, Max. *Degeneration*. 4th edn, translated from the 2nd German edn. New York: D. Appleton, 1895.

Norton, Ann V. 'Anita Brookner Reads Edith Wharton and Henry James: The Problem of Moral Imagination'. *Tulsa Studies in Women's Literature* 29.1 (2010): 19–33.

Nunokawa, Jeff. 'Sexuality and the Victorian Novel'. In *The Cambridge Companion to the Victorian Novel*. Edited by Deidre David. Cambridge: Cambridge University Press, 2001: 125–48.

Oates, Joyce Carol. 'Writing for the Tortoise Market'. Review of Anita Brookner's *Undue Influence*. *Times Literary Supplement* (30 July 1999): 19.

Pater, Walter. *The Renaissance: Studies in Art and Poetry*. London: Macmillan, 1924.

Pender, E.E. 'Sappho and Anacreon in Plato's *Phaedrus*'. *Leeds International Classical Studies* 6.4 (2007): 1–57.

Petit, Laurence. 'Between Iconophilia and Iconophobia: Anita Brookner's Museum of Words'. *Word & Image* 30.1 (2014): 7–12: doi.org/10.1080/02666286.2013.771924.

—— 'Romance of a Family or Inverted "Family Romance": Familial Gaze and Narratorial Look in Anita Brookner's *Family and Friends*'. *Literature Interpretation Theory* 17 (2006): 379–97.

Piehler, Liana F. *Spatial Dynamics and Female Development in Victorian Art and Novels: Creating a Woman's Space*. New York: Peter Lang, 2003.

Plante, David. 'They Won Their Life on the Football Pools'. Review of Anita Brookner's *A Friend from England*. *New York Times Book Review* (20 March 1988): sect. 7.

Plato. *Phaedrus*. Translated by Christopher Rowe. London: Penguin, 2005.

Prendergast, Christopher. *Mirages and Mad Beliefs: Proust the Skeptic*. Princeton, NJ: Princeton University Press, 2013.

Prince, Gerald. *A Dictionary of Narratology*. Lincoln: University of Nebraska Press, 1987.

Prins, Yopie. *Victorian Sappho*. Princeton, NJ: Princeton University Press, 1999.

Proust, Marcel. *Swann's Way*. In *In Search of Lost Time*, vol. 1. Translated by C.K. Scott Moncrieff and Terence Kilmartin. Revised by D.J. Enright. New York: Modern Library, 2003.

Publishers Weekly. 'Falling Slowly'. Review of Anita Brookner's *Falling Slowly* (26 October 1998): 42.

Purdon, John James. 'John Aubrey's "Discourse in Paper"'. *Essays in Criticism* 55.3 (2005): 226–47.

Radway, Janice. *Reading the Romance: Women, Patriarchy, and Popular Literature*. Chapel Hill: University of North Carolina Press, 1991.
Ratner, Rochelle. 'The Next Big Thing'. Review of Anita Brookner's *The Next Big Thing*. *Library Journal* 128.12 (2003): 145.
Reid, Roddey. *Families in Jeopardy: Regulating the Social Body in France, 1750–1910*. Stanford, Calif.: Stanford University Press, 1993.
Riffaterre, Michael. 'Syllepsis'. *Critical Inquiry* 6.4 (1980): 625–38.
Robb, Graham. *Strangers: Homosexual Love in the Nineteenth Century*. London: Picador, 2003.
Rodd, Candice. 'Drawing-Room Despair'. Review of Anita Brookner's *Fraud*. *Times Literary Supplement* (21 August 1992): 17.
Rousseau, Jean-Jacques. *Reveries of the Solitary Walker*. Translated by Peter France. Harmondsworth: Penguin, 1979.
Rubin, Merle. 'The Search for a Suitable Suitor'. Review of Anita Brookner's *Falling Slowly*. *Wall Street Journal* (20 January 1999).
Sadler, Lynn Veach. *Anita Brookner*. Twayne's English Author Series, 473. Boston: Twayne, 1990.
Sappho. *The Poetry of Sappho*. Translated by Jim Powell. Oxford: Oxford University Press, 2007.
Schier, Rudolf. 'Giorgione's *Tempest*: A Virgilian Pastoral'. *Renaissance Studies* 22.4 (2008): 476–506.
Schor, Naomi. *Reading in Detail: Aesthetics and the Feminine*. New York: Methuen, 1987.
Schultz, Gretchen. 'Daughters of Bilitis: Literary Genealogy and Lesbian Authenticity'. *GLQ: A Journal of Lesbian and Gay Studies* 7.3 (2001): 377–89.
Schwob, Marcel. *Imaginary Lives*. Translated by Lorimer Hammond. New York: Avon Book Division, 1952.
Scodel, Ruth. 'Self-Correction, Spontaneity, and Orality in Archaic Poetry'. In *Voice into Text: Orality and Literacy in Ancient Greece*. Edited by Ian Worthington. Leiden: E.J. Brill, 1996: 59–80.
Seaman, Donna. 'Undue Influence'. Review of Anita Brookner's *Undue Influence*. *Booklist* (15 October 1999): 394.
Sedgwick, Eve Kosofsky. *Epistemology of the Closet*. Berkeley: University of California Press, 1990.
Seewald, Jacqueline. 'Private View'. Review of Anita Brookner's *A Private View*. *Library Journal* 122.6 (1997): 145.
Settis, Salvatore. *Giorgione's 'Tempest': Interpreting the Hidden Subject*. Translated by Ellen Bianchini. Cambridge: Polity Press, 1990.
Seymour, Miranda. 'The Mistress of Gloom'. Review of Anita Brookner's *The Bay of Angels*. *Atlantic Monthly* (June 2001): 107–09.
Sheppard, R. Z. 'A Friend from England'. Review of Anita Brookner's *A Friend from England*. *Time* (21 March 1988): 76.

Simons, Patricia. 'Lesbian (In)Visibility in Italian Renaissance Culture: Diana and Other Cases of *donna con donna*'. In *Gay and Lesbian Studies in Art History*. Edited by Whitney Davis. New York: Harrington Park Press, 1994: 81–122.
Sinfield, Alan. *The Wilde Century: Effeminacy, Oscar Wilde and the Queer Moment*. New York: Columbia University Press, 1994.
Singmaster, Deborah. 'Sorting Out the Arrangements'. Review of Anita Brookner's *A Friend from England*. *Times Literary Supplement* (21 August 1989): 899.
Skinner, John. *The Fictions of Anita Brookner: Illusions of Romance*. Basingstoke: Macmillan, 1992.
Smith, Patricia Juliana. *Lesbian Panic: Homoeroticism in Modern British Women's Fiction*. New York: Columbia University Press, 1997.
Southworth, Helen. *The Intersecting Realities and Fictions of Virginia Woolf and Colette*. Columbus: Ohio State University Press, 2004.
Spacks, Patricia Meyer. *Boredom: The Literary History of a State of Mind*. Chicago: University of Chicago Press, 1995.
Staël, Madame de. *Corinne, or Italy*. Translated by Sylvia Raphael. Oxford: Oxford University Press, 2008.
Stambolian, George and Elaine Marks. Introduction to *Homosexualities and French Literature: Cultural Contexts/Critical Texts*. Edited by George Stambolian and Elaine Marks. Ithaca, NY: Cornell University Press, 1979: 23–34.
Steiner, Wendy. 'She Who Won't Be Obeyed'. Review of Anita Brookner's *Undue Influence*. *New York Times Book Review* (23 January 2000): 34.
Stendhal. *The Life of Henri Brulard*. Translated by Catherine Alison Phillips. New York: Vintage Books, 1955.
—— *On Love*. Translated by Sophie Lewis. London: Hesperus Press, 2009.
—— *Scarlet and Black: A Chronicle of the Nineteenth Century*. Translated by Margaret R.B. Shaw. Harmondsworth: Penguin, 1953.
Stetz, Margaret D. 'Anita Brookner's Visual World'. *Tulsa Studies in Women's Literature* 29.1 (2010): 35–46.
Stewart, Charles. 'Nymphomania: Sexuality, Insanity and Problems in Folklore Analysis'. In *The Text and Its Margins: Post-Structuralist Approaches to Twentieth-Century Greek Literature*. Edited by Margaret Alexiou and Vassilis Lambropoulos. New York: Pella, 1985: 219–52.
Summers-Bremner, Eluned. 'Love's Pleasure, Love's Pain'. *Dalhousie Review* 84.3 (2004): 441–62.
Sylvester, Louise. 'Troping the Other: Anita Brookner's Jews'. *English: The Journal of the English Association* 50.196 (2001): 47–58.
Symonds, John Addington. *Studies of the Greek Poets*, vol. 1. 3rd edn. London: Adam and Charles Black, 1893.

Szogyi, Alex. 'Fiction: In Short'. *New York Times Book Review* (21 April 1985): 24.

Thornton, R.K.R. *The Decadent Dilemma*. London: Edward Arnold, 1983.

Tierney, Tom. *French Fashion Designers: Paper Dolls, 1900–1950*. Mineola, NY: Dover Publications, 2002.

—— *Great Fashion Designs of the Twenties: Paper Dolls in Full Color*. New York: Dover Publications, 1983.

Time. 'Brief Lives'. Review of Anita Brookner's *Brief Lives* (5 August 1991): 14.

Tindall, Gillian. 'Safe Sorrow'. Review of Anita Brookner's *Falling Slowly*. *Times Literary Supplement* (10 July 1998): 23.

Tintner, Adeline R. 'Henry James's Fiction "Swallowed, Digested and Assimilated": A Strong "Whiff" of Henry James in 1997's Overflow'. *Henry James Review* 19.3 (1998): 255–63.

Tonkin, Boyd. 'Anita Brookner: "You Should Play Russian Roulette with Your Life"'. *Independent Magazine* (29 June 2002): www.independent.co.uk/arts-entertainment/books/features/anita-brookner-you-should-play-russian-roulette-with-your-life-182287.html.

Tuite, Clara. 'Decadent Austen Entails: Forster, James, Firbank, and the "Queer Tale" of *Sanditon* (comp. 1817, publ. 1925)'. In *Janeites: Austen's Disciples and Devotees*. Edited by Deidre Lynch. Princeton, NJ: Princeton University Press, 2000: 115–40.

—— 'Trials of the Dandy: George Brummell's Scandalous Celebrity'. In *Romanticism and Celebrity Culture, 1750–1850*. Edited by T. Mole. Cambridge: Cambridge University Press, 2009: 143–67.

Tyler, Anne. 'A Solitary Life is Still Worth Living', *New York Times* online (3 February 1985): www.nytimes.com/1985/02/03/books/a-solitary-life-is-still-worth-living.html (subscription required).

Usandizaga, Aranzuzu. 'The Female *Bildungsroman* at the Fin de Siècle: The "Utopian Imperative" in Anita Brookner's *A Closed Eye* and *Fraud*'. *Critique: Studies in Contemporary Fiction* 39.4 (1998): 325–41.

Vaughn, William. 'Turnabouts in Taste: The Case of the Late Turner'. In *Romanticism and Postmodernism*. Edited by Edward Larrissy. Cambridge: Cambridge University Press, 1999: 29–46.

Vicinus, Martha. 'The Adolescent Boy: Fin-de-Siècle Femme Fatale?' In *Victorian Sexual Dissidence*. Edited by Richard Dellamora. Chicago: University of Chicago Press, 1999: 83–106.

Vidaud, Richard. 'L'écriture palimpsestueuese d'Anita Brookner: de la transtextualité à l'autotextualité'. *Études britanniques contemporaines* 19 (2000): 81–96.

Vivien, Renée. *The Muse of the Violets*. Translated by Margaret Porter and Catherine Kroger. Tallahassee, Fla.: Naiad Press, 1982.

―― *A Woman Appeared to Me*. Introduction by Gayle Rubin. Translated by Jeanette H. Foster. Tallahassee, Fla.: Naiad Press, 1982.

Watson, Daphne. *Their Own Worst Enemies: Women's Writers of Women's Fiction*. London: Pluto Press, 1995.

Watteau, Antoine and Anita Brookner. *Watteau*. Colour Library of Art. Feltham: Hamlyn, 1967.

White, Chris. Introduction to *Nineteenth Century Writings on Homosexuality: A Sourcebook*. Edited by Chris White. London: Routledge, 1999.

Wilcox, John. 'The Beginnings of L'art pour l'art'. *Journal of Aestheticism and Art Criticism* 11 (1952–53): 363–65.

Wilde, Oscar. *The Picture of Dorian Gray*. Ware: Wordsworth Classics, 1992.

Wilhelmus, Tom. 'Brief Lives'. Review of Brookner's *Brief Lives*. *Hudson Review* 45.1 (1992): 138.

Williams, Raymond. *Marxism and Literature*. Oxford: Oxford University Press, 1977.

Williams, Rosalind H. *Dream Worlds: Mass Consumption in Late Nineteenth-Century France*. Berkeley: University of California Press, 1982.

Williams-Wanquet, Eileen. *Art and Life in the Novels of Anita Brookner: Reading for Life, Subversive Re-writing to Live*. Berne: Peter Lang, 2004.

Winkler, Jack. 'Gardens of Nymphs: Public and Private in Sappho's Lyrics'. *Women's Studies* 8.1–2 (1981): 65–91.

Wittig, Monique. 'Paradigm'. In *Homosexualities and French Literature: Cultural Contexts/Critical Texts*. Edited by George Stambolian and Elaine Marks. Ithaca, NY: Cornell University Press, 1979: 114–21.

Wittig, Monique and Sande Zeig. *Lesbian Peoples: Material for a Dictionary*. New York: Avon, 1978.

Woolf, Virginia. *Mrs. Dalloway*. Orlando, Fla.: Harcourt, 1925.

Woollard, Alison. 'Review: Brief Lives'. Review of performance of *Brief Lives*, written and directed by Patrick Garland. *BBC* (12 February 2008): www.bbc.co.uk/essex/content/articles/2008/02/12/review_brief_lives_feature.shtml.

Wyatt-Brown, Anne M. 'Creativity in Midlife: The Novels of Anita Brookner'. *Journal of Aging Studies* 3.2 (1989): 175–81.

Index

adventure narrative 26, 43, 46, 47, 48, 51, 56, 57, 224
aesthete 2, 22, 24, 28, 73, 78, 79, 80, 81, 82, 86, 87, 88, 89, 90, 91, 92, 93, 96, 99, 100, 101, 103, 104, 105, 106, 107, 108, 109, 110, 111, 113, 115, 116, 134, 174, 191, 193, 194, 212, 233
aestheticism 3, 17, 28, 31, 67, 79, 92, 94, 95, 96, 111, 133, 134, 135, 140, 144, 153, 164, 171, 175, 180, 182, 203
Albert, Nicole 76, 77
anachronism 22, 140, 141, 208, 246
anagnorisis 227, 228, 245
analysand 22, 24, 25, 26, 27, 37, 38, 57, 58, 59, 60, 61, 62, 63, 64, 66, 73
Anxiety of Influence, The xii, 30, 165, 171, 248
apophrades 179, 189
Arabian Nights, The 225, 226, 227, 228, 237, 242
art for art's sake 79, 87, 90
artifice 2, 90, 206, 211
asexual sexuality 142
askesis 179, 188, 240
Aubrey, John 29 122, 127, 129, 131, 132, 136, 137, 248, 253, 256
'Author of Beltraffio, The' 81
autobiographical 12, 77, 78, 85, 125, 126, 145, 164

backwards turn 78, 87, 107, 108, 110, 140, 213
Bahti, Thomas 28, 79, 98, 99, 100, 101, 106, 109, 247
Bakhtin, Mikhail 20, 28, 79
Barbey d'Aurevilly, Jules 29, 122, 132
Barney, Natalie 91, 92, 97
Barthes, Roland 23, 29, 109, 122, 132, 135, 220
Baudelaire, Charles xii, 1, 2, 3, 23, 26, 28, 29, 30, 37, 38, 77, 78, 79, 89, 90, 92, 93, 96, 100, 101, 103, 108, 110, 122, 133, 134, 136, 139, 154, 164, 165, 169, 170, 171, 172, 173, 174, 175, 176, 177, 180, 195, 207, 248, 249, 250, 252, 255
Bay of Angels, The 4, 168, 254, 255, 257
Bayley, John 84, 85, 248
Beamish, Sally 5, 27, 74, 76, 83, 94, 97, 103, 105, 108, 109, 111, 112, 115
Benjamin, Walter 3, 28, 79, 97, 225, 226, 247
Bennett, Kate 29, 127
Björkblom, Inger 124, 167
blessedness 28, 79, 80, 100, 106, 109, 111, 115
Bloom, Harold xii, 23, 30, 31, 40, 165, 166, 171, 172, 173, 174, 175, 176, 177, 178, 179, 180, 181, 182, 183, 184, 185, 187, 188, 189, 190, 191, 248

Booker Prize, The 9, 11, 84, 225, 231, 245
boredom 28, 29, 122, 134, 137, 138, 206
boring 10, 17, 28, 102, 129, 137, 138, 144, 145
Bourdieu, Pierre 79, 90, 100
bourgeois 2, 8, 49, 79, 87, 90, 93, 100, 101, 102, 105, 109, 110, 111, 113, 118, 123, 135, 139, 140, 142, 167, 187
brevity 124, 130, 131, 134, 143, 146
Brief Lives viii, xii, xiii, 6, 8, 21, 28, 29, 117, 118, 119, 120, 122, 123, 124, 125, 126, 127, 128, 129, 131, 132, 134, 135, 136, 137, 138, 139, 140, 141, 142, 143, 144, 145, 147, 148, 149, 151, 152, 153, 155, 156, 158, 173, 228, 234, 236, 243, 249, 250, 251, 253, 256, 259, 260
British Museum, The 108
Brooknerine 4, 14, 19, 22, 136, 200, 229, 234, 235, 246
Brooks, Peter 235, 236, 249
Butler, Judith 16, 19, 20, 210, 246, 250

Caldwell, Gail 13, 249
capitalist 2, 44, 91, 114, 139, 141, 142, 201
celebrity 10, 137, 145, 238
childless 6, 64, 85, 142, 165, 216, 244
Christian 106, 107, 169, 177, 201, 250
clinamen 179, 181, 182
Colette 18, 23, 32, 226, 227, 228, 230, 231, 233, 234, 236, 238, 239, 240, 241, 245, 247, 250, 251, 254, 258
consumption 2, 62, 123, 134, 152, 153, 239
context 2, 4, 10, 12, 14, 15, 17, 19, 20, 21, 22, 23, 24, 25, 36, 37, 41, 43, 46, 59, 68, 79, 84, 91, 96, 125, 126, 136, 142, 143, 176, 181, 193, 195, 201, 203, 210, 214, 216, 217, 221, 231, 241, 242, 245, 246
convalescence 111, 115
Corinne ou l'Italia 81, 82, 226, 258
Craig, Patricia 87, 124
cravat 147, 148
critics 3, 4, 11, 12, 13, 14, 15, 16, 19, 22, 25, 31, 40, 41, 42, 60, 78, 83, 85, 86, 87, 94, 119, 124, 125, 135, 138, 165, 166, 167, 168, 169, 200, 219
cross-historical 20, 22, 57
crossing 22, 180

daemonisation 179, 187
dandy 23, 24, 26, 28, 29, 30, 45, 65, 86, 122, 124, 132, 133, 134, 135, 136, 137, 138, 139, 140, 141, 142, 143, 144, 145, 146, 147, 148, 150, 151, 152, 153, 154, 155, 156, 157, 158, 159, 164, 170, 191, 212, 233, 236
de Certeau, Michel 30, 161, 162, 164, 171, 176, 190
decadence 17, 91, 208
degeneration 148, 149, 150, 197, 200, 202, 203, 204, 205, 207, 213, 216, 218, 219, 220
DeJean, Joan 77
Derrida, Jacques 215, 216
despair 55, 99, 103, 194, 205, 219, 232
detail 9, 28, 29, 46, 63, 110, 122, 125, 126, 127, 128, 129, 131, 132, 133, 134, 137, 141, 145, 147, 148, 155, 156, 201, 202, 228, 233
Dickens, Charles 12, 18, 64
diseuse 6, 117, 139, 146
distinction 29, 82, 106, 122, 130, 132, 133, 134, 137, 141, 154, 156, 216
divorce 40, 74, 83, 87, 102, 103, 104
dressing 29, 30, 120, 122, 123, 133, 143, 147, 150, 151, 156, 207, 228
Duguid, Lindsay 10, 124

INDEX

eating 29, 30, 118, 119, 122, 133, 150, 151, 152, 158, 236, 244
Eberstadt, Fernanda 86
eccentric 5, 59, 64, 65, 105, 119, 131
Ellmann, Richard 81, 94, 251
ephebe 171, 173, 174, 179, 181, 182, 184, 187, 188, 189, 190, 191
ephemeral 30, 122, 130, 137, 143, 146, 154, 155, 158, 159, 189, 219, 222, 233
ephemeral endurance 30, 122, 137, 143, 155, 158, 159
Esseintes, Duc Jean des 194
exile 7, 50, 77, 80, 81, 87, 101, 104, 105, 106, 118, 135, 143, 158, 164, 206, 225, 228, 231, 242, 244
extempore 130, 144, 145, 146

Faderman, Lillian 91
Falling Slowly vii, xii, xiv, 7, 8, 17, 31, 139, 192, 193, 194, 196, 198, 200, 201, 202, 206, 207, 208, 209, 210, 212, 213, 215, 216, 217, 218, 221, 232, 234, 240, 243, 248, 249, 250, 251, 254, 255, 256, 257, 259
family 4, 6, 7, 8, 20, 22, 30, 31, 37, 38, 39, 40, 42, 44, 45, 46, 48, 57, 59, 64, 68, 69, 70, 71, 73, 90, 102, 112, 141, 142, 172, 177, 182, 183, 188, 190, 192, 193, 198, 208, 209, 210, 212, 217, 218, 227
Felski, Rita 3, 93, 135
female friendship 6, 7
femininity 2, 8, 10, 19, 44, 47, 85, 86, 104, 112, 126, 134, 135, 136, 140, 142, 152, 153, 168, 169, 173, 234
feminism 13, 27, 41, 48
feminist 5, 8, 10, 13, 14, 23, 28, 39, 71, 86, 92
Fictions of Sappho, 1546–1937 77, 79, 82, 84, 89, 92, 95, 96, 101, 250
fin-de-siècle 79, 105, 132, 194, 195, 203, 206, 218

first-person 68, 77, 125, 126, 144, 164, 168
Fisher-Wirth, Ann 11, 13, 25, 40, 41, 251
flâneur vii, 160, 162, 164, 165, 169, 181
Flowers of Evil, The 3, 89, 90, 91, 250
Fontane, Theodor 18, 160
food 119, 120, 151, 152, 153, 206
Foucault, Michel 2, 193
Fowles, John, 127, 128, 247
fragment 109, 182, 222, 240
Freadman, Anne 226, 251
Friend from England, A xii, xiii, 5, 6, 16, 25, 26, 27, 33, 37, 38, 39, 40, 41, 42, 44, 45, 47, 48, 49, 50, 51, 55, 57, 58, 59, 60, 61, 62, 63, 65, 66, 67, 68, 70, 71, 72, 73, 173, 224, 234, 240, 243, 248, 249, 256, 257, 258

Garland, Patrick 129, 256, 260
gaze 28, 79, 96, 97, 106, 108, 111, 223
gender 2, 4, 10, 12, 13, 16, 19, 20, 21, 22, 36, 37, 42, 47, 48, 57, 64, 72, 78, 84, 86, 93, 122, 126, 134, 135, 136, 137, 138, 139, 140, 141, 150, 166, 168, 177, 178, 180, 183, 191, 200, 207, 208, 210, 211, 225, 232, 233, 244, 246
generation 22, 38, 113, 141, 212, 213
Genius of the Future, The xii, 26, 169, 249
Gibson, Martin 30, 89, 160, 162, 163, 165, 166, 168, 175, 178, 179, 180, 181, 182, 183, 184, 185, 186, 187, 188, 189, 190, 191, 243, 248
Giltrow, Janet 243, 245, 252
glamour 30, 122, 137, 143, 147, 152, 153, 155, 157
Gower Street 30, 160, 163, 166, 175
Greek Nymphs: Myth, Cult, Lore 75, 76, 254

Grès, Madame ix, 118, 120, 140, 148, 158, 255
Grover, Jan Zita 12, 252
guilt 28, 79, 80, 100, 101, 105, 110, 111, 234
Guys, Constantin 154, 170, 175

Haffenden, John 13, 18, 228, 249
Haralson, Eric 81, 193
Hardy, Barbara 10, 12, 103
heat 74, 87, 89, 91, 94, 95, 114, 116, 237
Heine, Heinrich 160
Hellenic 28, 79, 82, 96, 99, 100, 110, 112
Hellenism 79, 95, 113
hendiadys 13, 26, 43, 44, 50, 51, 52, 55, 61, 224
heterocentric 12, 51, 197
hetero-chronic symbolic 125
heterosexual romance 6, 30, 47, 82, 102, 103, 104, 110, 154, 166, 167, 168, 169, 177, 178, 179, 180, 186, 191, 201, 202, 203, 209, 210, 211, 212, 213, 216, 217, 221, 232, 233, 237, 243, 246
Higonnet, Patrice 12, 252
homoerotic 3, 35, 36, 37, 42, 51, 57, 58, 73, 82, 95, 97, 99, 108, 110, 111, 150, 151, 211, 228, 235, 240, 241, 242, 246
homosexuality 2, 3, 29, 64, 65, 66, 71, 72, 73, 136, 150, 151, 176, 207, 231, 241
homosocial 5, 70, 93, 112, 176, 211, 239
Hope, Edith 7, 8, 11, 14, 20, 225, 229, 231, 234
Hotel du Lac xii, xiv, 7, 8, 9, 11, 12, 14, 20, 32, 81, 103, 224, 225, 226, 227, 228, 229, 230, 231, 232, 233, 234, 236, 237, 238, 239, 240, 243, 244, 245, 252, 253

Huysmans, Karl-Joris xii, 1, 2, 3, 23, 31, 67, 194, 195, 196, 198, 207, 212, 218, 219, 249, 251, 252, 253

Imaginary Lives 29, 122, 131, 132, 257
imagination 6, 12, 30, 62, 64, 95, 158, 160, 161, 164, 165, 168, 169, 170, 171, 172, 175, 177, 178, 179, 180, 182, 183, 184, 185, 186, 191, 227, 228, 237, 238
inactivity 103, 189, 206
incapacity 105
inconsequential 6, 21, 28, 122, 125, 127, 137, 144
industrialisation 44, 132, 151
insignificant 52, 125, 128
interiors 120, 127, 128, 133
intertextuality 17, 24, 45, 78, 93, 97, 164, 167, 171, 175, 226
interview 1, 6, 7, 9, 10, 12, 13, 14, 20, 34, 77, 83, 84, 194, 231, 232

James, Henry xii, 2, 3, 4, 5, 12, 15, 17, 18, 23, 37, 38, 51, 57, 64, 65, 81, 88, 94, 105, 114, 172, 193, 230, 235, 251, 252, 253, 256, 259
Jameson, Frederic 12
Jesse, Captain William 136
Jewish 1, 13, 16, 80, 81, 255

Kennedy, Rachel 21, 25, 33, 39, 42, 44, 45, 46, 48, 61, 231
Kermode, Frank 83, 84, 85, 253
kinosis 179
Klee, Paul 98
knot 147, 148

labia 76, 88
Lacan, Jacques 100, 101, 254
lack 11, 12, 25, 54, 62, 69, 84, 102, 139, 147, 149, 153, 166, 186, 202, 211, 230
Ladenson, Elisabeth 2, 230

INDEX

Larson, Jennifer 75, 76, 254
Lee, Hermione 1, 6, 11, 20, 249
Lelong, Lucien ix, 119
lesbian 2, 3, 10, 21, 27, 28, 31, 38, 44, 60, 64, 65, 67, 72, 76, 77, 78, 79, 80, 87, 89, 90, 91, 93, 95, 97, 99, 140, 141, 197, 198, 208, 209, 216, 221, 224, 226, 228, 229, 235, 236, 240, 241, 246
lesbianism 64, 67, 76, 89, 90, 93, 97, 134, 141, 208, 226, 227, 233
Lesbos 88, 89, 92, 94, 207
Life of George Brummell 136, 137, 150
Livingstone, Heather 5, 21, 25, 33, 37, 39, 45, 48, 57, 62, 63
lyric 77, 144

madness 75, 109, 110, 111
maps 30, 72, 106, 148, 162, 200, 211
Marks, Elaine 2, 81, 226, 258, 260
marriage 8, 11, 14, 40, 41, 47, 51, 52, 53, 54, 55, 69, 70, 73, 86, 92, 93, 100, 102, 103, 104, 123, 126, 153, 178, 198, 210, 211, 212, 216, 228, 229, 232, 233, 242, 243, 244, 245
masculinity 2, 29, 38, 44, 47, 48, 49, 55, 69, 70, 79, 81, 92, 93, 122, 135, 136, 138, 140, 141, 149, 152, 153, 164, 172, 193, 207
Mayne, Richard 9, 26, 231, 248, 255
memory 16, 60, 76, 109, 128, 130, 194, 216, 221, 222, 227, 240, 241
Messud, Claire 201, 255
metalepsis xiii, 98, 99, 111
metaleptic prolepsis 28, 79, 87, 98, 99, 100, 104, 110, 174, 212
metamorphosis 28, 79, 87, 100, 101, 103, 108, 111, 115, 116, 224
military man 22, 24, 25, 26, 34, 36, 37, 38, 47, 48, 50, 53, 54, 55, 57, 59, 60, 63, 66, 72, 73
Misalliance, A vii, xii, xiii, 1, 5, 6, 8, 14, 21, 27, 74, 78, 79, 80, 82, 83, 84, 85, 86, 87, 88, 89, 90, 94, 97, 101, 102, 103, 104, 105, 106, 107, 108, 109, 111, 113, 116, 224, 226, 228, 234, 240, 243, 248, 249, 250, 251, 253
mise en scène 36, 89
Moers, Ellen 81
Montagu Mansions 160, 162, 166, 175, 185
Morgan, Thaïs E. 3, 77
Morton, Julia 6, 21, 28, 117, 123, 140
Muse of the Violets, The xii, 91, 259

narrative orality 32, 229, 245
National Gallery, The 5, 74, 75, 83, 95, 97, 107, 108
nature 5, 20, 23, 28, 31, 44, 52, 53, 76, 88, 93, 95, 101, 110, 123, 127, 129, 130, 146, 165, 178, 184, 195, 198, 204, 207, 212, 219, 221, 222, 225, 226, 230, 234, 235, 237, 244, 246
nineteenth century 2, 3, 4, 12, 13, 15, 17, 18, 20, 24, 25, 26, 27, 28, 29, 30, 31, 33, 37, 53, 55, 57, 64, 66, 68, 71, 72, 73, 77, 78, 79, 81, 86, 87, 88, 93, 97, 108, 112, 113, 114, 119, 131, 134, 135, 136, 140, 145, 147, 150, 152, 166, 167, 170, 172, 178, 179, 180, 182, 191, 194, 203, 208, 209, 218, 219, 220, 228, 230, 235, 246
No Future: Queer Theory and the Death Drive 24, 197, 202, 213, 214, 251
Nordau, Max xii, 23, 31, 105, 195, 203, 239
normative 8, 20, 22, 23, 25, 37, 42, 47, 48, 57, 65, 72, 86, 112, 139, 140, 141, 168, 173, 176, 177, 204, 210, 211, 213, 234, 246
Norton, Ann V. 15, 16, 17, 254, 256
Novus, Angelus 98

Nunokawa, Jeff 113
nympholepsy 74, 76
nymphs 5, 14, 27, 74, 75, 76, 78, 80, 82, 83, 85, 87, 88, 89, 92, 95, 100, 102, 103, 105, 106, 108, 114, 115

obituary 11, 123, 159
old-fashioned 10, 21, 104, 118, 141
On Dandyism and George Brummell 29, 137, 143, 247
Onslow Square 120, 149, 150, 154, 155, 156, 157, 158
oral 27, 130, 143, 144, 145, 146, 154, 158, 159, 225, 235, 236
original reception 11, 25, 59, 78, 86, 216, 234
outdated 21

pagan 75, 107
Painter of Modern Life, The xii, 26, 29, 30, 37, 101, 133, 154, 170, 172, 173, 180, 248
Paris Review 8, 83, 84, 194, 231, 232, 249
Pater, Walter 23, 78, 94, 112
Patou, Jean ix, 118, 121, 140
patriarchal 10, 11, 14, 24, 28, 64, 80, 82, 93, 105, 106, 110, 164, 218
Pender, E.E. 88, 89, 97, 108, 111, 256
periodisation 72, 136
peripatetic 30, 170, 171, 176, 179
peripeteia 31, 165, 176, 179, 212, 237
Petit, Laurence x, 7, 15, 256
Phaedrus 82, 88, 89, 97, 108, 109, 110, 112, 115, 256
Piehler, Liana 235, 237, 256
Pitt, Claire 6, 20, 30, 160, 162, 172, 173, 231, 237, 238
Plato 18, 78, 80, 82, 88, 89, 97, 100, 105, 108, 109, 110, 111, 115, 256
pleasure 2, 49, 52, 61, 74, 78, 81, 83, 97, 108, 112, 114, 152, 153, 156, 215, 230, 234, 240, 241, 245

plotless 10, 126
poet 2, 29, 34, 76, 77, 78, 80, 84, 91, 97, 99, 122, 130, 132, 144, 161, 164, 165, 170, 171, 172, 173, 174, 176, 177, 179, 181, 182, 184, 185, 187, 188, 189, 191, 215
poetry 76, 79, 80, 81, 88, 91, 144, 173, 179
Portrait of a Lady, The 81, 230, 253
postmodern 23, 138
Powell, Anthony 83, 84, 129, 257
precursor 88, 89, 131, 137, 171, 172, 173, 174, 176, 179, 181, 182, 183, 184, 185, 187, 188, 189, 190
preterition xiii, 65
Prins, Yopie 77, 78, 79, 82, 84, 99, 100, 256
production 2, 20, 45, 59, 73, 79, 93, 98, 100, 106, 107, 109, 120, 125, 129, 133, 134, 135, 136, 137, 141, 142, 145, 152, 153, 154, 155, 168, 173, 177, 179, 180, 191, 194, 198, 204, 208, 210, 211, 212, 217, 222
prolepsis 13, 98, 99, 100, 111
Proust, Marcel 18, 23, 83, 108, 194, 227, 228, 229, 230, 256
Providence 18, 77, 249
punishment 28, 79, 80, 100, 103, 104, 105, 110, 111
Purdon, John James 29, 127, 129
Pure and the Impure, The 226, 227, 230, 231, 233, 234, 238, 239, 240, 241, 247, 250, 251
purification 28, 80, 100, 106, 109, 111, 113, 114, 115

queer theory 3, 16, 22, 214, 221
queering 3, 37, 57, 64, 73, 110, 112, 151, 220

radiance 69, 74, 109, 114
Reading in Detail 44, 125, 201, 257

recollection 82, 97, 108, 111, 118, 217, 221
recursive 78, 82, 99
redemption 28, 79, 100, 103, 106, 107, 108, 110, 111
renaissance 5, 27, 33, 34, 35, 74, 76, 91, 94, 95, 96, 97, 106, 112, 251, 252, 256, 257, 258
repetitive 10, 17, 44, 58, 61, 64, 145, 224
reproductive 30, 86, 105, 107, 110, 112, 113, 141, 142, 153, 177, 201, 208, 213
restlessness 68, 103, 206
reversal xiii, 31, 52, 101, 165, 173, 174, 175, 176, 179, 180, 184, 189, 190, 237, 238
reviewers 10, 37
reviews 9, 10, 15, 77, 84, 85, 86, 168
revisionary ratios 31, 166, 179, 180, 181, 189
Riffaterre, Michael 171, 215, 216, 257
Rimbaud 18, 105
rise-and-fall 30, 122, 123, 134, 136, 137, 138, 143, 147, 148, 149, 150, 151, 153, 154, 158, 212, 224
Rodd, Candice 11, 257
Romanticism xii, 1, 2, 12, 13, 17, 19, 20, 21, 29, 79, 96, 119, 131, 139, 154, 170, 171, 172, 177, 208, 218, 231, 246, 249, 250, 252, 259
Romanticism and Its Discontents 12, 17, 19, 96, 139, 154, 170, 172, 177, 252
Romantics 1, 2, 3, 72, 160, 195, 196, 203, 218
Rubin, Merle 257
ruination 30, 122, 137, 143, 147, 148, 149, 154, 155, 157

Sadler, Lynn Veach 4, 13, 41, 59, 85, 86, 257

same-sex desire 3, 38, 58, 59, 61, 63, 64, 73, 76, 106, 108, 109, 112, 216
sapphic 2, 79, 89, 111
scandalous 6, 7, 15, 28, 127, 128, 129, 132, 136, 137, 143, 146, 148, 229, 234
Schudel, Matt 11
Schwob, Marcel 29, 122, 131, 132, 136
Scodel, Ruth 144
senses 21, 28, 52, 76, 79, 87, 88, 95, 219, 233
sensual 27, 74, 76, 78, 83, 87, 88, 89, 91, 119, 152, 153
sexual identity 2, 20, 58, 72
sexuality 2, 4, 7, 10, 11, 14, 20, 21, 22, 29, 37, 38, 39, 42, 63, 64, 71, 75, 76, 86, 90, 93, 110, 112, 113, 122, 141, 142, 150, 151, 203, 207, 208, 216, 238, 240, 246
Seymour, Miranda 4, 139, 257
Sharpe, Beatrice 194, 202, 206, 218
Sharpe, Miriam 7, 17, 31, 193, 206, 231, 232
shipping forecast 217, 218, 220, 223
shock 56, 75, 109, 242
signifying matrix 78, 96, 119, 122, 138, 165, 207, 225
Skinner, John 15, 25, 40, 59, 60, 86, 230, 232, 234, 236, 244, 258
Smith, Patricia Juliana x, 4, 12, 16, 25, 38, 39, 41, 71, 72, 81, 258
solitary 6, 7, 30, 161, 170, 172, 188, 235, 236, 259
Soundings 81, 82, 226, 249
spectator 74, 87, 96, 255
Staël, Madame de 3, 18, 81, 82, 86, 95, 101, 105, 226, 236, 255, 258
Start in Life, A 1, 18, 247, 249, 251
Steiner, Wendy 13, 167, 168, 169, 258
Stendhal xii, 1, 18, 23, 26, 37, 38, 42, 43, 44, 45, 46, 48, 49, 50, 51, 53, 54, 55, 56, 240, 249, 258
Stetz, Margaret D. 15, 16, 17, 254, 258

Stewart, Charles 75
Studies of the Greek Poets 88, 258
subjectification 96, 99, 100, 104, 106, 107, 111, 115, 174
Summers-Bremner, Eluned 166, 167, 169, 258
suspension 67, 72, 104, 175
Swann's Way 83, 108, 256
swerve 109, 174, 175, 176, 177, 181, 182, 184, 237
Swinburne, Algernon Charles 91
syllepsis xiv, 171, 215, 216, 257
Sylvester, Louise 16, 258
Symonds, John Addington 88

talking 12, 29, 30, 122, 133, 159, 185
Tempest ix, 33, 34, 35, 36, 48, 49, 50, 51, 55, 60, 73, 257
temporal 10, 17, 19, 20, 21, 22, 39, 48, 64, 66, 67, 68, 72, 90, 91, 99, 100, 101, 106, 107, 109, 110, 130, 134, 140, 141, 142, 165, 180, 191, 208, 209, 213, 214, 231, 246
tessera 179, 182, 183
'Theses on the Philosophy of History' 28, 97
Tindall, Gillian 31, 200
Tonkin, Boyd 15, 259
Tragic Muse, The 81, 253
transference 59, 63, 108, 110
transgression 29, 68, 122, 134, 135, 140, 175
transgressive 3, 28, 30, 90, 113, 128, 135, 136, 138, 150, 173, 198, 209, 246
Treatise on Elegant Living 29, 132, 133, 139, 148, 154, 155, 156, 247
Tuite, Clara x, 29, 122, 133, 150, 176
Turner, J.M.W. 18, 94, 218, 219, 220, 221, 253, 259

Undue Influence vii, ix, xii, xiii, 6, 20, 30, 61, 160, 162, 164, 165, 166, 167, 168, 169, 172, 175, 177, 178, 179, 180, 181, 183, 184, 188, 191, 228, 234, 237, 238, 243, 249, 250, 253, 255, 256, 257, 258
utilitarian 90, 113, 135, 139, 142, 153

Vernon, Blanche 5, 14, 27, 74, 80, 82, 84, 85, 87, 102, 107, 224, 226, 231, 243
Vidaud, Richard 15, 259
Vivien, Renée xii, 3, 23, 78, 80, 91, 255

walking 29, 30, 122, 128, 133, 154, 155, 158, 160, 161, 162, 164, 165, 167, 171, 172, 176, 177, 178, 179, 184, 190
Watson, Daphne 11, 13, 260
Wilde, Oscar 2, 3, 23, 27, 37, 38, 57, 65, 66, 67, 68, 71, 131, 156, 157, 230, 238, 251, 252, 258, 260
Williams-Wanquet, Eileen 15, 167, 168, 169, 230, 232, 245, 260
winged 88, 97, 100, 108, 109, 110, 116
Wings of the Dove, The 114
Wittig, Monique 76
Woman Appeared to Me, A xii, 80, 84, 91, 92, 260
'Women Damned' 89, 93, 96
women's writer 14, 22, 28, 32, 77, 78, 79, 82, 84, 85, 87, 93, 99, 125, 126, 164, 167, 228, 229, 236, 245, 246
women's writing 6, 84, 85, 125, 126, 136, 164, 165, 180, 226, 227, 232, 233
Wood, Anthony 128
Woolf, Virginia 9, 10, 160, 161, 229, 230, 231, 236, 240, 244, 254, 258, 260
Wyatt-Brown, Anne 86

9781789620597